Business Development Opportunities and Market Entry Challenges in Latin America

Mauricio Garita
Universidad del Valle de Guatemala, Guatemala

Jose Godinez
Merrimack College, USA

BUSINESS SCIENCE
Reference
An Imprint of IGI Global

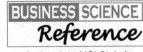

Managing Director: Lindsay Johnston
Managing Editor: Keith Greenberg
Director of Intellectual Property & Contracts: Jan Travers
Acquisitions Editor: Kayla Wolfe
Production Editor: Christina Henning
Development Editor: Courtney Tychinski
Cover Design: Jason Mull

Published in the United States of America by
        Business Science Reference (an imprint of IGI Global)
        701 E. Chocolate Avenue
        Hershey PA 17033
        Tel: 717-533-8845
        Fax: 717-533-8661
        E-mail: cust@igi-global.com
        Web site: http://www.igi-global.com

                  Library of Congress Cataloging-in-Publication Data

Business development opportunities and market entry challenges in Latin America / Mauricio Garita and Jose Godinez, editors.
        pages cm
   Includes bibliographical references and index.
   Summary: "This book provides a practical, in-depth look at the different challenges and opportunities present in the Latin American economy"-- Provided by publisher.
    ISBN 978-1-4666-8820-9 (hardcover) -- ISBN 978-1-4666-8821-6 (ebook) 1. Economic development--Latin America. 2. Investments, Foreign--Latin America. 3. International business enterprises--Latin America. 4. Latin America--Commerce. 5. Latin America--Economic conditions--21st century. I. Garita, Mauricio, editor. II. Godinez, Jose, 1979- editor.

   HC125.B775 2016
   330.98--dc23

                           2015023729

British Cataloguing in Publication Data
A Cataloguing in Publication record for this book is available from the British Library.

All work contributed to this book is new, previously-unpublished material. The views expressed in this book are those of the authors, but not necessarily of the publisher.

Editorial Advisory Board

Table of Contents

Detailed Table of Contents

Chapter 1
Theoretical Aspects on Bottom of the Pyramid in Emerging Economies: An
Overview of Microfinance in Latin America 1

    Milo Paviera, University of Edinburgh, UK
    Mahmoud Khalik, University of St. Andrews, UK

Despite the growing body of literature on the Bottom of the Pyramid (BoP), much
remains unclear and more research is needed in a number of areas as this chapter
will highlight. Firstly, the broad literature is reviewed which includes looking at
definitions and different strands of research undertaken in the field. The chapter then
presents three key sectors that the authors believe have the most potential to aid
poverty alleviation, while proposing that other types of studies can be conducted for
other sectors that are more likely to lead to consumer satisfaction. Points of departure
are offered, before discussing microfinance and then latterly in the context of Latin
America. The chapter uses secondary data to show key countries and institutions
serving the BoP, and to highlight important aspects that merit further attention.
Implications for policy makers and practitioners are offered, and this is followed
by a number of directions for future research.

Chapter 2
Corruption in Latin America and How It Affects Foreign Direct Investment
(FDI): Causes, Consequences, and Possible Solutions 30

    Jose Godinez, Merrimack College, USA

Foreign direct investment has aided in a significant manner the economic development
of Latin America since the early 1990s because capital in this region is limited
(Blanco, 2012). Despite some criticism literature on FDI has overwhelmingly

demonstrated that FDI has positive effects on host countries (Tan & Meyer, 2011) especially in Latin America (Wooster & Diebel, 2010). Authors researching the effects of FDI in Latin America have stated that this investment helps to growth on productivity (Blonigen & Wang, 2005) and thus, might help developing countries to begin their road to development. Therefore, scholars have devoted great efforts to understanding the determinants of FDI to Latin America and a brief overview will be provided in this study. This paper will present a detailed account of FDI flows to the region, a clear definition of corruption and how it is manifested in Latin America. After these definitions, suggestions are provided to deal with the problem of corruption in the region.

Chapter 3

Otto Mena, Tallinn University of Technology, Estonia
Leon Miller, Tallinn University of Technology, Estonia

The text states the problem in connection with defining the dilemma of small states, the advantages and disadvantages of being small and gives a brief background of how the problem developed, a brief history of how dependency developed and at the same time offers a solution, a futuristic perspective on development planning that eliminates the problem of dependency. The authors argue that the attempts of supra national institutions and NGO's to foster a Neo Liberal approach to development without implementing strategies for bolstering the social institutions of particular states has crippled their effort to create sustained economic development, although it has contributed to spiking material assets and creating a bubble for the financial sector and certain segments of production but per capita income of the general public has not benefited from such strategies and indeed on some cases their interest of the general public has been hurt.

Chapter 4

Jose Godinez, Merrimack College, USA
Theodore Terpstra, University of Connecticut, USA

Historically, Chinese corporations have been relatively unknown in Latin America. Total foreign direct investment (FDI) in Latin America was 18.1% of the world total in 2012 (UNCTAD, 2013). However, Chinese FDI in Latin America has averaged about US$10 billion per year since 2010, only a small part of Latin America's total FDI inflows (ECLAC, 2013). Yet the presence and economic leverage of Chinese corporations has become very substantial in several industries in the region, particularly the oil and mining industries. Trade between China and Latin America has also grown dramatically since 1999 (Luo, et al., 2010). Despite the growing economic connectivity between Latin America and China, the motivation, strategy and procedures behind China's FDI in the region have not yet been fully understood.

Chapter 5
 Harish C. Chandan, Argosy University, USA

Trust is the expectation of honest and co-operative future behavior based on commonly shared norms (Fukuyama, 1995). In Latin American region, people who believe that most people can be trusted ranges from 4 to 19% as compared with 34% for USA and 60% for China and Sweden (World Values Survey, 2010-2014; Jamison, 2011; Cardenas et al., 2009). Trust consists of a mix of inter-personal trust and institutional trust. An understanding of business culture, national culture and religion is essential for developing trust in business relationships (Hurtado, 2010; Searing, 2013; Weck, 2013, Ransi and Kobti, 2014). Trust among various business stakeholders within a firm or between firms in a local, national or international setting is an essential component of business development activities that are rooted in the relationships between exchange partners (Barron, 2014; Taylor, 2013; Friman et al., 2002;). The monitoring mechanisms on trust, i.e., "trust but verify" are conductive to maintaining trust in a business relationship (Kusari, et al. 2014).

Chapter 6
 Heather C. Webb, Higher Colleges of Technology, Dubai, UAE

With the increase of economic growth in Latin America, the mobile finance (m-finance) sectoral system of innovation model is applied as an analytical framework in order to focus in on the technological infrastructure and regulatory structure. The SSI approach links innovation to the interactions of the different actors in the system. Innovation is either the process of creating or the recombining of knowledge for some new use to become an outcome of that process. Innovation does not sit within the boundaries of an organization nor does it sit neatly at one level, but instead it is a multifaceted construct. Therefore, this chapter presents aspects of the sectoral system of innovation (SSI) of mobile finances within the Latin America region.

Chapter 7

Michele Lobina, Sapienza University of Rome, Italy
Marco Bottone, Sapienza University of Rome, Italy

This chapter studies the process of trust building in politics by using large data set
on political behaviour in Latin America. The results yielded by developed models
indicate specific elements as the most influential on the popular trust in institutions.
These observed determinants were enclosed in five macro classes: cohesion of
society; economic factors; electoral transparency; efficiency of judicial organs; and
crime diffusion. The analysis of the public support in governments and parliaments
revealed that certain variables have a direct impact on the stability of the Latin
American democracies, while other factors merely determine the likelihood of a
government's reappointment.

Chapter 8

Mauricio Garita-Gutierrez, Universidad del Valle de Guatemala,
Guatemala

The present chapter analyzes the different areas concerning competitiveness. This
analysis is based on the two visions of competitiveness. The first vision establishes
that the only form of competitiveness is to engage in lowering costs and therefore
establishing a competitive advantage through costs. The second vision is a more
integral one that sees a competitive advantage in the capacity of the workers in the
specialization of labor. This second vision enforces the idea of investing in education
and health to compete in more profitable markets. Based on these visions, the question
to ask is: Is Central America ready?

Chapter 9

Luis Javier Sanchez-Barrios, Universidad del Norte, Colombia
Eduardo Gomez-Araujo, Universidad del Norte, Colombia
Liyis Gomez-Nuñez, Universidad del Norte, Colombia
Sandra Rodriguez, Universidad del Norte, Colombia

This chapter explores various aspects that might be associated with entrepreneurial
activity and non-entrepreneurial engagement in Colombia between 2010 and 2012.
These ratios were calculated from the GEM-Colombia report between 2010 and
2012. Aspects were obtained from the National Expert Survey (NES) of the GEM
project and from the Doing Business Study. Sommer's d correlation was used to
test significant association. Results show that in general, context conditions in

Colombia are adequate to start a business. Positive aspects include public policies to stimulate business creation, skilled specialist teams and reduction in processes required to formally establish an SME. Yet further substantial advance need to be made in terms of access to financial resources, access to technology that is relevant for microbusinesses, implementation of innovation policies and education in entrepreneurship. This is required to enhance the creation of high growth businesses that result in a knowledge-based economy in contrast with a prevalent traditional economy as is the case at present.

Chapter 10

The chapter will be a case study from an Ordoliberal perspective of the conception, implementation and policy output of the newly created Private Council of Competitiveness (PCC) in Guatemala, a country wracked by mistrust of the public sector by the private sector. The PCC was founded as a private sector initiative, in conjunction with academia, to work with the government to spawn new efforts aimed at augmenting Guatemala's national competitiveness, by fomenting innovation, entrepreneurship and closer ties between academia and the public and private sectors. The chapter utilizes first hand interviews with the members of the PCC and key public sector players, academics, and other top representatives from the private sector to show how working together built the trust necessary to make the PCC a successful working body with the potential to produce important initiatives in matters of competitiveness, innovation and entrepreneurship.

Chapter 11

This chapter describes the market entry process of Portuguese small and medium-sized enterprise (SME) into the Brazilian. This chapter explores an under-researched strand in the studies of internationalization of SMEs, namely how trust and commitment leveraged the relationship orientation of the Portuguese SME in entering into the Brazilian market. Through a Case Study the chapter explores the concept of relationship orientation, trust and commitment to analyze how a Portuguese SME managed to turn around a difficult situation transforming its associates in business partners and prevented a process of desinternationalization.

Considering Latin American economies have introduced various forms of attaining combat the economic crisis mostly through short-term policies based on credit incentive and increased public expenditure in order to revive the same; however, a long-term strategy where inclusive and sustainable growth which can be clearly discerned through innovation can play a key role prioritizing necessary. Thus in the course of this chapter create an analysis of the benefits of innovation and technological development taking into account the current state in Latin America and the possible scenarios in which technology serves as an important tool for economic and social development which translates into basic cornerstone for business and growth enhancer.

Latin America and the Caribbean (LAC) as an emergent region has showed a high economic growth at the recent history. Its economic growth has been higher than the world general performance during a half of a century. Since 1960 to 1980, LAC was the region with the highest economic growth per decade. Unfortunately, the great economic growth stopped with the Debt Crisis which macroeconomic non desirable effects were sensible during the next decade. As a solution at international level. One of the barriers to start a business is the financial factor. The crowdfunding is a group of people dedicated to create a network in order to get financial help from people that are willing to support a business idea.

International remittances to developing countries are growing and are more than foreign direct investment or the official development aid. More of the 3.2% of global population are living abroad and the trends will increase in the next decades, involving skilled and no skilled workers. Developing countries in Latin America receives 15% of all international remittances and six countries (México, Guatemala, Dominican Republic, Colombia, El Salvador and Honduras) in the region received more of the 70% of all the remittances in 2013. By coincidence, this six countries have a lack to develop and large pockets of poverty, much of which is concentrated in those areas from which migrants come. The remittances are palliatives to poverty in their countries and help their families to reduce their poverty. In many cases, the remittances are the seed for new small and medium enterprises in Latin America, with not enough access to financial services.

Foreword

This new book, titled *Business Development Opportunities and Market Entry Challenges in Latin America*, and edited by the distinguished researcher in Sociology by the Pontifical University of Salamanca, Mauricio Garita, and distinguished PhD in Management Jose Godinez, covers a topic of great interest to those interested in the social and economic reality of Latin America. Equipped with a general and broad vision of the social and economic problems emerged in these sister countries, the book analyzes the economic structure of Latin American nations, and especially Brazil, Colombia and Guatemala, in order to show the reader new business areas in an economic business world characterized by "glocalization", a term exceeding the concept of globalization. In fact, today's business world is characterized by thinking in a global background, while acting in local environments. Companies that follow this strategy survive in hostile environments, and grow sustainably over time, while expanding their market niches and satisfying stakeholders' expectations. As a result of "glocalization", mainly investors, shareholders and many executives have become citizens of the world to work, thanks to the Information and Communication Technologies (ICT)s in internationally-business environments worldwide. This type of readers is those who are especially targeted the book.

After decades of economic, political and financial instability in Latin American countries, it is now the time to invest in the continent to counterbalance the growing Asian economic power in the world. But one of the main problems to achieve this goal is the economic, political and social corruption existing, with different intensity, in the region. Aware of this fact, the book analyzes in chapter 2 how this triple corruption affects foreign direct investment and, what it is more interesting, suggests possible solutions to eliminate corruption practices. As a result, only when corruption will be deleted from the economic, political and social structures of these countries, stakeholders' trust in Latin America will be developed, as the book shows in chapter 5.

In this process of attracting foreign investment to Latin American countries, economic and social policies carried out by national and multilateral governments are of fundamental importance, always having in mind the economic and social well-being of their citizens. In this sense, it is outstanding the significance of institutionalism for increasing social and economic wealth in a multi-level perspective in Latin American small states, analysis in the book in chapter 3. Building trust in politics (chapter 9), while eliminating corruption practices, is essential to economically transform Latin America, and to attract foreign direct investment and richness to the region.

This transformation process must be also rooted on microfinance (chapters 1) and competitiveness (chapter 8). Offshoring strategies and initiatives based on solidarity and social economics, as an emerging research trend to be applied in the Latin American region, are of key importance to augment social welfare and competitiveness in these countries. The key is to transform these economies of survival to nations characterized by welfare, as in the European Union case. And this will be only possible if there is stronger private-public cooperation, alongside a quality university education for society.

Moreover, business strategies based on innovation (chapter 6) and on searching of blue and purple oceans by adopting mobile financial sectorial systems of innovation, as in India, is a cornerstone for achieving good results in terms of economic growth and social welfare. Innovation techniques connected with entrepreneurship policies related to business incubators and accelerators, as the future of a prosperous and developed Latin America depends on both good both university and vocational education. In fact, as in *Proverbs* 16, 16 is stated: *Posside sapientiam, quia auro melior est* [Possess wisdom is better than owning gold].

In this Latin American transformation process, China is taking an increasing role, as shown in chapter 4, especially in Venezuela, Bolivia, and Ecuador. From a geopolitical point of view, there are two types of power (soft power and hard power) in the world, and China has opted for soft power in a process of slow, effective, intelligent, and social acculturation. In the next generation, which is in fifteen years, China will be the first economy in the world in GDP terms, as in this decade is having a growing economic, political and social influence in the world. Chinese citizens working outside China, usually speak at least one foreign language, and are generally characterized by their strong ability for hard-working, team spirit, and their deep respect for national cultures in which they are established.

Finally, this interesting and outstanding book finishes with the analysis of three cases: [1] business opportunities and challenges for entrepreneurial activity and non-entrepreneurial engagement in Colombia (chapter 9); [2] public-private-academic cooperation, as a trust building mechanism for Guatemala (chapter 10), and [3] the market entry in Brazil through commitment-trust dynamics in an internationalization process (chapter 11). The analyses carried out in these pages are very interesting, especially for the Brazilian and Colombian cases, as they are, with Mexico and Peru, the so-called Eagles (Emerging and Growth-leading Countries) in Latin America.

In short, Latin American citizens deserve new opportunities to enjoy a better quality of life for achieving their individual goals in peace and prosperity through education. As taught by the popular adage in the European Middle Ages: *Quod nova testa capit, inveterata sapit* [What is learned in the cradle, lasts forever], while writing this book, the author had his ideas, working and learning experience, thoughts and reflections in mind to serve for a righteous cause: to fight poverty and hopelessness in Latin American countries for its citizens to enjoy better standards of economic and social welfare in the future. And sincerely, this book is one more step to achieve it.

José Manuel Saiz-Alvarez
Nebrija University, Spain & Catholic University of Santiago de Guayaquil,
    Ecuador

Preface

Latin America is one of the most interesting regions in the world. Since the beginning of history, Latin America was seen as a game changer in the international economics. During the era of Christopher Columbus, Latin America became an important opportunity for economic growth. Islands such as Puerto Rico, Haiti and Dominican Republic were strategic to the growth of the Spanish Colonies. The search for gold and other precious metal led expeditions with the purpose of encountering a new business opportunity.

Today Latin America is as attractive as it was three hundred years ago. During the 1980´s the region confronted what is called the "lost decade" given the lack of growth and the failure of the states. Since then Latin America has changed led by countries such as Peru, Panamá, Brazil, Colombia and Chile. These Countries faced a restructuration of its foundations and a new business conception. Colombia was considered a country submerged in drug war during the 1990´s with a violent panorama. In approximately 20 years Colombia changed and surpassed its problems and is known one of the most competitive countries in the world.

Panama is another interesting history in Latin America. A country that needed a discussion centered on a vision of what the world expected from them. Panama engaged in two important efforts being the financial structure that they developed and the Panama Canal. Given this changes Panama started growing in 2005 at 7.2% reaching its peak in 2007% with a growth of 12.1%. When the 2008 financial crisis struck Panama and Guatemala were two of the countries that did not enter into a recession. Panama grew 9.1% in 2008 and the next year the country encountered the lowest with a growth of 4%. The country recovered and again peaked in 2011 with a growth of 10.8%. The country is still growing at a steady and strong pace.

Brazil is another example of growth and change. The poverty headcount ratio of Brazil was 21% in 2005. Since then the effort of a more inclusive economy became a reality by diminishing this ratio to 17.3% in 2006, 14.1% in 2008 to 8.9% in 2013. Brazil became an example in eradicating poverty and an important hub for engaging in business in Latin America.

This region is a promising region for the next years. The forecasts for the year 2016 predict that Dominican Republic will be having a growth similar to the last three years of 4.9%. Bolivia will have the same behavior with a steady growth of 4.3%. This demonstrates that the region is a solid region with an important potential for doing business.

The interesting aspect for the region and a question that is the main topic for the book is: What are the challenges and opportunities when entering the region? In the present book the reader will find an important analysis of what the region offers, the different challenges that could affect is decisions and how to surpass them. The book will lead the reader to an understanding of the region both theoretically and practically since various author of the book are from the region and work in the region. This gives a practical approach that will differentiate from other books in the market.

The topics discussed in the book include competitiveness, corruption, foreign direct investment, institutionalism, wealth, financial sectorial systems, politics and private cooperation. The reader will have a book that deepens into the different aspects of Latin American and that invites to discuss of what other challenges and opportunities the region offers. The book is on important pillar on the research of Latin America because of the content, the capacity of the researchers and the knowledge of the region.

The future of the region is a bright one but the decision making of the manager has to be cautious, informed and strategic. The information given in this book will help elaborate this strategic decisions and advise into the different paths managers have when entering this beautiful and inspiring region.

AN APPROACH TO THE CHAPTERS

The first chapter of the book is titled *Theoretical aspects on bottom of the pyramid in emerging economies: An overview of microfinance in Latin America* which offers and interesting analysis of the different aspects in Bottom of the Pyramid (BoP) research. The literature revision gives and important idea of to apply Bottom of the Pyramid research and the importance of its application. The approach by the authors is centered on poverty alleviation an important challenge in Latin America. By its BoP analysis the authors offer a more comprehensive approach on what three (3) sectors could make an important change in the poverty area in Latin America. This chapter was chosen as an opening of the book because it tackles on of the biggest challenges using secondary data and what is more important, the authors offer solutions that could be implemented in the region.

The second chapter centers in the Corruption in Latin America. Corruption is an important challenge in the region that has to be taken into account when entering the country. There are different aspects of corruption and the levels of corruption vary from one country to the other. This chapter analyzes the different aspects of corruption and leads to important findings on what is the result of corruption in the region when compared to Foreign Direct Investment (FDI). This chapter is extremely important for understanding the behavior of corruption in Latin America.

The fourth chapter states the problem in connection with defining the dilemma of small states, the advantages and disadvantages of being small and gives a brief background of how the problem developed, a brief history of how dependency developed and at the same time offers a solution, a futuristic perspective on development planning that eliminates the problem of dependency. The authors argue that the attempts of supra national institutions and NGO's to foster a Neo Liberal approach to development without implementing strategies for bolstering the social institutions of particular states has crippled their effort to create sustained economic development, although it has contributed to spiking material assets and creating a bubble for the financial sector and certain segments of production but per capita income of the general public has not benefited from such strategies and indeed on some cases their interest of the general public has been hurt.

The fifth chapter is based on trust. Trust is the expectation of honest and co-operative future behavior based on commonly shared norms. In Latin American region, people who believe that most people can be trusted ranges from 4 to 19% as compared with 34% for USA and 60% for China and Sweden. Trust among various business stakeholders within a firm or between firms in a local, national or international setting is an essential component of business development activities that are rooted in the relationships between exchange partners. This chapter demonstrates an important aspect of the economy In Latin America.

The sixth chapter demonstrates that with the increase of economic growth in Latin America, the mobile finance (m-finance) sectoral system of innovation model is applied as an analytical framework in order to focus in on the technological infrastructure and regulatory structure. The SSI approach links innovation to the interactions of the different actors in the system. Innovation is either the process of creating or the recombining of knowledge for some new use to become an outcome of that process. A new approach on the future of the economy of Latin America is essential for understating the new dynamics.

The seventh chapter is also based on trust. This chapter studies the process of trust building in politics by using large data set on political behaviour in Latin America. The results yielded by developed models indicate specific elements as the most influential on the popular trust in institutions. These observed determinants were enclosed in five macro classes: cohesion of society; economic factors; electoral transparency; efficiency of judicial organs; and crime diffusion. The analysis of the public support in governments and parliaments revealed that certain variables have a direct impact on the stability of the Latin American democracies, while other factors merely determine the likelihood of a government's reappointment.

The eight chapter of the book centers in a specific area of Latin America that is Central America. Central America is the union between South and North America and connects both markets. Central America has been a convulsive region that was almost completely at war during three decades. The construction of a post-war Central America has been a challenge in the region, but they have demonstrated that with effort change can be made. This chapter analysis the different countries in Central America and compares them in different competitive aspects such as education and health. The comparison of these aspects leads to an interesting conclusion on how to be more competitive.

Chapter nine explores various aspects that might be associated with entrepreneurial activity and non-entrepreneurial engagement in Colombia between 2010 and 2012. These ratios were calculated from the GEM-Colombia report between 2010 and 2012. The approach of the information applied to Colombia offers an important aspect when discussing the future of the region.

Chapter ten is a case study from an Ordoliberal perspective of the conception, implementation and policy output of the newly created Private Council of Competitiveness (PCC) in Guatemala, a country wracked by mistrust of the public sector by the private sector. This chapter demonstrates that alliances in Latin America are important and that they will have an important result when dealing with different circumstances in the region.

Chapter eleven describes the market entry process of Portuguese small and medium-sized enterprise (SME) into the Brazilian. This chapter explores an under-researched strand in the studies of internationalization of SMEs, namely how trust and commitment leveraged the relationship orientation of the Portuguese SME in entering into the Brazilian market.

Chapter twelve discusses the benefits of innovation and technological development taking into account the current state in Latin America and the possible scenarios in which technology serves as an important tool for economic and social development which translates into basic cornerstone for business and growth enhancer.

Chapter thirteen describes Latin America and the Caribbean as an emergent region showing a high economic growth in recent history. It has been higher than the world general performance during a half of a century. From 1960- 1980, LAC had the highest economic growth per decade, but the growth stopped with the Debt Crisis which macroeconomic non desirable effects were sensible during the next decade. The crowdfunding is a group of people dedicated to creating a network in order to get financial help from people that are willing to support a business idea.

Chapter fourteen describes how international remittances to developing countries are growing and are more than foreign direct investment or the official development aid. More than 3.2% of global population are living abroad and the trends will increase involving skilled and unskilled workers. The remittances are palliatives to poverty in their countries and help their families to reduce their poverty. In many cases, the remittances are the seed for new small and medium enterprises in Latin America, with not enough access to financial services.

Mauricio Garita
Universidad del Valle de Guatemala, Guatemala

Jose Godinez
Merrimack College, USA

Acknowledgment

Mauricio Garita:

I thank my wife Sonia for the patience during the construction of this book. Without her this would have been impossible.

Jose Godinez:

To Indigo.

The Editors:

We want to thank and acknowledge the work of each of the authors that contributed to the book. We thank their dedication, their patience and the ideas that led this book to be a pillar of knowledge in Latin America. We thank our editorial board that revised each work and that dedicate time by exchanging comments for a better and more accurate book.

Mauricio Garita
Universidad del Valle de Guatemala, Guatemala

Jose Godinez
Merrimack College, USA

Chapter 1
Theoretical Aspects on Bottom of the Pyramid in Emerging Economies:
An Overview of Microfinance in Latin America

Milo Paviera
University of Edinburgh, UK

Mahmoud Khalik
University of St. Andrews, UK

ABSTRACT

Despite the growing body of literature on the Bottom of the Pyramid (BoP), much remains unclear and more research is needed in a number of areas as this chapter will highlight. Firstly, the broad literature is reviewed which includes looking at definitions and different strands of research undertaken in the field. The chapter then presents three key sectors that the authors believe have the most potential to aid poverty alleviation, while proposing that other types of studies can be conducted for other sectors that are more likely to lead to consumer satisfaction. Points of departure are offered, before discussing microfinance and then latterly in the context of Latin America. The chapter uses secondary data to show key countries and institutions serving the BoP, and to highlight important aspects that merit further attention. Implications for policy makers and practitioners are offered, and this is followed by a number of directions for future research.

DOI: 10.4018/978-1-4666-8820-9.ch001

INTRODUCTION

The concept of the Bottom of the pyramid (BoP) first introduced by C.K. Prahalad has led many scholars to undertake research on the low-income consumers and underserved communities, and this has become a promising area of study. This chapter aims to uncover two important objectives: firstly, to review the concept of BoP, and secondly to map out a number of microfinance institutions that serve this segment in the region of Latin America. We begin this chapter with a review of BoP from its inception, and the controversy surrounding the definition, before delving into the literature on the BoP, including Prahalad's work and the main theoretical developments. Attention then turns to microfinance and the BoP in emerging markets, before focusing more specifically on Latin America as an important region of study. The chapter then using secondary data maps out the microfinance companies serving the BoP, and the Latin American countries in which they operate. This will allow scholars undertaking research on this area to more easily identify which companies and countries merit further and more narrow research at different levels, including a firm and individual level. Finally, we conclude with policy implications and future research directions.

BOTTOM OF THE PYRAMID: PRAHALAD AND BEYOND

The Peruvian economist Hernando de Soto (2000) calculated that up to half of the total economic activity undertaken in emerging markets takes place outside the formal economy. The scholar further states that the total unregistered assets among the world's poor accounts for US$9 trillion, a point acknowledged by Prahalad (2010). London and Hart (2004) have consequently suggested that within such an informal context, governments and firms should primarily build relationships based on social, rather than legal contracts. The work of these scholars has set the foundations and contributed significantly to research on how firms in emerging economies should look in a constructive manner at the people living at the bottom of the socio-economic pyramid.

There are different ways to define the bottom of the pyramid, and initially Prahalad and Hart (2002) in their seminal paper outlined the BoP as people living with an annual income of less than US$1,500 measured on purchasing power parity (PPP) basis. However, much debate has centred on this PPP threshold and this is due to the lack of rigour. The World Bank and other scholars use different thresholds and so there is clearly a lack of consistency, which is neatly pointed out by Karnani (2007). The World Resource Institute (WRI) and its partners have proposed a new definition and this threshold is based on an annual income of US$ 3,000 PPP in 2002 U.S. dollars, which is $3,260 when adjusted to 2005 U.S. dollars (London, 2007). According to the WRI threshold, the total amount of people living at the BoP across Africa, Asia, Eastern Europe, Latin America and the Caribbean accounts for nearly 4 billion people (Hammond, Kramer, Katz, Tran, & Walker, 2007).

Nevertheless, it remains very opaque, and it is complex to establish a consistent BoP definition when purely based on an income basis. An important issue to point out is that the national context in various emerging economies is different, with certain regions of the world exposed to higher levels of extreme poverty (people living on less than US$1.25 per day). At the same time there are studies that apply a rather general definition of BoP that is well above the US$ 3,000 annual income (Hart, 2005). Furthermore, there are important differences when we take into account rural poverty contexts (often the case with African countries), and urban poverty (often the case with the Latin America region). This distinction is fundamental, and well explained by Kolk, Rivera-Santos, and Rufin (2013) who point out that "the spending power on consumer goods in the shantytown of the three largest cities in Venezuela is between 5 and 10 times higher than that of the whole Indian rural BoP population" (p.15). It is the case also that some studies tend to segment the BoP and just focus on one specific tier (either taking the lowest or highest). These limitations illustrate how difficult it is to arrive at a universal definition for the BoP. It is due to this complexity we feel that the definition proposed by London (2007/2010) that views the Base of the pyramid as the poor at the base of the global socio-economic ladder, who primarily transact in an informal market economy as the most effective and reliable one.

One of the specific topics surrounding the base of the pyramid is how firms build businesses that target the BoP. Kolk, Rivera-Santos, and Rufin (2013) show that research views the BoP from two dimensions; the first refers to the role or position of the poor in the value network, meaning the extent to which the poor are viewed as customers. The second is the mode of engagement, which examines the extent to which targeting the BOP is based on existing or the 'co-invention' of products.

The opportunities at the BoP and the low-income segments are an intriguing proposition. However, what is less clear is how companies and particularly MNEs can effectively serve this large mass of informal workers and consumers. Prahalad (2005) suggested that there is an untapped purchasing power at the BoP, and that private firms can attain profits by selling to the poor. The underlying argument is based on the assumption that by selling to the low-income segments, companies can bring prosperity to the poor and this can contribute to alleviating poverty. From this perspective, it is suggested that MNEs should play a key role in this process. However, it is noteworthy that some authors like Karnani (2009a) view this with scepticism.

Other scholars, such as London and Hart (2004) have emphasised that strategies in emerging economies have to reinvent the transnational model if they want to target the BoP. The aforementioned authors suggest that MNEs that successfully devise strategies that rely "on leveraging the strengths of the existing market environment outperform those that focus on overcoming weakness" (London & Hart, 2004, p. 350). The same authors advocate three important strategies for the BoP, which include developing relationships with non-traditional partners, such as (NGO's, the local government, suppliers), co-inventing custom solutions, and building local capacity. The BoP approach suggests implicitly a market solution to poverty; however, since its inception the BoP has considered the poor mainly as consumers. More recently, it has been advocated that poor people should also be considered as producers (Karnani, 2007/2009a), self-employed poor people, otherwise known as micro-entrepreneurs (Gibson, 2007), or even looking at the poor in different points of value chains (UNDP, 2008).

Simanis and Hart (2009) formalized the idea that the poor should not be regarded just as consumers, but also as co-inventors of BoP initiatives. Karnani (2007/2009a) suggests that to alleviate poverty, it is necessary to raise the income of the poor and points out that buying from the poor is far more relevant than selling to them. He emphasizes that the majority of examples of BoP are based on the poor as consumers. The author goes further to suggest that the effective way to reduce poverty is through employment, and that the most effective organizational form to achieve this is small and medium enterprises (SMEs) in labour- intensive sectors. Karnani (2007/2009a) offers the example of China as one of the countries that have implemented the most effective poverty reduction strategy, where poor people have been given the chance to work in labour-intensive rather than in capital-intensive industries. This approach has been effective yielding strong results in China. Other emerging economies, such as India opted for different strategies (generating jobs through larger businesses), which has not achieved the same result. In his more recent work, Karnani (2009b) brings to light the example of Technoserve, an NGO that is able to generate thousands of jobs through specific investments in human capital to boost the creation of local SMEs in different developing countries, such as Asia, Africa and Latin America. However, the downsides are that it assumes a certain level of government involvement in the creation of a business environment for SMEs to grow, and the examples presented in the literature are scarce.

A small group of scholars have pointed out the relevance of microfranchising as an approach to alleviate poverty. Gibson (2007) explains that microfranchising brings two parties together and brings mutual benefits to each party. It pairs talented microentrepreneurs who want to expand their business, but may lack managerial skills and capital to achieve this; with people who lack entrepreneurial skills, but desire self-employment. Kistruck, Webb, Sutter, and Duane Ireland (2011) advocate that microfranchising might provide a number of social benefits to microfranchisees and underserved communities.

Banerjee and Duflo (2007) show that the poor can be entrepreneurial, and show BOP consumers as being able to undertake several different types of jobs. However, it is a result of the lack of specialization and training that prevents them from obtaining higher incomes. An interesting finding in the literature is that the large majority of entrepreneurship examples at the BoP are not initiatives introduced by the poor (Anderson & Billou, 2007; Dolan & Scott, 2009), but examples showing the poor as producers (Altman, Rego, & Ross, 2009). Kolk, Rivera-Santos, and Rufin (2013) suggest that while there is a call for MNEs to collaborate and co-create with the poor, very little examples of this can be found in the current literature.

The review so far illustrates that there are different perspectives with respect to understanding the poor at the BoP, and how to alleviate poverty through different approaches. However, they all recognise to different degrees the potential or relevance of the BoP (Nghia, 2010). The majority of the studies conducted have viewed the poor as consumers, and much less have focused on the poor generating income, or the poor as key actors along the value chain, such as distributors, suppliers or employees (Kolk, Rivera-Santos, & Rufin, 2013).

Another strand of literature within the BoP is linked with the initiators of BoP activities. In the initial work, Prahalad and Hart (2002) called for the active role of MNEs, and during the last decade few examples have appeared alongside those well known in the literature, such as Avon in South Africa, Cemex in Mexico, Hindustan Lever Ltd in India (Unilever in India). Despite these cases being MNEs, the majority of initiatives at the base of the pyramid seem to be developed by small and local firms. Cases have been studied, particularly in Asia and Africa showing how small companies have developed innovative solutions to alleviate poverty, particularly in the case of communication technology and mobile phone services (Anderson & Markides, 2007; Arnould & Mohr, 2005; Brinkerhoff, 2008). Another group of studies instead have shown initiatives that have been developed by not-for-profit organizations, and this is quite remarkable given that this goes against the initial idea of BoP. One thing that is clearly shown in the literature is that much more work is needed, in order to enhance our understanding with respect to the roles each of the following can play in BoP projects: MNEs, SMEs or NGOs, social entrepreneurs.

Finally, there is literature associated with the type of outcome related to the initiatives at the base of the pyramid. This is an extremely important section within the BoP literature since an ample of definitions or lens might be used to understand the BoP outcomes. The issue of the assessment and impact measurement of BoP initiatives is relevant and it has been raised by scholars as an important way to legitimize the market approaches to the BoP (London, 2009). Kolk, Rivera-Santos, and Rufin

(2013) analyzed a comprehensive number of articles containing explicit measures of the economic impact of BoP initiatives, and they found that half of them did not actually measure the economic impact on the firm. Out of 34 articles that reported the economic impact on the firm, 25 reported a positive outcome for the company. The companies range from a microfinance company reporting positive profit margins (but without showing the actual profit margin) to a renewable energy firm in India reporting positive profit, but without any substantive data (Akula, 2008; Hart, 2005).

The social impact of BoP ventures was found in 48 out of a total of 104 initiatives, and this has been measured in terms of the impact on the local populations (Kolk, Rivera-Santos, & Rufin, 2013). The literature shows that different assessment criteria has been used from healthcare output to education, access to water and sanitation, to employment and income generation, and empowerment. However, only 28 of these articles were able to fully provide measurable results. One of the issues that need further attention in this research area is objective assessments of BoP initiatives, since the BoP concept deals fundamentally with poverty reduction. A minority of studies have focused on the environmental impact of BoP initiatives, and this may partially be explained by the main structural challenges often poor people have to face in their everyday life, which is linked with basic needs rather than with sustainable aspects of their life. The findings in this area show that empirical evidence of the economic, social, and environmental impact of BoP ventures is rather weak, and more work is needed here to better capture both impact assessment and trade-offs that firms must confront (Kolk, Rivera-Santos, & Rufin, 2013).

SECTORIAL PATHS AND THE BASE OF THE PYRAMID

It is clear to the authors that the most relevant and pending issues related to research on the base of the pyramid have been the sectorial application. We believe that doing business at the base of the pyramid in different sectors has different impacts on the poor, for example, the healthcare sector is not the same as the consumer retail sector. The reason for this is that when a sector provides poor people with access to a business solution (either a product or a service) that improves one's life then that specific venture is having an impact at the base of pyramid while conducting business. On the other hand, when a poor person has access to either a product or service related to discretionary spending (such as tobacco or alcohol) this will not improve their life, and can cause more harm (Karnani 2009b). For this reason, we believe that the key sectors that are better linked with the philosophy of the base of pyramid are: healthcare, education, and financial services. Retailing and consumer products still merit attention, but with the objective of better understanding how firms devise strategies to serve low-income segments. We believe that this is more relevant to the field of marketing, and such studies could adopt psychology perspectives which could be fruitful.

Figure 1 demonstrates the type of impact in terms of sector, with two different types of outcomes (Poverty alleviation vs. Consumer satisfaction), the latter relates to improving the purchasing experience of the poor). Applying this to the BoP would have a series of implications: on the one hand it may potentially and effectively improve the quality of life for the poor in terms of health, access to education, access to basic literacy, and knowledge with respect to the use of finance. On the other hand this embraces a more consumption based perspective (which we would argue resembles a 'pure free market ideology' applied to poor consumers), with the argument that the poor also need to have a decent customer experience. Given this dual approach to the BoP, we propose a simple framework that shows the likely approaches and the possible outcomes resulting from sectorial applications. In summary, figure 1 demonstrates that there are opportunities to alleviate poverty and improve the quality of life, or to provide a better purchasing experience for poor people.

Figure 1. Sectorial paths and the base of the pyramid
(Source: Authors elaboration).

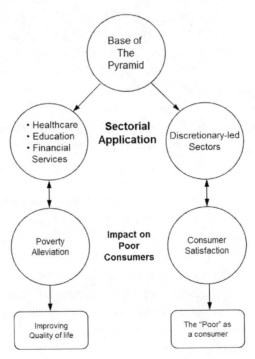

We believe that the sectors previously mentioned, which are ones whereby poor people have more difficulty in finding good custom solutions at effective prices can realistically alleviate poverty. In the case of the healthcare, the case of Aravind Eye care system, pointed out by Prahalad (2005/2010) shows how radical business models may effectively improve the life for thousands of poor people, while being a viable business. Without these types of business solutions, many poor people would eventually die earlier than they should simply because for them it is not feasible to have access to certain healthcare services, which can be regarded as basic for Western standards. Education is intriguing and appears to be an untapped potential for the base of the pyramid (Stanfield, 2010). While for some readers the association of the terms 'business' and 'education' may seem overstated, there are a number of examples in rural India of private solutions in the education sector. The authors have found private schools serving low-income communities in developing countries (India in particular), which outperform public counterparts. This offers interesting insights with respect to how private sector education may contribute to the development of people living in low-income communities. This offers the poor learning opportunities that are affordable, compared with public schools and this is having a tremendous impact (Stanfield 2010).

Similarly, the financial service industry and in particular microfinance has a lot to offer. When using the term microfinance we are referring to financial services for micro-entrepreneurs, small businesses, and poor people that do not have access to formal banking channels and related services. The case of Grameen Bank has been well documented, and has become a popular case that has shown not only how microfinance in Bangladesh has helped thousands of micro-entrepreneurs to grow their business, but also how to start a culture of saving.

The following section of this chapter discusses microfinance, but before delving into this we summarise some important points from the BoP literature, and these are as follows:

- Prahalad deserves merit for bringing the attention with respect to how businesses and particularly MNEs may find untapped opportunities at the base of the pyramid; meaning the low-income based socio-economic groups in society.
- BoP casts light on the large amount of people living below the poverty line or barely above it, and that have commercial needs.
- Early perspectives on BoP have failed to build a more constructive and sustainable approach for this segment as it considers engaging with the poor, mainly as customers (Karnani, 2007/2009a).

- Later approaches i.e. (Karnani, 2007; London and Hart, 2004/2011), have demonstrated that the base of the pyramid requires either co-building solutions with poor people or generating real employment opportunities for the poor, in order to raise their income level.
- We question the extent to which industries can aid poverty alleviation with respect to wants (discretionary spending). We believe that some sectors may require more marketing and psychology perspectives to better understand how companies can sell to the poor. Other sectors, such as financial services and more specifically microfinance offer more potential to tackle the issue of poverty.
- Important sectors to study include: education, financial services, healthcare. Further research is needed on the role of SMEs, microfranchising, and microfinance which have strong potential to alleviate poverty.

MICROFINANCE AND BOP

With the term microfinance, we are referring to the source of financial services for microentrepreneurs, small businesses, and poor people that cannot obtain access to formal banking channels and related services. In certain countries, such as Bangladesh or Bolivia microfinance has been extremely successful, and today represents an important segment with respect to bringing financial services to microentrepreneurs and poor people. Advocates of microfinance believe that access to financial services may contribute to poverty alleviation and improve financial inclusion. The microfinance business model is based on providing loans to people who do not have collateral to guarantee banks repayment of a loan. Microfinance can contribute significantly to the lives of poor people, for example weddings, emergencies, and even more long term investment opportunities such as improving a business or buying a land. Furthermore, microfinance is vital to poor people due to their lack of income stability, whereby they may not have money or sufficient funds when they face a specific need, and therefore need to borrow.

One of the best cases that resonates the importance of microfinance is the success of Muhammad Yunus and his Grameen Bank. Microfinance has often been linked with poverty alleviation and has received strong support from governments, NGOs, development agencies, economic and financial institutions. There is a general belief that microfinance represents a method that can aid with alleviating poverty and boost entrepreneurship, and a number of successes have been well documented. The microfinance concept was essentially designed in developing nations for developing nations, essentially to provide financial services to those that are left behind by the formal and mainstream channels and it has worked as a mechanism to fight poverty and achieve social inclusion. According to the Consultative Group to Assist the Poor (CGAP, 2011) 2.7 billion adults do not have full access to formal financial services. This view that providing financial services to people who do not own any assets as collateral is believed to contribute to poverty alleviation, for a number of reasons.

Carruthers and Kim (2011) believe that access to credit is sensible for the long-term prosperity of a business, and gives people the chance to plan for the future. Furthermore, it may also contribute to the accumulation of equipment and tools to improve business productivity and so there are opportunities for a rise in income (CGAP, 2014). Authors, such as Hermes, Lensink, and Meesters (2011) also link microfinance services with an improvement in terms of access to healthcare services and housing. The logic of microfinance challenges mainstream finance, and sets the foundation for low-income individuals to access credit for different purposes. The rise of microfinance in developing nations also has been accompanied by a certain degree of failure. It could be argued that state owned banks have neglected delivering services and products that target low-income individuals, and instead have increasingly served more the middle and high income classes. Microfinance is probably the most prominent tool that can aid with poverty reduction and business development. According to Berger, Goldmark, and Miller-Sanabria (2006) microfinance has enabled poor microentrepreneurs to access financial services to support the growth of their businesses and increase productivity.

Roodman (2012) points out that microfinance serves at least 150 million clients around the globe. The mechanism of microfinance is based on small loans to poor people that often do not have the formal assets or guarantees to obtain credit through formal channels (banks but also other credit vehicles). In this sense, microfinance is able to provide a small amount of money that can allow microentrepreneurs to grow their business until they move out of poverty. While this concept looks attractive the reality is more complex, as different authors have shown that microfinance outcomes are not fully clear. Banerjee and Duflo (2011) show that in different cases and certain regions, microfinance loans are taken for consumption purposes rather than for productive purpose (i.e. increasing the productivity of a business). Karnani (2007/2009a) also pointed out that the outcome of microfinance is not clear and while in some cases it has proved to be successful, in other cases there was no evidence of poverty reduction at all.

Microfinance has grown remarkably since its foundation in the 1970s. By the end of 2009, more than 3,500 Microfinance institutions (MFIs) reached around 190 million households and 640 million poor people according to the microcredit Summit Campaign Report (Reed, 2011). In 2009, Wharton Business school published a list of the top 30 innovations over the past 30 years and microfinance made this list, with an entry at number 17 (Wharton, 2009). It is quite fascinating how the industry has evolved tremendously since the initial concept can be viewed negatively by both parties involved: institutions offering loans to poor people with no credit history or collateral and poor people wary of accumulating debt. However, organizations that provide such a service to the poor are known as microfinance institutions, which can vary in size. The positive results from expanding portfolio of microloans accessed by the poor have remedied the perception of the poor as a risky segment (Helms, 2006; Pantelić, 2013). Overall, we believe that this sector has much to offer in terms of alleviating poverty and improving the lives of the poor; whether it is the poor accessing capital for business development or emergency needs.

MICROFINANCE AND BOP: THE LATIN AMERICAN CASE

Latin America represents one of the most dynamic regions within the emerging economies, and this due to its unique business environment. Latin America is characterized by institutional voids, corruption, lack of rules of the game, high microeconomic volatility, arbitrage opportunities, large natural resource availability, and numerous low-income consumers (Vassolo et al, 2011). Interestingly, other business research strands such as entrepreneurship and family business which have started to dedicate research toward Latin America, share this view. For instance, authors such as Nordqvist et al (2011) explain that Latin America needs to overcome many obstacles as industry environments are uncertain and hostile. Problems in Latin America include weak property rights and business networks, lack of access to financing, rigid regulations and security issues among others. Despite this, the aforementioned authors argue that there is potential for research and cite a report by Ernst and Young (2010) which argues that it may be the best time to start or grow a business in the region as trade relationships have increased and economic institutions have become stronger.

As it has been emphasized in other studies, Latin America is characterized by an overall large informal economy (UN, 2009), and a large number of informal microenterprises (de Soto, 2000). The GDP estimates of the informal economy account for around 51% of employment in Latin America (Webb, Bruton, Tihanyi, & Duane Ireland, 2012). Informality is defined as the entrepreneurial activities that cover certain market-based initiatives that take place within informal boundaries and outside formal institutional ones (Bruton, Khavul, & Chavez, 2011). Therefore, Latin America represents an appropriate environment for research where the informal economy is widely accepted and acknowledged as a norm among the poor. In the literature, a large proportion of the BoP initiatives studied have centred on India, and much less attention is given to Latin America (Kolk, Rivera-Santos, & Rufin, 2013).

The 2013 edition of *Microscope, a* comprehensive report on the world's microfinance business environment produced by the Economist Intelligence Unit (EIU) demonstrates that Peru and Bolivia are the top two countries among the 55 countries in the world. Peru has held the top spot for six consecutive years, while Colombia, El Salvador, and the Dominican Republic all occupy places in the top ten (IDB, 2013).

Microfinance institutions in Latin America have had much success in expanding financial services to underserved communities. Latin America and South East Asia are the two regions whereby microfinance has expanded the most, and since the 1980s the number of clients has grown gradually (Navajas & Tejerina, 2006). Brazil was the country that pioneered and developed microfinance in Latin America during the 70s. However, due to difficult social conditions, microfinance only expanded throughout the region from the 80s (LAB, 2012). By 2009, microfinance institutions in Latin America had served around 10.5 million people and reached a loan volume that exceeded US$12.3 billion. This is a result of the expansion in the number of institutions offering microfinance, and the number of customers or clients that are served (Cotler & Aguilar, 2013). However, as the aforementioned authors point out that there are many differences between countries, and explain that Peru performs well in terms of the institutional development and rank highly in terms of the regulatory framework. Mexico, meanwhile ranks significantly lower in terms of the regulatory framework for microfinance, and even more poorly compared with Peru with respect to the institutional development of the sector. This is an interesting observation as Mexico is a much larger market, and likely has a greater need for microfinance services, yet it is underdeveloped when compared with Peru.

Despite the hype around microfinance and authors advocating its importance, it is unclear to what extent it can alleviate poverty. This remains unclear as most evaluations are based on the financial performance of MFIs, rather than evaluating the level or effect on poverty alleviation (Pantelić, 2013). There are those who are more sceptical with respect to the effect of the industry's potential to alleviate poverty, and advocate that microfinance may not be a sufficient way to establish economic and social development in a manner that can be sustained (Bateman, 2010; Bateman & Chang 2009). Although the same authors acknowledge that microfinance plays an important role in Latin American economies with respect to boosting business activities, at least in the short term. We believe that microfinance is one of the three key industries that have the potential to alleviate poverty, but agree that more comprehensive and longitudinal studies are needed that measure and focus on the impact of the industry with respect to reducing poverty.

In the following section the authors provide factors that entrepreneurs need to be aware of when engaging with the microfinance industry in Latin America.

MICROFINANCE AND ENTREPRENEURSHIP IN LATIN AMERICA

In the majority of emerging economies in Asia, Africa and Latin America, a large number of the employment comes from the informal economy, and a large number of these people work as microentrepreneurs. Another feature of many emerging economies is that important segments of the population live below the poverty line or slightly above it. This represents an important challenge as the economic and demographic profile is different when compared to developed nations. However, these are potential business opportunities that result from large segments of the population who are willing to increase their level of consumption.

The presence of institutional voids in emerging economies often leads to ineffective and/or inefficient goods and financial markets, which generate unproductive mechanisms that connect supply and demand. Entrepreneurs often have to face challenges to successfully fill these voids. However, these gaps in the functioning of markets and institutions provide opportunities to entrepreneurs. One of these opportunities is precisely the ability to provide access to capital for micro-entrepreneurs and poor consumers. From a business perspective, entrepreneurs potentially have the chance to fill this 'gap' on the lack of access to capital for people without collateral or assets, and who normally would not have access to capital through commercial banks by putting in place a profitable business model. This implies that entrepreneurs working and providing microfinance services can potentially act as social entrepreneurs, or agents of social change that improve the life of poor people, and at the same time build successful and profitable business models. Entrepreneurs interested in filling business opportunities in the microfinance sector should take into account the following factors:

1. **Microfinance in Different Contexts:** There is a need to understand the different ways in which microfinance is implemented in different countries within Latin America. It is important to stress that income per capita is not the only variable for entrepreneurs looking at microfinance as a business opportunity. For example, Bolivia is a country where people are very familiar to the solidarity-based mechanisms behind microfinance through systems such as the 'pasanaku'. Local communities in rural areas are used to obtaining loans where the community guarantees the repayment of the person who took out the loan. This type of deeply rooted mechanisms, while they do not represent the success of microfinance in Bolivia per se, they still provide a more complex picture of why microfinance institutions can work well in certain countries. On the other hand, evidence from Argentina (and specifically from the province of Buenos Aires) where a number of poor people used to be middle class, shows

that this specific type of social composition often does not fit with the profile of potential microfinance customers (Curat, Lupano & Adúriz, 2006). This explains the partial failure of microfinance in Argentina compared to many other countries in Latin America, such as Ecuador, Bolivia, or Peru. Therefore, it is important to understand the type of poverty within each context and the specific mechanisms of social organization within communities.

2. **Methods of Scaling-Up Microfinance Institutions:** One of the biggest challenges in Latin America is to gain access to enough capital to allow microfinance institutions to obtain long term growth. This is due to the limited size of the financial markets within the region and the number of requirements needed to secure this capital. This represents a potential a major barrier for entrepreneurs and can be overcome by forming strategic alliances with key market players in industries such as food processing and retail.

3. **Product Diversification and Promotional Methods:** While in Latin America microfinance often means providing credits to individuals (or group credit), it is more difficult to identify microfinance institutions with a large and sophisticated portfolio of loans dedicated to microentrepreneurs and micro firms. Entrepreneurs should make a strategic choice about the type of offering to their clients depending on the risk appetite. Entrepreneurs should increase their offering to include other services such as savings or investment, while minimizing losses on their loans and applying customised based solutions to local needs. Entrepreneurs need to promote their products beyond the mainstream outlets (television and radio advertisements). Instead they should promote the services in places that are truly relevant to the local community, for example promoting services in local schools, churches, or other venues that has a strong relevance to that community.

4. **Leveraging Social Reputation:** Latin American entrepreneurs' reputation is not usually perceived highly among local populations. However, social leaders' reputation within the region is often regarded more favourably. Therefore, it is advised that entrepreneurs should establish ties with social leaders in order to have a greater impact on the society. This could be achieved by working with local NGOs and other social leaders.

The following section of this chapter turns to the secondary analysis with the main objective of identifying the state of microfinance in various countries within Latin America. At the same time the authors aim to identify important companies and some of their characteristics that can be used in future studies, particularly those focusing more on a firm level.

MAPPING OUT COUNTRIES AND MICROFINANCE INSTITUTIONS

In this section we set to map out the main microfinance institutions in Latin America. Figure 2 shows the number of microfinance institutions ranked by the Multilateral Investment Fund of the Inter-American Development Bank in Latin America. The data compiled and presented shows that there are a group of countries in Latin America that are clearly represented (see Figure 2). The most standout countries include Ecuador, Bolivia, Mexico, Colombia and Peru, whereby the number of microfinance institutions is relatively high. There is a second group of countries with a smaller number of institutions, but with a significant representation, and these are El Salvador, Nicaragua, Honduras, Paraguay, Guatemala and the Dominican Republic. Finally, there is a group of countries with a more limited number of successful and large microfinance institutions, and these are Chile, Argentina, Brazil, Panama and Haiti.

There are a number of reasons why microfinance is more developed in some countries compared with others, and here we will offer a possible source of analysis to understand these differences. Using secondary data offered by different organizations, such as the Inter-American Development Bank, the World Bank, or the

Figure 2. The number of microfinance institutions by country (Source: Authors based on MIF-IDB data, 2013).

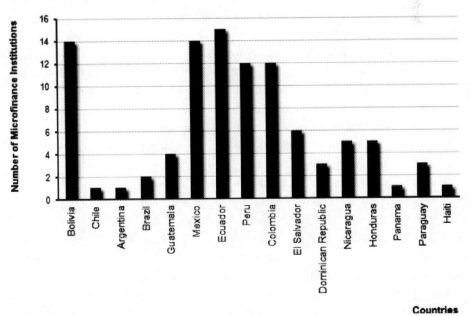

Figure 3. Number of microfinance institutions and ease of starting a business
Source: Authors analysis based on MIF-IDB data, 2013 and World Bank Data Ease of Doing Business, 2013.

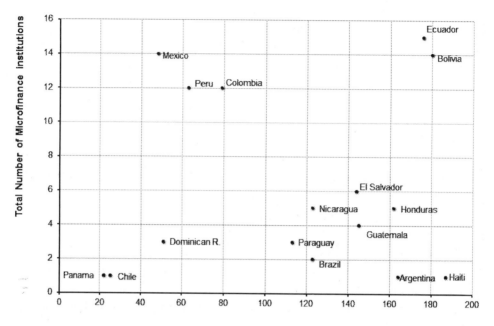

World Economic Forum, Figure 3 shows on one axis the number of microfinance institutions in each country and on the other the rank of each country in 'starting a business' according to the World Bank. Starting a business which is related to entrepreneurship represents one of the main sources of growth and development in countries around the world, and this becomes even more important in the case of developing countries. For entrepreneurs, the access to capital is a critical aspect for their activity, and therefore we aim to understand how in terms of 'ease' it is to start a business in different developing countries within Latin America. This allows us to understand possible links with the presence of a strong or weak microfinance industry in a given country.

The data shows no potential link between the number of microfinance institutions and the ease of starting a business in a country. Microfinance seems to prosper both in Bolivia, which ranks 180th in the world for starting a business, and in Mexico, a country that ranks pretty well in terms of 'starting a business'. In a similar fashion Peru and Colombia show an important number of microfinance institutions and a positive performance in starting business procedures. The data however does not support the perspective that there could be a link between the number of procedures and days required to start a business and the number of microfinance institutions.

Countries, such as Chile and Panama that rank very well in starting a business have a low and similar number of institutions, while Argentina and Haiti, which have a low ranking in terms of ease of starting a new business, rank very poorly.

An element that may be linked with the development of microfinance institutions in Latin America is the financial market development of a given country. To measure the financial market development, we used the indicator offered by the WEF Ranking on Competitiveness 2013-14, and this includes the following variables:

- Availability of financial services
- Affordability of financial services
- Financing through local equity market
- Ease of access to loans
- Venture capital availability
- Soundness of banks
- Regulation of securities exchanges
- Legal rights

Figure 4 shows that in the countries where microfinance is more developed there is a medium level of financial market development, and these countries include Ecuador, Mexico, Colombia, Peru and to some extent Bolivia. A number of countries, such as Argentina, Chile, Haiti, and Panama all rank poorly. The Central American countries, such as El Salvador, Nicaragua, Honduras and Guatemala have a decent number of microfinance institutions and show a medium level of development with respect to their financial markets.

The data analysed could support the idea that further empirical studies are needed to test the effect of the relationship between the level of financial development in a given country and the development of the microfinance institutions there. Figure 4 may offer different interpretations about the impact of financial development on the microfinance industry. However, clearly there are also other factors to take into account, such as the rule of law, corruption levels, the number of micro-entrepreneurs, SMEs, and MNEs in a given country, the overall levels of poverty, and type of poverty (rural/urban). These issues could be part of a larger empirical study that could be conducted to further assess the impact of the financial market development.

The analysis undertaken based on the Inter-American Development Bank data interestingly demonstrates that in Latin America the main microfinance institutions offer loans targeting micro-enterprises rather than individual consumers. It appears to be that only in a few countries, including Mexico, Ecuador, Peru, Colombia and Paraguay there is a growing presence of microfinance institutions that focus their portfolios toward the pure consumption side, rather than microenterprises (see Figure 5).

Figure 4. Number of microfinance institutions and financial market development
(Source: Authors analysis based on MIF-IDB data, 2013 and WEF Competitiveness Report data, 2014).

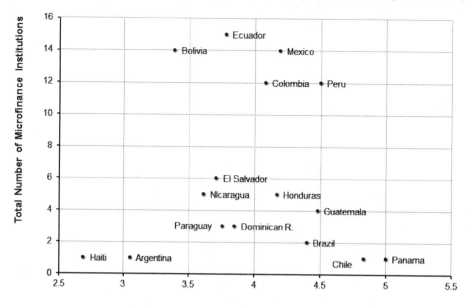

Figure 5. Microfinance led loans
(Source: Authors analysis based on MIF-IDB data, 2013).

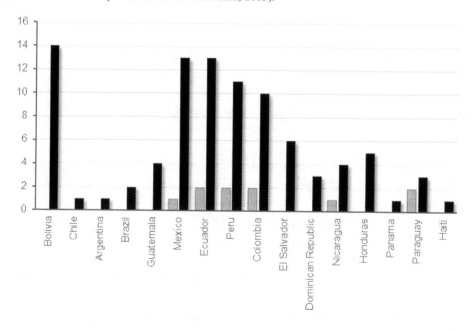

Figure 6. Microfianance institutions based on efficiency and scope
(*Source: Authors analysis based on MIF-IDB data, 2013*).

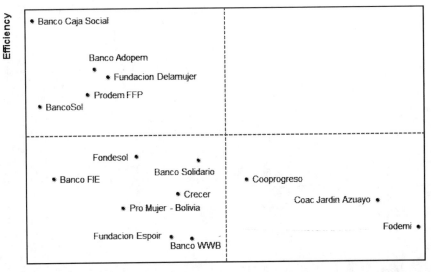

Our view is that government should bring more incentives to further expand microenterprise led MIFs as they can further contribute to the development and growth of entrepreneurs who will be responsible for generating more prosperity and jobs in a country.

Figure 6 is company based and shows the top 20 companies ranked by the Inter-American Development Bank in terms of scope and efficiency. One of the most interesting insights from the data is that there is a polarization between the microfinance institutions in Latin America. There are insitutions that tend to be very efficient and those which tend to expand their scope; however, none of them seem to be capable of combining these two aspects (see Figure 6). Furthermore, we introduce Figures 7 and 8, which go further by mapping out the microfinance institutions according to the loans provided by the gross portfolio of loans (Figure 7 illustrates this for microenterprise loans, while Figure 8 illustrates this for consumption loans).

We conclude this section with a case study on BancoSol (Box 1). This briefly illustrates that despite the difficult institutional environment and the number of economic problems the country has faced, BancoSol has emerged as one of the best microfinance institutions in the world. Following this, we move on to implications and future directions before concluding this chapter.

Figure 7. Loans to microenterprises and gross portfolio of microenterprise loans
(*Source: Authors analysis based on MIF-IDB data, 2013*).

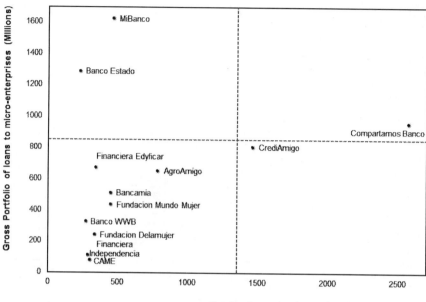

Figure 8. Loans for consumption and gross portfolio of consumption loans
(*Source: Authors analysis based on MIF-IDB data, 2013*).

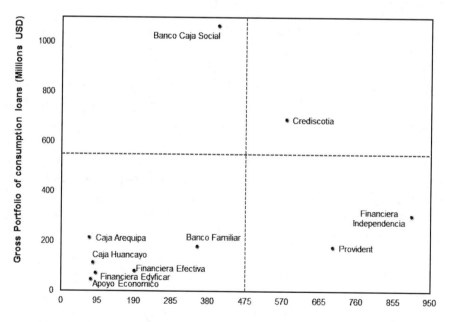

Box 1. BancoSol in Bolivia

Bolivia used to be considered as one of the least developed countries in Latin America. With a population of 9.5 million inhabitants made of members belonging to different ethnic groups in the country, Bolivia represents a unique nation with different geographical, economic and social challenges. In 1985, the country suffered one of the worst economic crises in its history. The country experienced hyper-inflation, and between 1982 and 1986 the GDP showed a negative rate of -3.4% and public debt reached 25% of the GDP. During the years 1993-1998, the country experienced a strong period of growth, only to fall again in 1998 into an economic crisis driven by different external and internal shocks. The political side like the economy also showed a similar instability

With this historical events and a mix of poor policies, the country generated a large mass of unemployment and people who did not have any access to credit. During the 80s the first NGOs offered microfinance services, while later several of them transformed into "Fondos Financieros Privados" (FFP), a small financial entity specialized in offering micro-loans and financial services. These institutions were able to serve these consumers through a mix of methodologies, including: solidarity-based groups, individual loans, and city-banks. The three approaches used different guaranty systems for the bank.

BancoSol was initially funded through the funding of PRODEM, the USAID, and other NGOs. Banco Sol initially offered only 3 types of products: medium-term deposits, solidarity-based loans, and short-term deposits. The typical loan was on average US$100 with a return period of 2 months. The banks employees undertook long periods of fieldwork sessions in order to better know and understand the local community, who were their clients. 75% of the people working for BancoSol were women with social science backgrounds. The group proved to be successful until the end of the 90s when Banco Sol started to face serious problems.

During 2000-2004 BancoSol developed a new strategy to regain competitiveness once again. Among the measures taken that allowed the company to grow again was the methodology known as "CAMEL", which was based on a more complex approach to evaluating clients, but also changes in the commercial areas with a new portfolio of products, and a strong innovation with respect to the bank's information system. It can be argued that BancoSol is one of the most successful microfinance institutions in the world.

Source: based on Caballero, and Melgarejo (2005). Banco Solidario S.A. La estrategia de recuperación, 2000 – 2004. INCAE Business School.

IMPLICATIONS FOR POLICYMAKERS AND PRACTITIONERS

Policymakers in Latin America need to devote attention to the creation of more microfinance institutions, and this can be accomplished by offering tax incentives for entrepreneurs. There is a need to devise and implement strategies that allow local financial markets to be more transparent and improve the access to capital.

It is recommended that governments actively create financial markets designed specifically for microfinance institutions. As commercial banks have access to capital at low interest rates, this is not available or specifically designed for smaller microfinance companies. It is suggested that governments implement policies to create such an environment whereby microfinance institutions can access capital from a wider range of sources, including people from the general public. The authors believe this to be a possible avenue that governments can explore further as it allows benefits to both parties involved in the exchange process. The general public are given opportunities to invest with the aim of making a return on their investment (different to no-profit organisations), and can do so with a conscience and a feel good effect. At the same time this provides microfinance companies with capital from a wider range of sources.

Programmes are needed that allow people at the BoP to understand the procedures and benefits of using formal lenders to access capital. There should be nationwide programmes that are included in schools so that those at the BoP can understand microfinance at an early age and become more familiar with this channel for accessing credit.

It is important that new policies implemented take into account the successful companies that are profitable and have a proven track record. Studying these cases will offer much on two fronts; firstly, it allows policymakers to understand how successful strategies were devised and how these can be replicated and contribute to frameworks and guidelines for other firms to follow. Particular attention needs to be paid to innovative non-profit organisations, such as Kiva which connects people by leveraging the internet and a worldwide network of microfinance institutions to reduce poverty. People can help create opportunities around the world by lending as little as US$25 (Kiva, 2014). This idea of utilizing the web and building networks with microfinance institutions are a model to be studied with objective of contributing to policies that can aid access to credit. Secondly, it will allow policymakers to understand what aspects of microfinance models needs to be addressed so that existing barriers can be tackled and removed.

For practitioners, the importance of business scope and efficiency merits significant attention. More is needed in terms of understanding and studying microfinance business models and the way they operate. In our chapter we pointed out that existing firms in Latin America are only able to focus on efficiency or scope but not both, and what is needed is a deeper understanding as to why this appears to be the case. Is there a way that existing models can be adapted or changed in such a way that both are achieved? Practitioners working with microfinance institutions need to devote more effort to understanding this issue. Understanding polar cases would yield interesting perspectives, for example, the microfinance company Banco Caja social in Colombia ranks high in terms of efficiency, but poorly in terms of scope, and this is in sharp contrast with the Ecuadorian firm FODEMI.

FUTURE RESEARCH: MOVING FORWARD

It is clear that a deeper understanding of strategic segmentation of the microfinance institutions is needed, according to their portfolio orientation. The field would highly benefit from a firm and individual level or unit of analysis. For example, it would be interesting for research to investigate and compare at a firm level the successful and unsuccessful firm strategies devised and implemented. In addition to this, formal lending institutions could be compared with informal lenders, as this will allow the field to better understand the practices of both types (Ayyagari, Demirguc-Kunt, & Maksimovic, 2007; Tsai, 2004). Longitudinal studies are needed that study firms serving the BoP over time, in order to uncover if strategies implemented are not only successful, but are ethical and sustainable. Therefore, we encourage firms to serve the BoP, and to do so in such a way that corporate social responsibility is at the heart of their ethos. Measuring the impact of microfinance institutions in terms of reducing poverty requires further attention, as some scholars believe this has been exaggerated and remains unclear. There needs to be a shift away from measuring success based on the growing number of loans and institutions, and a move toward measuring poverty reduction.

Research on SMEs and the decision making process at an individual level would be insightful. More research is needed that uncovers the way managers evaluate opportunities and perceive risk. Studies are needed that investigate those at the BoP as producers, rather than viewing poor people only as consumers. Research needs to be undertaken in many regions, not only Latin America, but Africa and the Middle East so that the best practices adopted by successful firms can be identified and possibly tested in other parts of the world. Although it can be argued that every emerging market is unique with its own institutional and cultural environment, it is still possible that some universal themes or principles that are relevant to other contexts can emerge.

An increasing number of scholars within the field of International Business (IB) have emphasised the need to move research forward. Buckley (2002) explained that the IB research agenda had stalled due to the lack of 'big questions' to guide future research. In addition to this, Buckley and Ghauri (2004) suggested that the big question could indeed be globalisation and its driving forces. Indeed a number of IB scholars have undertaken research and shown interest on MNEs and global poverty reduction (Ghauri and Buckley, 2006; Jain and Vachani, 2006; O'Brien and Beamish, 2006), and this has potential to offer exciting and fruitful research opportunities. MNEs and SMEs targeting the BoP and contributing to poverty alleviation in a sustainable and ethical manner should be another big IB research strand. For example, there is plenty of scope for international business scholars to be involved, particularly those researching firm behaviour. Future research could investigate the paths of internationalization pursued by microfinance companies, and how they adjust their strategies and organisational structures in foreign markets to serve BoP consumers. It is here we argue that there is a potential for a strong intersection of two fields: strategy and IB. If again we turn our attention to the example of Kiva, we can see opportunities with respect to understanding the internationalisation process of lending institutions that make use of the web for people at the BoP.

CONCLUSION: A FINAL THOUGHT

The purpose of this chapter was to review literature on the BoP, and we began broadly before specifically focusing on microfinance. Using secondary sources, we mapped out microfinance companies operating in Latin America that serve the BoP. We strongly believe that a number of sectors can help alleviate poverty, while other sectors are not deemed as effective or are better understood from marketing perspectives, such as discretionary led sectors. There are still plenty of research opportunities as stated in the future research section of this chapter. We advocate that scholars continue to explore concepts and approaches to BoP that enlighten the field with a better understanding of e.g. the role of SMEs, and how firms devise and implement successful, responsible, and ethical strategies, to name a few.

Trust is an important underlying theme and is central to microfinance and the BoP, and this is supported by Sriram (2005). From the lenders perspective, they need to trust that the poor can repay their loans, while in turn the poor need to trust companies if they are to engage with them and move away from informal lenders, which have been prevalent in some countries. Trust is the foundation, and this is why we advocate that firms adopt long term visions and adopt strategies in an ethical and responsible manner. We strongly recommend that more exploratory research on the BoP is conducted with strong policy implications. Only then can we offer pragmatic solutions to tackle poverty, and move one step closer towards alleviating it.

REFERENCES

Akula, V. (2008). Business basics at the Base of the Pyramid. *Harvard Business Review, 86*(6), 53–57.

Altman, D. G., Rego, L., & Ross, P. (2009). Expanding opportunity at the Base of the Pyramid. *People & Strategy, 32*(2), 46–51.

Anderson, J., & Billou, N. (2007). Serving the world's poor: Innovation at the Base of the Economic Pyramid. *The Journal of Business Strategy, 28*(2), 14–21. doi:10.1108/02756660710732611

Ayyagari, M., Demirguc-Kunt, A., & Maksimovic, V. (2007). *Formal versus informal finance: Evidence from China*. World Bank Mimeo.

Banerjee, A. V., & Duflo, E. (2007). The economic lives of the poor. *The Journal of Economic Perspectives, 21*(1), 141–167. doi:10.1257/jep.21.1.141 PMID:19212450

Banerjee, A. V., & Duflo, E. (2011). *Poor economics: A radical rethinking of the way to fight global poverty*. New York: PublicAffairs.

Bateman, M. (2010). *Why doesn't microfinance work? The destructive rise of local neoliberalism*. New York: Zed Books.

Bateman, M., & Chang, H. J. (2009). *The Microfinance Illusion*. Available online at: http://www.microfinancetransparency.com/evidence/PDF/App.3%20Chang%20 Bateman%20article.pdf (accessed 15 October 2014)

Berger, M., Goldmark, L., & Miller-Sanabria. (Eds.). (2006). *An inside view of Latin American microfinance*. Washington, DC: Inter-American Development Bank.

Bruton, K., Khavul, S., & Chavez, H. (2011). Microlending in emerging economies: Building a new line of inquiry from the ground up. *Journal of International Business Studies, 42*(5), 718–739. doi:10.1057/jibs.2010.58

Buckley, P. J. (2002). Is the International Business research agenda running out of steam? *Journal of International Business Studies, 33*(2), 365–373. doi:10.1057/ palgrave.jibs.8491021

Buckley, P. J., & Ghauri, P. N. (2004). Globalisation, economic geography and the strategy of multinational enterprises. *Journal of International Business Studies, 35*(2), 81–98. doi:10.1057/palgrave.jibs.8400076

Caballero, K., & Melgarejo, M. (2005). La estrategia de recuperación, 2000 - 2004. In INCAE Business School (Eds.), *CGAP Portal de Microfinanzas*. Available at: http://www.microfinancegateway.org/sites/default/files/mfg-es-documento-caso-bancosol-2-2005.pdf

Carruthers, B. G., & Kim, J. C. (2011). The sociology of finance. *Annual Review of Sociology, 37*(1), 239–259. doi:10.1146/annurev-soc-081309-150129

CGAP. (2011). What do we know about the impact of microfinance? In *Consultative group to assist the poor - About microfinance*. Available online at: www.cgap. org/p/site/c/template.rc/1.26.1306

CGAP. (2014). *Financial Inclusion and Development: Recent Impact Evidence*. Available online at: http://www.cgap.org/sites/default/files/FocusNote-Financial-Inclusion-and-Development-April-2014.pdf

Cotler, P., & Aguilar, G. (2013). The microfinance sectors in Peru and Mexico: Why have they followed different paths? In R. Manos, J.-P. Gueyie, & J. Yaron (Eds.), *Promoting microfinance: Challenges and innovations in developing countries and countries in transition*. Palgrave Macmillan. doi:10.1057/9781137034915.0008

Curat, P., Lupano, J., & Adúriz, I. (2006). *Demanda potencial por microcréditos en el Conurbano Bonaerense*. Fundación Andares.

De Soto, H. (2000). *The mystery of capital: Why Capitalism triumphs in the West and fails everywhere else*. London: Bantam Press – Black Swan edition.

Dolan, C., & Scott, L. (2009). Lipstick evangelism: Avon trading circles and gender empowerment in South Africa. *Gender and Development, 17*(2), 203–218. doi:10.1080/13552070903032504

Ghauri, P. N., & Buckley, P. J. (2006). Globalization, multinational enterprises and world poverty. In S. C. Jain & S. Vachani (Eds.), *Multinational corporations and global poverty reduction* (pp. 204–232). Cheltenham, UK: Edward Elgar Publishing.

Gibson, S. (2007). Microfranchising: The Next Step on the Development Ladder. In J. Fairbourne, S. Gibson, & G. Dyer (Eds.), *Microfranching: Creating Wealth at the Bottom of the Pyramid* (pp. 235–239). Northampton, MA: Edward Elgar Publishing. doi:10.4337/9781847205360.00012

Hammond, A. L., Kramer, W. J., Katz, R. S., Tran, J. T., & Walker, C. (2007). The next 4 billion: Market size and business strategy and the Base of the Pyramid. World resources institute and international finance corporation/World bank. *Group*.

Hart, S. L. (2005). *Capitalism at the Crossroads. The Unlimited Business Opportunities in Solving the World's Most Difficult Problems*. Upper Saddle River, NJ: Wharton School Publishing.

Helms, B. (2006). *Access for all: Building inclusive financial systems*. Washington, DC: World Bank. doi:10.1596/978-0-8213-6360-7

Hermes, N., Lensink, R., & Meesters, A. (2011). Outreach and efficiency of microfinance institutions. *World Development, 39*(6), 938–948. doi:10.1016/j.worlddev.2009.10.018

IDB. (2013). *Global Microscope: Continued Growth and Innovation in Financial Markets for Low-income Populations*. Available online at: http://www.iadb.org

Jain, S. C., & Vachani, S. (2006). The role of MNCs in alleviating global poverty. In S. C. Jain & S. Vachani (Eds.), *Multinational corporations and global poverty reduction* (pp. 3–28). Cheltenham, UK: Edward Elgar Publishing.

Karnani, A. (2007). The mirage of marketing to the Bottom of the Pyramid: How the private sector can alleviate poverty. *California Management Review, 49*(4), 90–111. doi:10.2307/41166407

Karnani, A. (2009a). Romanticizing the poor. *Business Strategy Review*, *19*(2), 48–53. doi:10.1111/j.1467-8616.2008.00535.x

Karnani, A. (2009b). Romanticizing the poor harms the poor. *Journal of International Development*, *21*(1), 76–86. doi:10.1002/jid.1491

Kistruck, G. M., Webb, J. W., Sutter, C., & Duane Ireland, R. (2011). Microfranchising in Base-of-the- Pyramid markets: Institutional challenges and adaptations to the franchise model. *Entrepreneurship Theory and Practice*, *35*(3), 503–531. doi:10.1111/j.1540-6520.2011.00446.x

Kiva. (2014). *About Us*. Available online at: www.kiva.org

Kolk, A., Rivera-Santos, M., & Rufin, C. R. (2013). Reviewing a Decade of Research on the 'Base/Bottom of the Pyramid' (BOP) Concept. *Business & Society*, *20*(10), 1–40.

LAB. (2012). *An Overview of Microfinance in Latin America*. Latin American Bureau. Available online at: http://lab.org.uk

London, T. (2009). Making better investments at the base of the pyramid. *Harvard Business Review*, *87*(5), 106–113.

London, T., & Hart, S. L. (2004). Reinventing strategies for emerging markets: Beyond the transnational model. *Journal of International Business Studies*, *35*(5), 350–370. doi:10.1057/palgrave.jibs.8400099

London. (2007). *A base of-the-pyramid perspective on poverty Alleviation*. The William Davidson Institute-University of Michigan.

London. (2010). Business Model Development for the base of the pyramid market entry. *Academy of Management Proceedings*, (1), 1-6.

MIF-IDB. (2013). *Fondo Multilateral de Inversiones (FOMIN) - Banco Interamericano de Desarrollo (BID) - Microfinanzas Americas, Las 100 Mejores, 2013*. Available at: http://www10.iadb.org/intal/intalcdi/PE/2013/12790es.pdf

Navajas, S., & Tejerina, L. (2006). *Microfinance in Latin America and the Caribbean: How Large Is the Market?* Washington, DC: Inter-American Development Bank. Sustainable Development Department Best Practices Series.

Nghia, N. C. (2010). Management research about solutions for the eradication of global poverty: A literature review. *Journal of Sustainable Development*, *3*(1), 17–28. doi:10.5539/jsd.v3n1p17

Nordqvist, M., Marzano, G., Brenes, E., Jimenez, G., & Fonseca-Paredes, M. (2011). *Understanding entrepreneurial family businesses in uncertain environment: Opportunities and resources in Latin America* (pp. 1–29). Cheltenham, UK: Elgar Publishing in Association with the Global STEP Project. doi:10.4337/9781849804738

O'Brien, J., & Beamish, P. W. (2006). Linking poverty and Foreign Direct Investment in developing countries. In S. C. Jain & S. Vachani (Eds.), *Multinational corporations and global poverty reduction* (pp. 105–122). Cheltenham, UK: Edward Elgar Publishing.

Pantelić, A. (2013). The implications of a growing microfinance market in Latin America and the Caribbean. In R. Manos, J.-P. Gueyie, & J. Yaron (Eds.), *Promoting microfinance: Challenges and innovations in developing countries and countries in transition*. Palgrave Macmillan. doi:10.1057/9781137034915.0006

Prahalad, C. K. (2005). *The fortune at the Bottom of the Pyramid: Eradicating Poverty Through Profits*. Upper Saddle River, NJ: Wharton School Publishing.

Prahalad, C. K. (2010). *The fortune at the Bottom of the Pyramid: Eradicating poverty through profits (5th Anniversary Edition)*. Upper Saddle River, NJ: Wharton School Publishing.

Prahalad, C. K., & Hart, S. L. (2002). The fortune at the Bottom of the Pyramid. *Strategy and Business*, (26), 1-13.

Reed, L. R. (2011). *State of the Microcredit Summit Campaign Report*. Washington, DC: Microcredit Summit Campaign. Available online at: http://www.microcredit-summit.org/uploads/resource/document/socr-2011-english_41396.pdf

Roodman, D. M. (2012). *Due diligence: An impertinent inquiry into microfinance*. Washington, DC: Center for Global Development.

Simanis, E., & Hart, S. L. (2009). Innovation from the inside out. *MIT Sloan Management Review*, *50*(4), 77–86.

Sriram, M. S. (2005). Information Asymmetry and trust: A framework for understanding microfinance in India. *Vikapla*, *30*(4), 77–85.

Stanfield, J. (2010). *Self Help and Sustainability in Education in Developing Countries, E.G. West Centre EFA Working Paper, 10*. Available online at: http://egwestcentre.com/publications-3/working-papers/

Tsai, K. S. (2004). Imperfect Substitutes: The local political economy for informal finance and microfinance in rural China and India. *World Development*, *32*(9), 1487–1507. doi:10.1016/j.worlddev.2004.06.001

UNDP. (2008). *Creating value for all: strategies for doing business with the poor - Growing Inclusive Markets*. New York: United Nations Development Programme. Available at http://growinginclusivemarkets.org/media/gimlaunch/Report_2008/GIM%20Report%20Final%20August%202008.pdf

United Nations. (2009). *Rethinking Poverty: Report on the World Social Situation*. Available online at: www.un.org/esa/socdev/rwss/docs/2010/fullreport.pdf

Vassolo, R. S., De Castro, J. O., & Gomez-Mejia, L. (2011). Managing in Latin America: Common issues and a research agenda. *The Academy of Management Perspectives*, *25*(4), 22–36. doi:10.5465/amp.2011.0129

Wharton. (2009). *A world transformed: What are the top 30 innovations of the last 30 years?* Knowledge@wharton - University of Pennsylvania. Available online at: http://knowledge.wharton.upenn.edu

Chapter 2
Corruption in Latin America and How It Affects Foreign Direct Investment (FDI):
Causes, Consequences, and Possible Solutions

Jose Godinez
Merrimack College, USA

ABSTRACT

Foreign direct investment has aided in a significant manner the economic development of Latin America since the early 1990s because capital in this region is limited (Blanco, 2012). Despite some criticism literature on FDI has overwhelmingly demonstrated that FDI has positive effects on host countries (Tan & Meyer, 2011) especially in Latin America (Wooster & Diebel, 2010). Authors researching the effects of FDI in Latin America have stated that this investment helps to growth on productivity (Blonigen & Wang, 2005) and thus, might help developing countries to begin their road to development. Therefore, scholars have devoted great efforts to understanding the determinants of FDI to Latin America and a brief overview will be provided in this study. This paper will present a detailed account of FDI flows to the region, a clear definition of corruption and how it is manifested in Latin America. After these definitions, suggestions are provided to deal with the problem of corruption in the region.

DOI: 10.4018/978-1-4666-8820-9.ch002

1. INTRODUCTION

In this chapter a description of foreign direct investment (FDI) flows, its determinants, and corruption in Latin America will be provided. The rationale for analysing how corruption affects the attraction of FDI to Latin America is due to the size of the region and its substantial FDI inflows, which can provide a clear macroeconomic picture of the issue. Also, all the countries in Latin America are considered developing and thus with high levels of corruption (Except Chile that does not present high levels of corruption but is still considered developing) (Transparency International, 2011). Therefore, this region represents an ideal location to study how corruption affects FDI depending on the corruption levels of the home countries.

Foreign direct investment has aided in a significant manner the economic development of Latin America since the early 1990s because capital in this region is limited (Blanco, 2012). Despite some criticism literature on FDI has overwhelmingly demonstrated that FDI has positive effects on host countries (Tan & Meyer, 2011) especially in Latin America (Wooster & Diebel, 2010). Authors researching the effects of FDI in Latin America have stated that this investment helps to growth on productivity (Blonigen & Wang, 2005) and thus, might help developing countries to begin their road to development. Therefore, scholars have devoted great efforts to understanding the determinants of FDI to Latin America and a brief overview will be provided in this study.

Also, studies have consistently demonstrated that corruption has a detrimental effect on FDI flows. Therefore, studying corruption and its causes in Latin America can be viewed as the first step to start dealing with this problem. This paper will present a detailed account of FDI flows to the region, a clear definition of corruption and how it is manifested in Latin America. After these definitions, suggestions are provided to deal with the problem of corruption in the region.

2. DEFINITIONS

2.1 Foreign Direct Investment (FDI)

Foreign direct investment (FDI) is defined by the Organization for Economic Cooperation and Development (OECD) as "cross-border investment by a resident entity in one economy with the objective of obtaining a lasting interest in an enterprise resident in another economy" (OECD, 2014). By lasting interest the OECD means that a long-term interest and significant influence between the direct investor and the enterprise should exist. Therefore, to be considered FDI, the foreign investor should at least have 10% of the voting power in an investment made overseas.

Foreign direct investment is a crucial element in international economic integration. FDI generates direct, stable and long-term links between countries. FDI also fosters technology and know-how transfer between economies and it permits the host economy to disseminate its products and services more freely in international markets (OECD, 2014). Moreover, FDI can also be an extra source of funds for investment for the host country, which means that FDI can be seen as an important medium for development.

While a number of scholars argue that inward FDI is necessary for a country to develop, this idea also has its detractors. Several studies have analyzed whether or not inward FDI benefits a host country or region yielding mixing results. According to Balasubramanyam, et al., (1999), FDI is necessary for a developing economy to grow. Others, however, have argued that FDI does not necessarily help the host economy since the rewards do not reach the general public (Borensztein, et al., 1998). However, the general consensus is that FDI would be favorable for the host economy if certain conditions are met. Such conditions include economic policies and development levels of financial and institutional development (Curevo-Cazurra, 2008). Therefore, for a host region to truly benefit from inward FDI, such region must have an adequate institutional structure to support growth. However, the presence of corruption in a host location undermines its institutions and thus, diminishes the potential benefits of FDI flowing to such region.

2.2 Corruption

Corruption can be defined as the abuse of public power for personal gain (Godinez & Liu, 2014). This definition is appropriate for this study because it includes bribery, nepotism, extortion, fraud, embezzlement, cronyism, influence pending, and misappropriation of public resources (Myint, 2000). However, it is necessary to point out that it does not include behavior that can be seen as offensive to moral standards since it may not be illegal. One important aspect that needs attention is that concepts of corruption are generally viewed from a 'western' point of view, which might fail to account for cultural practices of non-western societies (Zurawicki & Habib, 2010). Nevertheless, western standards are at least partly relevant in most developing economies, which can make this definition as inclusive as possible.

Corruption can relate to individual acts or to a state of society as a whole (Kurer, 2005). Corruption reflects a society that has failed to maintain a standard of goodness but at the same time it can reflect only individual actions (Collins & Uhlenbruck, 2004). Corruption can be carried out by one or more parties. Corrupt activities such as fraud, embezzlement, and misappropriation of public assets can be carried out by an official alone without the involvement of a second party. On the other hand, bribery, extortion, cronyism, influence pending, and nepotism need at least the involvement of two parties (Gray & Kaufman, 1998). Notwithstanding which of these activities are carried out by a public official and even in their simplest form, they can influence government policy and/or misallocate public resources (Jain, 2001). Moreover, if any of these activities are discovered they at least should be considered illegal and cause public disapproval.

3. DETERMINANTS OF CORRUPTION

To exist, corruption needs three elements. Firstly a public official has to have discretionary power. Roughly defined, discretionary powers include the authority to devise and administer regulations. Secondly, this power must be associated with possible economic rents. Thirdly, the probability of being caught and punished for the illicit acts must be low (Myint, 2000). In other words, corruption exists when higher rents are associated with discretionary powers and the possibility of being penalized is minimal.

Several types of corruption have been identified in literature. Shleifer and Vishny (1993) make a distinction of corruption with or without theft. In the corruption with theft context, the corrupt official keeps the amount of the bribe and provides the amount of the service to the government. On the other hand, in the corruption with theft context the official keeps the whole amount paid. Rose-Ackerman (2008) differentiates between bribery to modify existing rules and bribery to shape the application of such rules. One problem encountered with these classifications is that they were considered at the transaction level as opposed to the country level (Curevo-Cazurra, 2008). To account for this problem scholars have distinguished between two dimensions of corruption: Arbitrariness and Pervasiveness (Doh, et al., 2003).

Corruption is different in different countries. Corruption changes widely across different locations in its scope in an economy as well as in the level of uncertainty it creates (Uhlenbruck, et al., 2006). The uncertainty created by corruption is also called arbitrariness (Wei, 1997), which echoes the amount of ambiguity linked with corrupt deals in any given location (Rodriguez, et al., 2005). Arbitrary corruption is viewed as the uncertainty created by corruption regarding how to operate in a given location (Uhlenbruck, et al., 2006). In this sense, foreign investors, when operating in a country with high arbitrary corruption, will not know whether or not they will be asked for illegal payments or if the service agreed on will be delivered after making the illegal payment.

A high level of arbitrary corruption can be described as 'disorganized corruption' where different parties across the public sector may ask for illegal payments independently from one another (Shleifer & Vishny, 1993). As a result from this, a foreign investor cannot be certain that, after making an illegal payment to a local official, another payment will be required for the same service or if additional payments will need to be made. This leads to what Uhlenbruck et al., (2006) define as ineffectual corrupt transactions.

Pervasive corruption is defined as the likelihood of an MNE to encounter corruption in a foreign location (Rodriguez, et al., 2005). Pervasive corruption increases the costs of operating in a country. In other words, pervasive corruption represents the known costs of host country corruption and thus, MNEs have an idea of what to expect from corrupt public officials (Curevo-Cazurra, 2008). Also, in countries with high levels of pervasive corruption, the chances of facing consequences for corrupt activities are lower (Lee, et al., 2013). Furthermore, Murphy, et al., (1993) argue that corrupt behavior can be institutionalized and thus becoming a normal practice in certain locations.

The pervasiveness level of corruption in a location is likely to affect each MNE's assessment of the costs and benefits of participating in corrupt deals (Doh, et al., 2003). However, not all MNEs perceive corruption in the same manner. MNEs have organizational practices defined at their founding that will be replicated overseas. For this reason recent studies have concluded that MNEs located in countries with low levels of corruption would avoid investing in highly corrupt countries (Habib & Zurawicki, 2002). Nevertheless, high pervasiveness of corruption enables foreign MNEs to gain access to local government without the need of a local partner (Uhlenbruck, et al., 2006). This could imply that countries used to pervasive environments might have a competitive advantage when operating in similar environments. Furthermore, MNEs located in countries considered corrupt might carry over their own practices when investing abroad. Hence, such firms may not avoid investing in corrupt locations.

4. BACKGROUND INFORMATION

4.1 Brief History of Foreign Direct Investment to Latin America

The Latin American region has a long history of FDI dating back to the 19th century (Behrman, 1974). Initially FDI was mainly export-oriented, and/or natural resource seeking by MNEs from developed countries. After WWII, however, FDI to the region shifted towards manufacturing for local consumption (Biglaiser & De Rouen, 2006). Despite the attractiveness of the region, local governments had a detrimental influence on foreign businesses by exercising significant regulative powers and enforcing them randomly (Grosse, 1989). It was until the 1980s that local governments began opening the region to foreign MNEs fuelled by the need of local governments of foreign exchange (Trevino & Mixon, 2004).

Figure 1. Map of Latin America

Due to the prohibition of most imports and by restricting FDI to the region, many countries created an unattractive business climate to foreign MNEs. Exacerbating this problem, a shortage in foreign currency created an important crisis throughout the Latin American region. These policies led to closed economies that did not open to foreign commerce until the 1980s (Trevino & Mixon, 2004). Nevertheless, during the past three decades, several Latin American countries have employed market-oriented reforms hoping that such reforms would indicate their good intentions towards prospective foreign investors (Rodrik, 1996).These reforms included changes in tax laws, liberalization of trade, privatization, financial reform, and the removal of barriers to international capital flows (Biglaiser & De Rouen, 2006). FDI flows to the area fluctuated up and down in the 1970s and 1980s with no distinctive tendency to rise. However, the region saw an explosion of inward FDI during the 1990s. The magnitude of this capital flows to the region has been well defined in literature; nevertheless, this phenomenon is still quite unusual for any region in the world (Rivera-Batiz, 2000).

Latin America also experienced changes due to the deregulation it experienced during the 1990s. During the last decade of the last century the area underwent several reforms that opened its doors to trade with foreign MNEs (The Ecomomist, 2012). Furthermore, the region has also shown stability during the last five years. This stability is shown with the region's GDP growth averaging 4%, also demonstrating its endurance in the face of the global crisis of 2008 when the markets bounced back rapidly (The Ecomomist, 2012).

Figure 2. Latin America and the Caribbean Inward and Outward FDI, 1992-2009 in billions of US$
(*Source: Economic Commission for Latin America and the Caribbean (ECLAC) 2010*).

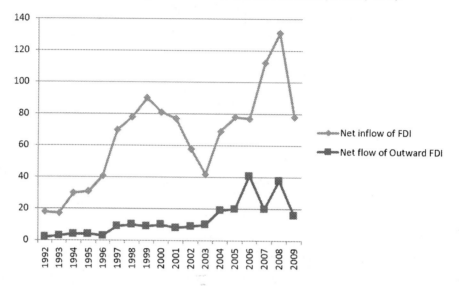

4.2 Foreign Direct Investment Flows to Latin America

According to the Economic Commission for Latin America and the Caribbean (ECLAC) (2010), due to the global recession, FDI flows to Latin America in 2009 reached US$77.675 billion, which represents a 41% decline compared to an all-time high in 2008 as presented in Figure 2. In South America FDI decreased 40% to US$54.454 billion, being Brazil, Chile, and Colombia the region's largest recipients. Mexico also felt the consequences of the global recession by receiving US$12.522 billion, which is 47% less FDI than in 2008; however, this made Mexico the third largest recipient of FDI in the region after Brazil and Chile. Central America was also affected by the recession and FDI to the region shrank 33% compared to the previous year amounting to US$5.05 billion. In the region, Costa Rica, Guatemala, and Panama were the largest recipients of FDI. Finally, the Caribbean also saw a decline in FDI flows by 43% to US$5.662 billion.

Even though FDI flows to the region decreased drastically in 2009 from the previous year, FDI levels to the region were the fifth highest in history (ECLAC, 2010). In fact, FDI flows to the region have trended upwards during the past two decades, and the post-crisis recovery was remarkable (ECLAC, 2012). This was achieved by steady structural characteristics of this kind of investment in the region, comprised mainly of commodities and low and medium-low technology manufac-turing with investment in asset seeking investment that generate research and development (R&D) almost inexistent (ECLAC, 2010). This trend means that the region did not suffer from the global recession as badly as other regions because firms tend to cut expenses in R&D activities first when facing financial problems. However, even though the region benefited by the structure of FDI received, Latin America has a strong potential to attract more FDI to its technology sector in order to transition to more technological activities, which would strengthen the region's absorptive capacities.

4.3 Trends and Characteristics of Inward FDI flows to Latin America and the Caribbean

The global financial crisis overturned the rising trend of inward FDI flows to the Latin American region. According to the United Nations Conference on Trade and Development (UNCTAD) (2013), even though the region saw a sharp decline in FDI inflows in 2009, the average flows were above annual averages for the decade. Furthermore, FDI received in the region were the fifth highest ever received and this is excluding the main financial centers in Latin America. This section will analyze FDI inflows into the region.

As presented in Figure 3, the decrease on FDI to Latin America is evident in every sub-region despite the different sectors and specializations that each of these sub-regions possess. In fact, FDI inflows to South America reached US$54.454 billion in 2009, which is 40% less than the previous year. Mexico and the Caribbean Basin received US$23.211 billion in the same year, seeing a decrease of 43% in FDI inflows compared to 2008 (ECLAC, 2010). The decrease in FDI to the region can be explained by (a) problems in obtaining access to credit and the high levels of uncertainty at the time; (b) the abrupt decrease in commodity prices, which caused a reduction in natural resource-seeking FDI; (c) the North American recession; and (d) the recession in many other world's countries (ECLAC, 2010). Even though FDI flows to South America dropped in 2009 all this sub-region, the sub-region has been steadily been one of the most important recipients of FDI worldwide during the past three decades. Figure 4 presents the distribution of inward FDI to Latin America from 1999 to 2009.

In South America, Brazil, Chile, and Colombia have been the largest recipients of FDI, even though in 2009 these countries saw a deep decline in FDI inflows. According to ECLAC (2010), South America experienced a decline of FDI inflows compared to 2008. Also, UNCTAD (2013) says that the region receives most of its FDI in the primary and services sectors and due to the global recession, the region's economy contracted from a 5.1% growth in 2008, to a-0.2% decrease the following year. This contraction in the country's economy deterred market seeking FDI in 2009. Mexico and Central America have also been important recipients of FDI in

Figure 3. Latin America and the Caribbean Inward FDI by sub-region, 1992-2009 in billions of US$
Source: *Economic Commission for Latin America and the Caribbean (ECLAC) 2010.*

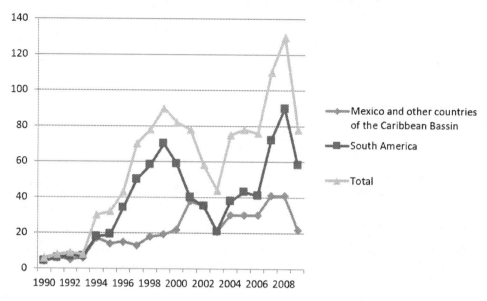

Figure 4. Latin America and the Caribbean: Sectoral Distribution of FDI, 1999-2009 (Percentages)
Source: *Economic Commission for Latin America and the Caribbean (ECLAC) 2010.*

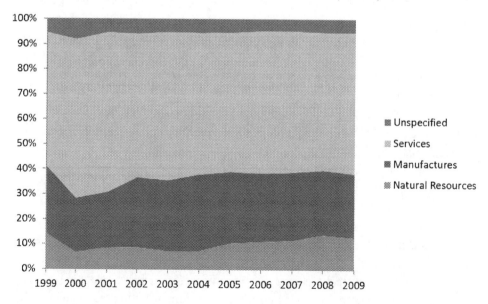

the Latin American region. The main investor in this sub-region is the United States, and for that reason the recession that hit the North American giant also affected these Latin American countries. Nonetheless, similarly to the South American Sub-region, Central America has seen a steady increase in FDI flows in the past three decades and even though this rise was stopped in 2009, the region still receives considerable amounts of FDI especially in export platforms. Nevertheless, according to the UNCTAD (2013), the amounts of FDI received by the region are still extremely high compared to what the region has historically attracted and compared to other regions in the world. Figure 5 presents the country of origin of FDI to the region from 1998 to 2009.

Foreign direct investment has aided in a significant manner the economic development of Latin America since the early 1990s because capital in this region is limited (Blanco, 2012). Despite some criticism literature on FDI has overwhelmingly demonstrated that FDI has positive effects on host countries (Tan & Meyer, 2011) especially in Latin America (Wooster & Diebel, 2010). Authors researching the effects of FDI in Latin America have stated that this investment helps to growth on productivity (Blonigen & Wang, 2005) and thus, might help developing countries to begin their road to development. However, it has been argued that the high levels of corruption in the region have deterred even greater flows of this kind of investment (Godinez & Liu, 2014).

Figure 5. Latin America and the Caribbean: Origin of FDI, 1998-2009
Source: Economic Commission for Latin America and the Caribbean (ECLAC) 2010.

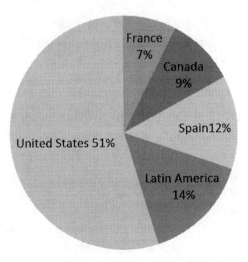

5. CORRUPTION IN LATIN AMERICA: CAUSES AND CONSEQUENCES

Corruption is increasingly seen as one of the most significant threats that Latin America is currently facing (Selingson, 2006). In fact, Weyland (1998) says that democracies in the Latin American region are threatened by a staggering growth in corruption that has arisen since the dictators of the past left power. Weyland (1998), argues that corruption has increased under the new democratic states in Latin America due to the dispersion of power that was concentrated in the hands of a few during the dictatorships; the liberal reforms that have opened many areas of the local economies to bribery; and the prominent role that expensive TV ads play in electing candidates to public office who to perpetuate their power seek illegal forms of economic support to afford such TV exposure.

According to Selingson (2006), corruption is increasing in Latin America because the people who are in charge (with monopoly powers) of controlling it are in fact benefiting from corrupt deals. In fact, in his study, Selingson (2006) finds that throughout Latin America members of the government elite, the judiciary system, and the bureaucracy are perceived to be involved in corrupt acts in the whole region. Furthermore, the author states that corruption corrodes trust and confidence in the political system of the Latin American countries he studied. However, this author did not provide an answer of whether or not corruption affected the attraction of FDI to the region and if it did how it affected this kind of investment.

States transitioning after an internal conflict usually have very weak institutions and a rising influx of foreign investment, which is a source of potential rents. These two circumstances, according to Rose-Ackerman (2008), provide incentives to local officials to make corrupt deals for their personal gain. This can be explained because the conflict might have nurtured a culture of impunity and secrecy on which illegal acts are fairly easy to cover. Furthermore, the end of such conflict might not encourage the enactment of a transparent government with accountability for its actions, especially if those who benefitted financially from the conflict remain in power. Hence, even though incentives to participate in corrupt deals exist everywhere, the frequency and magnitude of corruption may be especially elevated in post-conflict countries (Rose-Ackerman, 2008), which is the case of many Latin American countries. Even though all Latin American countries have constitutions clearly stating that corruption is illegal, corruption is rampant in the region (Transparency International, 2011). Moreover, even though most of these countries have held democratic elections since the 1980s, most political analysts argue that military and criminal powers influence all major political parties in the majority of these countries (Peacock & Beltrán, 2003).

Unsurprisingly, a considerable number of Latin Americans claim to not trust their politicians and central authorities in all three main areas of the government: The political elite, bureaucrats, and members of the judicial system. Furthermore, according to Migliorisi and Prabhu (2011), both local and foreign investors take advantage of the rampant corruption in Latin America to advance their own interests. Although, as mentioned before, no study linking how corruption affects the attraction of FDI was found in relevant literature, the World Bank published a significant study of how widespread corruption is in the region. According to the World Bank (2005), foreign and local investors in Latin America perceive the government elite to be highly corrupt. In fact, all the respondents in this study expressed that the business climate in the region is dominated by illegal payments to members of the government elite and bribes are a common practice amongst them.

When discussing about corruption in the judiciary system in Latin America, respondents to the World Bank's Transparency, Corruption, and Governability study also expressed high levels of corruption in this branch of the government (World Bank, 2005). According to the World Bank's study, respondents expressed that corruption in the judiciary system is rampant in the region. The rationale for these expressions is based on the lack of independence that members of the judiciary system have in the country (even though this branch of the government should be totally independent) and how members of other branches of the government and of the private sector can influence judicial decisions. The World Bank's report also mentions that investors in Latin America perceived high levels of corruption in the bureaucratic sector (World Bank, 2005). The report says that two thirds of investors in Latin America perceive high levels of corruption in the bureaucratic sector and that more than one third of bureaucrats reported to have witnessed corrupt acts in their organizations. Nevertheless, as mentioned before,

As mentioned before, arbitrary corruption is described as the level of uncertainty created by corruption (Uhlenbruck, et al., 2006). In this sense, foreign investors might be deterred by the lack of knowledge of how to cope with corruption rather than the level of corruption itself. On the other hand, pervasive corruption is classified as the likeliness of a foreign investor to encounter corruption in a foreign location. Pervasive corruption, in this sense, pervasive corruption may affect how a foreign investor assesses the costs associated to operating in a highly corrupt foreign location (Doh, et al., 2003). Nevertheless, according to the World Bank's Transparency, Corruption, and Governability study investors in Latin America have a general idea of how the dimensions of corruption (World Bank, 2005).

5.1 Possible Solutions

While corruption exists in all countries to a certain degree, it is more rampant in poorer countries, such as those in Latin America. The reason for this is not that citizens of low-income countries are more dishonest than those in richer countries. The reason for the widespread of corruption in poor countries is that these countries present more favorable conditions for this problem to flourish. According to Myint (Myint, 2000), crimes associated with corruption are not crimes of passion, but crimes of calculation. Therefore, if the availability of rents is high and the possibility of getting caught is small many people will choose to participate in corrupt deals.

Poorer countries, such as those in Latin America, are usually highly regulated economies that provide fertile grounds to obtain monopoly rents. Moreover, accountability in such countries is usually low. Also, civil liberties are generally restricted and political competition is discouraged. Furthermore, independent organizations dedicated to obtain and disseminate information geared towards detecting bribery and enforcing anti-corruption legislation are usually inhibited. However, even though the chances of winning the battle against corruption for Latin American countries might seem discouraging, there are some steps that can be taken to deal with this problem.

While some members of the general public might argue that there is not much to be done to curb corruption in Latin America, there are some steps that could be taken to attempt to alleviate the problem. Some developing countries like Singapore and Hong Kong have been able to deal with corruption by developing democratic institutions with the purpose of lowering possible economic rents from corrupt deals (Myint, 2000). This is encouraged by political leaders that actively proposed to talk about corruption and its consequences. Therefore, the first step to start dealing with corruption in the region is to encourage communication. It is important for politicians in Latin America to begin a dialogue with their constituencies regarding corruption and how it affects them.

After a serious dialogue has been established, local politicians should strive to attain credibility. To do so, governments should be adamant about fighting corruption by punishing actors in both ends (supply and demand) of a corrupt deal. However, to avoid persecuting political adversaries, people from the general public and the press should be involved. Also, inviting oversight bodies should be invited to help supervise the effectiveness of anti-corruption policies in place. These policies should also include improving institutions such as the legal framework and improving bureaucratic procedures in the all the Latin American countries.

6. CONCLUSION

This chapter provided a description of FDI flows to Latin America and the wide-spread problem of corruption in the region. The chapter also presented scholarly literature dealing with the determinants of FDI to the Latin American region as well as an account of how corruption affects the area. Latin America is an extremely important receptor of FDI; however, it also presents astonishing amounts of corruption. Therefore, understanding how corruption affects FDI flows to the region would help to combat this problem.

Latin America represents a very important recipient of FDI flows in the world (UNCTAD, 2013). FDI flows to the region reached US$77.675 billion in 2009. Nevertheless, the levels of corruption in the region are staggering, which might interfere in the reception of FDI to the region. According to Transparency International, Latin America would is currently the second most corrupt region in the world behind Africa. In fact, if Chile's corruption levels are not taken into account, then Latin America would be the most corrupt location in the world (Transparency International, 2011).

In today's business environment potential host countries should take a close look not only at their corruption levels, but also at the causes for such corruption. Foreign investors are concerned about the total level of corruption and at its dimensions. Latin American countries present very high levels of corruption and that might discourage potential foreign investors. These levels of corruption are described due to the high monopolistic powers that a few officials have over key government position. Also, since the possibilities of being caught and punished are low, corruption has flourished in the region. Therefore, political leaders in Latin American countries should aim to establish a dialogue about the problem to begin to establish credibility. Efforts should be made towards decreasing discretionary powers in officials, and to increase accountability. Also, non-governmental institutions should aid in observing and reporting corrupt practices in the region.

REFERENCES

Balasubramanyam, V., Salisu, M., & Sapsford, D. (1999). Foreign Direct Investment as an Engine of Growth. *The Journal of International Trade & Economic Development*, *8*(1), 27–40. doi:10.1080/09638199900000003

Behrman, J. (1974). *Decision criteria for foreign direct investment in Latin America*. New York: Council of the Americas.

Biglaiser, G., & De Rouen, K. (2006). Economic reforms and inflows of foreign direct investment in Latin America. *Latin American Research Review*, *41*(1), 51–75. doi:10.1353/lar.2006.0001

Blanco, L. (2012). The Spatial Interdependence of FDI in Latin America. *World Development*, *40*(7), 1337–1351. doi:10.1016/j.worlddev.2012.02.003

Blonigen, B., & Wang, M. (2005). Inappropriate pooling of wealthy and poor countries in empirical studies. In T. Moran, E. Graham, & M. Blomstron (Eds.), *Does Foreign Direct Investment Promote Development?* (pp. 221–244). Washington, DC: Institute for International Economics.

Borensztein, E., De Gregorio, J., & Lee, J. (1998). How does foreign direct investment affect economic growth? *Journal of International Economics*, *45*(1), 115–135. doi:10.1016/S0022-1996(97)00033-0

Collins, J., & Uhlenbruck, K. (2004). *How firms respond to government corruption: Insights from India*. Academy of Management Best Paper Procedings.

Curevo-Cazurra, A. (2008). Better the Devil You Don't Know: Type of Corruption and FDI in Transition Economies. *Journal of International Management*, *14*(1), 12–27. doi:10.1016/j.intman.2007.02.003

Doh, J., Rodriguez, P., Uhlenbruck, K., Collins, J., & Eden, L. (2003). Coping with corruption in foreign markets. *The Academy of Management Executive*, *17*(3), 114–127. doi:10.5465/AME.2003.10954775

ECLAC. (2010). *Foreign Direct Investment in Latin America and the Caribbean*. [Online] Available at: http://www.eclac.org/publicaciones/xml/0/43290/2011-138-LIEI_2010-WEB_INGLES.pdf

ECLAC. (2012). *Economic Comission for Latin America and the Caribbean*. [Online] Available at: http://www.eclac.cl/prensa/noticias/comunicados/4/46574/tabla_ied2011_en.pdf

Godinez, J., & Liu, L. (2014). Corruption distance and FDI flows into Latin America. *International Business Review*.

Gray, C., & Kaufman, D. (1998). *Corruption and Development*. Washington, DC: World Bank.

Grosse, R. (1989). *Multinational in Latin America*. London: Routledge.

Habib, M., & Zurawicki, L. (2002). Corruption and Foreign Direct Investment. *Journal of International Business Review*, *33*(2), 291–307. doi:10.1057/palgrave.jibs.8491017

Jain, A. (2001). Journal of Economic Surveys. *Corruption. RE:view*, *15*, 71–121.

Kurer, O. (2005). Corruption: An Alternative Approach to its Definition and Measurement. *Political Studies*, *53*(1), 222–239. doi:10.1111/j.1467-9248.2005.00525.x

Lee, E., Rhee, Y., & Lee, S. (2013). Beyond Ricardian Model: An Optimal Commodity Distribution Based on Absolute Advantage for Multi-Country Multi-Commodity. *International Journal of Business and Management*, *8*(14), 110–114. doi:10.5539/ijbm.v8n14p110

Migliorisi, S., & Prabhu, A. (2011). *Guatemala: World Bank Country-Level Engagement in Governance and Anticorruption*. Washington, DC: World Bank.

Murphy, K., Shleifer, A., & Vishny, R. (1993). Why is Rent-Seeking so Costly to Growth? *The American Economic Review*, 409–414.

Myint, U. (2000). Corruption: Causes, consequences and cures. *Asia-Pacific Development Journal*, *7*(2), 1020–1046.

OECD. (2014). *Secretary General's Report to Ministers*. Paris: Organization for Economic Cooperation and Development.

Peacock, S., & Beltrán, A. (2003). *Hidden Powers in Post Conflict Guatemala – Illegal Armed Groups and the Forces Behind Them*. Washington, DC: Washington Office on Latin America.

Rivera-Batiz, F. (2000). *Foreign Direct Investment in Latin America: Current Trends and Future Prospects*. New York: Columbia University Press.

Rodriguez, P., Uhlenbruck, K., & Eden, L. (2005). Government Corruption and the Entry Strategies of Multinationals. *Academy of Management Review*, *30*(2), 383–396. doi:10.5465/AMR.2005.16387894

Rodrik, D. (1996). Understanding Economic Policy Reform. *Journal of Economic Literature*, *34*, 9–41.

Rose-Ackerman, S., (2008). Corruption and Government. *Journal of International Peacekeeping*, 328-343.

Rose-Ackerman, S. (2008). *Corruption and Post-Conflict Peace-Building*. New Haven, CT: Yale Law School Legal Scholarship Repository.

45

Selingson, M. (2006). The Measurement and Impact of Corruption Victimization: Survey Evidence from Latin America. *World Development*, *34*(2), 381–404. doi:10.1016/j.worlddev.2005.03.012

Shleifer, A., & Vishny, R. (1993). Corruption. *The Quarterly Journal of Economics*, *108*(3), 599–617. doi:10.2307/2118402

Tan, D., & Meyer, K. (2011). Country-of-origin and industry FDI agglomeration of foreign investors in an emerging economy. *Journal of International Business Studies*, *42*(4), 504–520. doi:10.1057/jibs.2011.4

The Ecomomist. (2012). *The Economist Intelligence Unit.* [Online] Available at: https://www.eiu.com/public/topical_report.aspx?campaignid=LatAmFDI2012

Transparency International. (2011). *Transparency International.* [Online] Available at: http://www.transparency.org/cpi2011/in_detail

Trevino, L., & Mixon, F. Jr. (2004). Strategic factors affecting foreign direct investment decisions by multi-national enterprises in Latin America. *Journal of World Business*, *39*(3), 233–243. doi:10.1016/j.jwb.2004.04.003

Uhlenbruck, K., Rodriguez, P., Doh, J., & Eden, L. (2006). The impact of corruption on entry strategy: Evidence from telecommunication projects in emerging economies. *Organization Science*, *17*(3), 402–414. doi:10.1287/orsc.1060.0186

UNCTAD. (2013). Global Investment Trends Monitor. Geneva: *United Nations Conference on Trade and Development.*

Wei, S. (1997). *Why is corruption so much more taxing than tax? Arbitrariness Kills.* Cambridge, MA: National Bureau of Economic Research. doi:10.3386/w6255

Weyland, K. (1998). The politics of corruption in Latin America. *Journal of Democracy*, *2*(2), 108–121. doi:10.1353/jod.1998.0034

World Bank. (2005). *Diagnostico Sobre Transparencia, Corrupcion y Gobernabilidad en Latinoamerica.* Washington, DC: World Bank.

Zurawicki, L., & Habib, M. (2010). Corruption and Foreign Direct Investment: What Have We Learned? *International Business and Economics Research Journal*, *9*(7), 1–10.

Chapter 3
The Significance of Institutionalism for Increasing Wealth at Multi-Levels of Latin American Small States

Otto Mena
Tallinn University of Technology, Estonia

Leon Miller
Tallinn University of Technology, Estonia

ABSTRACT

The text states the problem in connection with defining the dilemma of small states, the advantages and disadvantages of being small and gives a brief background of how the problem developed, a brief history of how dependency developed and at the same time offers a solution, a futuristic perspective on development planning that eliminates the problem of dependency. The authors argue that the attempts of supra national institutions and NGO's to foster a Neo Liberal approach to development without implementing strategies for bolstering the social institutions of particular states has crippled their effort to create sustained economic development, although it has contributed to spiking material assets and creating a bubble for the financial sector and certain segments of production but per capita income of the general public has not benefited from such strategies and indeed on some cases their interest of the general public has been hurt.

DOI: 10.4018/978-1-4666-8820-9.ch003

Economic activity has to be planned in such a way "as to protect every member of the society from the injustice or oppression of every other member. Justice ... is the main pillar that upholds the whole edifice. If it is removed, the great, the immense fabric of human society ... must in a moment crumble into atoms." (Smith 1976, 687). Smith (1979, 86) (Smith 1979: 13ff.).

1. INTRODUCTION

This chapter addresses the issue of the role of institutions in the social and economic development of the small states of Latin America. The authors argue that the attempts of supra national institutions and NGO's to foster a Neo Liberal market approach to development without the implementation of strategies for bolstering the social institutions of particular states has crippled their effort to create sustained economic development (although it has contributed to a sharp rise in financial assets, in creating a bubble for the financial sector, and in improving performance for certain segments of production) but per capita income of the general public has not benefited from such strategies and indeed in some cases the interest of the general public has been hurt (Streeten 2005, 4).

Recently research articles on development published by respected development economists argue that underdevelopment follows as the result of weak institutions. This acknowledgement, which is particularly endorsed by social economists, has led scholars to conclude that by applying the Neo Liberal agenda to contexts that do not have the corresponding strong social institutional structures development tends to create conditions that favor *special interest groups* without corresponding benefit to the overall economy. That is to say that development experts claim that a lack of viable institutions is a cause of underdevelopment.

This study analyzes the role that institutionalism plays in the political economy of small Latin American states. This chapter defines small states, analyzes their characteristics, reviews the historic role of institutions in small states, emphasizes the consequences of their openness, and examines the consequential social economic conditions that occurred in the aftermath of their attempt to modernize (after their colonial past). This chapter claims that the cause of the vulnerability and insecurity of small Latin American States is directly related to the lack of an approach to institutionalism that complements the culture, values, and the heritage of small Latin American states. In addition this research will analyze: the factors that cause the economic failures of small Latin American states (including examining the extent to which institutionalism is a factor) as well as what factors contribute to social economic success and sustainable development.

That is to say that this chapter analyzes the challenges faced by small Latin American sates in their effort to innovate, create flourishing economies, increase the educational level of the populace, and improve the quality of life for their people. The basic premise of this study is that strong institutions and economic development go hand-and-hand. In the words of Nobel Prize winner Amartya Sen to increase wealth in a way that safeguards liberties and guarantees freedom it is necessary to develop strong institutions. "Individuals live and operate in a world of institutions. Opportunities and prospects depend crucially on what institutions exist and how they function" (Sen 199, 142).

"Even though different commentators have chosen to focus on particular institutions (such as the market, or the democratic system, or the media, or the public distribution system), we have to view them together" (Sen 1999, 142). Famed economist Joseph Schumpeter held a similar view concerning what generates improved economic performance and the factors that stimulate innovation and entrepreneurial activity. Schumpeter believed that "Economic analysis deals with how people behave and the economic effects [of] behaving so; in other words economic sociology deals with how they came to behave as they do. If we define human behavior widely enough it includes not only actions, motives and propensities but also the social institutions that are relevant to economic behavior" (Schumpeter 1986, 19).

This means that effective social economic systems are based on institutional normative principles that are manifest in particular market features: e. g. social institutions that employ the normative principle of freedom of association which results in what is called the free market, in other words, the freedom to conduct profitable market activities—that the Libertarians call for—while promoting the levels of economic justice that is necessary for the flourishing of the overall society—what Liberal Economics demands. In other words social economic planning that safeguards a society's social and economic interests. Ha-Joon Chang argues that one of the features most evident in successful economies is the impact of their institutions which have created strong economies with long histories of success. Rich countries at some point were at a similar level of material development as the developing countries (socially, economically, and institutionally). They grew to reach high levels of development [by building] good institutions (in tandem with, after, or—at the very least—as a counterpart to their economic success). This indicates that the quality of institutional development is a causal factor in overall social economic development. That is to say that the inadequacy of institutions is clearly a factor that explains stunted economic growth or failure of small states (Chang, 2010).

This chapter proceeds as follows: section two (the following section) defines small states (but in a way that makes clear their unique predicament) with special emphasis on Latin American states but includes a comparison with small states in general from the perspective of global political economy. The primary factors analyzed are: the effort that small Latin American states make to transform the consequences of colonialism (e.g. stagnated economic and cultural development plus some degree of economic dependency) into models of progressive sustainable development and models of development that are consistent with the values and normative principles of the overall society, their heritage, and their cultural values. This section argues that without effective institutions (clearly articulated principles that reconcile the dichotomy between social/human values and economic, market oriented, commercial values) the impact of foreign direct investment and of guidance by regional and international institutions will not create progressive social and economic development but instead perpetuate the problem of small Latin American states experiencing insecurity and vulnerability.

Section three offers a historical description of the development of social institutions in small Latin American states (emphasizing the impact of colonialism and international institutions (especially economic institutions like the IMF, The World Bank, The World Trade Organization, and The International Commission against Impunity in *Guatemala,* etc.). This section will highlight the advantages and disadvantages of relying on more powerful states and highlights the disadvantages of uniformed models that fail in application because of a lack of well administrated application of top down prescriptions. The final section summarizes the issues and proposes a model of development that takes full advantage of the resources and opportunities made available by the technological age economy. The study contributes to the sparse body of literature on the role of institutionalism in small Latin American states and provides a theoretical framework for generating wealth in ways that increase benefits for the overall society.

2. SMALL STATES IN THE GLOBAL POLITICAL ECONOMY

Never in the history of America has a small state been subjected to such enormous pressure. (Árbenz 2013, 20)

Jacobo Árbenz envisioned that capitalism could work according to the way it was prescribed by Adam Smith to promote *The Wealth of a Nation* and increase shareholder profits but in a way that also results in the common good in spite of the nation's size. However, unlike Smith, Árbenz was reluctant to grant economics laissez-faire operating privileges which would allow economics to be autonmous and independent of the other social institutions of the society. That is to say that the wealth that capitalism affords would put a small state under enormous internal and external pressure unless the market sector (financial sector) was firmly embedded in society (as one aspect of the overall institutional structure of society).

In other words, according to Árbenz, at the very least, increasing the wealth of a nation requires making decisions about what types of structures, systems, and institutional policies are needed to facilitate economic development: e.g. (interstate) roads, what energy systems are best for fueling economic growth, education (who to train and what training institutions to devote public resources to), communications, and public transportation, etc. This challenge is especially apparent in the small states of Latin America. Therefore, it is not a matter of whether or not there is a necessity for institutional structures in a society (all nations have their legislature, judicial systems, sectors for health, education, and welfare). In fact, there is little or no dispute that there must be certain policy decisions in place (i.e. about things like property rights, enforcing contracts, and protecting trademarks) (Chang 2007, 3). What is at issue is what types of systems work best for not only creating wealth in material terms but for enhancing the lives of the members of the overall society in a way the increases their experience of and/or their enjoyment of "the good life."

In addition, the extent to which the economic policies are laissez-faire or oriented toward social-welfare reflects the state's convictions regarding whether or not the wealth of the nation is believed to be based on a more liberal or regulative approach to economics: whether or not to increase social spending, or to tax international corporations more or less, the extent to which a country wants to protect domestic industries, and whether or not to enforce a minimum wage are all unavoidable decisions. In other words, as pointed out by Joseph Schumpeter, the economic development of a society does not happen in isolation but occurs in connection with interrelated processes that include the development of social institutions (Shionoya 2008, 15-18).

Some states are small by any metric[1] but for others it is not clear thus it is hard to perform an analysis by applying a simple standard or qualifier. For instance, in the table shown below, countries are classified as demonstrating features of small countries but not a small state per se. However, some of those countries are considered small by WTO documentation (Crowards 2002, 172). Regarding references to small states in the literature on Latin America there is a very clear consensus that the countries comprising all of Central America, as well as, the Caribbean states, and the South America states of Ecuador, Bolivia, Paraguay and Uruguay are small (see table 1).

Although the success or failure of a state is not determined by its size small states are burdened with particular challenges that are invariably evident in their economic performance (see table 2 below). This is because smallness results in particular factors that have an impact on economic development; these factors intensify with the influence of core-periphery relationships in terms of geography, the level of development, and the technological and industrial specialization of the state (Tõnurist 2010, 20). In addition, due to their reliance on foreign trade partners and

Table 1. Countries associated with groups of small countries but not classified as small

Country	Population (mn, 1995)	Land Area ('000 km²)	Total GDP (US$bn, 1995)
Bolivia [a]	7.2	1,099	5.4
Cuba [a,c]	10.1	110	?
Dominican Republic [a]	7.7	49	9.5
Guatemala [a]	10.3	109	11.3
Mauritania [b]	2.2	1,026	0.9
Nepal [a]	21.4	141	3.7
Nicaragua [a]	4.3	130	1.8
Papua New Guinea [c]	4.2	463	5.1
Singapore [c]	2.8	0.6	55.1
Sri Lanka [a]	18.1	66	10.5

(Crowards 2002, 172).

Notes:

[a]Countries associated with documents relating to small states circulated at the WTO.

[b]Countries listed as small in the IMF Framework.

[c]Members of AOSIS.

their need for foreign direct investments, small states tend to suffer greater volatility of their growth rates and trade shocks experienced by small states are much greater than for larger states (Easterly 2000, 11). As a result developmental economists have recognized that smallness in size and vulnerability are equated of (McCann 1995, 8). Thus, a characteristic of smallness is "Associated with the extent to which there is an external focus of the economy, the penetrability of the political system (by external forces), and the permeability of the social system" (Sutton & Payne 1993, 582).

Thus, there is clearly a discrepancy over where to draw the line between normal sized and small states. According to UNIDO when a population is under 20 million it is considered small (Tõnurist 2010, 10; original source from UNIDO 1979). However, world expert Streeten defines a small state as having less than 10 million inhabitants (1993, 197). Thus, exactly what is a small state in today's interdependent global economy is not exactly clear (Tõnurist 2010, 8). The ambiguity of determining a small state is indicated by the explanation of a small state given by Paul Streeten, "We know a small country when we see it" (Streeten 1993, 197).

However, in economic terms (according to Forbes Magazine's Latin American edition) in spite of their size Central America has enormous economic potential (Forbes Mexico, 2014).

Figure 1. Real GDP/capita growth 2008-13, selected countries/regions which indicates how much small states need a more effective model of social economic development (Source: The Economist 2014).

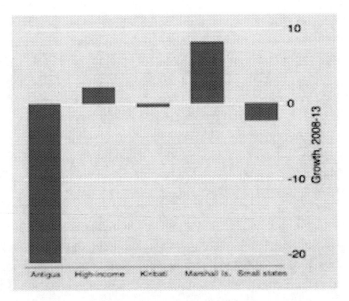

Guatemala alone represents 35% of Central America economy (Diplomat magazine, 2013)[2]. That is to say that the size of the country is not the sole determinant of economic success or failure (Srinivasan 1986, 207). In this respect Paul Streeten's perspective is particularly important in that he argues that there are a number of factors that must be taken into consideration other than size per se (Sreeten 1979, 37-44); Streeten's perspective is the standard applied in each of the following sections of this chapter). In this respect when referring to the challenges of small states it is not merely a matter of geographical space or populations but there are various economic factors that play a role with size being only one variable.

Some authors (e. g. Micheal Handel) prefer to use the concept weak states rather than small states because of the understanding that the concept of size can be relative to what neighborhood the country is in. For instance some of the countries in Central Asia are not considered small by the criteria listed above but compared to their large powerful neighbor (namely Russia) they are both weak and dwarfed. However, in terms of the findings of this research project weak is also not directly correlated with size thus does not apply to the problems this research addresses in regards to small countries in Latin America (Handel 1981, 257).

As a matter of fact, as is clearly indicated by Paul Streeten, there are advantages to size that can be capitalized on if the small state develops a market system that operates on the basis of certain essential principles and if its normative policies are effective for protecting its economy from the utilitarian tendency of more power-ful economic agents to seek relative advantage (especially in accordance with an economy of scale). Amongst the advantages Streeten lists are: flexibility, solidarity, a large percentage of its work force is able to benefit from even a small amount of industrialization and concentration on labor-intensive exports, the remittances of workers who are abroad, and small developing states are likely to receive foreign grants and donations, etc. (Streeten 1993, 200).

However, as Streeten goes on to stress, there are disadvantages that are particularly exasperated unless certain institutional precautions are put into place. A primary disadvantage is the necessary external orientation of developing economies which results in economic dependence which is a general condition that affects almost every developing country (Sutton & Payne 1993, 582). Dependence means that certain policy decisions are heavily influenced by the foreign market forces on which the small state is dependent. Maurice Shiff claims that the dependency factor is what increases the vulnerability and is one of the basic characteristics of small states that contributes to insecurity (Schiff 2002, 4). Along these lines Streeten points out that a small developing state tends to experience insecurity that comes from a lack of self-reliance especially when small Latin American states develop a dependency on their more powerful trade partners and financiers in the north (1993 200-201). Without strong institutions—structured on the basis of a clear vision of the appro-priate policies needed for creating mutually beneficial outcomes—the state that is reliant will tend to "Make excessive concessions to multinational firms that desire to locate footloose production activities for export in small developing countries (Streeten 1993, 201).

This generic characterization of the small states of Latin America applies regardless of the fact that, at the same time, each of the states of Latin America simultaneously exhibit significant differences from each other (e.g. historical, cultural, and cur-rently differences in key aspects of their social and economic structures, political and party systems, and the role of the armed forces, (Sierra 1999, 3).

3. THE HISTORY OF INSTITUTIONALISM IN SMALL LATIN AMERICAN STATES

This section argues that small Latin American states, like all other social economic systems, have demonstrated that they have a particular approach toward what they believe to be necessary institutional systems that define their social-economic interests and activity as well as their plans for development and sustained economic growth. However, rather than being able to put their vision into effect (thus be clearly self-determined) their colonial and postcolonial policies, systems, and procedures have been dominated by external influence thus have left small Latin American states more vulnerable and insecure. This section of the chapter describes the historical background of small Latin American states with an emphasis on their effort to overcome the handicaps suffered from colonialism, their problem of vulnerability (due to reliance on the powerful north for what are usually believed to be superior approaches to economic activity and planning), and how reliance on foreign guidance has not increased social and economic security but weakened it (leaving small Latin American states suffering from insecurity, a lack of self-determination, a lack of confidence).

The importance of institutions is that they create order and stability for a nation that is attempting to establish the best normative principles and policies necessary for the political sector to contribute best to strategizing about how to strengthen the economic sector. Institutionalism is based on the assumption that a society has a foundation upon which to build its procedures and systems that make manifest its understanding of social economic prosperity (i.e. making use of the best knowledge available from scholarship; locally and internationally trained social economic strategists; from the learned views on development that are put forth by reputable international NGO's; as well as, the result of knowledge derived from its history; and from some sense of heritage, tradition, worldview (cultural values), and/or identity. Although these factors (along with principles that are deeply rooted in the value perspective of the society) are manifest as the material aspects of what defines prosperity they are all essential aspects of institutionalism in that they are the means through which the national values are made apparent, through which the national character is made evident, and through which the identity of the people is expressed.

Institutionalization is significant because "Institutions effect social stability by reproducing processes that function as stable patterns" (Powell 2007, 1). This means that there is not only a necessary quantitative aspect to planning social and economic activity but as well a necessary qualitative dimension to social-formation. In fact, the quantitative measures satisfy the society's basic material needs but the qualitative measures appeal to higher order needs. Thus, successful economic planning and effective development strategies must take into account the full range of the human experience and must measure values in both social as well as material terms. That is to say that the wealth and/or poverty of a state cannot be discussed in any meaningful way independently of being inclusive of the full scope of both positive and normative economics (the social and economic values that are ultimately determined by the principles that shape the institutional systems that structure a society (Reinert 2007, 223).

In this respect an institutional approach assumes that political life is neither deterministic (caused by external forces and laws), controlled by powerful interests groups in a society, nor random (governed by the laws of chance), and that political institutions are neither completely static nor in constant flux (Olsen 2009, 5). In fact, because the history of Latin American states is clearly an expression of a heritage (in which many members of the society take pride) that is reflected in the values and worldview of the society in many ways Latin American small states have (at least within their heritage) the basis for a comprehensive approach to institutionalizing their normative principles that are the basis of its heritage and identity (even if the tradition and heritage have been overshadowed by colonialism and modernity). An example is the great importance given to the role of an individual in society. In Latin America the term "caudillismo" is reserved for a single person who has a position of authority in the community which results in influence over a political party or an institution (e.g. client network, patronages between groups, and patrons abound).

Historically speaking, the development dilemma of small was more effectively managed "Prior to the period when the Age of Reason culminated in the Modernity project—and its consequential mercantilism inspired drive to expand markets. At the prior stage local development was necessarily thought of in terms of integrative strategies for progress (Miller 2014, 155). That is to say that prior to the colonial influence prosperity was regarded as occurring on the basis of a natural progression that is in line with the culture's values and heritage. Thus, in all instances of social and economic development colonialism was a fundamental factor that was significant in many ways for creating the development dilemma (not least of which is the fact that it resulted in hindering a culture from naturally pursuing wealth and devising strategies for development on the basis of principles that are in line with its own sense of identity). Colonialism did produce systems that were clearly structured but not on the basis of benefits to the overall local society. During this period institutional systems tended to produce a low-level of performance, a deep sense of dependency, a lack of self-confidence on the part of the authorities and local people, plus a weakening of identity—"As the colonizers installed only the minimal institutions needed for resource extraction, rather than for the development of the local society in which the economy was embedded" (Chang 2010, 115).

Paul Streeten points out that after colonialism a type of paternal attitude toward the small Latin American states continued in the form of the assumption that the more developed north must supply the "missing components" (in terms of knowledge and technology transfer) to the developing south. "These missing components can be capital, foreign exchange, skills, or management" (Streeten 1979, 26). "Looked at in this way, the question became one of designing selective policies for aid, trade, foreign investment, transnational companies, technology, foreign education, movements of people, and so on. [What ended up being] neither complete insulation nor wide-open integration but a policy of enlightened discrimination" (Streeten 1985, 242). In this respect because of the privileged position it afforded oligarchs (most of whom are former Europeans who took on the nationality of the former colony) the status of an elite special interest group within the society who decided to align themselves with powerful trade partners (in counter-distinction to the local indigenous people who—for the most part—became marginalized).

In colonial times institutional frameworks were established with the aim of effectively managing the extraction of the country's raw materials. In fact, even after independence local elite and wealthy foreign merchants realized that in spite of the society having gained independence there remained an immense wealth producing capacity within the export industry. Thus, even though colonialism came to an end many of the systems and procedures geared to extract natural resources remained in place and/or were transformed into an economy based on producing the natural resources and exporting them abroad (Cardoso & Faletto 1979, 35).

Precolonial and Postcolonial studies of small states have been an important area of research for many of the World's regional financial and developmental analysts (e.g. scholars who research ASEAN, the European Union, The United Kingdom and its former Caribbean colonies—in addition to other regional studies on small states). If this is compared with research on Latin America then studies and literature on effective social economic development in Latin American States (especially in regard to small states) is limited. Although, for an extensive overview Cardoso et al. provides a good historical analysis of the social, political, and economic developments in Latin America. In *Dependency and Development in Latin America* Cardoso et al. point out that the attempt to institutionalize postcolonial development turned into a struggle to reconcile the tension between those who represented the power assertions of the oligarchic-export system and those who participated in efforts to establish viable social institutions (Cardoso et al. 1979, 76).

Cardoso et al. assert that there was recognition, during the period after independence, that small Latin American states could progress socially and economically if they could create institutional systems that were strong enough to offset the dominance of the *Latifundistas* (agricultural capitalists and/or extremely large landholders who were invariably of European decent, and who maintained large plantations during the postcolonial period, and reduced cost by using minimally paid workers who were local indigenous people, East Indians, and/or those of African descent) (Cardoso et al. 1979, 75 & 114-122). Those in favor of stronger national governments realized that an institutional framework might have been the only safeguard to protect the small state from the enormous pressure of their domestic oligarchic agricultural capitalists who were in collusion with the mercantilists of the powerful states.

The forces of the local oligarchs along with their international trade partners combined (plus were backed by their security forces) had the power to put into place policies in favor of their effort to operate on the basis of the Neo Liberal principle of gaining and maintaining the competitive advantage. The fact that the south developing in the way that it did—which resulted in remaining poor compared to the relatively wealthy north—is not a surprise to macroeconomists who realize that "The backwardness of the South is not something that developed in isolation: it is a necessary consequence of the process that also produced the industrialization of the North" (Krugman 1999, 98). According to world famous macroeconomist Paul Krugman the difference in wealth is not merely a matter of geography it is a matter of policy decisions that are either in favor of a particular geographical location or not. In other words, according to Krugman, "Because cumulative processes of concentration tend to produce winner and losers, [including] at the level of nation, there is an obvious incentive for policy-makers to try to make sure that their nation emerges as one of the winners" (1999, 105).

Thus, this study argues that progressive national institutional systems are clearly the means by which small states could have been able to transform mercantilism (Economic Realism) into practices that are in line with Economic Liberalism. Without a clear system of normative principles economic nationalism, Neo Liberalism, and post-colonial forms of mercantilism, ended up stagnating social and economic development, they contributed to increasing economic dependency, have invariably created strong security threats to legitimate authority, and clearly undermine the value principles upon which the Liberal Free Market is based. The lack of effective normative structures have, in fact, created systems that are in favor of domestic oligarchs and their powerful international partners (international agents who often are in control of more financial resources and more powerful security forces than some small states). The history of Latin America is filled with instances of powerful economic agents who intervene in local affairs in ways that have not resulted in what is best for the local economy (although clearly representing the vested interests the economic agent).

According to the research done by Evans and Rauch on 35 developing countries during the period 1970-1990 "The most challenging [aspect] of explaining [the factors for growth or stagnation for small Latin American states] involves trying to analyze the role that public institutions play in fostering (or impeding) economic growth" (1999, 748). In fact, there are, as Evens and Rauch emphasize, classical theorists who address the issue of administrative organization from the viewpoint of Max Weber (who is a renowned contributor to the debate on the role of institutions in political economy) and plays a key role in the attempt to resolve the debate over the role of institutionalism as an essential factor for overall social and economic development (and particularly whether or not the lack of certain key institutions is an enemy of growth) (Evans & Rauch 1999, 749). Weber believed that without resolving this controversy economic theory contributes to a divisiveness in economic strategizing in regards to the effectiveness of economic planning and sustainable development, at the very least, and at worst the dichotomy contributes to splintering economic science by making "two sciences out of one" (Miller 2014).

In this respect the position of the authors is that there is a strong correlation between the norms and principles that shape a society and its capacity to make the best use of the more recently developed technological advances to improve productivity and innovation. This factor is especially evident in the development performance of small states and particularly relevant in regards to the challenges facing the development of small Latin American States.

Therefore, as has been the basic argument of this chapter, the issue is not whether or not institutions play a role in economic growth and development but the issue is how to clearly determine the principles and policies that best contribute to small Latin American states gaining security while, at the same time, contributing to their effort to overcome vulnerability (by means of taking full advantage of the equalizing force of knowledge as the most valuable commodity today).

In this respect, the best approach to offsetting dependency and insecurity in the 21st century knowledge-based economy is not allowing the stigma of being labeled with the caption needing to "catch up" to create an attitude of ineptness and insecurity, and dependency in relationship to the more powerful north (because of the need to import knowledge, skills, and technology from more advanced countries). An alternative perspective that will increase self-determination is planning a mixture of technology and knowledge transfer along with the realization that a Constructivist approach to social economic activity has the potential of creating mutually beneficial and satisfactory outcomes. On the other hand a Constructivist approach is altering economic and market theory resulting in the concept of co-creation of desired outcomes for all stakeholders.

In fact, given the recent development claim that the market today is a networked knowledge-based and innovation driven it is possible to put into place the policy and procedures needed for small Latin American states to capitalize from their own knowledge, value, and relational assets. In other words without some clear sense of identity (in terms of principles for generating wealth that is inclusive of an increase in the overall well-being of its people, an increase in capabilities for increasing happiness, and an increase in longevity—factors that Sen asserted in his *Development as Freedom* 1999) Latin American countries will continue to be regarded as "lagging behind" and needing to "catch-up" in the eyes of those who will always be setting the pace (Reinert 2007, 58). This is the theme that will be addressed in the final part of this chapter.

Academic research that analyzes the role of institutionalism in successful development models are the main sources of information regarding how to effectively manage the development challenges of Latin American small states. However, in addition, the research is based on information drawn from an investigation into the development challenges of Latin America (although such researched sources are limited). Because of the lack of research and publications regarding Latin America this research project has followed the example established by the small number of scholars who have investigated Latin American social economic development (with reference made to editorials, local newspapers and magazines, UN reports, and research conducted by the World Bank).

This chapter continues by defining the social economic dynamics connected with small Latin American states and points out why institutionalism offers a solution to the most pressing current challenges in regards to the development of Latin small states. Previous research has found that small states suffer from their vulnerability (the fact that small states are subject to international economic forces is perceived as both a product of the market size of a small state and the implications that size has for the pattern of economic development (McCann 1995, 6). At the same time the authors add that small states should find a balanced model of development that takes advantage not only of foreign expertise, technology, and "know-how" but, as well, improve their position on the value chain by means of innovation and value creation (McCann 1995, 7). Such an approach to growth shapes out of what heretofore had been considered inefficiency features of efficiency that are proving to be effective for all countries employing the advantages of the knowledge-age economy (by creating innovation and entrepreneurial activity that generate growth and are creating immediate improvements in GDP (Easterly 2000, 15).

4. SUSTAINABLE DEVELOPMENT IN THE KNOWLEDGE AGE ECONOMY

Without a strong institutionalized plan for creating a networked economy—negotiated by university researchers, policy-makers, industry, and civil society—the investment the society makes in education will not produce the best results. One undesired outcome will be that the poor performance in science and technology will be perpetuated because the most talented will merely migrate to where they can find better opportunities, (Reinert 2007, 231).

Throughout the recorded history of the human experience improving economic performance has been a matter of a culture's ability to develop effective strategies for organizing relationships in such a way as to increase material satisfaction (e.g.

creating normative structures for organizing the relationship between the members of the society and their relationship to the environment) (Polanyi 1992, 29). During the earliest stages of existence such schemes were instituted into cultural norms and values however as civilization advanced they evolved into administrated policies and systems. In addition there were two contrasting features to economic activity that have been the key to a culture's ability to generate wealth. On the one hand, there has consistently been a fair amount of "blood, sweat, and tears" to use the phrasing of Amyrta Sen (see Sen 1997). This has especially been true at the earliest stages of development. However, on the other hand, early in human existence technology was also regarded as a means of improving and enriching social relations, improving communication, and assisting in humanity's economic endeavors. In fact, those with the technological advantage established a standard/model that surrounding cultures attempted to duplicate. Case in point is evident at the middle of the second decade of the 21st century when it is commonly accepted that "The technological gap between the rich and the poor countries [is] at the root of the economic distance between these two areas" (Patel 2006, 1).

Blood, sweat, and tears continued to play a role in economic activity, to some extent, right up until the time of Adam Smith's treatise on how to increase wealth. That is to say that hard work played a role in initiating the industrial era and it could be argued that labor combined with advances in technology was essential to the economic success of the industrial era (however it is clear that the economic success of the era was due to advances in technology which provided a means for mass producing merchandise). In addition, at the end of the last century and more clearly as humanity entered the 21st century the role of labor has been reduced and there has been a corresponding increase in the number of knowledge workers and a reliance on technology as dominant factors in successful organizational performance plus in accelerating economic prosperity and development. Thus, as could be expected, the emergence of the technological age economy has created the need for making policy decisions in regards to how to make the best use of the knowledge and technological advantages available for ensuring improved economic performance and for having a more highly trained/qualified workforce.

This section of the article argues that technology continues to play a role in improving the economic performance of a society and increasing the chances of experiencing material satisfaction. This concluding section deciphers the complexity of the widespread effort to "leapfrog" over the front-runners (as has been evident in sectors of other developing countries who are models of heightening GDP to impressive levels) by institutionalizing the means for generating innovation, knowledge, value creation, and entrepreneurial activity. That is to say that there has clearly been a shift (from the Frederick Taylor era of line workers and industrial production based on inciting laborers to work harder) to the conviction that wealth relies on generating knowledge, innovation, networking (which is knowledge generating), and making the best use of one's position on the value chain. "Such changes have created new challenges and opened up new opportunities for firms, universities, and governments around the world. Fresh thinking about the scope and objectives of policy has resulted in such new approaches in the last decade and a half" (Vonortas 2002, 435).

However, for small Latin American states the implementation of technologically advanced methods of production has to be carefully instituted so that such plans are put in place in such a way that they decrease the prospect of dependence on the technologically advanced North which could result is the less developed South becoming merely a service agent the North.

"First we have to stress the view that technological change is not an engineering wonder but a complex process that consist of technical, social, economic, and institutional factors all entwined and interacting" (Perez 2004, 2). In fact, according to Schumpeter (who is credited with being one of the first economist to herald the emergence of an age when innovation and entrepreneurial activity will be essential for generating wealth) technological advancement happens when it is facilitated by certain particular institutionalized principles that reflect the character, identity, ingenuity, creativity, and extent of freedom offed by a society (see Schumpeter 1934 & 1942).

At the organizational level the stimulus for increasing profit and generating wealth has to do with structuring certain procedures that create the value added factor (increasing profits for shareholders which is considered internal capital o, in other words increasing internal assets) which now, with the impact of technology of the economy, is believed to be achieved best by co-creating value and effectively managing knowledge networks/assets (which satisfies the interest of shareholders and is regarded as external capital or, in other words, increasing external assets). However, on the level of the economy an increase in innovation and entrepreneurial activity require certain institutional structures. Furthermore, the institutional factor is the basis of innovation generation—in that government, through public procurement policies, has been a primary force driving innovation in all developed and advanced countries. In fact the institutionalization of efforts to make the best use of technological advantages has created spillovers and interactions that benefit the private sector (Kalvet 2012, 153).

Peak economic performance in the technological age is clearly based on factors that are determined by intangible factors that are within the means of the people of the small state to determine. Economists realize that a new perspective on economic value theory is prompted by the fact that the proportion of labor devoted to handling and producing tangibles is decreasing and there is a sharp rise in recognition of the wealth producing potential that value and knowledge assets create (that are designated as intangible). Such factors are triggered by the normative principles upon which an economy operates, how it manages its human resources/human capital, a society's effectiveness in generating social capital, and the level of understanding it has regarding the importance of practices that integrate all of these factors into successful social economic planning. Together, small states that are considered as impressive models of balancing increased wealth with an increase in the overall well-being and happiness of the members of its society realize that creating such outcomes in the technological age requires a new type of economic value appraisal that is proving to be more profitable in the knowledge-based economy. Thus, the authors assert that the historical trend of extracting value from the society and economy by using natural resources and cheap labor, although heretofore clearly a source of wealth generation, must be supplemented with a value-based approach to sustainability (Bas et al. 2008, 52).

Given the fact that research is the key to making the best decisions on how to make the best use of technological opportunities social-economic advance requires not only input from policy-makers but from researchers (and the most available source are the universities). However, to take advantage of the possibility that the university is a resource for strengthening the nation's position in regards to science and technology policy-makers must decide to devote resources to university programs connected with research and development. Researchers analyzing development in the fast rising developing countries also point out that the funds devoted to the university must also include resources given to strengthening departments in public policy. When it comes to the connection between innovation, technology, and development the underlying idea is straightforward: university research results are meant to be directly tied into the interest of domestic industry and meant to fulfill their needs. This can be achieved through formal mechanisms such as licensing and spin-off creation (Kelli, et al, 2013).

Although the typical demander of innovation is the private sector another demander of innovation has traditionally been governments (through public procurement policies the mechanisms results in spillovers and interaction with the private sector) (Kalvet, 2012, p. 153). In addition, in many small countries it seems that innovation is driven by a network of partners who cooperate to produce the best results. This includes researchers, decision-makers, the private sector, and various suppliers who exist on some level of the value chain.

Because innovation processes are evolutionary and path-dependent they are best achieved through formal mechanisms of networked cooperation and knowledge generation (Kelli, et al, 2013). That is to say innovations are a complex socio economic phenomenon with entwined factors that cannot be left up to the economic interests of the private sector. Effectively implementing technologically advanced systems within itself requires technological age means of networking, knowledge generation, and value creation.

REFERENCES

Bas, T., Amoros, E., & Kunc, M. (2008). Innovation, Entrepreneurship and Clusters in Latin America Natural Resource-Implication and Future Challenges. *Journal of Technology Management and Innovation, 3*(3), 52–65.

Cardoso, F. & Faletto, E. (1979). *Dependency and Development in Latin America.* Berkeley, CA: Berkeley University Press.'

Chang, H.-J. (2007). *Institutional Change and Economic Development* (H.-J. Chang, Ed.). New York: United Nations University Press.

Chang, H.-J. (2010). *23 Things They Don't Tell You about Capitalism.* New York: Bloomsbury Press.

Crowards, T. (2002). Defining the Category of 'Small' States. *Journal of International Development, 14*(2), 143–179. doi:10.1002/jid.860

De Sierra, G. (1999). Limitaciones y potencialidades de un pequeño país en el marco de la integración regional. *Futuro de la sociedad uruguaya, CEE 1815.* EBO, Mdeo.

Diplomat Magazine. (2013). *Guatemala Land of the Eternal Spring...Land for Investments.* Available at http://www.diplomatmagazine.nl/2013/12/01/guatemala-land-eternal-springland-investments/

Easterly, W., & Kraay, A. (2000). Small States, Small Problems? Income, Growth, and Volatility in Small States. *World Development, Elsevier, 28*(11), 2013–2027. doi:10.1016/S0305-750X(00)00068-1

Evans, P., & Rauch, J. E. (1999). Bureaucracy and Growth: A Cross-National Analysis of the Effects of "Weberian" State Structures on Economic Growth. *American Sociological Review, 64*(5), 748–765. doi:10.2307/2657374

Handel, M. (1981). *Weak States in the International System.* London: Frank Cass Publishers.

Kalvet, T. (2012). Innovation: a factor explaining e-government success in Estonia. Electronic Government, 9(2), 142 - 157.

Kelli, A., Mets, T., Jonsson, L., Pisuke, H., & Adamsoo, R. (2013). The Changing Approach in Academia-Industry Collaboration: From Profit Orientation to Innovation Support. *TRAMES, 17*(3), 215–241.

Krugman, P. (1999). The Role of Geography in Development. *Annual World Bank Conference on Development Economics 1998.* Washington, DC: Published by the World Bank.

McCann, D. (1995). Small states, open markets, and the organization of business interests. Aldershot, UK: Dartmouth.

Mexico, F. (2014). *Los 12 millonarios más importantes de Centroamérica.* Available at from http://www.forbes.com.mx/los-12-millonarios-mas-importantes-de-centroamerica/

Miller, L. (2014). A Value-based Approach to Sustainability: The Role of Values and Culture in the Pursuit of Wealth. *Development and Society, 43*(1), 143–161.

Olsen, J. (2009). Change and continuity: An institutional approach to institutions of democratic government. *European Political Science Review, 1*(1), 3–32. doi:10.1017/S17557773909000022

Patel, S. (2006). Transfer of Technology to Developing Countries. *Mainstream Weekly., 45*(1), 1–6.

Perez, C. (2004). Technological revolutions, paradigm shifts and socio-institutional change. In E. Reinert (Ed.), *Globalization, Economic Development and Inequality: An alternative Perspective* (pp. 217–242). Cheltenham, UK: Edward Elgar. doi:10.4337/9781845421625.00016

Polanyi, K. (1992). The Economy as Instituted Process. In The Sociology of Economic Life. Boulder, CO: Westview Press.

Powell, W. (2007). The new institutionalism. The International Encyclopedia of Organization Studies. Sage Publishers. Available at http://www.stanford.edu/group/song/papers/NewInstitutionalism.pdf

Reinert, E. (2007). *How Rich Countries Got Rich... and Why Poor Countries Stay Poor*. London: Constable & Robinson Ltd.

Schiff, M. (2002). *Regional integration and development in small states.* Policy Research Working Paper Series 2797. The World Bank.

Schumpeter, J. (1986). *History of Economic Analysis.* Abingdon, UK: Routledge Publishing.

Sen, A. (1997). *Development thinking at the beginning of the 21st century* London, UK: Suntory and Toyota International Centres for Economics and Related Disciplines, London School of Economics and Political Science.

Sen, A. (1999). *Development as Freedom.* Oxford, UK: Oxford University Press.

Shionoya, Y. (2008). Schumpeter and Evolution: an ontological exploration. In Marshall and Schumpeter on Evolution: Economic Sociology of Capitalistic Development. Cheltenham, UK: Edward Elgar Press.

Smith, A. (1976). An Inquiry into the Nature and Causes of the Wealth of Nations (2 vols.). Oxford.

Smith, A. (1979). The Theory of Moral Sentiments. Oxford.

Srinivasan, T. N. (1986). *The Cost and Benefits of Being a Small, Remote, Island, Landlocked, or Ministate Economy.* World Bank, Development Policy Issues Series Discussion Paper. Number ERS 2.

Streeten, P. (1979). Development Ideas in Historical Perspective. In K. Hill (Ed.), *Toward a New Strategy for Development.* New York: Pergamon Press.

Streeten, P. (1985). Development Economics: The Intellectual Divisions. *Eastern Economic Journal, 11*(3), 235–247.

Streeten, P. (1993). The Special Problems of Small Countries. *World Development, 21*(2), 197–202. doi:10.1016/0305-750X(93)90014-Z

Sutton, P., & Payne, A. (1993). Lilliput under Threat: The Security Problems of Small Island and Enclave Developing States. *Political Studies, 41*(4), 579–593. doi:10.1111/j.1467-9248.1993.tb01657.x

Tõnurist, P. (2010). What Is a "Small State" in a Globalizing Economy? *Halduskultuur – Administrative Culture, 11*(1), 8-29.

Vonortas, N. (2002). Building competitive firms: Technology policy initiatives in Latin America. *Technology in Society, 24*(4), 433–459. doi:10.1016/S0160-791X(02)00034-9

ENDNOTES

[1] Geographical area, GDP, military force, population.
[2] According to the Ambassador of the Republic of Guatemala to the Kingdom of the Netherlands "Guatemala represents 35% of the Central America Region´s economy (US$50 of US$145 Billion) positioned as a business Hub in the Mesoamerican region".

Chapter 4

Foreign Direct Investment from China and Latin America:
Can Culture Be Deterring This Kind of Investment?

Jose Godinez
Merrimack College, USA

Theodore Terpstra
University of Connecticut, USA

ABSTRACT

Historically, Chinese corporations have been relatively unknown in Latin America. Total foreign direct investment (FDI) in Latin America was 18.1% of the world total in 2012 (UNCTAD, 2013). However, Chinese FDI in Latin America has averaged about US$10 billion per year since 2010, only a small part of Latin America's total FDI inflows (ECLAC, 2013). Yet the presence and economic leverage of Chinese corporations has become very substantial in several industries in the region, particularly the oil and mining industries. Trade between China and Latin America has also grown dramatically since 1999 (Luo, et al., 2010). Despite the growing economic connectivity between Latin America and China, the motivation, strategy and procedures behind China's FDI in the region have not yet been fully understood.

DOI: 10.4018/978-1-4666-8820-9.ch004

1. INTRODUCTION

Historically, Chinese corporations have been relatively unknown in Latin America. Total foreign direct investment (FDI) in Latin America was 18.1% of the world total in 2012 (UNCTAD, 2013). However, Chinese FDI in Latin America has averaged about US$10 billion per year since 2010, only a small part of Latin America's total FDI inflows (ECLAC, 2013). Yet the presence and economic leverage of Chinese corporations has become very substantial in several industries in the region, particularly the oil and mining industries. Trade between China and Latin America has also grown dramatically since 1999 (Luo, et al., 2010).

Despite the growing economic connectivity between Latin America and China, the motivation, strategy and procedures behind China's FDI in the region have not yet been fully understood. Moreover, compared to other regions such as Asia, Latin America is receiving only a small amount of investment from China. Chinese companies still need to gain a better understanding of the business environment and opportunities in Latin America (Kotschwar, et al., 2012). There is also the possibility that cultural differences could be a barrier for Chinese companies wishing to make entry into Latin America. Similarly, the host government's friendliness or unfriendliness towards the Chinese government could also influence FDI inflows from China. The purpose of this chapter will therefore be to understand both the motives and challenges of Chinese investment in Latin America.

2. CHINA AND ITS ROLE AS SOURCE OF FOREIGN DIRECT INVESTMENT

Recently, the motives and allocation of outward foreign direct investment (OFDI) from emerging economies has been deemed as one of the most intriguing questions in the international business (IB) research agenda (Mathews, 2006). This is derived from (a) the dramatic increase of OFDI from developing countries, which accounted to 16% of global FDI in 2008 (UNCTAD, 2009); and (b) how multinational enterprises (MNEs) from developing countries seem to have defied the basic theories of internationalization of firms (Ramasamy, et al., 2012). Therefore, the question of how firms without evident ownership advantages are able to succeed in the global arena still remains unanswered in the IB discipline.

While researchers have only begun to analyze OFDI from developing countries, no emerging economy has been more scrutinized than China (Ramasamy, et al., 2012). The reasons for such interest are twofold. Firstly, China has been one of the most popular destinations of FDI in the world. Secondly, as of 2008, China is considered the 13th largest source of FDI in the world, and third amongst developing countries

(UNCTAD, 2009). Nevertheless, despite of the growing importance of China's OFDI in the world, Chinese FDI to Latin America has been modest. According to the Economic Commission for Latin America and the Caribbean (ECLAC), Chinese FDI to Latin America has averaged US$10 billion per year since 2010 (ECLAC, 2013). Furthermore, ECLAC claims that the reason for the lack of Chinese investment in Latin America is because Chinese firms are still learning to do business in the region (ECLAC, 2013).

3. THE EXPANSION OF CHINESE OFDI

The People's Republic of China began its "open door" policies in the late 1970s and early 1980s in order to get the country more involved with the global economy (Buckley, et al., 2007). At first, only state-owned corporations were given permission to invest in other countries (Buckley, et al., 2007). Initially such investment was very strictly regulated and had a ceiling set at US$10 million (Luo, 2007). In the late 1980s to early 1990s the Chinese government allowed more state-owned corporations to invest abroad, and in a six year period from 1986-1991, US$1.2 billion of investment was approved (Buckley, et al., 2007). The Chinese government continued relaxing restrictions on outward investment by launching the "go global" initiative in 2000 (Luo, 2007). Following the loosening of restrictions in OFDI, China joined the WTO in 2001. However, private Chinese firms were not allowed to invest abroad until 2003 (Buckley, et. al., 2007).

From 2003 onwards, the Chinese government has actively encouraged companies to go global (Luo, et al., 2010). This encouragement is in the form of economic support to firms investing abroad such as discounted bank loans, credit funds, and single corporate tax to avoid double taxation (Luo, et al., 2010). Another measure taken by the Chinese government is the simplification of the approval process for investment, in order to cut down on the bureaucracy and speed up projects (Luo, 2007). The approval process had been reformed before in both 2004 and 2005 (Luo, et al., 2010). The aim of those reforms was to provide a foundation for future reforms and also decentralize the process (Luo, et. al. 2010). However, there are still complaints from Chinese firms that the approval process is overly complicated (Luo, et. al., 2010).

China has also created an information system of reports and pamphlets to aid firms that wish to invest overseas. Some examples of such a pamphlet would be the "Countries and Industries for Overseas Investment Guidance Catalogue", which evaluates investments overseas by Chinese companies and offers advice (Luo, et. al., 2010). A "Foreign Market Access Report" has been published annually since 2004 (Luo, et. al., 2010). This report catalogues the obstacles and barriers Chinese firms face in various countries. Some of these reports and pamphlets discuss Latin America specifically, such as the "Guiding Catalogue on Investment in Processing Trade of Textiles and Clothing in Some Latin-American Countries." (Luo, et. al., 2010) China continues to encourage both private and public firms to go global in accordance with the nation's five-year plan (Luo, et. al., 2010).

China only started publishing their data on OFDI, following IMF and OECD standards, in 2003 (Cheng & Kwan, 2000). According to these publications, China has invested in 142 countries from 2003 to 2006 (Kolstad & Wiig, 2012). Furthermore, the total OFDI from the Chinese economies has increased six times during the same period (Kolstad & Wiig, 2012). In terms of location of the investment, over 40% of Chinese OFDI was directed at the mining and petroleum sectors, 54% was allocated in several service industries (generally business services and finance), and only 4% in the manufacturing sector (Cheng & Kwan, 2000). Even though these figures do fluctuate from year to year, the investment trends from the Chinese economy strongly suggests that Chinese OFDI is mainly market and natural resource-seeking.

4. CHINESE FDI IN LATIN AMERICA

According to ECLAC (2013), Chinese OFDI was allocated mainly in other Asian countries, which received 71.4% of total FDI by the end of 2011. Latin America was the second largest recipient of Chinese FDI accounting for 13% of this kind of investment. However, the vast majority of Chinese FDI to Latin America was allocated in the British Virgin Islands and the Cayman Islands (92%), while the remaining 8% went to Brazil, Peru, Venezuela, and Argentina. One important point to be raised is that these countries have governments that sympathize with the authoritarian regime which governs the People's Republic of China.

In 2012 the total FDI inflows to Latin American and the Caribbean was US$244 billion (ECLAC, 2013). The main motivation for Chinese outward investment is to ensure a supply of domestically scarce resources in order to fuel the growing Chinese economy. For this reason, China's economic links with Latin America have been growing drastically since the late 1990s (Kolstad & Wiig, 2012). However, the Latin American region has not experienced the same levels of investment that other developing regions are receiving from China. In fact, the bulk of Chinese FDI outflow to Latin America ends up in "tax havens" like the Cayman Islands (Peng, 2010).

Since Chinese OFDI is mainly utilized to offset domestically scarce raw materials, it can be described as resource-seeking (Buckley, et. al. 2007). This type of OFDI focuses on natural resources such as oil and minerals. The main targets for this kind of investment in Latin America are Brazil, Peru, Chile, and Venezuela (Peng, 2010). Nonetheless, China has limited investment in Latin America's largest economies.

For example, only 1.1% of Mexican firms have Chinese capital (Peng, 2010). One plausible explanation for this apparent apathy of Chinese investment in the region is that smuggling is major problem in some Latin American industries. This fact might discourage China from making entry into those industries.

5. A THEORETICAL PERSPECTIVE ON THE MOTIVES AND OBSTACLES OF CHINESE FDI IN LATIN AMERICA

5.1 Determinants of FDI

The central question regarding FDI activity is why any given firm would select to service an overseas market via affiliate production instead of options such as licensing arrangements or exporting (Blonigen, 2005). The first theoretical effort to explain FDI flows was based on the Heckscher–Ohlin model of the neoclassical trade theory, on which FDI was assumed to be part of international capital trade (Bergstrand, 1990). This model proposed that a relatively capital-rich country would either export the capital-intensive good or move capital to locations where returns on capital would be higher and returns on labor would be lower until price equalization was achieved.

Building on the Heckscher-Ohlin model, but including the notion of ownership advantages, Caves (1971) focused on product differentiation. Therefore, MNEs would prefer FDI over export or licensing if their ownership advantage lies in product differentiation based upon knowledge. Even though each of these theories had their own merit, they did not fully integrate an economic theory to explain FDI (Hosseini, 1994). This later changed when scholars analyzed FDI from the viewpoint that markets were not efficient and perfect competition was inexistent. Despite there being several frameworks to analyze FDI activities, the most widely used tool in the IB literature to analyze this phenomenon has been Dunning's OLI Paradigm based on transaction cost economics.

The transaction cost theory as a predictive model proposes that the form and competitiveness of an MNE's international operations depends crucially upon the configuration of three elements (Rugman & Verbeke, 1992). The three elements of the transaction cost theory of the multinational enterprises are: Ownership, Locational, and Internalization advantages. Dunning's (1980; 1998) eclectic paradigm might be the most comprehensive framework to explain reasons for FDI (Ramasamy, et al., 2012). The eclectic paradigm, also known as the OLI paradigm, asserts that there are three factors that determine international activities of MNEs. These factors are: ownership (O) advantages, internalization (I) advantages, and locational (L) advantages. Within this context, the OLI paradigm explains outward FDI by

71

suggesting that MNEs must develop unique and competitive O advantages at their home countries and then transfer them to a foreign market (based on L advantages), which permits the MNE to internalize such O advantages (Rugman, 2010). In other words, the O advantages explain who will undertake FDI; the I advantage explains the mode on which international production will occur; and the L advantage explains where FDI will flow to.

5.2 Ownership Advantages

These unique ownership (O) advantages (also called competitive or monopolistic advantages) might compensate for the added costs related with setting up and running operations abroad while local firms do not incur in such costs (Stoian & Filippaios, 2008). In order to exploit these O advantages abroad, MNEs should choose to transfer them within their own organization rather than selling them or the right to use them to foreign-based firms (Dunning, 1988). This suggests that MNEs notice that foreign markets are not the most appropriate settings for transacting intermediate services or goods (Dunning, 1988).

In classic International Business literature, scholars have agreed that firms need O-advantages when investing abroad to offset their inherent liability of foreignness (Dunning, 1998). However, recent literature argues that in emerging markets MNEs may not have such advantages. Instead, scholars have proposed that firms from emerging markets have created a different set of O-specific advantages. These advantages allow them to operate in foreign countries in a more effective manner than other foreign companies from developed economies, and in certain cases even more effectively than local incumbents. Such advantages might include knowledge created while operating in their local markets, flexibility, and the ability to create relations with other firms that control certain resources operating in certain environments (Buckley, et al., 2007).

5.3 Internalization Advantages

Internalization (I) specific, advantages arise when a firm has developed a set of competitive O specific advantages, and the immobile attributes of a foreign location (L advantages) permit finding value-added or asset-augmenting activities in such place. Then this firm decides to undertake such activities within itself rather than letting another firm to perform them (Dunning, 2000). In other words, internalizing production will occur when an MNE believes that it is more convenient to transfer its O advantages within the firm across borders than selling it to a third-party (Stoian & Filippaios, 2008). In the words of Dunning himself, the internalization of O advantages will occur when the international market is not the most appropriate method for transacting intermediate goods or services (Dunning, 1998).

The internalization theory has provided a dominant explanation of why MNEs choose to participate in FDI rather than sell or buy intermediate products via a third party. The Internalization theory, as proposed by Buckley and Casson (1976), Rugman (1981), and Hennart (1982), is a theory at the firm-level that explains why MNEs will exercise ownership control over an intangible knowledge-based, firm-specific advantage (Rugman, 2010). Such knowledge advantage, according to Rugman (2010), results from a transaction cost economics explanation on which the public good nature of such knowledge is alleviated by means of the hierarchy of an MNE overcoming this situation of a market failure.

Building on earlier studies, Anderson and Gatignon (1986) propose a model based on transaction costs analysis in order to explain why an MNE would own and manage a facility in a foreign location instead of using other supply agreements with local firms already operating in such market. Their model blends components of contract law, industrial organisation and organisation theory. Based on their study, Anderson and Gatignon (1986), assert that MNEs will use a low level of control to operate in a foreign location unless the risks and transaction costs related with this option are too high. However, different MNEs might perceive different risks in different locations

5.4 Locational Advantages

In early attempts to describe the location of FDI, the question of where FDI is located based on a MNE's O and I advantages was not fully explored until the eclectic paradigm was put forward. The OLI paradigm acknowledged the importance of locational (L) advantages of countries as determinants of foreign production of MNEs, taking into account a firm's particular advantages (Dunning, 1998). Nevertheless, the rise of the knowledge-based global economy and asset augmenting FDI has required scholars to re-visit the issues of the placement of MNE activities and the competitive advantages of regions and/or nations. According to Buckley et al., (2007), FDI location is determined by three primary motivations:

- Market seeking;
- Resource seeking;
- Efficiency seeking.

This suggests that different selection criteria pertain for projects with different motivations. The L advantages play an important role when analyzing cross-border activities since they can define the attractiveness of a foreign market for a particular MNE (Dunning, 1998). Issues such as institutional differences, the size of the market, purchasing power, the rate of inflation, unemployment, and corruption gain more importance when doing business abroad than domestically. Moreover, these issues can be magnified when both the home and host countries have underdeveloped institutions. Therefore, advancing the knowledge of the L advantages and their influence on FDI between developing economies will expand our knowledge of international activities of the MNE in an ever-increasing international business context. This study seeks to advance the knowledge on the L advantages and their influence on FDI. To do so, corruption and corruption distance are included among the factors of the attractiveness of certain location.

5.5 Analyzing Determinants of FDI and Institutions

Despite of its prominence and usefulness, the OLI paradigm alone is not enough to explain FDI determinants, especially in emerging economies where the institutional environment plays a central role (Douma, et al., 2006). The Eclectic Paradigm explains the location of FDI in an economic efficiency matter; however, this approach can only provide a partial explanation for the location of FDI (Kang & Jiang, 2010). According to Kostova and Zaheer (1999), in addition to economic incentives, MNEs need institutional legitimacy to be able to carry operations in a foreign location. Therefore, the main difference between the institutional theory approach and the Eclectic paradigm, when describing a firm's motives to issue FDI, is the main criterion for selecting such location (Kang & Jiang, 2010).

Seeing as the eclectic paradigm focuses only on economic efficiency, the institutional theory takes into account the role that institutions play in a particular location (Kang & Jiang, 2010). Institutions are of great importance for an MNE considering starting operations abroad, since they are immobile. Institutions have an effect in the capacity of firms to interact and hence, they affect the transaction and coordination costs of production and innovation (Mudambi & Navarra, 2002).

While the OLI addresses an organization's concerns with efficiency, the institutional theory focuses on "how non-choice behaviors can occur and persist, through the exercise of habit, convention, convenience, or social obligation" (DiMaggio & Powell, 1983, p. 151). In its purest form, the institutional theory discards the premise that organizational occurrences are the result of rational choice grounded on technical considerations (Westney, 1993). Instead, the institutional theory places emphasis on the taken-for-granted nature of the decisions and/or on the pressures to gain legitimacy in a firm's operations (Roberts & Greenwood, 1997).

North (1990) defined institutions as the formal and informal "rules of the game." In his work, North (1990) states that formal institutions are explicit rules that constrain human economic behavior (such as laws and regulations), while informal institutions are tacit constraints (such as self-imposed codes of conduct). Despite the importance that institutions play in the internationalization of firms, early International Business studies assumed the institutional environment was 'background'. This assumption responded to the fact that such studies were carried out in developed economies on which institutions are reliable and market-based oriented (Luo, 2007). However, once researchers started analyzing emerging economies they realized that the institutions in such countries differ significantly from those in developed economies (Trevino, et al., 2008). It was then realized that institutions, both formal and informal, are crucial in shaping the strategy and performance of MNEs in emerging markets (Hoskisson, et al., 2000).

6. CULTURAL DIFFERENCES AS POSSIBLE REASON FOR LACK OF CHINESE FDI IN LATIN AMERICA

OLI paradigm studies argued that Chinese firms have developed O-specific advantages when investing in other developing economies, especially in other Asian countries and in Africa (Buckley, et al., 2007; Cheng & Kwan, 2000). It has been proposed that Chinese MNEs have developed O advantages to compensate for additional costs they may incur with starting operations in other developing countries. In fact, Kolstad and Wiig (2012) argue that Chinese MNEs have purposely developed knowledge on how to operate in other developing economies. Therefore, such firms might actively seek to invest in developing countries when given a choice. As mentioned previously, Chinese MNEs have not been very active in the Latin American region, which should be attractive for their activities.

The I sub paradigm of the OLI theory explores why an MNE would choose to own and operate a facility in a foreign country as opposed to utilizing other arrangements with local firms already established (Anderson & Gatignon, 1986). Furthermore, the internalization theory proposes that an MNE will choose a low level of control to service a foreign market unless the transaction costs related with such operations are considered too high. Evidence from literature suggests that Chinese MNEs prefer to have ownership control when internationalizing. Since the 'Go-Global' initiative, Chinese MNEs have deliberately located activities in other countries in order to generate greater rents. However, despite encouragement from their home government to invest abroad, Chinese MNEs have not invested in Latin America as much as they have in other developing regions such as Asia and Africa (See Table 1).

While the O and I aspects of the OLI Paradigm might not help one understand the lack of investment by Chinese MNEs in Latin America, the L section might offer clues to this mystery. The L-specific advantages section of the OLI Paradigm argues that there are certain aspects of the host location which MNEs find attractive when deciding to invest abroad. As mentioned previously, the list of these advan-

Table 1. Regional shares of Chinese outward FDI flows 2003 to 2006

	2003	2004	2005	2006	Total 2003-2006
Africa	0.03	0.06	0.03	0.03	0.03
Asia	0.53	0.55	0.37	0.44	0.44
Europe	0.05	0.03	0.03	0.03	0.03
Latin America and the Caribbean	0.36	0.32	0.53	0.48	0.46
North America	0.02	0.02	0.03	0.01	0.02
Oceania	0.01	0.02	0.02	0.01	0.01

Source: Kolstad and Wiig (2012).

tages has been closely scrutinized in existing literature. However, a new line of enquiry argues that the institutional environment of a country should also be taken into account to understand MNEs foreign activities (Peng, et al., 2008).

As noted before, poor institutions increase search, negotiation, and enforcement costs, therefore deterring FDI to certain locations (Meyer, 2001). However, it has been argued that institutions alone do not fully explain variation in the variation of FDI to foreign locations (Pournarakis & Varsakelis, 2004). Instead FDI decisions involve a simultaneous improvement in the market and institutions. Lately it has been established that MNEs undertake FDI not only to exploit existing resources, but to increase resources and capabilities, thus choosing locations to increase specific advantages (Rugman & Verbeke, 1992; Bevan, et al., 2004).

China is more likely to invest in a country if said country has a significant Chinese community (Anechiarico & Jacobs, 1996). The majority of Chinese diaspora live in other Asian countries while only a small percentage live in North and South America. This could explain why Chinese OFDI into Latin America has been limited when compared to other developing countries. Another plausible explanation is that Chinese FDI may be influenced by guanxi, an ancient system of ethnic and social networks (Buckley, et al., 2007). Lastly, Chinese firms may prefer to invest in the more familiar markets and cultures of its neighboring countries, meaning there is some geographic preference as well.

Since the Chinese central government has a great deal of influence in the investment decisions of Chinese firms abroad, Chinese firms typically will only invest in developing countries where they have affinity with the home government (Scott, 2002). An example would be Ghana, when the host government bent the mining rules for Chinese firms (Luo, et al., 2010). This strategy allows Chinese firms to have less international experience, but still do well and avoid learning-by-doing. However, because of the apparent control of firms by central government, some host governments are often suspicious of Chinese investment. For example, Chinese firms are often blocked from acquiring assets in developed countries, because of the host governments concerns over what will happen to acquired technology or knowledge (Luo, et al., 2010). For this reason, China places special interest in investments in developing countries with a more relaxed attitude towards Chinese OFDI.

One main deterrent could also be that the Chinese central government might not approve of investment in host countries that have accepted Taiwan as an independent state. Chinese OFDI has been allocated mainly to other developing countries, especially those rich with natural resources, which would make Latin America a clear target for Chinese investment. However, many Latin American countries either have relations with Taiwan or recognize Taiwan, which discourages China from exporting more from them (Kolstad & Wiig, 2012).

7. CONCLUSION

This chapter examined Chinese FDI to Latin America and why the Asian giant has not invested in the continent as heavily as in other regions. While the allocation of FDI has been widely studied in the International Business literature, the determinants of FDI from emerging economies still offers fertile grounds to understand how firms determine to invest in a given region (Matthews, 2006). Moreover, even though the determinants of Chinese FDI have been a very popular topic amongst scholars, the reason why China has limited its investment flows to Latin America has not yet been fully analyzed in literature.

Since China implemented its "open door" policies in the late 1970s and early 1980s, the country has steadily increased its investments in other economies (Buckley, et al., 2007). This trend has continued to increase making China the largest source of foreign investment from emerging markets (Kolstad & Wiig, 2012) focusing mainly in natural resources. Nevertheless, the bulk of the Chinese investment has been allocated in other Asian countries and in Africa. In Latin America, Chinese investment has mainly been directed at "tax heavens" like the Cayman Islands (Peng, 2010). Therefore, examining why China has not yet fully committed to investing in Latin America is still an unanswered question worth exploring.

With the aid of Dunning's OLI paradigm, this study argues that Chinese firms have ownership specific advantages when investing abroad, especially in other developing economies (Dunning, 1988). Also, this study claims that Chinese firms have the knowledge and resources to internalize activities abroad. Therefore, the answer as to why China has limited their investments to Latin America might be explained by the Location-specific advantages of the paradigm (Dunning, 1998). While Latin America might seem like an obvious choice for Chinese investment due to its richness in natural resources and low cost availability of labor, the present study claims that the main reason for the lack of Chinese investment in Latin America can be attributed to cultural differences.

Previous studies have concluded that Chinese FDI is more likely to flow to countries with a large Chinese population (Anechiarico & Jacobs, 1996; Buckley, et al., 2007). This means that other Asian countries, where Chinese communities are more numerous than Latin America would receive larger amounts of Chinese FDI. Another reasonable explanation of why Chinese FDI has not reached larges numbers in Latin America could be that Chinese firms might be influenced by guanxi, an ancient system of ethnic and social networks (Buckley, et al., 2007), that is not widely practiced in Latin America. Finally, Chinese firms may prefer to invest in the more familiar markets and cultures of its neighboring countries, meaning there is some geographic preference as well.

REFERENCES

Anderson, E., & Gatignon, H. (1986). Modes of foreign entry: A transaction cost analysis and propositions. *Journal of International Business Studies, 51*(1), 71–82.

Anechiarico, F., & Jacobs, J. (1996). *The Pursuit of Absolute Integrity.* Chicago: Chicago University Press.

Bergstrand, J. (1990). The Heckscher-Ohlin-Samuelson Model, The Linder Hypothesis and the Determinants of Bilateral Intra-Industry Trade. *The Economic Journal, 100*(403), 1216–1229. doi:10.2307/2233969

Bevan, A., Estrin, S., & Meyer, K. (2004). Foreign investment location and institutional development in transaction economies. *International Business Review, 13*(1), 43–64. doi:10.1016/j.ibusrev.2003.05.005

Blonigen, B. (2005). A Review of the Empirical Literature on FDI Determinants. *Atlantic Economic Journal, 33*(4), 383–403. doi:10.1007/s11293-005-2868-9

Buckley, P., & Casson, M. (1976). *The Future of Multinational Enterprises.* London: MacMillan.

Buckley, P., Clegg, L. J., Cross, A. R., Liu, X., Voss, H., & Zheng, P. (2007). The Determinants of Chinese Outward Foreign Direct Investment. *Journal of International Business Studies, 38*(4), 499–518. doi:10.1057/palgrave.jibs.8400277

Caves, R. (1971). International Corporations: The Industrial Economics of Foreign Investment. *Economica, 38*(179), 1–27. doi:10.2307/2551748

Cheng, L., & Kwan, Y. (2000). What are the determinants of the location of foreign direct investment? The Chinese experience. *Journal of International Economics, 51*(2), 379–400. doi:10.1016/S0022-1996(99)00032-X

DiMaggio, P., & Powell, W. (1983). The iron cage revisited: Institutional isomorphism and collective rationality in organizational fields. *American Sociological Review, 48*(2), 147–160. doi:10.2307/2095101

Douma, S., George, R., & Kabir, R. (2006). Foreign and domestic ownership, business groups, and firm performance: Evidence from a large emerging marke. *Strategic Management Journal, 27*(7), 637–657. doi:10.1002/smj.535

Dunning, J. (1988). *Explaining international production*. London: Unwin Hyman.

Dunning, J. (1998). Location and the multinational enterprise: a neglected factor. *Journal of* Dunning, J., 2000. The Eclectic (OLI) Paradigm of International Production: Past, Present and Future. *International Journal of the Economics of Business, 8*(2), 173–190. doi:10.1080/13571510110051441

ECLAC. (2013). *Chinese Foreign Direct Investment in Latin America and the Caribbean*. ECLAC.

Hennart, J. (1982). *A theory of multinational enterprise*. Ann Arbor, MI: University of Michigan Press.

Hoskisson, R., Eden, L., Lau, C., & Wright, M. (2000). Strategy in Emerging Economies. *Academy of Management Journal, 43*(3), 249–267. doi:10.2307/1556394

Hosseini, H. (1994). Foreign Direct Investment, Decision, Transaction-cost Economics and Political Uncertainty. *Humanomics, 10*(1), 61–82. doi:10.1108/eb018745

Kang, Y., & Jiang, F. (2010). FDI location choice of Chinese multinationals in East and Southeast Asia: Traditional economic factors and institutional perspective. *Journal of World Business, 47*(1), 45–53. doi:10.1016/j.jwb.2010.10.019

Kolstad, I., & Wiig, A. (2012). What determines Chinese outward FDI? *Journal of World Business, 47*(1), 26–34. doi:10.1016/j.jwb.2010.10.017

Kostova, T., & Zaheer, S. (1999). Organisational legitimacy under conditions of complexity: The case of the multinational enterprise. *Academy of Management Review, 24*, 64–81.

Kotschwar, B., Moran, T., & Muir, J. (2012). *Chinese Investment in Latin American Resources: The Good, The Bad and The Ugly*. Peterson Institute for International Economics.

Luo, Y. (2007). Are joint venture partners more opportunistic in a more volatile environment? *Strategic Management Journal, 28*(1), 39–60. doi:10.1002/smj.564

Luo, Y., Xue, Q., & Han, B. (2010). How emerging market governments promote outward FDI: Experience from China. *Journal of World Business, 45*(1), 68–79. doi:10.1016/j.jwb.2009.04.003

Mathews, J. (2006). Dragon multinationals: New players in 21st century globalization. *Asia Pacific Journal of Management, 23*(1), 5–27. doi:10.1007/s10490-006-6113-0

Meyer, K. (2001). Institutions, transactions and entry mode choice in Eastern Europe. *Journal of International Business Studies, 32*(2), 357–367. doi:10.1057/palgrave.jibs.8490957

Mudambi, R., & Navarra, P. (2002). Institutions and internation business: A theoretical overview. *International Business Review, 11*(6), 635–646. doi:10.1016/S0969-5931(02)00042-2

North, D. (1990). *Institutions, institutional change and economic performance.* Cambridge, UK: Cambridge University Press. doi:10.1017/CBO9780511808678

Peng, M. (2010). The global strategy of emerging multinationals from China. *Global Strategy Journal, 2*(2), 97–107. doi:10.1002/gsj.1030

Peng, M., Wang, D., & Jiang, Y (2008). An institution-based view of international business strategy: A focus on emerging economies. *Journal of International Business Studies, 39*(5), 920–936. doi:10.1057/palgrave.jibs.8400377

Pournarakis, M., & Varsakelis, N. (2004). Institutions, internationalization and FDI: The case of economies in transition. *Transnational Corporations, 13*, 77–94.

Ramasamy, B., Yeung, M., & Laforet, S. (2012). China's outward foreign direct investment: Location choice and firm ownership. *Journal of World Business, 47*(1), 17–25. doi:10.1016/j.jwb.2010.10.016

Roberts, P., & Greenwood, R. (1997). Integrating Transaction Cost and Institutional Theories: Toward a Constrained-Efficiency Framework for Understanding Organizational Design Adoption. *Academy of Management Review*, 346–373.

Rugman, A. (2010). Reconciling internatinalization theory and the eclectic paradigm. *Multinational Business Review, 18*(2), 1–12. doi:10.1108/1525383X201000007

Rugman, A., & Verbeke, A. (1992). A Note on the Transnational Solution and the Transaction Cost Theory of Multinational Management. *Journal of International Business Studies, 23*(4), 761–771. doi:10.1057/palgrave.jibs.8490287

Scott, W. (2002). The Changing World of Chinese Enterprises: An Institutional Perspective. In A. Tsui & M. Lau (Eds.), *Management of Enterprises in the People's Republic of China* (pp. 59–78). Boston: Kluwer Academic Press. doi:10.1007/978-1-4615-1095-6_4

Stoian, F., & Filippaios, F. (2008). Dunning's eclectic paradigm: A holistic, yet context specific framework for analysing the determinants of outward FDI. Evidence from international Greek investments. *International Business Review*, *17*(3), 349–367. doi:10.1016/j.ibusrev.2007.12.005

Trevino, L., Thomas, D., & Cullen, J. (2008). The three pillars of institutional theory and FDI in Latin America: An institutionalization process. *International Business Review*, *17*(1), 118–113. doi:10.1016/j.ibusrev.2007.10.002

UNCTAD. (2009). *World investment report 2009: Transnational corporations, agricultural production and development*. New York: UN Publications.

Westney, D. (1993). Institutionalization theory and the multinational corporation. In *Organization theory and the multinational corporation* (pp. 53–75). New York: St. Martin's Press.

Chapter 5
Antecedents of Stakeholder Trust in Business Development in Latin America

Harish C. Chandan
Argosy University, USA

ABSTRACT

Trust is the expectation of honest and co-operative future behavior based on commonly shared norms (Fukuyama, 1995). In Latin American region, people who believe that most people can be trusted ranges from 4 to 19% as compared with 34% for USA and 60% for China and Sweden (World Values Survey, 2010-2014; Jamison, 2011; Cardenas et al., 2009). Trust consists of a mix of inter-personal trust and institutional trust. An understanding of business culture, national culture and religion is essential for developing trust in business relationships (Hurtado, 2010; Searing, 2013; Weck, 2013, Ransi and Kobti, 2014). Trust among various business stakeholders within a firm or between firms in a local, national or international setting is an essential component of business development activities that are rooted in the relationships between exchange partners (Barron, 2014; Taylor, 2013; Friman et al., 2002;). The monitoring mechanisms on trust, i.e., "trust but verify" are conductive to maintaining trust in a business relationship (Kusari, et al. 2014).

DOI: 10.4018/978-1-4666-8820-9.ch005

INTRODUCTION

From a utilitarian perspective, trust can be viewed as 'mutual glue' that holds a relationship together. In a business exchange, trust is a multi-dimensional psychological concept concerned with shared human feelings between exchange partners making them either 'in-group' or 'out-group'. Trust is a dynamic concept, and is influenced by the past, present and future interactions. Each business interaction has consequences for trust. Trust increases by synergistic and ethical behavior. Trust decreases by opportunistic and unethical behavior (Khodyakov, 2007). In a business context, the entrepreneurs use mutual trust to sustain their enterprises and socioeconomic networks. Maintaining trust with all the stakeholders is essential for running an existing business profitably. To develop a new business, trust has to be established first before the deal is completed. In Latin American countries, the interpersonal trust is low, which has implications for existing businesses and new business development (Jamison, 2011). Low trust in Latin American countries significantly hampers efforts to achieve sustainable, long-term economic growth (Neace, 2004).

In this chapter, the role of stakeholder trust in the performance of the existing businesses and the development of new business in Latin America is reviewed. Some of the stakeholders in a business include the customers and clients, employees, supply chain partners, local communities, government and regulators, non-governmental organizations (NGO's), creditors and investors. A conceptual framework of trust, based on transaction-cost theory, social-exchange theory and commitment-trust theory is discussed for understanding the needs and concerns of different stakeholders regarding trust (Phelps and Campbell, 2012). The influence of culture and religion in the LA region on the stakeholder trust is discussed. The role of trust in leadership, organizational performance, business development activities including marketing and supply chain management are discussed. The determinants of the trust are discussed in the context of B2C, B2B and e-Business (Jones et al., 2000).

LOW TRUST LEVELS IN LATIN AMERICA

The low inter-personal trust in LA region reflects the colonial history and the lack of trust at the institutional and government level (Lagos, 2001). The LA citizens do not trust their public institutions, financial and legal institutions, government, police and the media (Power and Jamison, 2005). The expression *viveza criolla* (native cunning) is an example of LA mistrust. It expresses a belief that a person who does something shady and gets away with it, is successful while others who act in good faith are naïve, miss out on the opportunities and end up failing. Trickery and deceit inspire admiration than admonition in this frame of reference. There is a popular Spanish saying, "el que no tranza no avanza" (one that does not act unethically does not succeed). In a trust study conducted in Bogota, Buenos Aires, Caracas, Montevideo, Lima and San Jose, the most robust explanatory variables of trust and group formation across cities were related to pre-determined expectations about the outcomes. Trust and group participation are predictors of economic transactions and other social interactions (Cárdenas et al., 2009).

Based on World Values Survey (2010-2014), the mean trust level for the world is 24.5%. Table 1 lists the individual values for the LA region countries along with USA, China and Sweden. The value for Brazil was not reported in this publication. In the LA region, Argentina (19.2) has the highest trust level followed by Uruguay (13.8). Mexico and Chile have the same value of 12.4. The USA (34.8) represents a trust level higher than the world average (24.5). Both China (60.3) and Sweden (60.1) represent a very high trust level. Trust is crucial to business performance and the development of new business. The reasons for low trust can be intrinsic or cultural and a legacy from the past. Low trust can also be caused by the performance of political institutions and economic policies for the citizens. The intrinsic or structural (cultural, socio-economic) and extrinsic factors (citizen's evaluations of performance) contribute to the low levels of interpersonal trust. (Uslaner, 2003).

Table 1. Percent of People who believe that "Most People Can be Trusted, Source: World Values Survey (2010-2014), p 32 and 136 of 416

Latin American Country	Percent of People Who Believe that "Most People Can Be Trusted"	Percent of People Who" Trust Somewhat" People of Another Nationality
World Mean	**24.5**	30
Argentina	19.2	40
Chile	12.4	35.6
Colombia	4.1	20.2
Ecuador	7.2	22.6
Mexico	12.4	20
Peru	8.4	9.4
Uruguay	13.8	32.4
Other Countries		
USA	34.8	60.5
China	60.3	7.6
Sweden	60.1	62.6

The second column in Table 1, represents the percent of people who" trust somewhat" people of another nationality. This has implications regarding the development of new business in Latin America by foreign companies. The world mean is 30%. Argentina (40), Chile (35.6) and Uruguay (32.4) score higher than the world mean (30). Peru (9.4) represents a very low value. Ecuador (22.6), Colombia (20.2) and Mexico (20) are lower than the world mean (30). U.S.A. (60.5) and Sweden (62.6) values are twice the world mean whereas China (7.6) represents a low value for trusting foreigners (World Values Survey, 2010-14).

LATIN AMERICAN ECONOMIES

Latin America (LA) includes countries in South America, Central America and Mexico. LA and Caribbean regions are often discussed together due to their geographical proximity (LANIC, 2014). LA represents a mosaic of countries with distinct geo-political, technological, social, cultural and economic environments. The term "Latin" in Latin America refers to the Latin language, which is the common source of the spoken languages in LA countries. The majority language in most of the LA countries is Spanish except in Brazil where Portuguese is dominant. Five LA countries that represent the LA region well include Argentina, Brazil, Mexico, Colombia and Bolivia. Argentina, Brazil and Mexico are relatively prosperous. Colombia is in the middle and Bolivia falls in the poor category. Some of the major emerging economies in LA include Argentina, Brazil, Chile, Peru and Mexico.

In terms of the size of the economy (GDP), the big three countries include Argentina, Brazil and Mexico, the mid-sized countries include Colombia, Peru and Venezuela and much smaller countries include Bolivia, Uruguay and Paraguay (ECLAC, 2014). Argentina, Brazil, Mexico, Colombia and Bolivia together account for almost 75% of the region's population and about 82% of the GDP. Brazil and Mexico have a large population of 196 million and 118 million respectively and are the two largest economies in LA with GDP's exceeding trillion U.S. dollars (World Population Data Sheet, 2014). In terms of relative prosperity (GDP/capita), Chile and Uruguay lead the LA region. According to the Economic Commission for LA and the Caribbean (ECLAC, 2014), increasing the sustainable rate of economic growth, reducing the volatility of growth, reducing poverty, corruption and social/ economic inequality are some of the main challenges for the region.

The socio-cultural and historical backgrounds of LA countries include predominantly European Argentina (Italian and Spanish), European and African Brazil through the mixed "Meztizo" (Indianland European) nations of Colombia and Mexico to predominantly indigenous Bolivia. The most important values still present in LA nations are the family unity and religiosity. The majority of the population in

LA belongs to the Roman Catholic Church. Most of the Latin American countries were colonies of different European nations and many had dictatorships after the colonial rule. However, most LA countries have democratic governments now. The corruption is quite high in LA region countries except in Chile and Uruguay that have good local economic system, political structure, ethics legislation and regulations, business climate and business ethics. In Latin America, 68% of the region's inhabitants identify themselves as low-class, 30% as belonging to the growing middle class and 2% as high class. Democracy is constrained by inequality of access to political process as well as economic goods. Precariousness, poverty, inequality and discrimination continue to be the region's Achilles heel. In 2013, 30% identified economic problems as their country's most important problem, down from 38% in 2007. "There are two Latin Americas, one which enjoys the benefits of economic growth and the one which watches while the other enjoys it". Overall, the 2013 survey indicates that poverty is dropping, education is increasing and economic growth is rising, taking Latin American's satisfaction with life to the highest level since 1995(Latinobarometro, 2013). The ratio of the income of top 10% to bottom 10% is 35 in Latin America and Caribbean as compared to 8 in the USA (Watkins, 2005).

CONEPTUAL FRAMEWORK OF TRUST IN BUSINESS

Trust has been defined in several ways. We will explore a few perspectives. Trust is one of the most frequently cited dimensions in an exchange relationship in a business transaction. Trust is defined as the willingness to rely on an exchange partner in whom one has confidence. Trust exists when "one party has confidence in the exchange partner's reliability and integrity" (Morgan and Hunt, 1994). Trust has also been described as a belief and an expectation about the other party's reciprocity, honesty and benevolence (Ganesan, 1994; Dahlstrom and Nygaard, 1995; Kumar, Scheer and Steenkamp, 1995). Trust represents a "confidence in the integrity and reliability of another party, rather than confidence in the partner's ability to perform a specific action" (Hausman and Johnston, 2010).

Trust influences the working relationship at the individual and/or firm level. At firm level, trust represents a firm's belief that a partner will perform actions that benefit the firm. In addition, trust represents the belief that the partner will not act unexpectedly to cause negative outcomes or risks for the firm (Lancastre and Lages, 2006). Trust between partners constitutes one of the key factors for becoming long-term partners (Hausman and Johnston, 2010; Ybarra and Turk, 2009). Trust in a product or service represents an expectation of consistently good quality. Another widely cited definition of trust states that "trust is a particular level of the subjective probability with which an agent assesses that another agent or a group of agents will perform a particular action, both before he can monitor such action (or independently of his capacity ever to be able to monitor it) and in a context in which it affects his own action" (Gambetta, 1988).

Trust represents the conviction that the promise given by a business partner is reliable and the partner will meet its obligation (Bialaszewski and Giallourakis, 1985). Trust is an expectation of positive outcome that one can receive based on the expected action of another stakeholder in an interaction characterized by dynamic conditions with uncertainty. (Bhattacharya et al., 1998). Trust determines a firm's confidence in partner cooperation and organizations in a high-trust environment are significantly more effective in problem solving (Bibb & Kourdi, 2004).

Another viewpoint states that there are two dimensions of trust - competence and benevolence (Moorman et al., 1993). The competence trust is the extent to which the buyer believes that the supplier is able to do what is asked. The buyer will have competence trust in the supplier if it seems credible for the supplier to claim to have the required expertise to perform the job effectively and reliably. The competence dimension of trust reflects technical competency and is based on the other party's predictability and dependability. By comparison, benevolence trust is the buyer's belief that the supplier will indeed engage in the agreed upon behaviors, demonstrating genuine concern toward the mutual business partnership and will not take any actions that will harm the buyer. Benevolence trust is rooted in emotional attachment and concern about the other party's welfare. There is intrinsic value to emotional bonds that develop with frequent, longer-term interaction. As emotional connections deepen, trust may even go beyond a level that is justified by knowledge and experience. In short, competence trust reflects the sense of whether a partner can behave as hoped, exemplified by reliability and credibility, and benevolence trust captures the sense of whether the partner will behave as hoped, manifest as caring and integrity (Koh, Fichman and Kraut, 2012).

Buyer-Seller business relationships require the psychological factors of both trust and commitment (Dweyer et al. 1987; Ganesan, 1994). Trust is an antecedent of commitment (Morgan and Hunt, 1994). The development of trust and commitment can be explained using a combination of the Transaction Cost Theory (TCT), Social Exchange Theory (SET) and Agency theory.

TRANSACTION COST THEORY: RATIONAL ECONOMIC VIEW

Transaction cost theory's viewpoint about trust is that trust and distrust are essentially rational. Trust is a three-part relation: A trusts B to do X. Based on the street-level epistemology of trust, you trust someone if you have adequate reason to believe that it will be in that person's interest to be trustworthy in the relevant way at the relevant time. One's trust turns not only on one's own interests but also on the interests of the trusted. Trust is strategic in the sense that it requires seeing the choices of others from their perspective to comprehend their incentives. Others will be trustworthy when their incentives are right (Hardin, 1993).

Transaction cost theory (TCT) originates in transaction cost economics and it focuses mainly on the economic aspect of stakeholder relationships. TCT is used to explain why corporations exist. TCT has three distinct dimensions – behavior uncertainty, Information sharing and asset specificity. These three dimensions influence the amount of transaction cost. (Williamson, 1989; Kwon and Suh, 2004). TCT emphasizes outcomes and institutional arrangements instead of processes and the environment and disregards trust as irrelevant (Chao et al., 2013). Trust influences the social exchange where the attitudes and behaviors are determined by the rewards of the interaction minus the penalty of the cost of the interaction (Griffith, et al. 2006).

SOCIAL EXCHANGE THEORY: PSYCHOLOGICAL COMMITMENT

Business interactions require the psychological factors of both trust and commitment (Ganesan, 1994). Commitment is defined as perceived importance of a relationship (Dweyer et al., 1987). Commitment also includes the desire to continue the relationship and to work to ensure the continuance (Moorman et al., 1993). For a long-term business relationship, shared values, benefits and termination costs contribute to commitment. Shared values, communication and opportunistic behavior to maximize one's benefit contribute to trust. The shared values come from an understanding of the cultural values of the members of the economic exchange. Trust is an antecedent of commitment, i.e. trust leads to commitment for a long-term relationship Shared values contribute to both commitment and trust. The committed exchange partner believes, "that an ongoing relationship with another is so important as to warrant maximum efforts at maintaining it (Morgan and Hunt, 1994). In the context of supply chain management, commitment is defined as "partners who are willing to devote themselves to a sustainable partnership and maintain cooperation through temporary compromises" (Chao et al., 2013). Commitment is the key to successful supply chain integration (Kwon and Suh, 2004).

The Social Exchange theory (SET) explains the inter-firm relationships including supplier-buyer and manufacturer-distributor relationships (Kwon and Suh, 2004; Narasimhan et al., 2009). It also explains inter-partner relationships in strategic alliances (Kwon, 2008). One of the core assumptions of SET is that the benefits given are contingent upon the expectation of a future unspecified benefit (Shiau and Luo,

2012; Zapata et al., 2013). The characteristics of social exchange in a buyer-supplier relationship include communication, partner reputation, perceived benefit fairness and relationship tenure (Chao et al., 2013)

Trust is a social practice and process involving the commitment of both parties. To trust is to anticipate that the other party will exhibit benevolence supported by moral competence in the form of loyalty, generosity, and honesty (Jones, 1996). Trust is a multi-dimensional psychological concept concerned with shared human feeling between exchange partners making them either in-group or out-group. Trust is dynamic and is influenced by past, present and future interactions (Khodyakov, 2007).

DYNAMIC VIEW OF TRUST AS A PROCESS: AGENCY THEORY

Trust has a dynamic foundation, which involves the idea of trust building. There are three elements of agency that can describe trust as a process – iteration, projectivity, and practical evaluation (Emirbayer and Mische, 1998). Based on this agency theory, "trust is a process of constant imaginative anticipation of the reliability of the other party's actions based on the reputation of the partner and the actor, the evaluation of current circumstances of action, the assumptions about the partner's actions, and the belief in the honesty and morality of the other side. Trust consists of a mix of inter-personal trust and institutional trust. The inter-personal trust consists of thin interpersonal trust (reputation) and thick interpersonal trust (familiarity and similarity). The institutional trust represents perceived legitimacy of the institution. In this approach, trust is treated as a process rather than a variable. Trust is dynamic and is influenced by past, present and future interactions (Khodyakov, 2007).

Trust is a belief that the other party in the transaction will come through despite uncertainty. When the partner in the transaction comes through, the trust grows for the future interactions. Trust is a dynamic, psychological attribute of a relationship. In the context of business development, trust represents the comfort factor for interactions between the exchange partners. Such interaction can be between business and consumer, business and its employees, business and business B2C, B2B and e-Business. Employee trust affects bottom line (Moran and Gossieaux, 2013). The various relational safeguards, such as relationship-specific investments, explicit contracts, and relational norms, influence relationship satisfaction. Important questions remain about how trust is different in its antecedents and consequences, and particularly in understanding the dynamics and processes behind its creation, maintenance, and restoration across a multiplicity of important contexts and in key relationships. The development and nurturing of trust depend on the type of business interaction, cultural, social and religious context (Wagner et al., 2011; Gullett et al., 2010; Jambulingam, 2011).

The low levels of trust in the LA region can hinder economic development. For the sake of organizational effectiveness, the business leadership and the organizations can work towards increasing interpersonal trust by understanding the cultural values of the people in the LA region. The cross-cultural business interactions can also benefit from the cultural intelligence. Unlike reputation, which is based on an aggregate of past experiences with a company, trust is a forward facing metric of stakeholder expectation. Trust is a dynamic process and is influenced by past, present and future interactions (Khodyakov, 2007). An understanding of the concept of trust and the Lain American cultural values are essential to increase the low levels of inter-personal trust (Hurtado, 2010; Searing, 2013).Trust is believed to reduce inefficiencies and opportunism associated with agency relationships. Trust enhances cooperation, expectations of continuity, future purchase intentions, and customer loyalty and commitment (Hung et al. 2012).

ORGANIZATIONAL TRUST AND ORGANIZATIONAL CULTURE

In an organizational context, trust is an important part of professional relationships between co-workers, between managers and employees, or between employees and managers. Trust can be either interpersonal or institutional in nature. There are different dimensions of trust -competence, benevolence, and integrity. There are different types of trust- horizontal trust between co-workers, vertical trust between managers and employees, and vertical trust between employees and managers. The different dimensions of trust play a different role in different types of trust (Krot and Lewicka, 2012).Trust and control have been conceptualized as either substituting or complementing each other. The relation between trust and control is an interactive process, in contrast to earlier conceptualizations of trust and control as two relatively static and isolated concepts (Jagad, 2010).

The business development in Latin America is more about establishing personal connections and understanding the organizational and national culture. The organizational culture represents the practices within an organization or the ways things get done in the organization. The national culture is the "collective programming of the mind" distinguishing the members of one nation from others". Managing cross-cultural business relationships depends on the ability of people who think differently to act together (Hofstede, 1980). Organizational culture is determined essentially by the top leadership. Leadership is a relationship between the leader and the followers. Trust between the leader and the follower establishes credibility of the business leader. The organizational culture is also influenced by the national cultural values that have evolved over time. The violent colonial history, the demographic mix and the political instability influenced the cultural values for each country in the LA region.

TRUST AND NATIONAL CULTURE

The cultural differences between nations exist at the level of values, which represent the belief systems of the citizens. The values or belief systems are not visible but they guide their behavior. However, organizational practices are more tangible than cultural values. An organization can be means-oriented vs. goal-oriented, internally driven vs. externally driven, local vs. Professional, open-system or closed system, and employee-oriented vs. work-oriented. The degree of acceptance of leadership style and the degree of identification with the organization can vary. The organization can have easygoing work-discipline vs. strict work-discipline (Hofstede, 2014).

The cultural values that differentiate one nation from the other can be described by six categories- Power distance, Individualism vs. Collectivism, Masculinity vs. Femininity, Uncertainty Avoidance, Pragmatic vs. Normative, and Indulgence vs. Restraint (Hofstede, 2014). Table 2 compares the values for these cultural dimensions for various countries in the LA region and the U.S., China and India.

Note that each country in the LA region has unique dimensions of culture. The first dimension of national culture is Power Distance (PD). This is the degree to which people accept and expect inequality in the distribution of authority. In societies with high PD, decision-making is centralized rather than consultative, hierarchies are stable and clearly defined, and respect for leaders is highly valued. In contrast, low-PD societies place more emphasis on decision by consensus, hierarchies are less rigid, and leaders are expected to be on more equal footing with subordinates. Although the U.S. scores below the global average on PD, most Latin American countries surveyed by Hofstede had high to very high PD ratings. Generally, Latin

Table 2. A Comparison of Hofstede's Cultural Dimensions for Countries in LA region, USA, China and India (Hofstede, 2014)

	Power Distance	Individualism vs. Collectivism	Masculinity vs. Femininity	Uncertainty Avoidance	Pragmatic (Long-Term) vs. Normative (Short-Term) Orientation	Indulgence vs. Restraint
Brazil	69	38	49	76	44	59
Mexico	81	30	69	82	24	97
Argentina	49	46	56	86	20	62
Chile	63	23	28	86	31	68
USA	40	91	62	46	26	68
China	80	20	66	30	87	24
India	77	48	56	40	51	26

American authority figures expect to be respected and are accustomed to making decisions without soliciting the input of those under their authority. This does not mean that leaders are indifferent to those under their charge, however; on the contrary, they are expected to demonstrate concern and regard. But involving subordinates in decision-making is generally less common, and there is a greater emphasis on showing proper respect for those in authority than in the U.S.

A high Power Distance value affects the way meetings are organized. In a high power distance country, information flows primarily from the top down in meetings. In other words, it would generally be considered inappropriate and disrespectful in that country for an employee to correct a supervisor or make a suggestion in front of other employees. At meetings, supervisors expect subordinates to listen attentively, more than offering input. Meetings in Latin America are typically not thought of as a way for supervisors and employees to exchange ideas. Participatory management styles and employee empowerment are perceived as neither helpful nor desirable. In some instances, global companies have successfully implemented these kinds of managerial techniques in Latin American subsidiaries, but in other cases attempts to solicit employee input and involve workers in decision-making have been met with hostility. The deference afforded to managers often has an impact on attitudes toward formal rules and regulations. Persons in authority are more likely to be obeyed than a written policy, because of the respect they are given and the position they occupy. This attitude contrasts with the U.S., where most people tend to believe that rules should be applied impartially and without exception, in order to ensure fairness and justice.

Hofstede defined Individualism (IND) as follows: in high IND societies, there is more emphasis on individuality rather than identifying with a group, and high IND countries place more value on creativity and initiative. Although the U.S. earned the highest IND rating in the world, because of the celebration of individuality and personal expression, most countries in Latin America have a low IND rating. This means that in Latin America, conformity and loyalty to the group are generally more highly valued than expressing one's individuality.

Hofstede (1980) defined masculinity (MAS) in terms of how clearly gender roles are defined and how much of a distinction there is in a given society between men's and women's behavior. Despite the famous Latin "machismo," the U.S. actually rates higher for MAS than some LA countries except Mexico. The masculinity also represents the degree to which social and economic survival requires aggression, and the level of monetary reward attached to success. In the U.S., social survival requires a higher degree of aggression than in most LA countries, and monetary rewards are more highly valued. However, gender roles tend to be more distinct in LA than in the U.S., and men hold greater authority, especially in the lower socioeconomic class. However, in the upper socioeconomic class, LA women can have greater authority. Several LA countries have elected women presidents.

The "Uncertainty Avoidance" (UA) dimension of culture describes how open societies are to risk. Societies that rate high on UA prefer clearly defined situations and roles, and favor security over risk-taking. Latin America's high UA rating reflects the strong preference for clarity and safety and reflects the fact that people in LA countries "do not readily accept change and are very risk adverse." In U.S., people, in general, accept risk, prefer for more loosely defined rules, and show greater tolerance for new ideas. In the workplace, Latin America's high UA means that workers typically prefer specific instructions and close supervision, rather than management styles that stress worker initiative or independence. LA countries score very high on Uncertainty Avoidance (UA), which suggests that most Latin Americans prefer security and avoiding risk. This influences the attitudes toward technology and change. This may help explain why technology is not as prevalent in Latin America as in the U.S. Due to the high UA rating, many LA may perceive less of a need to upgrade, modernize, and replace old technology.

Low Individuality (IND) rating is prevalent in Latin America. Because of the group orientation, the employer-worker relationship tends to be more paternal in Latin America than in the U.S. In the workplace, low IND means employees tend to value harmony and good relationships more than personal advancement, and are expected to be loyal, hard-working, and willing to do whatever they are asked to do. In return for their hard work and loyalty, Latin American workers generally expect their employers to be loyal to them as well. Latin American firms typically treat employees as a sort of extended family, which often involves a wider range of benefits, such as subsidized, or free lunches, more inclusive medical coverage, and holiday bonuses.

In addition to Hofstede's cultural dimensions, the importance of family and personal relationships also impacts the workplace. Most people in Latin America place a higher priority on family than the majority of Americans. U.S. citizens are more likely to sacrifice family time for work or live farther away from family than what is common in Latin America. The family is considered by most Latin Americans to be the most important social group, and generally takes precedence over work and other obligations.

A large number of SME's are family-owned. It is more common in Latin America to seek employment with family members, hire family members, and look to the family for help in times of need. Many Latin Americans feel more comfortable doing business with people they know personally, and developing that relationship is often considered an essential first step. Establishing business contacts and closing deals in LA are best done in person, and may take more time than is customary in the U.S. Trying to speed up things and 'getting to the point' quickly may cause frustration in Latin Americans. The importance Latin Americans place on family and personal relationships helps explain the prevailing attitude toward punctuality.

Latin Americans are more inclined to place the relationship above arriving on time. Punctuality is definitely more flexible in social settings than in the workplace. The schedules tend to be less rigid in small towns and smaller companies than in larger, more industrialized cities and bigger firms with an international focus. Some Latin American countries are making a significant public effort to combat tardiness, and in some places the afternoon siesta is being eliminated. These changes are particularly noticeable in Argentina, Chile, Colombia, and Mexico. Of course, there are variations from one country to another, and even within countries.

In Latin America, the religion and family are very important. In most Hispanic countries, 90% or more of the population is Catholic, and religion plays a central role in many families. Religious traditions and holidays also tend to be more predominant in public life than in America. In the U.S., many public forms of religious observance have been curtailed or outlawed, but throughout Latin America there are significant religious holidays and public ceremonies. For many Latin Americans, the definition of "success" is connected much more to relationships and time with family. Most Latin Americans measure their happiness by having have enough income to support a comfortable lifestyle and spend plenty of time with their family, and would not be as willing to sacrifice family time now in order to achieve greater monetary success later. The LA work ethic may reflect the 'work to live' philosophy rather than the 'live to work' philosophy in the U.S.

The pace of life in the L.A. region is relatively slower than that in U.S.

TRUST AND BUSINESS DEVELOPMENT

Business development activities require trust and commitment. Trust is an antecedent of commitment. Trust leads to commitment for a long-term relationship (Morgan and Hunt, 1994). Trust is strategic in the sense that it requires seeing the choices of others from their perspective to comprehend their incentives. Others will be trustworthy when their incentives are right (Hardin, 1993). Trust is not just an independent or dependent variable but it is a dynamic process. Trust is like a bank account that grows or shrinks based on the positive or negative interactions. When the trust is low, it can be developed and maintained by understanding the needs and concerns of each stakeholder in the business interaction from their unique perspective (Jones et al., 2000). Social media provides businesses with an opportunity to strengthen bond with consumers and build trust (Korzeniowski, 2013).

In the business context, trust exists when "one party has confidence in the exchange partner's reliability and integrity" (Morgan and Hunt, 1994; Heffernan et al., 2008, MacIntosh, 2009). These relational exchanges can take many forms, including those between firms and their customers, firms and their employees, and between firms, such as buyer–supplier, manufacturer–distributor, and wholesaler–retailer relationships (Korzeniowski, 2013; Moran and Gossieaux, F., 2013). Such interactions occur in the context of products and services (Niazi et al., 2013), supply chain management (Chao et al., 2013), inter-partner strategic alliances, international B2B interactions (Theron et al., 2011), both in-person and virtual.

The antecedents of trust vary with the type of business development activity. For example, trust is determined by different factors for business-to-customer (B2C) and business-to-business (B2B) transactions. The trust between a manufacturer and distributor is determined by factors that are different from the factors for inter-partner strategic alliance. The trust in a firm's product is determined by factors that are different from that for service provided by a firm. Table 3 lists the antecedents of trust for various business development activities.

To support trade with Latin American small-to medium size enterprises (SME), an understanding of LA business culture, linguistic competence and cultural adaptation are helpful. Firms have to operate within the framework of the host culture and the local market environment (Swift and Lawrence, 2003). The strategic community of practice concept facilitated knowledge sharing among rival firms and developed trust and commitment. This helps with business transformations in Latin America (Arroyo & Walker, 2009). In developing cross-cultural joint ventures and strategic alliances, "we" needs to be replaced with "us-and them" since trust is about our perception about the other party and their perception about us. In the context of intercultural business relationships, to develop and maintain trust between partner firms, an understanding of the business culture of a partner firm and moderate level of cultural adaptation is necessary (Weck & Ivanova, 2013).

TRUST IN E BUSINESS

With the increased use of Internet, the e-business is growing. The e-business is defined as carrying out business activities that lead to an exchange of value, where the parties interact electronically using network or telecommunication technologies. The exchange includes goods, services that have market value. It also includes information, which may not have market value per se but is of value to exchange partners in specific commercial activities such as formation of a virtual organization. The new paradigm of e-commerce is built not just on transactions but also on building, sustaining and improving relationships. Examples of e-commerce include business-business (electronic trading, virtual enterprises), business-consumer (online retailing); intra-organizational (logistics management); business administration (submission of trading information); consumer-administration and consumer-consumer (online auctions). In business-to-business relationships involving technology

Table 3. Factors Promoting Trust in Various Business Developments Activities

Business Development Activity	Factors Promoting Trust	Reference/Theory
Business Culture in Latin America: Interactive Learning for UK SME's	Local language, Cultural understanding	Swift and Lawrence, 2003
Strategic Community of Practice in facilitating Business transformations in Latin America.	Knowledge sharing, community of practice	Arroyo & Walker, 2009
Business Relationships between Inter-cultural Partner Firms, Finland	Understanding and adaptation of business culture of the partner firm	Weck & Ivanova, 2013
International B2B, Technology and service in an international context, Sweden, Australia and U. K.	Communication, Commitment, Trust, Relation termination costs and benefits, shared values,	Friman et al., 2002, Commitment-Trust theory
e-Business	Confidentiality integrity, availability of information, authentication of payment information, Quality of digital goods, Identification and traceability of digital objects, Prevention of unauthorized copying, management of risks to critical information	Jones et al., 2000
Online customer repurchase intentions	Firm's Professional ability, Integrity, benevolence, security of on-line business information system, privacy protection, third party guarantees & recommendation, perceived waiting.	Hung et al., 2012
Buyer-Supplier Relationship, Supply chain-management	Communication, asset specificity, Behavioral certainty, Information sharing, Partner reputation, Perceived benefits, fairness	Chao et al., 2013, Social Exchange theory
Supply chain management, Metallurgical enterprises, Poland	Long-term contracts, Transfer of right information, Increase of knowledge about participants, more benefits than costs, trust but verify, commitment by all members for the product/service	Gajdzik, B. & Grzybowska, K., 2012
B2-B Financial Services	Communication, Satisfaction, Customization, Competence, and Shared Values	Theron et al., 2011
Customer Trust for a Service provider	Good communication of Information develop trust and commitment, avoids switching providers	Zillifro & Morais(2004) Agency theory, Trust-commitment theory
Trust Value of Service Providers	Interaction trust, word-of mouth trust	Ransi & Kobti, 2014

and service, the antecedents of trust and commitment between exchange partners include communication, shared values, and relation termination costs and benefits (Friman et al., 2002). International B2B relationships have to deal with language barriers and cultural differences. Manufacturing firms often grow internationally by acquisitions, mergers and franchising.

To develop trust between e-businesses and consumers, a shared understanding of the requirements of all the stakeholders involved has to be developed. One has to identify the stakeholders and the business processes involved. The generic requirements for trust in e-business include confidentiality, integrity, and availability of information, identification, traceability and quality of digital goods, prevention of unauthorized copying, security and authentication of payment system, and management of risks to critical information (Jones et al., 2000). Online shopping customers are not able to physically see and feel the products and have to wait to receive the products they purchase. The determinants of trust for the on-line store included the security of the business information system, privacy protection, third part guarantees and recommendations and perceived waiting to receive the product (Hung, et al., 2012).

TRUST IN B2B INTERACTIONS

B2 B transactions often involve customization. The two partners in the transaction develop trust through competence and shared values (Theron et al., 2011). Trust between customers and service providers involve communication of relevant information, interaction trust and word-of-mouth trust (Ransi & Kobti, 2014; Zillifro & Morais, 2004).

The involved parties invest in relationships in the hopes of maximizing long-term benefits and the collaborations are believed to represent a source of competitive advantage that consequently should be managed strategically. An important element of these relationships, and one central to our research, is the notion that they vary over the relationship life cycle (Dwyer et al. 1987). In buyer–supplier relationships, an increasing number of manufacturing firms are relying on a smaller number of suppliers, forging fewer but closer relational ties. Researchers have studied many factors that contribute to effective relational exchanges, including shared values (Morgan and Hunt 1994), commitment (Dwyer et al. 1987), cooperation, and power ; Ganesan1994). In particular, trust has assumed a central role in the success of long-term relationships in business-to-business (B2B) marketing contexts (Moorman, Deshpandé, and Zaltman 1993). There is a great deal of consensus in the marketing literature, that the construct of trust is best conceptualized as multidimensional. In particular, trust is consistently described and tested as being partitioned into facets of competence and benevolence, roughly addressing the issues of "Can my partner do as I'm trusting?," and "Will my partner do so?"

In B2B partnerships, such as buyer–supplier relationships, it may seem logical that competence trust would dominate, because these are business relationships embedded more in economic exchanges than in pure social exchanges, yet the representatives of each partnering firm are still human, and trusting behaviors operate at a personal level, so benevolence contributes to trust judgments as well. Indeed, it may be that the benevolence component of trust grows more important as the relationship progresses, as a natural result of repeated satisfactory interactions. When baseline expectations about the other party's reliability and competence are met, beliefs about the partner's motives, mutual support, and personal commitments to each other assume a more important role for high performance collaborations (Kusari et al., 2014). Therefore, it is important to unravel the effects of competence as well as benevolence considerations on buyer–supplier relationships. Marketing scholars also recognize that trust need not be naïve; for example, previous research has investigated the role of various relational safeguards, such as relationship-specific investments, explicit contracts, and relational norms, in influencing relationship satisfaction. Thus, we will also consider the mitigating role of monitoring mechanisms on trust; i.e., "trust but verify." Finally, the premise identified early on (Dwyer et al. 1987) that business relationships evolve over time is so important and attracts such consensus as to nearly be a truism. Researchers have suggested that as relationships go through different phases of a relationship life cycle, they are characterized by distinct behaviors, orientations, and outcomes. Yet, tracking relationships over time and identifying structural changes between the partners is a rare empirical undertaking, presumably in large part due to the extensive requirements in data collection. In this study, we will collect the necessary data to test the modification in form of relational elements. Specifically, we demonstrate that the efficacy of the combined trust–monitoring mechanism interacts with each dimension of trust (competence and benevolence) and that the results are contingent on the phase of the relationship life cycle (Kusari et al., 2014).

TRUST IN GLOBAL SUPPLY CHAIN

With increased globalization, the supply chain often involves partners across continents. Trust among the partners in all the links in the supply chain ensures proper coordination and functioning of the entire supply chain. The geographically distributed supply chain stakeholders represent a virtual organizations connected by Internet and information communication technology (ICT) and trust among all the stakeholders. Trust is a significant factor in achieving supply chain integration. Cooperation of the stakeholders in the supply chain determines their exposure to business and market risk. As the number of links in the supply chain increases, the trust relationships can get more complex. Some partners rely on trust based on direct interactions (e.g. A-B). Other business interactions rely on derivative trust, which affect A through B's interaction with C. A successful supply chain management offers all the stakeholder firms a competitive edge. Among medical equipment suppliers, communication, behavioral certainty, asset specificity, partner reputation and perceived benefits contributed to positive trust. The relationship tenure did not have a significant effect on trust (Chao et al., 2013). The stakeholders in the supply chain for metallurgical enterprises depend on the direct trust and derivative trust for smooth functioning of the entire supply chain (Gajdzik & Grzybowska, 2012).

A context dependent, multi perspective multilevel trust measurement instrument has been developed to measure supply chain members' trust from risk perspective, i.e. risk related to characteristics, rational and institutions/security considering the relationship as "Risky", "Risk-worthy" and "Not risky". Research on trust emphasizes to focus on a member's characteristics such as benevolence, integrity, ability, reliability, and credibility. The decision to trust requires multiple judgments. The trust should be measured from various context dependent perspectives at multiple levels in relationship from trustor's perceptions. The key perspectives of trust in supply chain relationship are; characteristics trust, rational trust (cost and benefit, dynamic capabilities, technology) and institutional trust/security system (Laeequddin et al., 2010).

SUMMARY

In the multi-polar economic development of the world, the expanding domestic markets and exports of natural resource commodities have made Latin America (LA) an international economic force. Most countries in LA have higher GDP/capita than China. However, the inter-personal trust in LA region is low due to the colonial history and the lack of trust at the institutional and societal level (Lagos, 2001). Low trust in LA region can be explained by the intrinsic or structural (cultural, socioeconomic) and extrinsic explanations (citizens' evaluations of performance). Trust level in individual countries cannot be explained with general models that treat LA region as one entity. Differences in levels of trust between countries may be explained by the socio-demographic differences and by the differences inside each country. An individual in Brazil has a different context of reference than an individual from Mexico, Argentina or Chile. The low levels of inter-personal trust may hinder economic and political development. Low levels of economic and political performance may be not only a consequence of low trust but also a cause of low trust (Jamison, 2011). In the context of intercultural business relationships, trust develops between partner firms by understanding the business culture of a partner firm. The adaptation of the each other's culture results in developing and maintains trust (Weck & Ivanova, 2013).

A concept for a common currency exists for Mercosur or the Southern Common Market including Brazil, Argentina, Paraguay, Uruguay and Chile (Holcova, 2011). Business development opportunities in LA will continue to grow for the upcoming economic superpowers like China, Russia and India. China has already established trade relationships with Venezuela and has oil rigs in the Caribbean. Venezuela and Russia have established military and energy collaborations. Brazil and Mexico's gross domestic product (GDP) is expected to grow at a rate of at least 4.1%. Brazil is becoming one of the leading producers of bio-fuels and alternative energy sources. Mexico is expected to overtake the stable economies such as Germany, Great Britain and France. In these inter-cultural transactions, trust requires cultural intelligence and adaptation including language fluency. Trust is believed to reduce inefficiencies and opportunism associated with agency relationships. Trust is an asset that enterprises must understand and properly manage in order to be successful in today's complex operating environment (Barron, 2014). The monitoring mechanisms on trust, i.e., "trust but verify" are conductive to maintaining trust in a business relationship (Kusari, et al. 2014).

REFERENCES

Arroyo, A. C., & Walker, D. H. T. (2010). The Role of Atlantic Corridor Project as a Form of Strategic Community of Practice in Business Transformations in Latin America. *International Journal of Managing Projects in Business*, *3*(2), 333–348. doi:10.1108/17538371011036626

Barron, J. (2014). All in the Family: Trading Legal Security for Trust and Export Growth in Latin America. *Business Credit*, *116*(5), 31–32.

Bhattacharya, R., Devinney, T. M., & Pillutla, M. M. (1998). A Formal Model of Trust Based on Outcomes. *Academy of Management Review*, *23*(3), 459–472.

Bialaszewski, D., & Giallourakis, M. (1985). Perceived Communication Skills and Resultant Trust Perceptions Whiting the Channel Distribution. *Journal of the Academy of Marketing Science*, *13*(1/2), 206–217. doi:10.1007/BF02729715

Bibb, S., & Kourdi, J. (2004). *Trust Matters for Organizational and Personal Success*. New York: Palgrave.

Cardenas, J. C., Chong, A., Nopo, H., Horowitz, A. W., & Lederman, D. (2009). To What Extent Do Latin Americans Trust, Reciprocate and Cooperate? Evidence from Experiments in Six Latin American Countries/ Comments. *Economia*, *9*(2), 45–94.

Chao, C. M., Yu, C. T., Cheng, B. W., & Chuang, P.-C. (2013). Trust and Commitment in Relationships among Medical Equipment Suppliers: Transaction Cost and Social Exchange Theories. *Social Behavior and Personality*, *4*(7), 1057–1070. doi:10.2224/sbp.2013.41.7.1057

Dahlstrom, R., & Nygaard, A. (1995). An Exploratory Investigation of Interpersonal Trust in New and Mature Markets. *Journal of Retailing*, *71*(4), 339–361. doi:10.1016/0022-4359(95)90018-7

Dweyer, F. R., Schurr, P. H., & Oh, S. (1987). Developing Buyer-Seller Relationships. *Journal of Marketing*, *51*(2), 11–27. doi:10.2307/1251126

ECLAC (Economic Commission for Latin America and Caribbean). (2014). Retrieved from http://www.eclac.org

Emirbayer, M., & Mische, A. (1998). What is Agency? *American Journal of Sociology*, *103*(4), 962–1023. doi:10.1086/231294

Friman, M., Garling, T., Millet, B., Mattson, J., & Johnston, R. (2002). An Analysis of International Business- to Business Relationship Based on the Commitment-Trust Theory. *Industrial Marketing Management*, *31*(5), 403–409. doi:10.1016/S0019-8501(01)00154-7

Gajdzik, B., & Grzybowska, K. (2012). Example Models of Building Trust in Supply Chains of Metallurgical Enterprises. *Metalurgija*, *51*(4), 563–566.

Gambetta, D. (1988). Can we trust 'Trust'?. In D. Gambetta (Ed.), Trust, Making and Breaking Cooperative Relations, (pp. 213-237). Basil Blackwell.

Ganesan, S. (1994). Determinants of Long-Term Orientation in Buyer-Seller Relationships. *Journal of Marketing*, *58*(2), 1–19. doi:10.2307/1252265

Griffith, D. A., Harvey, M. G., & Lisch, R. F. (2006). Social Exchange in Supply Chain Relationships: The Resulting Benefit of Procedural and Distributive Justice. *Journal of Operations Management*, *24*(2), 85–98. doi:10.1016/j.jom.2005.03.003

Gullett, J., Do, L., Canuto-Caranco, M., Brister, M., Turnet, S., & Caldwell, C. (2009). The Buyer-Supplier Relationship: An Integrative Model of Ethics and Trust. *Journal of Business Ethics*, *90*(S3), 329–341. doi:10.1007/s10551-010-0430-4

Hardin, R. (1993). The Street-Level Epistemology of Trust. *Politics & Society*, *21*(4), 505–529. doi:10.1177/0032329293021004006

Hausman, A., & Johnston, W. J. (2010). The Impact of Coercive and Non-Coercive Forms of Influence on Trust, Commitment, and Compliance in Supply Chains. *Industrial Marketing Management*, *39*(3), 519–526. doi:10.1016/j.indmarman.2009.05.007

Heffernan, T., O'Neill, G., Travaglione, T., & Droulers, M. (2008). Relationship Marketing: The Impact of Emotional Intelligence and Trust on Bank Performance. *International Journal of Bank Marketing*, *26*(3), 183–199. doi:10.1108/02652320810864652

Hofstede, G. (1980). *Culture's Consequences: International Differences in Work-Related Values*. Newbury Park, CA: Sage Publications.

Hofstede. (2014). Retrieved from http://geert-hofstede.com/organisational-culture-dimensions.html

Hung, S. W., Cheng, M. J., & Chen, P. C. (2012). Reexamining the Factors for Trust in Cultivating Online Customer Repurchase Intentions: The Moderating Effect of Perceived Waiting. *International Journal of Human-Computer Interaction*, *28*(10), 666–677. doi:10.1080/10447318.2011.654201

Hurtado, O. (2010). Latin America in the Mirror of Culture. *The American Interest*, (Jan/Feb), 92-102.

Jagad, S. (2010). Balancing Trust and Control in Organizations: Towards a Process Perspective. *Society and Business Review, 5*(3), 259-269.

Jambulingam, T., Kathuria, R., & Nevin, J. R. (2011). Fairness-Trust-Loyalty Relationship Under Varying Conditions of Supplier-Buyer Interdependence. *Journal of Marketing Theory and Practice*, *19*(1), 39–56. doi:10.2753/MTP1069-6679190103

Jamison, G. D. (2011). Interpersonal Trust in Latin America: Analyzing Variations in Trust Using Data from the Lationbarometro. *Journal of Multidisciplinary Research*, *3*(3), 65–80.

Jones, K. (1996). Trust as an affective attitude. *Ethics*, *107*(1), 4–25. doi:10.1086/233694

Jones, S., Wilikens, M., Morris, P., & Masera, M. (2000). Trust Requirements in e-Business. *Communications of the ACM*, *43*(12), 80–87. doi:10.1145/355112.355128

Khodyakov, D. (2007). Trust as a Process: A Three Dimensional Approach. *Sociology, British Sociological Association*, *41*(1), 115–132.

Koh, T. K., Fichman, M., & Kraut, R. E. (2012). Trust Across Borders: Buyer-Supplier Trust in Global Business-to-Business E-Commerce. *Journal of the Association for Information Systems, 13*(11), 886–922.

Korzeniowski, P., (2013). The Complex Challenge of Repairing Customer Trust. *Customer Relationship Management,* 26-30.

Krot, K., & Lewicka, D. (2012). The Importance of Trust in Manager-Employee Relationships. *International Journal of Electronic Business Management, 10*(3), 224–233.

Kumar, N., Scheer, L. K., & Steenkamp, J. B. E. M. (1995). The Effects of Perceived Interdependence on Dealer Attitudes. *JMR, Journal of Marketing Research, 32*(3), 348–356. doi:10.2307/3151986

Kusari, S., Hoeffler, S., & Iacobucci, D. (2014). Trusting and Monitoring Business Partners throughout the Relationship Life Cycle. *Journal of Business-to-Business Marketing.* Retrieved from http://www.tandfonline.com/loi/wbbm20

Kwon, I.-W. G., & Suh, T. (2004). Factors Affecting the Level of Trust and Commitment in Supply Chain Relationships. *Journal of Supply Chain Management, 40*(2), 4–14. doi:10.1111/j.1745-493X.2004.tb00165.x

Kwon, Y.-C. (2008). Antecedents and Consequences of International Joint Venture Partnerships: A Social Exchange Perspective. *International Business Review, 17*(5), 559–573. doi:10.1016/j.ibusrev.2008.07.002

Laeequddin, M., Sahay, B. S., Sahay, V., & Waheed, K. A. (2010). Measuring Trust in Supply Chain Partners' Relationships. *Measuring Business Excellence, 14*(3), 53–69. doi:10.1108/13683041011074218

Lagos, M. (2001). Between Stability and Crisis in Latin America. *Journal of Democracy, 12*(1), 137–145. doi:10.1353/jod.2001.0009

Lancastre, A., & Lages, L. F. (2006). The Relationship between Buyer and B2B e-Marketplace: Cooperation Determinants in an Electronic Market Context. *Industrial Marketing Management, 35*(6), 774–789. doi:10.1016/j.indmarman.2005.03.011

LANIC (Latin American Network Information Center). (n.d.). Retrieved from http://lanic.utxas.edu

Latinobarometro Corporation. (2013). *2013 Report.* Retrieved from http://www.latinobarometro.org/latino/LATDatos.jsp

MacIntosh, G. (2009). Examining the Antecedents of Trust and Rapport in Services: Discovering New Relationships. *Journal of Retailing and Consumer Services, 16*(4), 298–305. doi:10.1016/j.jretconser.2009.02.001

Moorman, C., Deshpande, R., & Zaltman, R. (1993). Factors Affecting Trust in Market Relationships. *Journal of Marketing, 57*(1), 81–101. doi:10.2307/1252059

Moran, E. K. & Gossieaux, F. (2013). How Employee Trust Affects the Bottom Line. *Communication World*, 18-21.

Morgan, R. M., & Hunt, S. D. (1994). The Commitment-Trust Theory of Relationship Marketing. *Journal of Marketing, 58*(3), 20–38. doi:10.2307/1252308

Narasimhan, R., Nair, A., Griffith, D. A., Arlbjorn, J. S., & Bendoly, E. (2009). Lock-in Situations in Supply Chains: A Social Exchange Theoretical Study Sourcing Arrangements in Buyer-Supplier Relationships. *Journal of Operations Management, 27*(5), 374–389. doi:10.1016/j.jom.2008.10.004

Neace, M. B. (2004). The Impact of Low Trust on Economic Development: The Case of Latin America. *Review of Policy Research, 21*(5), 699-713.

Niazi, M., Ikram, N., Bano, M., Imtiaz, S., & Khan, S. U. (2013). Establishing Trust in Offshore Software Outsourcing Relationships: An Exploratory Study Using a Systematic Literature Review. *IET Software, 7*(5), 283–293. doi:10.1049/iet-sen.2012.0136

Phelps, S. F., & Campbell, N. (2012). Commitment and Trust in Librarian-Faculty Relationships: A Systematic Review of the Literature. *Journal of Academic Librarianship, 38*(1), 13–19. doi:10.1016/j.acalib.2011.11.003

Power, T. J., & Jamison, J. D. (2005). Political Mistrust in Latin America. *Comparative Sociology, 4*(1-2), 47–72.

Ransi, G. S., & Kobti, Z. (2014). A Hybrid Artificial Reputation Model Involving Interaction Trust, Witness Information and the Trust Model to Calculate the Trust Value of Service Providers. *Axioms, 3*(1), 50–63. doi:10.3390/axioms3010050

Searing, E. A. M. (2013). Love Thy Neighbor? Recessions and Interpersonal Trust in Latin America. *Journal of Economic Behavior & Organization, 94*, 68–79. doi:10.1016/j.jebo.2013.07.010

Shiau, W. L., & Luo, M. M. (2012). Factors Affecting Online Group Buying Intention and Satisfaction: A Social Exchange Theory Perspective. *Computers in Human Behavior, 28*(6), 2431–2444. doi:10.1016/j.chb.2012.07.030

Swift, J. S., & Lawrence, K. (2003). Business Culture in Latin America: Interactive Learning for UK SME's. *Journal of European Industrial Training, 27*(8/9), 389–397. doi:10.1108/03090590310498522

Theron, E., Terblanche, N., & Boshoff, C. (2011). The Antecedents of Trust in Business-to Business Financial Services. *Journal of Business-To-Business Marketing, 18*(2), 188–213. doi:10.1080/1051712X.2010.499837

Uslaner, E. M. (2003). Trust, Democracy and Governance: Can Government Policies Influence Generalized Trust? In M. Hooghe & D. Stolle (Eds.), *Generating Social Capital: Civil Society and Institutions in Comparative Perspective*. Palgrave Macmillan.

Wagner, S. M., Coley, L. S., & Lindemann, E. (2011). Effects of Suppliers' Reputation on the Future of Buyer-Supplier Relationships: The Mediating Roles of Outcome Fairness and Trust. *Journal of Supply Chain Management, 47*(2), 29–48. doi:10.1111/j.1745-493X.2011.03225.x

Watkins, K. (2005). *Human Development Report- International Cooperation at Crossroads: Aid, Trade and Security in an Unequal World*. Retrieved from http://www.undp.org/en/reports/global/hdr2005

Weck, M., & Ivanova, M. (2013). The Importance of Cultural Adaptation for the Trust Development within Business relationships. *Journal of Business and Industrial Marketing, 28*(3), 210–220. doi:10.1108/08858621311302868

Williamson, O. E. (1989). Transaction Cost Economics. In R. Schmalensee & R. Willig (Eds.), Handbook of Industrial Organization, (pp. 136-182). Elsevier.

World Population Data Sheet Interactive World Map. (2014). Retrieved from www.prb.org

World Values Survey. (2010-2014). Retrieved from http://www.worldvaluessurvey.org/

Ybarra, C. E., & Turk, T. A. (2009). The Evolution of Trust in Information Technology Alliances. *The Journal of High Technology Management Research, 20*(1), 62–74. doi:10.1016/j.hitech.2009.02.003

Zapata, C. P., Olsen, J. E., & Martin, L. L. (2013). Social Exchange From the supervisor's Perspective: Employee Trustworthiness as a Predictor of Interpersonal and Informational Justice. *Organizational Behavior and Human Decision Processes*, *121*(1), 1–12. doi:10.1016/j.obhdp.2012.11.001

Zillifro, T., & Morais, D. B. (2004). Building Customer Trust and Relationship Commitment to a Nature-Based Tourism Provider: The Role of Information Investments. *Journal of Hospitality & Leisure Marketing*, *11*(2/3), 159–172. doi:10.1300/J150v11n02_11

Chapter 6
Mobile Financial Sectoral System of Innovation:
What Latin America Can Learn from India

Heather C. Webb
Higher Colleges of Technology, Dubai, UAE

ABSTRACT

With the increase of economic growth in Latin America, the mobile finance (m-finance) sectoral system of innovation model is applied as an analytical framework in order to focus in on the technological infrastructure and regulatory structure. The SSI approach links innovation to the interactions of the different actors in the system. Innovation is either the process of creating or the recombining of knowledge for some new use to become an outcome of that process. Innovation does not sit within the boundaries of an organization nor does it sit neatly at one level, but instead it is a multifaceted construct. Therefore, this chapter presents aspects of the sectoral system of innovation (SSI) of mobile finances within the Latin America region.

1. INTRODUCTION

Financial services are one of the most rapidly growing industries worldwide, specifically mobile finance (m-finance) services. M-finance, which includes mobile payment (m-payment), mobile banking (m-banking) and mobile wallet (m-wallet), have generated a lot of hype, yet not all supportive infrastructures are in place where

DOI: 10.4018/978-1-4666-8820-9.ch006

one company's service can be applied globally. Technology has provoked major changes in this industry with how companies operate and innovate as well as how they adapt their strategy. Additionally, how mobile services expand into and understanding the ways new services are developed in different countries are becoming increasingly relevant especially in regards of regulation. Thus, m-finance is part of a system of innovation.

This chapter evaluates the m-finance sectoral system of innovation (SSI) in the Latin American region. The SSI framework is usable by policy-makers, and especially companies exploring their value or service chain positioning. Though Breschi and Malerba (1997) define SSI as a supply side technological system, Geels (2004) develops the notion of SSI composing of both supply and demand institutions with social and technical parameters such as markets, user-stakeholders, university-industry links and sources of risk capital. Thus, SSI is a useable framework for observing the evolution of m-finance.

According to the World Bank (2014), 60% or around 250 million people, lack access to basic banking services in Latin America. Mobile devices are widely available as normal, everyday items. For this reason, it creates a perfect opportunity for banks, financial institutions and other m-payment providers to offer mobile services. Cash is still seen as the most common durable commodity, and where some even see cash as being more trustworthy than any kind of electronic forms of payments. Therefore, introducing an innovative payment requires a coordinated approach of consumers, retailers, merchants, banks and telecommunications networks, or a system of interoperability and innovation.

Historically, for financial services in developed countries, banks competed for customers primarily on the basis of branch location and customer service. Therefore, the branch location was key for customers to build their trust with the bank. Banks, at the time, were beginning to invest in innovative mainframe computing and automated record keeping. Additionally, the more branches a bank had, the better a competitive advantage they could create as well as trust with their customers. Trust is needed to create the willingness for people/organization to transfer and receive resources, and different levels of trust affect companies' effectiveness in resource acquisition and value creation (de Wever et al, 2005). Within an m-finance SSI, trust is important in order to implement these services, especially in developing countries. Therefore, relationships with businesses can be influenced by trust and longstanding personal connections. In addition, when two companies trust each other, they are willing to share resources without worrying that the other party will act opportunistically (Mayer et al, 1995), and thus can create a system of innovation as well as knowledge exchange.

For the Latin American region, similar to India, companies are leapfrogging basic financial services. However, m-finance is still a newer service, yet it is gaining more acceptance and recognition. Over time, this innovative financial service can specifically benefit the unbanked population, people at the bottom of the income pyramid (BoP), and people with limited credit histories (Prahalad and Hammond, 2002). Moreover, mobile services in Latin America can trickle down from the entrepreneurs to the BoP, but it will take the right strategy, regulation, and necessary partnerships to have these services become a success.

Overall, this chapter looks at m-financial services within a sectoral system of innovation in certain Latin American countries. For Latin America, there has been no research done neither on a SSI system nor on m-financial services. Uptake of m-finance varies widely within the Latin American region. Therefore, this chapter hopes to identify the main barriers faced by these countries when designing and implementing these kinds of mobile services. This chapter is not aimed at evaluating all Latin American countries, but rather, it aims to examine the approach and scope of an m-finance SSI in certain countries. In addition, the chapter looks at lessons from India in regards of their m-finance SSI in order to see what Latin America can learn from India's strengths and weaknesses.

2. MOBILE FINANCIAL SERVICES

Before reviewing the m-finance SSI, it is imperative to discuss who the main players are as well as what exactly is involved in the service. M-finance is still a fledgling service in most economies. In western countries, such as the US and Europe, very few mobile financial or mobile payment services have gained a significant customer base. Thus, when success in m-finance occurs, it can take dramatically different forms.

As technology has matured for mobile services, so too has it created further development of techniques to support this service context. As such, an m-payment transaction is more multifaceted than traditional banking or retail transactions because they typically involve a complete complex service chain executed in a remote manner. Several other factors contribute to the complexities of m-finance applications. Firstly, the mobile marketplace has been in a constant state of change where this change comes in the form of new functionality or new technologies. Secondly, m-finance solutions are inherently distributed and asynchronous requiring strict adherence to well-defined protocols as well as standards in maintaining application integrity. Thirdly, transactions can occur over a longer duration since the user can take advantage of the virtual experience whereas the traditional experience tends to be done in a shorter start-to-end timeframe. Finally, the integrity requirements of a mobile commerce system forces the application to constantly monitor and deal with errors often in real-time which requires an architectural infrastructure of resources that supports this kind of capability.

The m-financial payment framework is complex where it consists of many companies, or actors, within a system. Strategic alliances and partnerships are being formed between telecommunication operators (telcos), financial service companies, retailers, technology/software companies and other entities. These partnerships are enhancing value and expanding services in order to meet rising consumer demand. Undoubtedly, the convergence of companies in these diverse sectors is imperative only if companies are to successfully compete within the new business landscape while, at the same time, achieve the desired value propositions. The system is complex because it involves value chains, mobile retail, and technology actors colliding and vying for pole position. Some actors are involved primarily in enabling the payment service or involved in the payment transaction itself; and some are involved in both the payment and transaction.

As such, the mobile device manufacturer can gain a competitive advantage by building devices that support mobile payments such as near field communication (NFC)-enabled mobile devices with secure elements that store the payment application and account information. The telco provides the channel through which payment applications and consumer data from banks or financial institutions can be delivered to the secure element on the mobile device. Thus, the telco is responsible for the integrity of the keys and certificates that are used to protect communication across its network. The data itself is encrypted by the payment before transmission using another key known only to the payment application.

For the payment transaction, the actors involved are the merchant and technology companies. The merchants need to be within the existing contactless card payment infrastructure in order to accept NFC m-payments. The technology companies are involved in authorizing and settling the transaction through existing financial networks. In other words, these companies are involved in the operation of the bank-end payment processing.

The players involved in both the payment and the transaction are the financial institution (or bank), the wallet provider company, and the customer. The financial institution's role is very similar to their traditional role in the credit/debit card transactions. The wallet provider supplies an application or service that manages financial instruments such as credit/debit/coupon cards. The customer is the consumer of the m-payment service who plays a critical part in the payment transaction by enabling the start of the payment process. The customer initiates the requests for the issuance of payment credentials and can sometimes have the choice regarding the telco, mobile device, financial institution and merchant. Although in some countries, especially in Latin America, there are no choices or options when dealing with the telco and/ or financial institution.

The benefits of m-payments can be seen in every stakeholder, although it is mainly transparent to consumers, but the immediate benefits are most apparent to financial institutions and governments. For customers, the most important benefits are the increased convenience, greater personal safety and security and enhanced financial management capabilities. Merchants benefit from increased sales in securing transaction processes as well as reduced costs. Banks or financial institutions benefit from more efficient payment processing operations that has lowered costs and reduced risks. However, governments are perhaps the biggest beneficiaries because the large reductions in systemic risk enhance the ability of central banks to manage national financial and social systems, and thus, can improve country risk ratings.

Banking correspondents (BCs) are information communication telecommunication (ICT)-enabled points of service installed by banks on a partnership basis with non-bank businesses, such as supermarkets, pharmacies, grocery stores, post offices and other types of retail establishments in low-income areas underserved by traditional banking (Ivatury and Mas, 2008; Diniz et al, 2012). It is ICT-based where basic personal computers are operating as terminals and are installed in retails stores to permit financial transactions to be carried out (Diniz et al, 2012). The model is considered unique because of its reach and scale, the quality of services provided, and the technological platforms that have enabled these services (Kumar et al, 2006). Although different from bank-to-bank, the list of services offered by BCs is quite extensive: bill payments, account opening, access to balance and statements, fund transfer, deposits, government benefits withdrawal and credit (Thompson et al, 2003).

The availability and effectiveness of m-finance and/or BCs varies from country to country. This variance can, sometimes, reflect the relative efficiency of payment systems already in place, the differences of financial sectors and the size and geographical density of the market. Additionally, consumer preferences and cultural traits will affect the adoption rates and usages of these services. For that reason, customers draw value in different ways from m-finance. There is no single monopoly proposition. M-finance is about the ease of moving money across distances, where the purpose and the context of the transactions make a difference in the value proposition for the customers as well as for service providers. These service providers need to understand how to adequately tailor services, market the services and their value proposition. Moreover, the role that governments play in exploring and developing these services and market segments are outside the commercial limits, but where in time, these services can become commercially viable. However, it comes down to how strong interoperability is among the various stakeholders.

Regardless of exponential growth predictions in m-finance, fundamental challenges continue to hinder engagement in both developing and developed countries. For example, the power struggles that affect organizational engagement, specifically, between the banks and telcos with regards to the customer relationship is a challenge.

Also, m-finance is a complex structure because of the many actors involved in the process who need to generate interest economically on both the supply and demand sides of the market (Ondrus and Lyytinen, 2011). Additionally, growth potential depends on the type of consumers who use these innovative services.

2.1 Bottom of Income Pyramid

It has been estimated that 2.5 billion people in lower to middle income countries have no basic bank accounts (GSMA, 2013). These unbanked individuals lack the financial services they need to help them climb out of poverty. According to the banks, the infrastructure for traditional bricks-and-mortar banking is too expensive to serve them. Nonetheless, of the unbanked population, more than 1 billion have access to a mobile phone (CGAP, 2012).

In Latin America, poverty levels are decreasing while the ranks of the middle class are increasing. Businesses that focus on poverty reduction are, in essence, outlining Prahalad and Hammond's (2002) concept of the BoP. Prahalad and Hammond attempted to raise awareness of the world economic pyramid and the vastly untapped market of 4 billion people living on less than $1500 purchasing power parity per capita income. Innovation is almost a mandate condition for countries with strong BoP markets. Companies should focus on products or services that could be embedded into the BoP consumers' lives (Simanis and Milstein, 2012). For m-finance, the BoP primarily transact in an informal market economy due to the cost, complexity and unfamiliarity of transitioning to the formal economy. Therefore, these unmet societal needs are potential business opportunities.

3. SECTORAL SYSTEMS OF INNOVATION AND DEVELOPING COUNTRIES

Innovation systems are complex. The SSI framework provides a valuable analytical and prescriptive tool for identifying the needs and strengths inherent to a system. In addition, the SSI views intangible features as being important. However, SSI is complex because of the networks of actors and the linkages among these actors. As Malerba (2002) points out, the elements and structure of SSI include products, agents, knowledge and learning processes, basic technologies, mechanisms of interactions within companies and outside companies, processes of competition and selection, and institutions. All of these characteristics interact with each other in order to formulate the system where elements come together to develop the whole character of the system.

Most sectoral innovation research has, up until recently, been mainly from developed countries (Malerba and Mani, 2009), but there is growing interest in understanding how to apply the innovation system framework to improve policy and strengthen innovation in developing countries (Aorcena and Sutz, 2000; Aubert, 2005; Chaminade and Vang, 2008; Malerba and Mani, 2009). For a developing country, mapping the system and how the institutional environment evolves as well as analyzing how this evolution affects organizational fields and the broader society is especially challenging. Companies and institutions are largely conditioned by the specific properties of SSI because, to some extent, companies in developing countries can be considered as latecomers. Thus, it has been said that latecomers and institutions will therefore lack the competence to create major innovations to compete on a global level since they are dislocated from sources of technology and lack resource and development (Hobday, 1994). In addition, as compared to advanced countries, developing countries will have a disadvantage with the demands of users (von Hippel, 1988). For that reason, dislocation from advanced users is, often times, related to lack of competence to innovate in latecomer companies, but there are few exceptions within SSI.

Recently, researchers have shown that there is at least a need to assess to what degree the original concepts around innovating systems in a developing country context (Srinivas and Sutz, 2008; Chaminade and Vang, 2008; Lundvall et al, 2009). Others have also explored the difficulty of developing technological capacity in emerging economies. For example, the transition dilemma between the 'catch-up' phase and true leadership is explored by Hobday et al (2004) who describe how companies and sectors move between these stages. Ernst (2002) has explored the innovation systems of developing countries by studying the international networks that allow the import of mature technologies for reverse engineering. The key similarity between all of the frameworks described above is that the focus is on how latecomer companies become involved in the eventual creation of new knowledge. Knowledge is a foundational pillar for innovative and development success. In terms of emerging industries, SSI explains that knowledge is developed and then actors change the knowledge into economic value accordingly to the needed institutions being built and how the industry evolves. Often times, individuals are the most important feature because they are involved in several aspects of the technology as well as creating knowledge.

4. INDIAN M-FINANCIAL SSI

In India, the government has historically played a major, and in most cases, a singularly positive role in the formation of its innovation system. Ever since its independence from British rule, India has invested much time, resources and efforts in creating a knowledge society and building institutions of research and higher education. Nevertheless, India is faced with major challenges related to infrastructure and bureaucratic hurdles.

For India, efforts to include the unbanked into the formalized financial system followed after independence from the British. These efforts included the nationalization of the banking system and the creation of regional rural banks. The Reserve Bank of India implemented regulations designed to replace the countryside money lender with commercial bank branches. Therefore, for every new bank branch opened in a banking strong region, banks are required to open four new branches in areas heavily populated with unbanked individuals. Therefore, what happened was that bank branches in unbanked areas increased while money lenders decreased.

India's SSI has mainly been focused in the telecommunication industry. In the 1980s, the Indian government created the Centre for Development of Telematics (C-DOT) to mandate the design and development of digital exchanges. C-DOT is, in essence, a public laboratory. While the lab has been successful in not just generating technologies that are suited to Indian conditions, it has been able to effectively transfer the generated technology to a host of public and private sector companies. The laboratory is credited with establishing a modern telecommunications equipment industry in the country (Mani, 2007).

Currently, the government of India has shifted their focus on the use of technology models in order to improve social banking. They are trying to implement a nationwide identity system which links to the delivery of government payments. The National Payments of Corporation of India is promoting a national switch that is interoperable among all bank agents and financial services. Thus, India's technology initiatives are notably aimed at improving the effectiveness of social banking without increasing actors. Indeed, these innovative services are disrupting lives in a positive way as well as creating different business models. These services will have a positive, economic impact.

The presence of institutional factors is well documented within the Indian economy. There are various government funded institutions, especially educational for both the engineering and the management sectors. These institutions have produced world class graduates who have fuelled the international growth of the software industry by enabling Indian software companies to capitalise on the readily available pool of talented and comparatively cheaper software programmers. The abundance of highly skilled and comparatively low-cost labour pool has enabled a sustained form of competitive advantage for software companies and technology companies to compete in the global market. Moreover, these educational institutions have been a pillar for India's SSI.

India's m-finance SSI strives to include the poor and unbanked. However, there are constraints. Expansion constrains include the difficulties of marketing m-payment services to often illiterate, rural residents; and the absence of 2G network connectivity in many rural areas. The institutional and regulatory environment in India promotes the social justice goal of enabling BoP consumers to become 'banked' via m-finance. Regulations and institutional arrangements in India are supporting and driving m-finance innovation, and companies are responding with the appropriate technology. However, as elsewhere in Indian economic development, infrastructure is a major constraint.

5. LATIN AMERICA

Latin America is a region of countries where all have different stages of economic development occurring. Each country has its own unique characteristics which differentiates it from the rest. For m-finance, these characteristics can be seen in different payment methods employed by each country; however some countries have yet to implement a strong regulatory framework. Mobile services are influenced to the extent in which technology, the Internet, and mobile phones have already penetrated the market. Mobiles are ubiquitous which creates, at times, the sole link to any kind of financial services.

Latin America can be described has being a highly polarized distribution of income. Low banking penetration perpetuates the informal economy. This undermines government efforts to manage the economy, and at times, can hinder the development of financial innovations. Nonetheless, financial payment products availability and effectiveness varies substantially from country to country because of differences in the economy, regulation and social environment. Thus, what works in one country will not necessarily work in another country.

For the Latin American region, there is a noticeable absence of sectoral system of innovation in mobile financial services as compared to other regions of the world. Each country has a different regulatory approach to m-finance. These differences are not only due to the types of institutions that provide mobile services, but also their role within the SSI. In addition, these countries have various definitions of what constitutes m-finance. For instance, in some countries, m-finance implies deposit taking because money in mobile wallets may be stored for an indefinite period of time. This entails that mobile wallets may only be offered by companies authorized to accept deposits such as banks or other licensed financial institutions. In other countries, m-finance is defined as simply the transformation of physical money into electronic money. This definition allows both banking and non-banking institutions to provide m-finance. For example, Bolivia sees mobile financial services being similar to a payment service, and thus, a non-financial company can provide m-financial services; whereas in Peru, m-finance can only be provided by a bank. In countries where the government considers m-finance as a payment service, the central bank's authority is used as the governing body created under governmental law. Therefore, there is no standard definition of m-finance in the Latin American region.

The road in providing m-finance does not have to be the same for countries, but as one will see below, lack of certain institutional frameworks will hinder the success of any kind of m-finance. Therefore, one should consider what these countries can learn from India in regards of knowledge of interoperability and regulation as well as India's focus on social agenda for BoP or the unbanked. Not every country in Latin America is discussed below because of the deficient of data available. Therefore, the countries presented in this chapter only offer a snapshot on what is happening in regards of m-finance SSI in the Latin American region.

5.1 Argentina

In Argentina, mobile development and innovation is broad. Banks are interested in providing mobile services, but full implementation is taking time because of lack of investment in payment infrastructure as well as high cost of smartphone usage. Thus, the telcos are unsure of whether they need or want to partner with financial institutions. These issues are creating barriers to growth and development of an m-payment ecosystem. Therefore, the key for adoption will be in creating consumer confidence as well as increasing financial access through government policies.

5.2 Brazil

Brazil is becoming a leader in m-banking initiatives for the Latin American region. Banks and other financial institutions have made m-payment and m-banking a priority in their strategy development. However, actors in the SSI are still struggling with creating an effective business model. Therefore, developing strategic partnerships with retailers, and specifically telcos, will be key in order to focus on improving services and access. Technology will advance once companies and banks overcome challenges such as the convergence of systems and processes to create stronger interoperability.

The government is more involved by being progressive in implementing regulation. However, a main obstacle is still security concerns. With innovative services interacting with technology, innovative fraud risk also grows. In addition, lack of knowledge about transaction security is a concern. In 2013, Brazil signed into law an emphasis on interoperability between telcos, bank card issuers, acquirers and card brand providers. The result of this law is to spur more consumer adoption, especially among the 65 million unbanked adults that the government wants to include in the financial mainstream.

By late 2013, the Brazilian government established regulations directed at clarifying expectations for m-payment services. The Central Bank of Brazil is responsible for oversight of mobile commerce and created a new classification of mobile money companies called "payment institutions." These payment institutions will have fewer capital restrictions, but similar protections to traditional financial institutions. The government's long term goal is to create interoperability between all competing platforms. By creating a friendlier regulatory environment, this should eventually translate to a viable financial service option for the unbanked population as well as the banked population.

Banks have achieved significant growth through the agent networks. However, banks are facing challenges. Firstly, unions claim that captive bank agents are employees according to labor laws, and therefore, should be paid the same wages as bank workers. Secondly, various groups are advocating for legislative caps on bank agent fees. There is a lack of clarity on prices and contract fees of agent which creates a lack of investment from the banks. The regulatory framework allows non-bank entities to issue electronic money. Importantly, it does not treat money as deposits which have a far greater regulatory restriction. The law only grants non-bank entities access to the domestic processing network and settlement at the Central Bank if they apply for a payment institution license. The regulation does not mandate interoperability because the Brazilian government does not want to restrict a market that is still very much, in their perspective, in a development phase. However, specifically for the BoP, there is no legislative clarity. Compared to India, Brazil can learn to incorporate the requirement of banks and other financial institutions which require a certain percentage of their customers to be from the BoP. Brazil also can build a stronger agent network with more specific clarity as to who can become a banking agent.

5.3 Colombia

In Colombia, regulations, issued by the Ministry of Treasure and Public Credit and the Financial Superintendence, are diverse in regards of m-finance. Electronic deposits are defined within the authorized transactions for intermediation entities. In 2006, the government issued regulations regarding the use of banking agents. However, it was evident that achieving financial presence in all of the country's municipalities by 2010 was going to require a lot more than just authorizing the usage of agents. The agent model in Colombia is similarly organized as India's banking correspondent model with the bank issuing the agent a credit line. The limit of the credit line is set by the bank as a maximum amount of cash that can used by the agents at any given time. When the agent carries out cash withdrawals or pays out remittances, then this frees up credit. When the maximum cash limit is reached, the system does not allow for any more transactions until the accumulated cash is taken to the nearest bank branch. Once at the bank, the point limit is adjusted and reset to where the agent can perform transactions again.

For Colombia, it has been a slow expansion of the agent network. However, the Banca de las Oportuniadades (BdO) begun to monitor the BCs sequentially to figure out the various challenges. A Banking Committee was established in order to facilitate a dialogue with the government. The BdO wanted the agent model to be designed with the idea that banks could set up agent networks in order to lower the risk and the perception of low profitability. The BdO incentive model was made to guarantee a specific number of transactions for a specific period of time at a specific price. Thus, these specified, guaranteed transactions would allow the agents to cover their break-even points if transactions were less than the guaranteed level. For instance, if the transactions were higher, then the government would not have to pay. Therefore, the risk perceived by the institutions operating in smaller municipalities would be insured.

There have been problems. Selecting and implementing the agents has become a concern. Agents have to be authorized to operate as an agent because most banks require the authorization of a credit limit. Therefore, an agent has to pass the bank's risk assessment and be willing to take on the cost and risk of transporting cash to the nearest branch. Banks have the control as to who is to become an agent, but there lacks knowledge on organizing the agent network and there lacks the ability to estimate the economic activity as well as serving the BoP communities. Other issues with the model include lack of profit, except when agents were used when nearby branches were busy, and lack of a commission structure. Banks have to realize that they were entrusting the bank's brand and customer service to third parties, which became more of a challenge to the bank. There was no allowance for an accurate estimate of the cost structure because of different technological options being utilized, and hence, lack of interoperability. In addition, lack of clarity regarding the right business models.

Lessons from the BdO incentives are that a favorable regulatory framework is needed that allows financial institutions to use a low-cost channel through agents. The use of incentives can accelerate the process and reduce the time needed to learn. Although the agent model is a low-cost channel compared to ATM or branch banking, there are still difficulties in smaller municipalities. Therefore, m-finance can be stronger if telecommunication coverage is more readily available. In addition, managing agent networks needs to be better where agents fund their own float and not need to use a line of credit from a bank. It limits the bank's risk by making each agent responsible for developing their own business according to their own capacity. The BC and agent model took time to find success in India, but Colombia can learn from India's knowledge in this area.

5.4 Guatemala

Guatemala is one of the poorest Latin American countries. It is a country of small, informal businesses where, similar to other developing countries, formal and informal lending practices coexist within the larger financial system. Guatemala has a history of granting concessions to companies who provide no service that they were contracted to provide. In 1986, the government granted a 15-year concession to Comunicaciones Celulares, S.A. to provide cellular services. This company provided no such service. However, by 2011, through opportunities created by the government, four companies (Comcel, Telgua, Telefonica and Bellsouth) were competitively offering mobile services.

The Office of the Superintendent of Banks (Superintendencia de Bancos, SIB) issued in 2011 the Regulations for Providing Mobile Financial Services. This regulation requires that operations be registered in real time, that there be infrastructure in place for customer assistance, that third parties participate in the oversight of financial institutions' obligations to their customers, and that financial institutions take responsibility for m-finance transactions. The regulation established that banks are the only ones who can provide mobile services. These services have to be tied to an individual bank account for deposits and/or lines of credit.

For m-finance, these regulations are focused at preventing money laundering. However, these are basic regulations and have very little to do with the m-finance model. There is no definition of m-finance which leaves it open for interpretation. The telcos view regulation for these services as a banking concern. There is lack of coordination with the telcos in implementing a joint regulatory framework where supervisory responsibilities are defined. In terms of the unbanked segment, the Monetary Board created the Regulations for Operations and Provision of Services by Banking Agents and the Regulations for Providing Mobile financial services. It has yet to be seen if the BoP communities are being serviced according to this regulation.

5.5 Mexico

Mexico does not have a clear strategy in defining the role of financial institutions nor defining m-finance services. Increased dialogue between banks, payment providers, merchants and telcos is critical for creating a stronger ecosystem and interoperability. Therefore, cultivating these relationships needs to be stronger or else implementation will be more difficult and costly. Banks and other financial institutions cannot provide m-payments or m-banking alone, yet no progress has developed. Currently, banks are more focused on SMS m-banking and not on advanced technology such as NFC. Although, SMS m-banking does offer growth and should not easily be dismissed because it can reach unbanked consumers, high cost of smartphones remains a significant challenge. Additionally, it comes down to consumer trust in changing perceptions about security and using the mobile channel for financial services. A strong ecosystem created through cooperation is necessary in order to realize the risk-sharing and resource-pooling benefits.

5.6 Peru

In Peru, telcos and/or third parties can participate in m-finance without the requirement of financial institutions. This is a similar process in Kenya, but not so in India. Peruvian regulation focuses on a simple law defining electronic money. The regulation aims to mainly benefit rural or isolated areas where commercial banking has no presence, by helping to make payments and transfers securely and at a low cost. Agents were established in 2005 through Superintendencia de Banca, Seguros y AFP (SBS) regulation. Agents are a low-cost channel for banks because banks do not charge customers for transactions using agents. The regulation also stipulates that a pre-paid card and airtime is not considered money. The extensive spread of mobile technology across the country creates opportunities to expand financial services and this is the basis for seeking to provide wider access. Nonetheless, the Peruvian banking sector has developed an extensive network of retail points and banking agents outside of the traditional brick-and-mortar branches.

Telcos have an opportunity to grow their services beyond communication. Their advantage lies in their experience to manage high-volume, low-value transactions which allow them to safely offer electronic money services with lower cost structures than banks (GSMA, 2010). Furthermore, the network systems needed are mostly in place (Alexandre et al., 2010). Telcos generally market themselves nationwide and commonly avoid niche strategies that are typical for financial institutions that are driven by specific customer and segment profitability within defined geographies (Ivatury and Mas, 2008).

The possible disadvantage of allowing the telcos to provide m-finance is that these companies really do not promote full entry into the banking industry. Thus, they lack the knowledge that banks have. However, electronic money services provided by the telcos can make the BoP communities better off by offering efficient payment and transfer services. In fact, this entry route to financial services may be more effective for consumers, since mobile networks have a consumer track record in payment and credit worthiness (Williams and Torma, 2007). In particular, credit information on these BoP consumers may help to reduce the barriers to accessing a larger set of financial services and get the country closer to achieving full financial inclusion. The fundamental principle that the financial regulator should follow when defining the regulation is to establish a level playing field for all types of service providers. For this purpose, a key approach is to focus the regulation on the service rather than on the service providers (GSMA, 2010). In order to guarantee that all players follow the same rules, they should have a common supervisor that will maintain a continuing dialogue with others such as the Central Bank that oversees the payment system and the telecommunications sector.

5.7 Paraguay

In regards of banking services, Paraguay has one of the lowest rates of banking penetration compared to others with only 22% of adults having a formal bank account (GSMA, 2014). Policymakers and regulators are focused on increasing the penetration levels by embarking on the National Strategy for Financial Inclusion and allowing telcos to provide financial services. Therefore, telcos have become licensed electronic money issuers (Entidades de Medios de Pagos Electróbucis).

Historically, when any kind of mobile financial services begun in Paraguay, there was no specific regulation. The Central Bank of Paraguay (BCP) have identified mobile services as a pillar strategy for the financial inclusion, yet decided to implement the "test and learn" approach, or cautiously allow the telcos to develop commercially without issuing any regulation. By 2010, BCP had to issue regulation in regards of remittances and money transfers.

The interesting aspect about Paraguay is that the regulation includes unique provisions that have not been previously tested in other markets (GSMA, 2014). Most noteworthy is that balances on accounts that have been inactive for 90 days or more are automatically transferred to a savings account at a formal financial institution. Therefore, if the electronic money account holder does not already have a bank account, EMPE must facilitate opening an account at a partner bank. This, in essence, is creating stronger interoperability because bank accounts will be necessary in order for this provision to work. In a way, Paraguay is mandating interoperability, yet it does not include the technical specifications of regulating the transfer or amount as seen in India. Overall, Paraguay is taking a critical approach by creating a framework for electronic money issuers. Thus, there is potential for Paraguay in becoming a leader within the Latin American region in providing financial services to people excluded from the formal financial system and BoP communities.

6. CONCLUSION

The adoption of m-financial services can greatly lower the costs of financial services as well as provide substantially greater access to companies and individuals. By increasing efficiency of operations, m-finance can increase economies of scale where it can lead to greater consolidation and evolvement of the financial services industry (Allen et al, 2002) within a sectoral system. With these findings and the ongoing evolution of the industry and sector, it seems likely over time that new services, new delivery channels, and new or hybrid institutions competing will significantly change the financial service industry. Thus, financial services are entering a period of Schumpeterian (Schumpeter, 1939) competition and creative destruction where innovations are radically changing the nature of competition.

In regards of the relationship between regulation and innovation, this relationship is ambiguous when it comes to such issues as competition. Pro-competitive regulation that prohibits anti-competitive behaviour encourages innovation by reducing barriers to entry for new, more innovative companies, and by allowing companies to choose more freely the strategy and business model which best facilitates innovation. Yet, the same regulation may restrict innovation by preventing businesses from collaborating closely at the research and development stages as well as preventing certain organizational structures or the forming of some agreements that could facilitate the transfer of knowledge and technologies.

There are two challenges in providing financial services for the unbanked. For one, it becomes difficult for consumers who have always dealt with cash to trust the service provider. Thus, personal relationships play an important role in building confidence in the service. Therefore, these banking agents are very important part of the business model and strategy in educating consumers on the value of these services. Second, some Latin American regulators have yet to introduce legislation for mobile services. The lack of regulation creates a barrier and puts a hold on providing the services because companies are waiting for legislation. Another barrier to overcome is educating the poor on the value of basic financial services. Companies have to create a product that makes sense for people to adopt and use. One way could be for banks and other financial institutions to lower account opening requirements, offering pay-as-you-go services, establishing agent networks and providing account access through mobile phones. However, banks need to overcome the misconceptions of saving since it is an intangible concept. Individuals who are not familiar or use to saving see it as a wasted opportunity. Moreover, these individuals believe their money is no longer actively working for them and instead will invest in more tangible investments such as livestock or the ability to grow additional crops. In addition, the concept of saving money is individualistic with banks, which creates hesitations among the unbanked that are use to pooling their savings in order to share resources. Consumer education will be required besides designing services based on their financial behavior.

Interoperability creates cost efficiencies and stronger risk management where it benefits all participants in the m-financial ecosystem including consumers, merchants, governments, and financial institutions. Central banks delegate regulation for payment systems and see interoperability as an economic objective to be cost-efficient. Thus, costs are kept low, and capabilities are minimized. Therefore, participation in an interoperable network is rarely regarded as a strategic concern. In terms of regulation, a too-early or a too-heavy approach to payment innovation can stifle market development as well as interoperability. Regulators are stronger working with industry associations to encourage interoperability. Furthermore, with absence of associations, interoperability can be long, difficult and messy. However, processes or technologies may not be compatible which delays achieving a robust system.

Latin America could become a regional leader for m-finances. Three characteristics suggest a favorable climate for growth. Firstly, the regions economies are advancing (Argentina, Brazil, Mexico) which is leading to personal income growth. Secondly, there are millions of customers that are unbanked which represents new customers for banks, telcos and/or m-financial suppliers. Thirdly, the mobile culture is already heavily rooted within these societies. However, the availability and effectiveness of a particular m-finance product varies substantially from country to country because of the differences in the level of concentration of the financial sector, the telecommunication sector and the government. In addition, the size and geographical density of the market will have an effect on the efficiency of mobile services more-so than just consumer preferences and cultural traits. Therefore, these kinds of differences confound direct country-to-country comparisons. A process or service that works in one country and market will not necessarily be appropriate for another country or market.

M-financial services are at the intersection of wireless technology combined with financial services; therefore it requires working hand in hand. There are a multitude of approaches in providing these services. Compared to other regions in the world, Latin America has lagged behind. Latin America has the right characteristics to succeed and can benefit greatly from m-financial services. The key aspect being that all stakeholders within the ecosystem need to overcome interoperability concerns and market fragmentation. There are encouraging signs that this is already happening such as being open to competition. It just takes time in creating the right interoperable system for the actors involved to operate cohesively and together.

REFERENCES

Alexandre, C., Mas, l. & Radcliffe, D. (2010). *Regulating New Banking Models that can Bring Financial Services to All.* Bill & Melinda Gates Foundation.

Allen, F., McAndrews, J., & Strahan, P. (2002). E-Finance: An Introduction. *Journal of Financial Services Research, 22*(1/2), 5–27. doi:10.1023/A:1016007126394

Aorcena, R., & Sutz, J. (2000). *Interactive Learning spaces and development policies in Latin America.* DRUID Working Paper, 00-13, Department of Business Studies: Aalborg.

Aubert, J.-E. (2005). *Promoting Innovation in Developing Countries: A Conceptual Framework.* World Bank Policy Research Working Paper, No. 3554.

Breschi, S., & Malerba, F. (1997). Sectoral Innovation Systems: Technological Regimes, Schumpeterian Dynamics and Spatial Boundaries. In C. Edquist (Ed.), *Systems of Innovation Pinter.* London.

CGAP. (2012). *The Consultative Group to Assist the Poor.* [online] Available at: http://www.cgap.org/blog/biggest-social-experiment-planet

Chaminade, C., & Vang, J. (2008). Globalisation of knowledge production and regional innovation policy: Supporting specialized hubs in the Bangalore software industry. *Research Policy, 37*(10), 1684–1696. doi:10.1016/j.respol.2008.08.014

De Wever, S., Martens, R., & Vandenbempt, K. (2005). The impact of trust on strategic resource acquisition through interorganizational networks: Towards a conceptual model. *Human Relations, 58*(12), 1523–1543. doi:10.1177/0018726705061316

Diniz, E., Birochi, R., & Pozzebon, M. (2012). Triggers and barriers to financial inclusion: The use of ICT-based branchless banking in an Amazon County. *Electronic Commerce Resource Application, 11*(5), 484–494. doi:10.1016/j.elerap.2011.07.006

Ernst, D. (2002). Global production networks and the changing geography of innovation systems. Implications for developing countries. *Economics of Innovation and New Technology, 11*(6), 497–523. doi:10.1080/10438590214341

Geels, F. W. (2004). Sectoral systems of innovation to socio-technical systems: Insights about dynamics and change from sociology and institutional theory. *Research Policy, 33*(6-7), 897–920. doi:10.1016/j.respol.2004.01.015

GSMA. (2010). *Mapping and Effectively Structuring Operator-Bank Relationships to Offer Mobile Money for the Unbanked.* [online] Available at: http://www.gsma.com/mobilefordevelopment/wp- content/uploads/2012/03/mappingandeffectivestructuringfinal2643.pdf

GSMA. (2013). *State of the Industry 2013: Mobile Financial Services for the Unbanked.* [online] Available at: http://www.gsma.com/mobilefordevelopment/wp- content/uploads/2014/02/SOTIR_2013.pdf

GSMA. (2014). *Financial Inclusion in Paraguay: New Mobile Money Regulation.* [online] Available at: http://www.gsma.com/latinamerica/financial-inclusion-in-paraguay-new-mobile-money-regulation

Hobday, M. (1994). Technological learning in Singapore: A test case of leapfrogging. *The Journal of Development Studies, 30*(4), 831–858. doi:10.1080/00220389408422340

Hobday, M., Rush, H., & Bessant, J. (2004). Approaching the innovation frontier in Korea: The transition phase to leadership. *Research Policy, 33*(10), 1433–1457. doi:10.1016/j.respol.2004.05.005

Ivatury, G., & Mas, I. (2008). *The Early Experience with Branchless Banking. Focus Note 46.* Washington, DC: CGAP.

Kumar, A., Nair, A., Parsons, A., & Urdapilleta, E. (2006). *Expanding Bank Outreach through Retail Partnerships: Correspondent Banking in Brazil.* World Bank Working Paper No. 85. Washington, DC: World Bank.

Lundvall, B.-A., Joseph, K. J., Chaminade, C., & Vang, J. (Eds.). (2009). *Handbook of Innovation Systems and Developing Countries. Learning. Edward Elgar.* doi:10.4337/9781849803427

Malerba, F. (2002). Sectoral systems of innovation and production. *Research Policy, 31*(2), 247–264. doi:10.1016/S0048-7333(01)00139-1

Malerba, F., & Mani, S. (2009). Sectoral systems of innovation and production in developing countries: an introduction. In F. Malerba & S. Mani (Eds.), *Sectoral Systems of Innovation and Production in Developing Countries: Actors, Structure and Evolution* (pp. 3–24). Cheltenham, UK: Edward Elgar. doi:10.4337/9781849802185.00006

Mani, S. (2007). *Innovation Capability in Developing Countries, A study of the Telecommunications Industry.* Cheltenham, UK: Edward Elgar.

Mayer, R. C., Davis, J. H., & Schoorman, F. D. (1995). An integrative model of organizational trust. *Academy of Management Review, 20*(3), 709–734.

Ondrus, J., & Lyytinen, K. (2011). Mobile payments market: Towards another clash of the Titans? *10th International Conference on Mobile Business*, (pp. 166-172). Academic Press.

Prahalad, C. K., & Hammond, A. (2002). Serving the World's Poor, profitably. *Harvard Business Review*, (September), 4–11. PMID:12227146

Schumpeter, J. A. (1939). *Business Cycles: A Theoretical, Historical and Statistical Analysis of the Capitalist Process*. London: McGraw-Hill.

Simanis, E. & Milstein, M. (2012). Back to Business Fundamentals: Making BoP Relevant to Core Business. *Field Actions Science Report*, (4), 8.

Srinivas, S., & Sutz, J. (2008). Developing countries and innovation: Searching for a new analytical approach. *Technology in Society*, *30*(2), 129–140. doi:10.1016/j.techsoc.2007.12.003

Thompsom, C. E. M., Barbosa Júnior, C. L., & Frota, I. L. N. (2003). *A parceria Bradesco e Correios no Bando Postal: uma abordagem estratégica, tecnológica e social*. Bauro, Brazil: X Simpósio de Engenharia de Produção.

Von Hippel, E. (1988). *The Sources of Innovation*. New York: Oxford University Press.

Williams, H., & Torma, M. (2007). Trust and Fidelity: From "under the mattress" to the mobile phone. In Vodafone policy paper series The Transformational Potential of M- Transactions, 6.

World Bank. (2014). *Poverty Data*. [online] Available at: http://data.worldbank.org/topic/poverty

Chapter 7

Building Trust in Politics:
Causes of Widespread Disillusionment in Latin American Countries

Michele Lobina
Sapienza University of Rome, Italy

Marco Bottone
Sapienza University of Rome, Italy

ABSTRACT

This chapter studies the process of trust building in politics by using large data set on political behaviour in Latin America. The results yielded by developed models indicate specific elements as the most influential on the popular trust in institutions. These observed determinants were enclosed in five macro classes: cohesion of society; economic factors; electoral transparency; efficiency of judicial organs; and crime diffusion. The analysis of the public support in governments and parliaments revealed that certain variables have a direct impact on the stability of the Latin American democracies, while other factors merely determine the likelihood of a government's reappointment.

INTRODUCTION

Citizens' attitude towards political elites has been thoroughly studied since the birth of the modern democracies. Nonetheless, dynamics of trust in political institutions remains a highly debated topic in many disciplines (e.g. marketing, linguistics,

DOI: 10.4018/978-1-4666-8820-9.ch007

kinesics, etc.), aiming at aiding politicians develop their public image that the vast public perceives as credible. Given the complexity of the public opinion, issues other than candidates' persona need to be considered; acknowledged efficiency of institutions, well-intentioned actions, and overall perception of a democratic order are only some of the requisites of overall trust in politics.

Generally, trust is a factor that entails personal risk (Levi, 1998), which in the political context, relates to the institutional power that electors attribute to the candidates of their choosing. Simply put – it is an exchange between the politicians and the rest of the population: the latter express their trust via ballots, the former validate this trust by efficiently representing popular interests. When the second part of the exchange is not achieved, perception of distrust emerges, explicating a rather asymmetric nature of trust that is arduously obtained yet so swiftly lost. Once the disillusion diffuses within a society, the endeavor of trust-building reveals to be rather challenging (Easton, 1975). This interpretation suggests that low levels of trust in politics usually represent repercussions of deep-rooted disenchantment in politicians' actions.

Surveying about politics can be very generic as the political system encloses a medley of institutions with divergent functions – the most important ones being the parliament and the government that respectively embody the executive and legislative power. This study aims at questioning the effective popular distinguishing of government and parliament efforts.

Plummeting levels of trust can forebode nefarious consequences on the economic and social settings (Citrin, 1974, Heterington, 1998). Disillusionment in a political elite can entice constituents to vote for marginal candidates and parties, reducing governing potential of those elected. Officials with limited powers tend to face difficulties in terms of the implementation of reforms and policies, which leads only to greater popular mistrust. A common final ramification takes forms of popular protests and, in case of extended intervals of unrest, exponential escalation of violence. Political instability of this sort can have deleterious impact on fragile democracies, resulting in coup d'état and possible military rule. For this reason, governments facing crises of confidence tend to focus on short-term policies, which, however, can induce a reduction of long-term growth and stem the process of development. Moreover political uncertainty greatly affects the business environment through different mechanisms. First of all weak governments are highly inefficient, this deters companies from invest or expand production capacity. The lack of ability to ensure future stability discourages R&D spending and foreign direct investment, preventing economies to improve domestic competitiveness. Less trusted executives are often unable to ensure basic conditions for the free markets, in the medium term it leads to the rise of oligopolistic or monopolistic structure, which can further hinder market reforms. These problems have serious consequences for the international economic integration, resulting in difficulties in the supply chain management, reducing overall system flexibility and burying opportunities coming from external trade. In extreme cases when disappointment in politics leads to riots and mass protests, business conditions can be completely compromised. For all these reasons it must be concluded that distrust in politics is a major threat for businesses and a stable government is a key element for the countries development and growth.

Therefore, the focus of this study is recognizing which Latin American countries boast higher trust in politics and identifying the main trust-inducing aspects. To this end, the models elaborated in this study offer insightful results and identify some of the determinants of the popular trust in institutions. Specifically, the effects on trust of social capital, perception of economic performance, the institutional efficiency, the electoral system, crime rate and the media will be presented. Finally, in order to explain if the considered aspects affect political institutions as well as the government, the aforementioned models will emphasize both the government and the parliament.

BACKGROUND

Over the years, numerous studies have delivered conflicting results in their analysis of factors that determine trust in government. This issue has been widely debated since the 60's and 70's, when dissatisfaction and disillusion in governments' actions spread to the advanced industrial democracies. A 1975 report of the "Trilateral Commission" entitled "The crisis of democracies" states that the lack of confidence had become a serious problem linked to the social transformation, triggered by widespread material well-being. Many data surveys provided proof of this social evolution in the US and gave rise to different interpretations: Miller (1974) attributed the decrease of nations' trust to the dissatisfaction with the available political options, which occurs when electors feel incapable of influencing government policies through the election process. According to him, a decreasing level of trust depends on the discrepancy between popular preferences and general perception of the positions taken by major political parties. A different point of view is affirmed by Citrin (1974) who calls into question the link between political cynicism and policy dissatisfaction, in this sense identifying four distinguishing attitudes: "dissatisfaction with current government policy positions, dissatisfaction with the outcomes of ongoing events and policies, mistrust of incumbent officeholders, and rejection of the entire political system" (p. 987). Under this logic, the disillusion noted in data surveys does not reflect the rejection of the entire political system, just the dissatisfaction with the representative party or a leader.

Complexity of the problem has induced researchers to analyze the trust in governments from different perspectives; previous studies identified many factors capable of influencing the evolution of citizen dissatisfaction such as: economic dynamics, social cohesion, cultural background, or relation with local institutions (Nye, Zikow, King et alter, 1997, Norris et alter, 1999). Economic performance is considered one of the main factors that can determine electoral outcomes, therefore strictly related with trust in political elites. However, it is important to acknowledge that mass media exercises a strong influence on the popular perception of the economy, which may not necessarily coincide with the real economic development. Previous works failed to provide a homogenous interpretation of various consequences of the economic turmoil, while many scholars agreed that a *sic et simpliciter* comparison between the effects of popular trust in third-wave democracies and stable democratic systems cannot be applied. Specifically, in the case of Latin America, empirical evidence obtained so far has proved that in the early 2000's negative economic performances has had adverse impact on the government trustworthiness (Graham and Sukhtankar, 2004).

Various scholars linked political distrust to social and cultural characteristics: numerous econometric analyses (as seen in Rice and Sumberg, 1997 and Knack, 2000 among others) indicate a positive correlation between the citizens' level of trust and their perception of institutional efficiency and political economy. From one aspect, good politics enable an increase of the level of trust in government, influenced by an improvement of the quality of life, a reduction of corruption and the black economy, as well as an increase in the interpersonal trust and social cohesion. In fact, interpersonal trust plays a key role in the determination of social capital (Putnam, 1994), the efficiency of politics and the formation of trust in government. It is therefore necessary to understand the interactions between interpersonal trust and trust in government, coupled with their contribution to the virtuous cycle mentioned above. In order to analyze this point, the influence of many variables is tested, together with the overall level of trust in other people and the participation in religious, humanitarian, environmental, and other social organizations.

Historically, media has had a fundamental role in trust building, mainly due to the fact that television channels and newspapers were the main sources of information. Nowadays, while notwithstanding their importance, it is important to stress the diffusion of Internet use in the last decade has offered novel and powerful tools for the easily accessible exchange of information: websites, blogs, forums and social networks. Users are no longer passive consumers; on the contrary –Web 2.0 transforms people in active participants of debates, thus eliminating any communication filters previously existing between citizens and politicians. What is the overall effect of the Internet usage on trust in political institutions? New opportunities of communication, when used properly, could strengthen the public image of a candidate and institutions, allowing them to inform citizens about their policies and actions in order to promote transparency. Nonetheless, some scholars link the diffusion of Internet with a possible change of relations between politics and individuals, namely – direct participation of citizens in the decision-making process (Thompson, 2008, Diamanti, 2014). This eventuality would introduce a new paradigm of governance, which would substitute the representative democracy with a type of direct democracy or a mixed system. In this case, distrust in political institutions would be a consequence of the transition to the new democratic paradigm. In some European countries (e.g. Island, Italy) popular movements seeking direct democracy have been mobilized, influencing the political behavior. For these reasons, the present study includes even an analysis of the role of Internet in trust building in politics.

Many recent studies highlight the importance of the impact of crime on political support in Latin American countries. Particularly Perez (2004) and Cruz (2003) indicated a strong negative connection between political disillusionment and the spread of violence in Central American countries. Carreras (2013) includes in his work other Latin American whose crime rate in the last decade increased, and notes that the democratic support system of the entire region is subject to crime-related variables. Citizens' disillusionment rises with decreasing public security, considered one of the main responsibilities of an elected government. This explains why a lack of security translates into a public view of an inefficient political elite. Furthermore, this disenchantment is related to the institutions whose role is to implement and effectively execute the law – mainly judicial organs and the police force itself.

Further aspects which could be relevant are individual characteristics, Booth and Seligson (2009) assess that gender, age, and education have an impact on government trust. In particular, young people and women tend to be more supportive. Moreover, the two authors demonstrate that less educated citizens have higher levels of confidence in the political system.

TRUST IN POLITICAL INSTITUTIONS IN LATIN AMERICAN COUNTRIES

Although Latin American countries ousted military regimes more than thirty years ago, the ongoing democratization is still considered fragile. UNDP has remarked the persistent risk of backsliding to authoritarianism, related to coup d'état in some countries (see UNDP, 2004, and UNDP-OAS, 2011). Additionally, issues have been raised about the independence of the electoral mechanisms, the media, judicial organs and other national institutions. Today, the main problems are related to the inclusion of the marginalized population into the political system. Possible solutions to this problem foresee policies, which tackle not only the inequality and human right abuses, but also the relation between the institution and citizens, a safe environment and the development of a more cohesive society. Until the political solution of these problems is presented, or at least until the overall living conditions are ameliorated, the increasing disillusionment in the political systems of these societies is not likely to be altered.

To help measure the level of citizens' disenchantment with politics, World Values Survey (WVS) provides useful data. The WVS is an international investigation project created by distributing a questionnaire to a representative part of the target-country population. The most recent survey available was created in the period from 2010 to 2014 and included a few Latin American countries. This study considers the results of Columbia, Chile, Mexico, Peru and Uruguay, due to the comprehensiveness of the needed information. The questionnaire examines the views individuals have on various institutions such as the parliament and the government by asking the question: "I am going to name a number of organizations. For each one, could you tell me how much confidence you have in them: a great deal of confidence; quite a lot of confidence; not much confidence; or no confidence at all?" (WVS 6, 2014, p.8) Clearly, the interviewees can decline to provide an answer, or define themselves incapable of providing one; however, these people are not included in the proposed model. In some instances, epistemological doubts have arisen over the distinction between trust and confidence. Nonetheless, the Spanish version of the questionnaire translates the two words using the same term, thus eliminating any linguistic uncertainty of the sort. Furthermore it is important remark that there is no accordance on the best way to measure trust in politics; however, the above-quoted question is widely used as valid indicator, which is why this work bases its conclusions on the provided answers.

According to the latest WVS, 6,635 people from the five Latin American countries studied, expressed their attitude towards the government and such high number of observations substantiates enough data to carry out statistically significant analysis. The answer distribution clearly shows a widespread problem of trust in Latin American governments (Table 2). In fact, only 9.34% of the interviewees has expressed their confidence in the government, while 29.25% declares to be quite confident, meaning that only 38.5% of the population perceives the government as a body efficiently working for a betterment of the living conditions. Furthermore, less than 10% is truly satisfied with the government performance. 35.21% of the interviewees lack faith in government, whereas 26.19% expresses complete mistrust. Popular dissatisfaction assumes more radical connotation since a quarter of the statistical population declares to be completely disappointed in the government.

Although all of these countries display objective issues with government trust, it is important to stress that there is a degree of heterogeneity in the data collected in these five nations. Inter alia Uruguayans trust their government more than other

Table 2. Trust in government and parliament, World Values Survey 6

WV6	Trust Government			Trust Parliament		
	Freq.	Percent	Cum.	Freq.	Percent	Cum.
All						
None at all	1,738	26.19	26.19	2,559	38.94	38.94
Not very much	2,336	35.21	61.40	2,409	36.66	75.60
Quite a lot	1,941	29.25	90.66	1,391	21.17	96.77
A great deal	620	9.34	100.00	212	3.23	100.00
Total	6,635	100.00		6,571	100.00	
Columbia						
None at all	372	24.80	24.80	675	45.42	45.42
Not very much	535	35.67	60.47	498	33.51	78.94
Quite a lot	438	29.20	89.67	262	17.63	96.57
A great deal	155	10.33	100.00	51	3.43	100.00
Total	1,500	100.00		1,486	100.00	
Chile						
None at all	253	25.69	25.69	287	29.35	29.35
Not very much	396	40.20	65.89	444	45.40	74.74
Quite a lot	284	28.83	94.72	229	23.42	98.16
A great deal	52	5.28	100.00	18	1.84	100.00
Total	985	100.00		978	100.00	
Mexico						
None at all	521	26.12	26.12	764	38.68	38.68
Not very much	700	35.09	61.20	711	36.00	74.68
Quite a lot	575	28.82	90.03	433	21.92	96.61
A great deal	199	9.97	100.00	67	3.39	100.00
Total	1,995	100.00		1,975	100.00	
Perù						
None at all	438	36.87	36.87	609	50.92	50.92
Not very much	482	40.57	77.44	440	36.79	87.71
Quite a lot	226	19.02	96.46	124	10.37	98.08
A great deal	42	3.54	100.00	23	1.92	100.00
Total	1,188	100.00		1,196	100.00	
Uruguay						
None at all	154	15.93	15.93	224	23.93	23.93
Not very much	223	23.06	38.99	316	33.76	57.69
Quite a lot	418	43.23	82.21	343	36.65	94.34
A great deal	172	17.79	100.00	53	5.66	100.00
Total	967	100.00		936	100.00	

Figure 1.

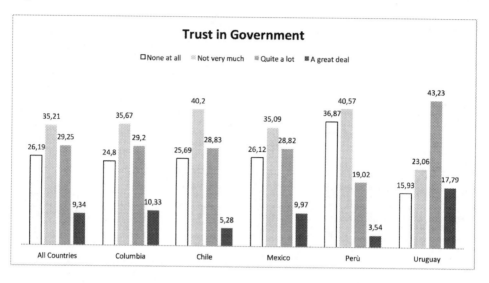

populations; 17.8% are completely satisfied with their executives, whereas mere 15.9% completely distrust the government. These levels of satisfaction are quite high relatively to the other countries – indeed Uruguay is the only country with more than 50% of the population showing some level of trust in their government. On the other spectrum, dissatisfaction is very strong in Peru as the WVS statistics report that just 3.5% of the interviewees claimed to have "a great deal of confidence", which is the lowest percentage in Latin America. Also, over 36% voiced their complete mistrust. It can be inferred that the overall trust level in Chile is rather low, as it is the case in Peru; while Columbian and Mexican citizens professed slightly higher trust. Ultimately, however, over 60% of the interviewees from Peru, Chile, Columbia and Mexico express mistrust in their governments.

The selected nations have similar democratic, presidential systems. Their governance model is the traditional tripartite system based on the notion of the separation of powers used by the Ancient Greeks and formalized by Montesquieu. As it is commonly known, this system assigns the role of the executive power to the government, whereas the parliament embodies the legislative power. The relation between the citizens and their government must not be confused with the relation with other political institutions, and one of the goals of this work is precisely to explain the difference between building trust in government and parliament. The first step is simply to compare the available descriptive statistical data; which is quite easy since the interviewees answered the above-mentioned question related to both government and parliament.

The overall citizens' opinion on parliament is very severe: just 3.23% of the interviewee from Latin America express their satisfaction, with 38.49% expressing a compete disappointment. Chile and Peru are again the nations with wider spread of disillusionment, confirming the complicated and strained relationship between political institutions and the citizens. Uruguayans remain the most trusting, yet, it is important to note that just 5.66% of the national statistical sample affirmed complete trust in their parliament.

As previously stated, the overall trust in politics has been declining since the 70's in the US and Europe as well, but how can this evolution be explained in Latin America? Data from the previous waves of the WVS shows that the last decade entailed consistent decline in the trust in government and the parliament in the five countries of the analysis, meaning that they followed a dynamic similar to that of the main industrial democracies. Nonetheless, popular disenchantment does not affect popular support of a democracy, still considered the optimal institutional system, but examines the efficiency of political institutions. Confidence erosion resulted in an increase of 5 percentage points of people who do not trust the government between the WVS survey conducted in 2005 and that of 2006. This is true for every country with the exception of Peru; actually, the least trusting country is the only one that has ameliorated the relationship between citizens and government. Quite a similar conclusion arises from the question regarding the parliament, which is why it can be stated that the overall political system has been losing citizens' trust.

Figure 2.

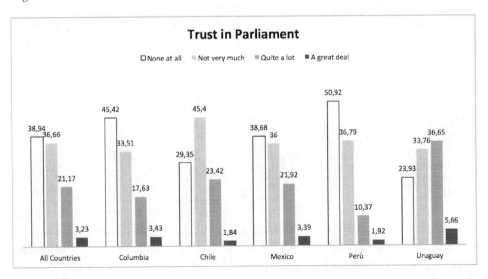

Since 2008, governments have faced a very difficult setting due to the global crisis. In this context, Latin America has not represented the region of the greatest economical losses, nonetheless, some may argue that the decrease of trust depends on the turmoil, not on the ongoing evolution of the relationship between citizens and the political system. In order to understand this point, further data has been analyzed from the WVS4, conducted in 2000. This survey, encapsulating only Chile, Mexico and Peru, used together with the comparison between interviewee's answers from WVS4, WVS5 and WVS6, indicates that the confidence decline began years before the 2008 crisis. In fact, the percentages of people mistrusting the government in these countries were respectively: 63.5% in 2000; 66.6% in 2006; and 76.7% in 2013.

This overview does not substantiate an interpretation of the cause of the lack of trust in politics. However, statistical information clearly shows the increasing popular disillusionment in the parliaments and the governments, which implies the importance of exploring possible determinants of this phenomenon. To that end, this study elaborates two econometric models that study the interviewees' relationship with the political system from different perspectives. Results from the last WVS are compared, when possible, to data from the previous survey, producing further evidence on the evolution of trust in politics.

Data and Methodology

The main instrument used in the analyses is the aforementioned World Values Survey (WVS), which provides useful information on popular trust in local government and other social and political aspects. The WVS (www.worldvaluessurvey.org) is a global organization composed of a network of social scientists interested in studying the alteration of values and their impact on social and political life. The survey was published by the World Values Survey Association, and it covers different countries including some in Latin America. The last available survey is the sixth wave, which includes all reports submitted from the 2010 up to 2014. The sixth wave comprises the following Latin American countries: Colombia, Chile, Ecuador, Mexico, Peru and Uruguay. Unfortunately, this study will disregard Ecuador since there is not enough data to substantiate a thorough analysis of this country. In order to develop an intertemporal comparison, data provided by the fifth wave of the survey (WVS 5), conducted from the 2005 up to 2009, is used. The results of the two waves are only partially comparable, since the questions submitted change, unlike the selected countries.

Various methodologies were used to measure trust in politics, however, two main approaches can be stressed: macro and micro based approaches. The macro-based methodology applies a Vector Autoregressive (VAR) structure to a multivariate time series concerning different levels of trust. Difficulties that this approach involves, such as those of finding the appropriate data in a time-series form, results in its less frequent use; nonetheless, it offers numerous benefits. In its general form, this model explicates the current value of the trust, the endogenous variables, using its lagged values and a set of explanatory variables considered to be the exogenous ones. Furthermore, this particular approach reduces the risk of omitting variable bias since it does not impose the structure between the endogenous variables a priori. What is more, it enables the specification of distinctly exogenous ones, clarifying the causal relation between the variables. For this reason, the macro-based approach can be used merely to explain the causes and consequences of changes in trust over time and it does not contain any information about individual-level variation in levels of trust at any given point. Conversely, the micro-based approach includes such information and can be developed with a variety of methods. Among them, the *ols* and the *logit* or *probit* methods are the most commonly used examples, especially when the independent variable measuring trust has binary outcome. The instances of models that involve panel data are rather rare due to the difficulties of finding data in a suitable form. Although the micro-based approaches do not provide information about the evolutionary dynamics of trust in politics, they represent the reference methodologies needed to investigate the determinants that have significantly contributed to the formation of the trust in government and parliament. Given the aim of this work and the cross-sectional structure of the dataset, the predominant approach is the micro one, even though some analyses of the dynamic properties of the model are made possible by the comparison with the results obtained using data of different time periods.

In order to measure trust in government and in the parliament, dependent variables used are the questions 115 and 117 of WVS: "I am going to name a number of organizations. For each one, could you tell me how much confidence you have in them: a great deal of confidence; quite a lot of confidence; not much confidence; or no confidence at all? The Government; The parliament".

Table 1 provides a list of variables used in the analyses and the relative question submitted by the interviewer. Most of the variables have been edited in order to achieve an easier interpretation of the coefficients. In particular, the scale of value of the two independent variables and some regressors were inverted following their original order. According to the new scale, the most negative answer has the lowest value and the most positive answer has the highest value. Therefore, the "trust in" variables (government, parliament, police, courts) are expressed in values from 1 to 4, with the answers being respectively "none at all" and "a great deal of confidence" (WVS 6, 2014, p.8). The same system was applied to the following institutional variables: National participation, Impartial vote counting, media, Impartial Officials, Genuine candidates. Therefore, as before, these variables take values from 1, if the answer is "Not at all often", to 4, if it is "very often".

Table 1. List of Variables

Variables	Questions and Explanation
Trust in government	Could you tell me how much confidence you have in the government: is it a great deal of confidence (4), quite a lot of confidence (3), not very much confidence (2) or none at all (1)?
Trust in parliament	Could you tell me how much confidence you have in the parliament: is it a great deal of confidence (4), quite a lot of confidence (3), not very much confidence (2) or none at all (1)?
Socio Economical Variables	
Trust	*Dummy Variable.* Generally speaking, would you say that most people can be trusted (1) or that you need to be very careful (0) when dealing with people?
Social organization	*Dummy Variable.* (1) if active or inactive member of: Church of religious organization; Art, music or educational organization; Humanitarian or charitable organization.
Activist organization	*Dummy Variable.* (1) if active or inactive member of: Labor union; Political party; Environmental organization; Consumer organization.
Satisfaction	All things considered, how satisfied are you with your life as a whole these days? Using this card on which 1 means you are "completely dissatisfied" and 10 means you are "completely satisfied" where would you put your satisfaction with your life as a whole?
Income	On this card is an income scale on which 1 indicates the lowest income group and 10 the highest income group in your country. We would like to know in what group your household belongs. Please, specify the appropriate number, counting all wages, salaries, pensions and other incomes.
Fin_sat	How satisfied are you with the financial situation of your household? Using this card on which 1 means you are "completely dissatisfied" and 10 means you are "completely satisfied" where would you put your satisfaction with your life as a whole?
Institutional Variables	
Trust in police	Could you tell me how much confidence you have in police: is it a great deal of confidence (4), quite a lot of confidence (3), not very much confidence (2) or none at all (1)?
Trust in courts	Could you tell me how much confidence you have in courts: is it a great deal of confidence (4), quite a lot of confidence (3), not very much confidence (2) or none at all (1)?
National participation	When elections take place, do you vote always (3), usually (2) or never (1)?
Impartial vote counting	In your view, how often are votes counted fairly? Not at all often (1), not often (2), fairly often (3), very often (4)?
Mass media	In your view, how often TV news favours the governing party? Not at all often (1), not often (2), fairly often (3), very often (4)?
Impartial officials	In your view, how often are election officials are fair? Not at all often (1), not often (2), fairly often (3), very often (4)?

continued on following page

Table 1. Continued

Variables	Questions and Explanation
Genuine candidates	In your view, how often are voters offered a genuine choice in the elections? Not at all often (1), not often (2), fairly often (3), very often (4)?
Internet	*Dummy Variable.* (1) if the Internet is used daily or weekly to obtain information and (0) if it is used monthly or less frequently.
Safe neighborhood	Could you tell me how safe you feel these days in your neighbourhood? Not at all safe (1), not very safe (2), Quite safe (3), very safe (4).
Crime victim	*Dummy Variable.* Were you a victim of a crime in the past year? Yes (1), No (0)
Control Variables	
Age	*Clustered Variable.* (1) if age $\leq$ 25; (2) if 25 < age $\leq$ 50; (3) if 50 < age $\leq$ 75; (4) if age > 75
Gender	*Dummy Variable.* (1) female, (0) male.
Married	*Dummy Variable.* (1) if the interviewee is married or widowed, (0) if she cohabitates or is single, divorced or separated.
Education	*Clustered Variable.* if the interviewee has no formal education the assigned value is (1) while increasing values are assigned if the highest educational level attained is the complete secondary school of technical or vocational type (2), complete secondary school of university – preparatory type (3) or university level education (4).

To avoid the proliferation of regressors, "social organization" and "activist organization" are used as a combination of other variables. In particular, "social organization" is a dummy variable that takes value of 1 in case the interviewer is a member (active or inactive) of one or more of the following categories of organizations: Church or a religious organization; Art, music or educational organization; Humanitarian or charitable organization. "Activist organization" is a dummy variable that, as the previous one, takes value of 1, if the interviewer is a member (active or inactive) of one or more of the following types of organizations: Labor union; Political party; Environmental organization; Consumer organization.

Finally, certain alterations involve control variables. In particular, the variables Age and Education are clustered in four categories in order to obtain a scale of values comparable to the dependent variables. Therefore, if the interviewee is under 25, the assigned value is 1; the following values increase to reach the value of 4 with one point of increase for 25 years (so, for example, the assigned value is 2 if the interviewee declares the age 25 < age $\leq$ 50 etc.). The final cluster 4 is upper unbounded, since it encapsulates all those over 75. The creation of homogeneous clusters is also useful for a precious insight in the behaviour of each category. Following this notion, the variable " Education" is similarly divided in homogeneous clusters.

Unlike the original division made by the survey, the variable used in the analyses assigns the value of 1 if the interviewee reports no formal education, increasing the value for the educational level of secondary school of technical or vocational type 2, a degree of a secondary school or university – preparatory type corresponds to 3 or in case of university level degree 4. The remaining control variables are two dummies – gender and marital status. The first one is simply a dummy variable that identifies females, thus it assigns the value of zero to a male interviewee. The second one is another dummy variable, however, it assigns the value of (1) in case the interviewee is married or a widowed person while the value (0) corresponds to those living with their partners, or are single, divorced or separated.

Regression Model

The regression model used in the analysis arises from the nature of the dependent variable. Specifically, variables "trust in government" and "trust in parliament" both assume separate values between 1 and 4, or simply put, they are arranged in four ordered categories. The estimation strategies useful for the analysis of multinomial responses are mainly: Multinomial logit/probit model or Ordered logit/probit model. The choice between the two models lucidly depends on the nature of the response variable: therefore, when the response categories represent mere labels (e.g. traveling by bus, train, or car), the fitting estimation strategy relies on the multinomial logit/probit model; conversely, if a response category possesses a natural ordering (e.g. low income, mid-level income, or high income), the ordered logit/probit model is favoured. Regarding this specific study, given that the response categories included the ordered increasing level of trust in government, the optimal regression model was identified in the ordered logit, or the ordered probit model.

To approach statistical properties of these models let y be composed by $j + 1 \geq 2$ ordered categories, labelled $j = 0, 1, 2, \ldots, J$. In order to derive the ordered logit/probit model for the expected values of y given a set of explanatory variables x, namely $E(y|x)$, we should consider a latent variable model assuming that y^*, the latent variable, is determined by $x\beta+e$, with $e|x \sim \text{Normal}(0,1)$ or $\text{Logistic}(\mu, s)$. The latent variable, or threshold crossing model implies that y is related to y^* through the following observation rule:

$$y = j \text{ if } y^* \in \left(c_{j-1}, c_j\right), j = 0, \ldots, J$$

where $c_{-1} < c_0 < c_1 < \ldots < c_J$ are $J+2$ unknown cut points (or threshold parameters) with $c_{-1} = -\infty$ and $c_J = \infty$.

The conditional distribution of y|x can be obtained by computing the response probabilities:

$$Pr\left(y = 0 \mid x\right) = Pr\left(y^* \leq c_0\right) = Pr\left(x\beta + e \leq c_0 \mid x\right) = F\left(c_0 - x\beta\right)$$

$$Pr\left(y = 1 \mid x\right) = Pr\left(c_0 < y^* \leq c_1\right) = Fc\left(_0 - x\beta\right) - \left(Fc_1 - x\beta\right)$$

...

$$Pr\left(y = J - 1 \mid x\right) = Pr\left(c_{J-2} < y^* \leq c_{J-1}\right) = F\left(c_{J-2} - x\beta\right) - F\left(c_{J-1} - x\beta\right)$$

$$Pr\left(y = J \mid x\right) = Pr\left(y^* < c_{J-1}\right) = 1 - F\left(c_{J-1} - x\beta\right)$$

where $F(.)$ is either a Standard Normal distribution function (Φ) or a Logit Function (Λ), depending on the assumption for e. It is easy to validate that the sum of all the probabilities is one and that for $J=1$ the model simplifies in the classical binary logit\probit model. At this point, it is clear that as long as e is e|x ~ Normal(0,1), F represents the Standard Normal d.f. (Φ) obtaining ordered probit model. However, if e|x ~Logistic(μ, s), then F represents the logit function (Λ) and results in the ordered logit model. Note that the matrix of explanatory variable x does not contain a constant, simply because the cut points remain the intercept inside the density function F.

The estimate of the parameters c and β can be obtained by maximizing the following log-likelihood function:

$$l_i\left(c, \beta\right) = 1\left[y_i = 0\right]\log\left[F\left(c_0 - x_i\beta\right)\right] +$$
$$1\left[y_i = 1\right]\log\left[F\left(c_0 - x_i\beta\right) - F\left(c_1 - x_i\beta\right)\right] + \cdots$$
$$+ 1\left[y_i = J\right]\log\left[1 - F\left(c_{J-1} - x_i\beta\right)\right]$$

The regression examinations showed in the next section are all based on the ordered logit model. The logit function was chosen instead of the standard normal due to the likelihood ratio test that indicates the ordered logit as the one that reaches higher values of the likelihood function on almost all the occasions. Under these circumstances of working with the response probabilities, the coefficients obtained after the maximization procedure indicate the expected alteration (in the ordered log-odds scale) of the response variables for a one-unit increase in the predictor, while the other variables of the model are held constant.

It is noteworthy that in some instances, one may be interested in the cumulative response probabilities, namely

$$\Pr\left(y \leq j \mid x\right) = \sum_{h=0}^{j} \Pr(y = h \mid x), j = 0, 1, 2, ..., J$$

where the elements in the summation are the response probabilities considered so far. Clearly, the cumulative response probability is equal to the response probability only for $j = 0$ and sums to 1 for $j = J$. The coefficients of this mode, also known as the proportional odds model, can be obtained by exponentiation of the ordered logit coefficients.

In this way, a coefficient greater than 1 suggests that for a unitary change of the relative regressor, the odds of belonging to a group with a greater value of the response variable is higher than the odds of belonging to a group with a lower one. For instance, if the proportional odds of satisfaction were 1.2, for a unit increase in satisfaction, the odds of higher level of trust in government would be 1.2 times greater than the odds of lower level of trust in government, provided that the other variables are held constant.

Theoretical Model

Given the description of the variables involved in the analysis and the provided econometric background this section briefly describe the implemented theoretical model. The observed variables y, trust in government and in parliament, are assumed to follow an unobserved latent component (y^*) described by two different sets of regressors plus some control variables:

$$y_t^* = X\beta + Z\gamma + S\delta + e, \text{ with } t = \text{government, parliament}$$

where X is a $n \times p$ matrix, with n observations and p socio economic variables; Z is an $n \times d$ matrix with d institutional regressors and S is an $n \times b$ matrix that accounts (controls) for b individual characteristics. The comparison of the results obtained with the two different independent variables (X, Z) reveals the ability of the people to discriminate between the two different bureaucratic apparatuses conditionally on a set of observables. The empirical strategy is for many aspects similar to those used by Alesina and La Ferrara (2005), Sukhtankar and Graham (2004) and many other authors. On the other hand, the theoretical justification of the explanatory power of the variables involved arise mainly from our intuitions and considerations but also on the most important results on the economic effects of trust (see Miller's, 1974, Citrin, 1974, Putnam, 1994, Booth and Seligson, 2009).

The results of the two different specifications of the regression model are presented in the next section.

MAIN RESULTS

The results presented in Tables 4 and 5 show the effect of two different sets of regressors on trust in government and parliament, as just clarified in the above section. The first model includes all socio economic variables, while the second model focuses on the relation between the trust in government and parliament and some

Table 4. Trust in Government and Parliament. Socio economical variables

Regressors	Trust in Government	Trust in Parliament
Trust	0.390*** (0.07)	0.532*** (0.05)
Social organization	0.027 (0.14)	-0.010 (0.16)
Activist organization	0.254* (0.12)	0.246** (0.09)
Satisfaction	0.049* (0.02)	0.033 (0.03)
Income	-0.007 (0.01)	0.019 (0.03)
Fin_sat	0.055** (0.02)	0.042*** (0.01)
Age	0.132 (0.09)	-0.013 (0.07)
Gender	0.035 (0.04)	0.031 (0.04)
Married	0.112** (0.04)	0.123* (0.06)
Education	0.100*** (0.02)	0.008 (0.07)
# of observations	4941	4941
Pseudo R^2	0.0103	0.0087
BIC	12720.8	11563.2

Legend: • p<0.1, * p<0.05, ** p<0.01, *** p<0.001

Table 5. Trust in Government and Parliament; institutional variables

Regressors	Trust in Government	Trust in Parliament
Trust in police	0.573*** (0.07)	0.370*** (0.10)
Trust in courts	1.225*** (0.10)	1.148*** (0.11)
National particip.	0.161*** (0.05)	0.159*** (0.02)
Impartial vote count	0.093• (0.05)	0.108* (0.04)
Mass media	-0.070* (0.03)	-0.063 (0.05)
Impartial officials	0.166*** (0.03)	0.174*** (0.05)
Genuine candidates	0.088• (0.05)	0.080 • (0.05)
Internet	-0.106 (0.16)	0.044 (0.10)
Neighbor. secure	0.137*** (0.04)	0.065 (0.05)
Crime victim	-0.176*** (0.05)	-0.132 (0.12)
Age	0.031 (0.08)	-0.085 (0.06)
Gender	-0.030 (0.04)	-0.039 (0.06)
Married	0.083 (0.07)	0.087 (0.06)
Education	0.112• (0.06)	0.002 (0.07)
# of observation	4941	4941
Pseudo R^2	0.1985	0.1651
BIC	10306.3	9729.4

Legend: • $p<0.1$, * $p<0.05$, ** $p<0.01$, *** $p<0.001$

institutional variables. Both models consider the individual heterogeneity, including four control variables that are: gender, age, marital status, and the educational level. These variables, education in particular, also play a key role in the explanation of dependent variables' movement.

The social economic model was applied to the previous edition of the World Value Survey (WVS 5), which was conducted between 2005 and 2009. The aim of this decision was to analyze the evolution of socio economic variables of the building trust in government and in the parliament. The first model enables the comparison between the two waves of the survey since there are enough selected variables and countries of both waves. Unfortunately, the same comparison cannot be done for the second model due to the absence of the institutional variables in the fifth wave of the survey. Nonetheless, it is important to remark that the results obtained separately by the two models are consistent with those that would have be obtained using a single, all inclusive, model.

As it has been stated, the estimation strategy used in the tables is the ordered logit regression. The coefficients are expressed in the ordered log-odds; therefore, proportional odds ratio are obtainable through the exponentiation of the coefficients. Country – induced heteroskedasticity is avoided using robust standard errors, showed in parenthesis below the coefficients.

SOCIO ECONOMIC MODEL

The socio economic model aims at investigating the consequences of changing in cohesion, social capital, and economic perception on trust level in political institutions. The results are shown in Table 4, with the second and third column containing the coefficients of the regression for respectively government and parliament.

In order to understand the interactions between social capital and trust in political institutions, three variables were used: Trust, Social organization, and Activist organization. The first one is a dummy that measures the interpersonal trust. Statistics show a highly significant and positive relation of both "trust in government" and "trust in parliament", which corroborates the claim that a cohesive society enables the institutions to obtain greater credibility in their actions. People who have greater trust in others are more trusting with their representatives in the parliament and feel that their government actually represents popular interests. From this point of view, political institutions are perceived as organizations composed of people concerned with the common problems, therefore the aforementioned discrepancy between people's preferences and politicians' positions decreases, which confirms Miller's (1974) finding, affirming a direct relation between interpersonal and politics trust. Moreover, further indirect interaction can be pointed out to explicate the way general trust influences satisfaction with politics. According to Putnam (1994), interpersonal trust is one of the fundamental determinants of social capital, which is why it affects both growth and wellbeing. Since people connect these concepts to political efficiency, it generates an increase in confidence in politics.

Citizens' participation in public organizations of various kinds reflects the way they generate social capital. However, only participation in certain organizations brings a higher trust in political institutions, which is elucidated by coefficients of social organizations and activist organizations. Taking part in social organizations such as, sports, religion, art etc., does not influence the level of confidence in government and parliament. This result is controversial, in terms of defining whether there can be a direct or an indirect relation connecting the increase of the social capital and trust in political dynamics. Conversely, positive and statistically significant relations were affirmed for those participating in activist organizations, i.e. labor union, political parties, environmental or consumer organizations. This outcome suggests that only the participation in organizations that allow interaction with the political setting influences the evolution of trust in government and parliament.

So far, the analysis fixated the social aspect of human relations and its influence on trust building, without considering the interviewee's satisfaction with their financial situation and life in general. To this end, the model was altered to include a variable measuring specifically the satisfaction of an individual with their life as a whole in the recent period. It is very important to consider this variable since a period of difficulties can drastically alter the way citizens perceive political institutions. It also ensures the specification of the model. Interestingly, a positive and significant correlation subsists with confidence in government; however the same cannot be applied to the parliament. At any rate, satisfaction is a variable that includes many elements and it does not distinguish what the relevant aspects of individual life are. The variable "fin_sat" has the same structure of "satisfaction" – namely the possible answers are the same, since it measures the financial satisfaction of the interviewee. This variable allows a definition of how trust in government depends specifically on financial satisfaction. The estimation considers the link to be stronger than general satisfaction, and it also includes the trust in parliament.

Economic performance has been widely perceived as an important determinant of trust in politics. One of the strengths of this model is its ability to consider the perception of the economic dynamics, which could not have been achievable with macro indicators. Disenchantment in politics is a phenomenon strictly linked to individual life; therefore, it is the individual financial satisfaction, rather than real past economy evolution, that determines the way citizens judge the efficiency of political institutions.

The interviewees also answered a question about the level of their income relative to the overall national population. An income scale is provided, based on which 1 indicates the lowest and 10 the highest income group, creating a total of ten groups in which individuals are clustered depending on their household income. The coefficient of this variable is not significant, so an increase in income seems to have no effects on the variation of trust in politics. This outcome is coherent with the hypothesis that the economic situation of households bears no impact, while the individual satisfaction does, suggesting that the income level does not necessarily need to be related to the financial satisfaction. A further proof of the above-discussed finding is that the correlation coefficients between "fin_sat" and "income" (0.2) are very low, corroborating that financial satisfaction does not depend on the income in Latin America.

Four control variables were included in the model: age, gender, marital status and education. Results suggest that the age is not a determining factor of trust in politics, which implies that young people are not more trusting than their elders. This finding refutes the idea of individuals being likely to develop refusal for politics as they age, which is clearly divergent from the previous work of Booth and Seligson (2009). These authors also found women to be more trusting than men; however this model debunks this claim as well, since gender appears to be irrelevant in terms of trust building.

An interesting outcome concerns the education of the interviewees: those highly educated declare the highest trust in government but not the parliament. This information offers many interpretations: firstly, it can be inferred that those with pronounced educational background differentiate the roles of the parliament and the government; secondly, a higher level of education leads to a deeper understanding of the difficulties governments face and the complexity of possible solutions to those problems, which induces them to judge less severely the governmental performance; lastly; highly educated citizens are more often a part of activist organizations, which, as previously stated, tends to increase the level of confidence in politics.

Some further considerations can be elaborated by comparing results from the last World Values Survey (the sixth one conducted in 2012), and the previous WVS (the fifth one from 2006). Nonetheless, it is important to stress the existing differences between the two models since WVS5 does not offer complete data on the financial satisfaction of interviewees. However, even if we exclude this variable, the results from the WVS6 model remain consistent, allowing the statistical comparability of the data from the two periods.

The main confirmation is that the majority of the findings of the WVS6 social-economic model are confirmed by the WVS5 model. Interpersonal trust remains an important determinant of trust in politics, showing that building a cohesive society is not a recent necessity, but that it should have been the primary target in the past as well. Participating in social organization is not relevant, while activist organization matter only for parliament; this result confirms the WVS6 and seems to disregard the indirect effect that social organizations could have on trust building. As previously stated, the level of satisfaction has an impact on confidence level; in this case, it affects even the parliament, while it previously affected merely the government. Unfortunately, nothing can be said about the financial satisfaction, yet, one of the most interesting results from the WVS6 is found: the income level does not determine changes in the mistrust.

Institutional Model

The second model this study developed considers variables related to specific institutions, crime rates, electoral mechanisms, and the media. The econometric analysis yielded thought-provoking results presented in the Table 5, which shows many statistically-significant coefficients as the socioeconomic model includes some control variables.

The first aspect studied is the role of institutions like police and courts. As expected, those interviewees that express greater confidence in these institutions tend to trust both government and parliament. This is not surprising – when citizens feel that justice system fails them, the implications of corruption are diffused to the entire political elite. In many Latin American countries, court inefficiencies and police bribery are crucial and unresolved problems, which is why this point assumes a significant importance in terms of the evolution of trust in politics. The effects of improving relations between citizens and law enforcement agents are positive for both government and parliament, but mostly the government, while increased credibility of the courts has an even greater impact. Further observation regards governmental role in terms of efficiency of these institutions, also in relation to crime diffusion.

In democracies, citizens express their political opinion by casting their votes; therefore, elections represent fundamental instruments of understanding the popular trust in politics. The transparency of the electoral process can influence the level of trust, as electors who believe the system to be rigged are less likely to acknowledge the winning candidates.

Data obtained from the WVS shows interesting facts about the way citizens comprehend elections. First, people who participate at national elections are more trusting of the government and the parliament. Nonetheless, it is also true that the outcome of an election is not a sufficient element to measure the level of trust in political institutions. This is because a part of the population, disappointed with political elites, refrains from voting, which suggests that the abstention is an essential component for evaluating real trust in politics. If winning parties or candidates underestimate the relevance of absenteeism, they could base their suppositions on the wrong perception of citizens satisfied with their political programs and actually exacerbate citizens' discontent, enabling a vicious circle that alienates voters from exercising their civic rights.

Further observations must be made regarding the electoral system, considered fraudulent as the interviewees declare convictions of frequent interferences with the count of votes, as well as a consistent concern with the corruption of electoral officials, who could influence the final outcome. Obviously, these contingencies negatively affect trust in politics. Coefficients of both government and parliament models are quite similar, suggesting that corruption problems affect the political world in general and not just the winning parties.

Issues relating the list of candidates to the presidency are also perceptible. It is fundamental for the electors to be able to choose among genuine candidates; a failure of which leads to alienation and eventually, abstention. Once again, lack of representative and honest candidates causes the decrease of trust in the political institutions, without distinguishing institutional roles. Corrupt candidates and fraudulent electoral systems cause disenchantment since the citizens feel unable to influence policies, breaking the trust relationship, which is the main trait of the paradigm of representative democracy.

As mentioned before, the evolution of trust levels depends on the popular perception of institutional efficiency, which is why the media has a central role in determining trust dynamics. Media filters news and provides partial points of view of government actions, using journalistic investigations, scoops and gossips to alter the public opinion. Interviewees were asked to express concern for possible interference of government in TV news, considered the main source of information. Answers show that citizens' conviction of the news programs favoring the governing party. As expected, this has an adverse influence on the level of trust in government, but not the parliament. This explicates citizens' concern with the eventuality that incumbent governments could try to directly manipulate news diffused through public or private televisions, which, if substantialized, could cause the public support of the governing party to plummet, triggering political instability.

Many scholars perceive the Internet as a potential source of changes in trust in politics, even though there is no accordance about the overall consequence of introducing the opportunity to discuss government actions through blogs or social media. One of the aspects analyzed by this model is the importance of using the web as a source of information in terms of trust in politics in America Latina. The results suggest that current Internet users do not display different trust levels compared to the other citizens, suggesting that the Internet does not affect the trust building process. This can be a peculiarity of the Latin American societies or just a reflection of poor diffusion of the Internet; nonetheless, the use of platforms such as social networks and blogs is recent and viral, so sudden changes in the relation between the web and the politics cannot be debarred.

Moving on, lack of safety and consistent crime rates are widespread problems of Latin American countries, and statistics show that the already high crime rate has been increasing in the region. Many studies focus on the devastating impact of violence on social wellbeing, and of course on the popular judgment of institutional actions. In order to measure the magnitude of the effect on trust in politics two variables were included. The first one discloses whether the interviewees had been victims of crime in the year prior to the submission of the questionnaire. When the answer is positive, trust in government decreases (which is why the coefficient is negative), while trust in parliament remains unaltered. The second question refers to the perception of the interviewees, specifically if they feel safe in their neighborhoods in that period of time. A positive answer also in this case influences just the trust in government, the safer the neighborhood is, the higher the individuals' trust is. Questions referred to two different aspects: the first to the real consequences of being subject of a crime, the second to the perception of safety. In both cases, the government is the only the institution considered responsible; there is not an overall effect on other political institutions. This remarkable result suggests that for Latin American governments, the fight against crime has fundamental political implications and that crime rates are one of the main sources of instability in the region.

Finally this model confirms some of the findings of the socio-economic model in the analysis of the role of age, gender and education. Particularly, it can be affirmed a lack of a relation between trust and age or gender, as well as that those with higher education tend to support their governments. Unfortunately, due to the lack of data from the previous survey of the WVS an inter-temporal comparison cannot be done in this case.

Solutions and Recommendations

The previous section analyzed some of the determinants of trust in politics, implying that countries with low trust levels could pay high costs in economic and social terms as consequence of the political instability. This is common in third-wave, and therefore fragile, democracies, which is why, as recent history shows, countries of Latin America should put forth immense efforts in order to definitely stabilize its local democracies.

The models outcomes stated the dramatic necessity of the justice system reform: precedents of courts' and police inefficiencies and corruption are widely considered one of the main issues of Latin American countries. From one perspective, the WVS data reveals a strong correlation between the spread of disillusionment in politician action and presence of corruption. Public perception of biased justice can potentially have nefarious consequences for the society, as lack of credibility that easily diffuses onto the entire managerial structure of the country can impel destabilization. This paper does not aim at proposing the optimal solution to this problem; however, the aforementioned results cast light to the high priority that should be given to the reform of justice system. In fact, corrupted or inefficient courts, in addition to the loss of wellbeing, generate great risk for the ongoing process of democratization in the region. On one side of the spectrum, popular trust in governments heavily relies on the reduction of crime rates. Governments are expected to manage the spread of violence with firmness and vigor, therefore failing at this task leads to stark decline of public support, and vice versa – a successful implementation of anti-crime initiatives increases the chances of the ruling parties to be reelected for another term. Nevertheless, it is important to note that crime rate bears no impact on trust in every political institution, since it is related only to governments' efficacy, while corruption fosters issues more deeply rooted in the democratic system itself.

Further measures should be implemented in relation to the electoral process. Lack of transparency negatively affects the level of trust in politics. Interviewees are certain of external interferences in previous elections; which advocates the importance of an "ad hoc" action aimed at increasing the electoral transparency. Similarly to what has been noted about justice system, unfair elections cause alienation from the political context in a general sense. In this case governments are not identified as liable for electoral interferences, suggesting an existence of a problem whose dynamics outstretch the limits of a governing party. Conversely, governments are called into question regarding the freedom of media; specifically, respondents are concerned with the influence most parties exercise on various TV news programs. This information would imply that a Latin American version of "glasnost" could greatly benefit national and regional stability, as well as popular support of governments.

A very interesting result derives from the economic variables – specifically, income level was proven to have a limited bearing on the trust level; while financial satisfaction significantly influences trust building. A lack of a correlation between financial satisfaction and income levels raises doubts about the nature of the satisfaction, questioning the phenomena behind the fact that richer citizens do not express greater satisfaction than their poorer fellow citizens. What, then, determines individuals' satisfaction of their economic situations? This kind of satisfaction can be related to one of the characterizing elements of Latin American countries – the inequality. The WVS questionnaire fails to thoroughly examine the relation between these two issues; however it does suggest that highest inequality in income distribution is commonly associated with financial dissatisfaction. In this sense, popular wisdom says "company in distress makes sorrow less", which is corroborated by a more formal interpretation suggesting that those with higher life standards who can afford greater luxuries awake the same desires and expectations in those with limited financial options, resulting in their overall dissatisfaction. This is why reducing inequalities in Latin America could have positive impact on financial satisfaction and indirectly on citizens' trust in politics.

FUTURE RESEARCH DIRECTIONS

Regarding the econometric approach used in this paper, the results obtained in different experimental models suggest its good robustness under different specifications, namely using different set of covariates. Nevertheless, the proposed statistical method may show misleading results in presence of measurement error or unobserved heterogeneity. Although the source of the data derives from the WVS, which is one of the most important and famous organizations that provide this kind of data, the presence of problems listed above cannot be excluded with absolute certainty. Hopefully, further research may elaborate different estimation strategies capable to overcome this kind of bias. There are at least two options to be used, panel and pseudo-panel, both of which are based on the information provided by the simultaneous use of the cross-section and the time series data dimension. WVS has only recently provided its first version of Longitudinal Multiple-Wave data, allowing a panel form of the data used in the analysis, which aggregates information from different surveys including those conducted in the period of 1981 – 2014. The Association declares that for the time being, this dataset should be used as a beta version – therefore it entails risks. A valid alternative, even if panel data is available, is based on grouping data to estimate on a pseudo panel. Particularly, using series of surveys deriving from the same population in different periods allows adding the time dimension to the cross section data. In order to obtain a pseudo panel, different individuals are grouped on the basis of a variable that is individual-specific and time-invariant such as the year or place of birth. The panel dimension of the dataset allows, for instance, the control of the unobserved time invariant heterogeneity after having applied the first difference to the data. Using the same method, the bias that may eventually arise from measurement error can in some specific case be obviated, resulting in a correct estimation of the parameter of interest.

The proposed econometric analysis includes factors strictly connected to the contemporaneous society; in future, study models specifications could drastically change in accordance to the change of the environment. An example is the impact of new technologies such as low cost smart-phones and tablets that offer web access to the majority of the population. Under these circumstances, Internet usage could become one of the main determinants in the following years, thus disproving actual results. Certainly, some elements need constant monitoring in Latin America, such as the consequence of high crime rates on the overall democratic stability; while other need further analysis such as the relation between income inequalities and trust building.

Table 3. Trust in government and parliament, World Values Survey 5

WV5	Trust Government			Trust Parliament		
	Freq.	**Percent**	**Cum.**	**Freq.**	**Percent**	**Cum.**
All						
None at all	1,786	22.47	22.47	2,734	35.01	35.01
Not very much	2,705	34.03	56.49	3,13	40.08	75.08
Quite a lot	2,51	31.57	88.06	1,654	21.18	96.26
A great deal	949	11.94	100.00	292	3.74	100.00
Total	7,95	100.00		7,81	100.00	
Columbia						
None at all	599	20.06	20.06	1,003	34.81	34.81
Not very much	863	28.90	48.96	1,147	39.81	74.63
Quite a lot	1,084	36.30	85.26	627	21.76	96.39
A great deal	440	14.74	100.00	104	3.61	100.00
Total	2,986	100.00		2,881	100.00	
Chile						
None at all	172	17.53	17.53	306	31.55	31.55
Not very much	336	34.25	51.78	410	42.27	73.81
Quite a lot	384	39.14	90.93	227	23.40	97.22
A great deal	89	9.07	100.00	27	2.78	100.00
Total	981	100.00		970	100.00	
Mexico						
None at all	312	20.38	20.38	568	37.20	37.20
Not very much	534	34.88	55.26	570	37.33	74.53
Quite a lot	520	33.96	89.22	332	21.74	96.27
A great deal	165	10.78	100.00	57	3.73	100.00
Total	1,531	100.00		1,527	100.00	
Perù						
None at all	539	36.84	36.84	653	44.85	44.85
Not very much	754	51.54	88.38	693	47.60	92.45
Quite a lot	118	8.07	96.45	78	5.36	97.80
A great deal	52	3.55	100.00	32	2.20	100.00
Total	1,463	100.00		1,456	100.00	
Uruguay						
None at all	164	16.58	16.58	204	20.90	20.90
Not very much	218	22.04	38.62	310	31.76	52.66
Quite a lot	404	40.85	79.47	390	39.96	92.62
A great deal	203	20.53	100.00	72	7.38	100.00
Total	989	100.00		976	100.00	

Table 6. Trust in Government and Parliament. Socio economical variables WVS 5

Regressors	Trust in Government	Trust in Parliament
Trust	0.525*** (0.15)	0.502** (0.15)
Social organization	0.021 (0.04)	-0.058 (0.06)
Activist organization	0.206 (0.14)	0.246* (0.11)
Satisfaction	0.080** (0.02)	0.045* (0.02)
Income	0.041 (0.04)	0.052 (0.04)
Age	0.174*** (0.05)	0.078 (0.11)
Gender	-0.042 (0.05)	-0.046 (0.06)
Married	0.007 (0.05)	0.004 (0.09)
Education	-0.077 (0.09)	-0.075 (0.10)
# of observation	6994	6994
Pseudo R^2	0.0124	0.0096
BIC	15803.5	14296.6

Legend: • $p<0.1$, * $p<0.05$, ** $p<0.01$, *** $p<0.001$

CONCLUSION

This study aimed at identifying the determinants of trust in Latin American politics using a set of variables provided by the World Values Survey. The results of the developed models show that the process of trust building in politics is strongly influenced by specific factors, some of which have been widely analyzed in socio-economic literature. The present contribution updates findings from previous researches and adds new elements that characterize the relations between citizens and politics of modern societies. Furthermore, differences between confidence in government and parliament are underscored, facilitating the distinction between the aspects that engender a general disillusion in political institutions from those generating disappointment in present governments.

Five classes of determinants are highlighted: the first one is the cohesion of the society, which confirmed the claim that Latin American citizens with higher interpersonal trust tend to trust their governments more frequently, as well as the claim that citizens involved in activist organizations express greater trust in their representatives. The second determinant are the economic factors, which influence trust in politics, explicating that the economic satisfaction increases the confidence level, however, the income level cannot boost satisfaction as the two are not mutually connected. Next, the absence of transparency in elections certainly triggers spread of disillusionment in politician system, and the issue of transparency expands onto the media, which is considered overly influenced by the political parties. Another class of determinants involves inefficiency and corruption of the justice system – the problems perceived as very diffused and instigating a general disenchantment with the entire political world. Conversely, the high crime rate, representing the last class of determinants, is intimately linked to the government inaction, since people do not attribute a direct responsibility for this phenomenon to the parliament. Contrary to the expectations, the analyzed data does not suggest any significant role of participation in social organizations and usage of Internet as informational source in trust in politics.

To summarize, while the overall stability of the Latin American democracies can be threated by corruption, unfair elections and social disintegration, the possibility of a government reappointment is positively influenced by effective policies crime-suppressing and transparency in media relations.

REFERENCES

Alesina, A., & La Ferrara, E. (2005). Preferences for redistribution in the land of opportunities. *Journal of Public Economics, Elsevier, 89*(5-6), 897–931. doi:10.1016/j.jpubeco.2004.05.009

Booth, J. A., & Seligson, M. A. (2009). *The Legitimacy Puzzle: Political Support and Democracy in Latin America.* New York: Cambridge University Press. doi:10.1017/CBO9780511818431

Carreras, M. (2013). The impact of criminal violence on regime legitimacy in Latin America. *Latin American Research Review, 48*(3), 85–107. doi:10.1353/lar.2013.0040

Citrin, J. (1974). The Political Relevance of Trust in Government. *The American Political Science Review, 68*(3), 973–988. doi:10.2307/1959141

Cruz, J. M. (2003). Violencia y democratización en Centroamérica: El impacto del crimen en la legitimidad de los regímenes de posguerra. *América Latina Hoy, 35,* 19–59.

Diamanti, I. (2014). *Democrazia Ibrida.* Rome: Editori Laterza.

Easton, D. (1975). A Re-Assessment of the Concept of Political Support. *British Journal of Political Science, 5*(04), 435–457. doi:10.1017/S0007123400008309

Heterington, M. J. (1998). The Political Relevance of Political Trust. *The American Political Science Review, 92*(4), 791–808. doi:10.2307/2586304

Hetherington, M. J. (1998). The Political Relevance of Political Trust. *The American Political Science Review, 92*(4), 791–808. doi:10.2307/2586304

Knack, S. (2000). *Social Capital and The Quality of Government: Evidence from the United States.* World Bank Policy Research Working Paper (2504).

Levi, M. (1998). A state of trust. *Trust and Governance,* 77-101.

Miller, A. H. (1974). Political Issues and Trust in Government: 1964-1970. *The American Political Science Review, 68*(3), 951–972. doi:10.2307/1959140

Norris, P. (1999). *Critical citizens global support for democratic government.* Oxford, UK: Oxford University Press. doi:10.1093/0198295685.001.0001

Nye, J. S., Zelikow, P. D., & King, D. C. (1997). *Why People Don't Trust Government.* Cambridge, MA: Harvard University Press.

Pérez, O. J. (2004). Democratic Legitimacy and Public Insecurity: Crime and Democracy in El Salvador and Guatemala. *Political Science Quarterly, 118*(4), 627–644. doi:10.1002/j.1538-165X.2003.tb00408.x

Putnam, R. D. (1994). Social Capital and Public Affairs. *Bulletin - American Academy of Arts and Sciences. American Academy of Arts and Sciences, 47*(8), 5–19. doi:10.2307/3824796

Rice, T., & Sumberg, A. (1997). Civic Culture and Government Performance in the American States. *The Journal of Federalism, 27*(1), 99–114. doi:10.1093/oxford-journals.pubjof.a029899

Sukhtankar, S., & Graham, C. (2004). Does Economic Crisis Reduce Support for Markets and Democracy in Latin America? Some Evidence from Surveys of Public Opinion and Well Being. *Journal of Latin American Studies,* 349–377.

Thompson, D. M. (2008). Is the Internet a Viable Threat to Representative Democracy? *Duke Law & Technology Review, 23*(1).

Trilateral Commission. (1975). *The crisis of democracy.* New York: New York University Press.

UNDP. (2004). *La democracia en América Latina: Hacia una democracia de ciudadanas y ciudadanos*. New York: UNPD.

UNDP-OAS. (2011). *Our democracy in Latin America*. Mexico: Fondo de Cultura Económica.

World Values Survey Association. (2014). *WVS - Wave 6* and *WVS - Wave 5*. Retrieved from http://www.worldvaluessurvey.org/WVSContents.jsp

WVS 6. (2012). *WV6 Official Questionnaire v4*. Retrieved from http://www.worldvaluessurvey.org/WVSDocumentationWV6.jsp

KEY TERMS AND DEFINITIONS

Democratization: The process of shaping a society in order to reach standards of the democracy and its principles.

Disillusion: To alter an illusion or a false belief. Citizens are disillusioned if they decide that politicians do not represent public interests.

Government Paradigm: Powers division structure of a country's governing institutions.

Logit Model: Econometric model suitable in case of binary outcome variable. It evolves in the ordered logit model when the outcome displays multinomial ordered values.

Representativeness: The quality to accurately represent. Representative politicians are able to focus on popular ideals and necessities.

Social-Cohesion: Level of inclusion of all society members, which determines social unity.

Trust: Reliance on actions and behaviors of a person or an organization. In the specific case of a relation between citizens and politics, trust is expressed through ballots.

Chapter 8
Rethinking Competitiveness:
Is Central America Ready?

Mauricio Garita-Gutierrez
Universidad del Valle de Guatemala, Guatemala

ABSTRACT

The present chapter analyzes the different areas concerning competitiveness. This analysis is based on the two visions of competitiveness. The first vision establishes that the only form of competitiveness is to engage in lowering costs and therefore establishing a competitive advantage through costs. The second vision is a more integral one that sees a competitive advantage in the capacity of the workers in the specialization of labor. This second vision enforces the idea of investing in education and health to compete in more profitable markets. Based on these visions, the question to ask is: Is Central America ready?

1. INTRODUCTION

The present chapter aims to demonstrate the important of a new idea in competitiveness for Central America. The chapter challenges the idea of competitiveness centered in the lowering of costs and taxes to attract investments and instead centers in the importance of education and health to secure the future of the country.

DOI: 10.4018/978-1-4666-8820-9.ch008

The chapter engages in a discussion concerning two different theories of competitiveness to offer a new approach, an approach that is centered in the importance of investing in education and in health services. As a consequence the chapter evidences the different countries that have engaged in an investment focuses in education and health and that have augmented their economic growth. This is important because it established a different approach that differs greatly from the mercantilist approach of the economy. In this sense a view that creates a more integral conception of the market and how a small region can take advantage of two important factors that will lead into a comparative advantage by the use of competitiveness.

Finally the chapter presents the analysis applied to the Central American region to conclude if the region is taking into this vision of investing in education and health or if it is focusing on other factors.

2. DEFINING COMPETITIVENESS

Competitiveness is often defined by the productivity in the use of human, capital and natural resources. (Porter, 2005) The purpose of competitiveness is to reach prosperity for a country in the shortest time possible. To engage in the definition of competitiveness one must understand the definition of productivity. Productivity can be defined as the rate at which goods are produced and the work is completed. (Mirriam-Webster, 2014)

To sum up the definition of competitiveness, it is to produce more goods with the use of human, capital and natural resources. This idea of competitiveness is found in the works of Adam Smith, specifically in his book "The Wealth of the Nations", and in the discussions of David Ricardo. Both authors were very critic to the idea of mercantilism, an economic model that focused on exporting goods to other countries with the exploitation of the markets. The main idea of the theory was based on the idea that the benefit for a country that is exporting to another is to have an absolute advantage. This absolute advantage refers to the concept of being able to create more products in less time, an idea that is similar to the definition of competitiveness. (Laguna, 2003)

Being in an absolute advantage will create a more competitive country. The country then will have certain dominance over its competitors based on its productivity. David Ricardo added that to engage in a higher productivity a country must have lower labor costs, a market structure and relative immobility of the factors. (Chacholiades, 1992) In this sense, David Ricardo added the importance of costs to the definition of Adam Smith. David Ricardo stated that is important to control the different factors, labor, capital and land, to be competitive. But these factors should be controlled through their costs. In conclusion, according to David Ricardo if a country has lower labor, capital or land it will be more competitive and as a consequence it will create more income.

Porter (2005) criticizes this approach and defines that competitiveness will create productivity and that productivity will support higher wages, attractive returns to capital and a higher standard of living. This definition takes into account the advances in technology that had led to a better understanding for competitiveness.

Despite the different ideas on competitiveness, there is still an important amount of support to the idea of David Ricardo. International commerce theory still supports that a country will continue to produce based on the idea of intensively using the factor which the country has relative abundance. The importance of cheaper inputs to guarantee lower prices has lead to creation and acceptance of cheap labor. (Inter-American Development Bank, 2010)

To this idea, Porter (2012) mentioned in a conference in Mexico the following statement:

A nation or a region is competitive to the extent that the different business are capable of competing successfully in a global economy meanwhile they can raise wages and human living for the average citizen.

Therefore, given globalization, the importance of a discussion concerning the view of competitiveness has been divided between the two theories. The new view of competitiveness considers economic health, which is the creation of jobs. This has changed the vision of competitiveness to a more integral one that is "the ability of a region to export more in value added terms than in imports." (Atkinson, 2013) This definition adds an important concept that is added value. In this case added value is seen as the importance of specialized labor in the products.

3. LABOR AS COMPETITIVENESS

The discussion of competitiveness is usually centered in stable institutions, sound macroeconomic policies, market opening and privatizations. (Porter, What is Competitiveness?, 2005) This has led the vision to other areas that are not related to the importance of labor. For this reason it is important to analyze the added value factor that a country may give to the competitiveness of a product.

The European Union has engaged in the discussion of lowering costs given the nature of the economic crisis that still doesn't recuperate. Greece, Ireland, Italy, Portugal and Spain are implementing politics based on the reduction of labor costs through wages, which has created an internal debate with the idea of competitiveness proposed by Michael Porter. Felipe and Kumar (2011) demonstrated that the rise of nominal wages in Greece and Portugal increased labor productivity.

In Latin America the idea of competitive advantage is based somewhere in between of the semi-skilled labor and the abundance of primary educated workers. Therefore the advantage is based on the production of goods that require that level of skill. (Inter-American Development Bank, 2010) This conclusion demonstrated that to have a competitive advantage it is important to create products based on the education level of the worker. Consequently one can assume that a rise in the education will lead to a competitive advantage to the country.

The relationship of education and specialized labor has been an important asset for countries to reach economic prosperity. One of the cases is Ukraine. During the Cold War, Ukraine was the technological center of the Soviet Union. The Soviet vision concerning education in Ukraine aimed it to be technical and oriented to engineering and computational science. During this period Ukraine only had state supported institutions with no religious affiliation. The educational system was divided into pre-school, elementary, secondary school, upper secondary education, vocational-technical, technical lyceum, and specialized technical and specialized education. (OSEAS, 2014)

The vision of more technical education in Ukraine during the Soviet period led to a mayor competitive advantage after the end of the Cold War. The creation of a product such as Skype and the contributions made to Shazam, the music-identifying app, come as no surprise that the creators and contributors come from Ukraine.

The important of higher education is represented in better wages for production. The top six higher hourly compensations in the manufacturing industry are highly productive countries: (U.S. Bureau of labor statistics, 2007)

- Norway: US$ 57;
- Switzerland: US$ 53;
- Belgium: US$ 51;
- Denmark: US$ 45;
- Sweden: US$ 43;
- Germany: US$ 45[1].

Concerning Latin America, Argentina has an hourly compensation cost of approximately US$ 13 and Mexico an approximate US$ 7 dollars. The United States reports a US$ 35, the United Kingdom an approximate of US$ 29 and China US$ 3. The difference between China and Germany establishes which kind of competitiveness each one is engaging. In the case of China, the competitiveness is similar to the idea of David Ricardo of lowering costs and in the case of Germany it is similar to the one proposed by Michael Porter. To engage in prosperity, it seems that Germany has a better social indicators than China.

Based on the Global Competitiveness Index (2013), China is ranked as the number 29 country meanwhile Germany is ranked as number 4. Switzerland is ranked as number 1, Norway as number 11, Belgium as number 17, and Denmark as number 21.

The major difference between this countries and China is the higher education level. China is ranked in higher education in number 70 of 148 countries. Germany is ranked as 3, Switzerland is ranked 4th, Norway is number 10, Belgium is 5th, and Denmark is 14. This demonstrates the importance of education as an asset for competitiveness.

4. EDUCATION AND SOCIAL SECURITY AS COMPETITIVENESS INPUTS

For an economy to be competitive it must engage in new economic vision. This economic vision is centered on education and innovation. This will create a comparative advantage for the country. The new economic growth theory promotes five different aspects for an economy to grow: (Martin, 2007)

- Expenditure in research and development;
- Innovation (patents);
- Educational level;
- Spending on investment in human capital (schooling and training);
- Effective dissemination of knowledge (knowledge centers).

The following theory is supported on the idea that European and Asian countries have grown under the implementation of better education. One of these countries is the case of Finland that invested in public education to promote the cellular mobile industry. This validates the idea that investing in high quality early education and child care-raising, the completion of basic and vocational education, increasing links between higher education and labor markets and wider vocational training opportunities will lead to higher economic growth. (World Economic Forum, 2002)

The investment of education is also an important variable in Latin America. The waged that were on the rise during the period of 1975 to 1995 were the higher education sector. The wages of the unskilled stagnated during this period. (Inter-American Development Bank, 2010)

In Europe the relation is the same, the increasing labor productivity is closely linked to the rise in education. (Wood, 2014) This relationship is repeated through the Eurozone as a signaling of education and growth. The consequence is a more stable market guided by specialized competitiveness that can handle recession.

Despite the fact that China has been guided into a differentiation by lower labor costs, they have invested during the past year in technological education. This effort has led China to surpass the United States in high-technology exports meanwhile the United States has a deficit in such exports. China graduates nearly three times as many four-year degrees in engineering, computer science and IT than in the United States (Attis, 2014).

The search for added value in innovation has guided the economies such as China and Ireland into investing in education related to the computer sciences and engineering. To innovate the country needs better skills that will amount in higher wages. This will eventually lead to higher competitive advantages (Council on Competitiveness, 2007).

Countries such as the Czech Republic have created initiatives like the Education for Competitiveness OP (ECOP) based on a system of lifelong learning, the creation of suitable environments for research, innovation, and cooperation. This investment is equivalent to 2.11 billion. (European Social Fund in the Czech Republic, 2013) The importance of a more educated country to give added value to product seems as the reasonable answer for the development of new projects for economic growth.

Ben Widalvsky (2010) called this competition for the brain race. The brain race is used as a description for the international competition for the best talents. But the idea centers on that the talents can emerge from the country and therefore they will be less keen to leave the country. This is the importance of local and technical education.

Another important factor considering competitiveness is health care. The importance of healthcare is based on the capacity that the child will get if he is nurtured under the right conditions. This condition could lead to the development of the brain so that the child can learn as it is intended. Nutrition becomes one of the most important aspects in healthcare. Later, in the workers phase, the worker will need less income to support his health care if the government covers it. This will lead to better to wage that does not include the cost of health. (Mankiw, 2009) In conclusion both education and healthcare are important factors for competitiveness because they maintain the comparative advantage.

Figure 1. 20 most critical aspects for choosing a country for investment
(*Source: Elaborated by the author with information from Central American Institute of Fiscal Studies, 2014*).

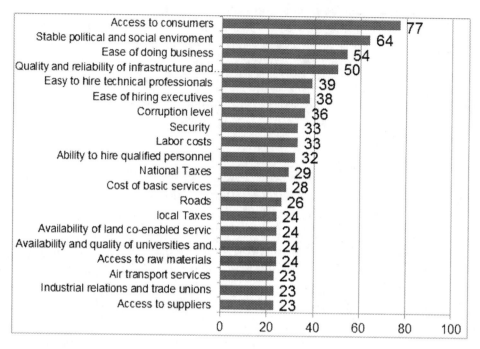

5. THE CHALLENGES FOR CENTRAL AMERICA

To analyze the challenges one must address the different aspects that are critical for investors when choosing a country for investment. Figure 1 reflects this importance, being the first five elements the access to consumers, a more stable political and social environment, the ease of doing business, quality and reliability in infrastructure and the ease of hiring technical professionals. Of these different aspects three have address the topic of education as the main cause. The ease for hiring technical professionals, the stable social environment and the ease of hiring executive has certain influence of education.

As discussed earlier the important of educated countries surpasses the need for labor costs and taxes. This demonstrates that the priority of investors in not related to the lowering of costs but to a more competitive country.

This gives us two main aspects for the analysis of education and labor costs. The fist being the investment in education that Central America has engaged over the last seven years. This amount will reflect the importance of education and the

Table 1. Public expenditure in education considering remittances (In percentages)

Public Expenditure in Education	2006-2011
Belize	26%
Costa Rica	8%
El Salvador	-5%
Guatemala	21%
Honduras	20%
Nicaragua	31%
Panamá	24%

Source: Elaborated by the author with information from (Central American Institute of Fiscal Studies).

competitiveness vision of the countries. The migratory population is concerned with education; mostly because they are working in more advanced countries and they see education as a way getting better jobs.

Table 1 demonstrates that the higher investment has been made by Nicaragua over the last seven years followed by Belize, Panamá, Honduras and Guatemala. The country that evidences a lower investment in education is El Salvador that presents a negative figure. This has to be analyzed that the remittances sent to this countries in Central America are meant for improving education that the government cannot cover.

Despite the fact that there is growth in the region, the data can mislead the argument. Considering the total investment, of the remittances, Belize amounts for only 0.3% of the public expenditure in the region. El Salvador, Guatemala and Honduras are equivalent to 85% of the investment in education in the region. If this is compared to the population that these three countries represent (66.7%), it seems logical such investment.

The public expenditure in health of remittances does not behave that different than education. Panamá has the lowest investment in public health related to its GDP. Panama only invests 1.2% of its GDP in public investment, followed by Costa Rica with 1.3% of the GDP, and Belize with 2.5%. The highest investors of remittances in public health in comparison with the GDP are El Salvador (14.3%) and Honduras (15.8%). Also these countries are the ones that represent most of the population that has migrated to other countries in search for opportunities. (Central American Institute for Fiscal Studies, 2014)

If the population that migrates sees education and health as an important asset for advancing in life, the question lies in how the government sees such investment. The poverty levels in the region are in countries like Honduras (61.9%), Guatemala (53.7%) and El Salvador (47.5%). Almost half of the citizens in the country are in poverty conditions. It becomes more dramatic when analyzing extreme poverty in which Honduras has 41.6% of the population living with one dollar a day.

Poverty has a toll on education, especially secondary education. Panamá and Costa Rica have the highest enrollment in secondary education with a 65.5% and 72.4%. In Guatemala the enrollment in secondary education is equivalent to 33.8% and in Honduras it is 44.7%. If we take into account that the enrollment in primary education in Guatemala is of 92.8% and in Honduras 88%, the fallout of students is extreme. Almost half of the students leave the educational system in primary school.

As a consequence, Honduras, El Salvador and Guatemala have the lowest literacy rate in the region with 84.5%, 89.2% and 89.2% of the adult population in conditions of reading and writing.

These same countries have the highest mortality rate. Guatemala has a 29.5 of mortality rate per 1,000 children born only followed by Honduras with a 24.3. Guatemala also has the highest maternal mortality, 139.5 for every 100,000 born. Only followed by Nicaragua with 62.7 and El Salvador 50.8.

The investment in education is not as high as it should be with an important difference between countries. Two countries are leading the investment in education and health care, Panamá and Costa Rica. The other four countries have a very different perception on this vision.

Figure 2 demonstrates the difference between Costa Rica and Panama with the rest of the region. This difference is also seen in the expenditure in health per capita in the region. Panama invests US$ 315, followed by Costa Rica with US$ 141, El Salvador with US$ 89, and Honduras with US$36, and Guatemala with US$ 35, and Nicaragua with US$ 31

The same difference is seen when analyzing the direct and indirect investment by the government per capita. Costa Rica has an investment of US$ 968.7, Honduras has US$ 252.7, and El Salvador has US$ 247.9, Guatemala with 142.3% and Nicaragua with US$93.6%.

Figure 2. Expenditure in Education per capita (2010)
(Source: Elaborated by the author with information from Central American Institute for Fiscal Studies).

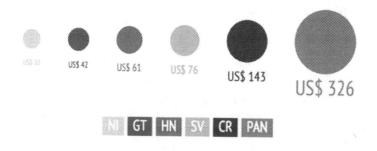

If we translate this into competitiveness, Guatemala is located in the position 86 of 144. Nicaragua is in the position 99, El Salvador in position 97, Honduras in 111, Costa Rica in position 54 and in position 46. Concerning the indicator of higher education and training Costa Rica is in ranked in 33, Panamá in 68, Nicaragua in 109, Honduras in 110, El Salvador in 100 and Guatemala in 105. (World Economic Forum, 2014)

This information demonstrates that competitiveness in Central America is centered in Panamá and Costa Rica. The other countries of the region have to invest in education and health to promote the same vision as a region. Therefore the challenge of investing in Central America lies in the country that is selected since it is an unequal region.

6. CONCLUSION

The chapter aimed to examine the new vision concerning competitiveness. Rethinking the vision of competitiveness into a more integral one that does not focuses only on the importance of cost but takes that into account important factors such as health and education. This new concept has demonstrated to be effective in Asia and Europe to surpass the crisis. Focusing on economies that are integrated into education and higher technical skills seem to be growing faster than those dedicated to lower education and lower costs. Therefore, rethinking the concept of education in Central America is extremely important.

To demonstrate this, the present chapter examined the different situations in which labor adjustments, higher salaries and a vision of more technical products have lead different countries into growing. After defining the importance of education and health care, the chapter made a profound analysis into the reality of Central America with the purpose of identifying if Central America is focusing on this concept of competitiveness.

In conclusion, two countries in Central America and focusing on the new trends of competitiveness. Only Panama and Costa Rica have a very high investment in education and social security. They also maintain the highest enrollment rates in secondary education that leads to a more technical education.

The countries that are urged to change this vision are Guatemala, Honduras, El Salvador and Nicaragua that have very high poverty and extreme poverty levels, very low enrollments in secondary education, very low investment in education per capita and a extremely low investment in health. If this countries want to have a better competitive level they have to invest in this areas a priority for at least the next ten years.

The chapter also demonstrates that it is not only important to invest focus on facilitating commerce but that for a futuristic vision, education and health are essential to guarantee the countries future.

REFERENCES

Atkinson, R. D. (2013). *Competitiveness, Innovation and Productivity: Clearing up the Confusion*. Washington, DC: The Information Technology & Innovation Foundation.

Attis, D. (2014). *Higher education and the future of U.S. competitiveness*. Educause.

Central American Institute for Fiscal Studies. (2014). *Participación de las remesas en salud*. Central American Instititute for Fiscal Studies. Central American Instititute for Fiscal Studies.

Central American Institute for Fiscal Studies. (n.d.). *Gasto Público, tendencias recientes y su impacto en equidad*. Central American Institute for Fiscal Studies.

Central American Institute of Fiscal Studies. (2014a). *Public Expenditure in Education*. Central American Institute of Fiscal Studies.

Central American Institute of Fiscal Studies. (2014b). *To a new vision of competitiveness*. Central American Institute of Fiscal Studies.

Chacholiades, M. (1992). *Economía Internacional*. Bogotá, Colombia: McGraw-Hill.

Council on Competitiveness. (2007). *Competitiveness Index: Where America Stands*. Boston: Council on Competitiveness.

European Social Fund in the Czech Republic. (2013). *Education for Competitiveness OP (ECOP)*. Recuperado el 23 de 10 de 2014, de The Education for Competitiveness Operational Programme (ECOP): http://www.esfcr.eu/07-13-en/ecop

Felipe, J., & Kumar, U. (2011). *Unit Labor Costs in the Eurozone: The Competitiveness Debate Again*. New York: Levy Economics Institute.

Inter-American Development Bank. (2010). *Labor Costs and Competitiveness*. Washington.

Laguna, C. (2003). Undamentos de la teoría clásica del comercio internacional. Buenos Aires: EUMED.

Mankiw, G. (2009). *Healthcare and Competitiveness*. Boston: Harvard.

Martin, R. L. (2007). *A Study on the Factors of Regional Competitiveness.* Cambridge, UK: Academic Press.

Mirriam-Webster. (2014). *Encyclopedia Britannica.* Mirriam-Webster.

OSEAS. (2014). *Educational system of Ukraine.* Tallin, Ukraine: OSEAS.

Porter, M. (2005). *What is Competitiveness?* Spain: IESE Business School.

Porter, M. (2012). *Regional competitiveness.* Obtenido de Harvard Business School: http://www.isc.hbs.edu/pdf/2012-0427---Michael_Porter_Puebla.pdf

U.S. Bureau of Labor Statistics. (2007). *Competitiveness in Manufacturing.* Washington, DC: U.S. Bureau of Labor Statistics.

Wildavsky, B. (2010). *The Great Brain Race: How Global Universities Are Reshaping the World.* Princeton University Press.

Wood, R. (2014). *Eurozone: Competitiveness Indicators and the Failure of Internal Devaluation.* EconoMonitor. EconoMonitor.

World Economic Forum. (2002). *The Global Competitiveness Report 2001-2002.* Oxford, UK: Oxford Press.

World Economic Forum. (2014). *The Global Competitiveness Report 2013–2014.* World Economic Forum.

ENDNOTE

[1]   The data presented is approximate.

Chapter 9
Opportunities and Challenges for Entrepreneurial Activity and Non-Entrepreneurial Engagement in Colombia

Luis Javier Sanchez-Barrios
Universidad del Norte, Colombia

Liyis Gomez-Nuñez
Universidad del Norte, Colombia

Eduardo Gomez-Araujo
Universidad del Norte, Colombia

Sandra Rodriguez
Universidad del Norte, Colombia

ABSTRACT

This chapter explores various aspects that might be associated with entrepreneurial activity and non-entrepreneurial engagement in Colombia between 2010 and 2012. These ratios were calculated from the GEM-Colombia report between 2010 and 2012. Aspects were obtained from the National Expert Survey (NES) of the GEM project and from the Doing Business Study. Sommer's d correlation was used to test significant association. Results show that in general, context conditions in Colombia are adequate to start a business. Positive aspects include public policies to stimulate business creation, skilled specialist teams and reduction in processes required to formally establish an SME. Yet further substantial advance need to be made in terms of access to financial resources, access to technology that is relevant for microbusinesses, implementation of innovation policies and education in entrepreneurship. This is required to enhance the creation of high growth businesses that result in a knowledge-based economy in contrast with a prevalent traditional economy as is the case at present.

DOI: 10.4018/978-1-4666-8820-9.ch009

INTRODUCTION

Entrepreneurship is a fundamental component of economic growth, productivity, generation of employment, innovation and socio-economic development (OECD, 2009). The Global Entrepreneurship Monitor (GEM) has been demonstrating since 1999 on a worldwide scale that there is a strong correlation between business start-up and economic growth (Amorós, Bosma and GERA, 2014). GEM also has demonstrated that the entrepreneurial activity varies widely across countries and regions. These entrepreneurial differences are not only found across countries, but also within countries across different regions and territories (Audretsch et al., 2012).

In recent years Colombia has presented one of the highest rates of the Total Early-Stage Entrepreneurship Activity (TEA) among countries in the Latin America and Caribbean Region (21%) (GEM- Colombia, 2013). TEA includes individuals involved in setting up a business (Nascent Entrepreneurship) and those running new businesses less than 3.5 years old (New Business Ownership) (Bosma et al., 2013) (see Figure 1). Within Colombia, entrepreneurial activity varies year after year between cities, territories and regions (GEM-Colombia, 2014).

In addition, the GEM methodology identifies individuals with entrepreneurial attitudes (i.e. potential entrepreneurs) and individuals involved as owner-managers in established firms (Bosma et al., 2012) (see Figure 1). Consequently, according to GEM the rate of individuals involved in entrepreneurial activities at different stages (i.e.: potential, new and nascent entrepreneurs, new business owners and owner-managers) normally varies each year among countries, between cities and territories in which GEM project is performed (Amorós, Bosma and GERA, 2014).

Figure 1. Phases of entrepreneurship in the GEM research framework
Source: Bosma et al. (2012).

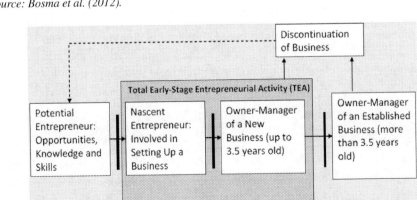

On the other hand, it has been confirmed that the potential for doing business varies between countries and different cities in the world (World Bank, 2013); "The Doing Business Project provides objective measures of business regulations and their enforcement across 189 economies and selected cities at the subnational and regional level" (World Bank, 2014). This study has a specific component namely Starting a Business, which is a ranking about the processes, cost and time associated specifically with starting a business. In 2014 Colombia occupied position 79 among countries. At the subnational level, four main Colombian cities, namely Bogotá, Medellin, Cali andi Barranquilla occupied positions 7, 11, 4 and 14 respectively within the ranking of starting a business (World Bank, 2013).What could explain the differences in entrepreneurial activities rates between cities in Colombia? The main objective of this chapter is to explore some factors that according to the existing literature might be decisive in explaining this phenomenon. Data were extracted from the Adult Population Survey (APS) and National Experts Survey (NES) (GEM-Colombia, 2010; GEM-Colombia, 2012) and the Doing Business Report (World Bank, 2010; World Bank, 2013) for years 2010 and 2012. These years were chosen because the latter report is prepared every two years.

The aim is to offer the reader useful insight as of the factors that might be affecting entrepreneurial activity among Colombian cities. This will shed light on further issues that should be considered within the research agenda and academic debate on the field. From a practitioners perspective, findings will be useful for policy making, design of education programmes and operating procedures that ultimately affect the entrepreneurial activity and hence, the economic growth of Colombia. For the purpose of this chapter, two approaches were used to measure entrepreneurial activity: First, in terms of TEA as explained before (i.e. the proportion of nascent entrepreneurs and new businesses among surveyed adults) and second, in terms of non-entrepreneurial engagement (i.e. the proportion of surveyed adults which are not potential entrepreneurs, nascent entrepreneurs or do not own new/established businesses). This is further expanded in the methods section.

This chapter is structured as follows: The following section presents the theoretical framework, followed by a section in methods for data collection and data analysis. Findings and discussion are then presented, followed by conclusions and implications.

BACKGROUND

Entrepreneurial activity or business start-up is a determinant of economic growth (Wennekers and Thurik, 1999; Audretsch and Keilbach, 2007; Fritsch and Mueller, 2008; Audretsch et al., 2012). What are the reasons behind this? From an academic perspective, there are three links between entrepreneurship and economic development: first, innovation; second, firm start-ups and job creation; and third, competitiveness (Karlsson et al., 2004). Some studies suggest that the function of entrepreneurship as the driving force of economic development is due to its role as the conveyor of innovation to the markets (Audretsch and Thurik, 2001; Thurik and Wennekers, 2001; Carree and Thurik, 2002; Acs and Amoros, 2008); correspondingly, small firms produce a large share of the total number of innovations (Acs, 1996). Moreover and according to Karlsson et al. (2004), empirical studies show that increased competition has been found to stimulate greater employment as well as enhance growth in total factor productivity. Hence, the wealth of an economy is highly linked to the promotion of innovation and entrepreneurship (Bamoul, 2004).

Entrepreneurial activity and its relationship with economic growth varies across different territorial levels such as countries, regions, cities, towns, rural and urban areas, etc. (Reynolds et al., 1994; Audretsch and Thurik; 2001; Freytag and Thurik, 2007; Fritsch, 2008; Bosma et al., 2010; Wennekers et al., 2010; Amorós, Bosma and GERA, 2014). According to Malecki (1994) the studies of entrepreneurship and new firm formation have demonstrated that not all places are alike in their potential to generate entrepreneurial activity and economic growth. This author suggests that these variations are possible to explain from three dimensions of territorial environment such as industrial structure, organizational structure and entrepreneurial climate or milieu. There is a complex relationship between social-economic structure, culture and entrepreneurship (Davidsson, 1995).

Therefore, creating a suitable business climate or ecosystem is a key factor in countries to stimulate entrepreneurial activity (Isenberg, 2010; World Bank, 2013; OECD & LEED, 2014; World Economic Forum, 2014). Achieving sustainable entrepreneurial activity not only depends on the involvement of government and the private sector, but also molds cultural norms and the education system, eliminates regulatory barriers, provides financial support for new business initiatives and effective market strategies and networks access and encourages the creation of clusters, among others (Isenberg, 2011). The following sections briefly present these aspects as determinants of a suitable climate for stimulating entrepreneurial activity.

Governmental Policies Focused on Entrepreneurial Activity

Among the factors that generate a suitable climate for entrepreneurial activity, governmental policies for entrepreneurs in a country or territory are a crucial aspect to consider (European Commission, 2004; Reynolds et al., 2005; Isenberg, 2010). Entrepreneurial policy is understood as every governmental action related to encouraging and supporting entrepreneurs in a territory. Encouraging and supporting entrepreneurship requires that government policy takes actions in the areas of awareness, education and training, business incubation, business growth, R&D transfer, networking, financial support, business infrastructure, regulation of business procedures and taxes, the structure of the labor force, and any other aspect required to improve the business climate and entrepreneurial ecosystem (Ribeiro-Soriano and Galindo-Martín, 2012; OECD & LEED, 2014).

Integrating these areas through a consistent entrepreneurial policy and performing effectively the required actions affect the development of entrepreneurial activity and hence economic growth in a territory (OECD, 2003; Acs and Szerb, 2007; Grilo and Thurik, R, 2008). A major issue and challenge in Latin American countries is to improve governmental policy through the efficient integration of areas and entities related to entrepreneurial encouragement and support (GEM-Colombia, 2011; Terjesen and Amoros, 2010). Also, some scholars have analyzed and verified the positive relationship between Government policy and the growth of entrepreneurship (Grilo and Thurik, R, 2008; Asghar et al., 2011; Ribeiro-Soriano and Galindo-Martín, 2012). Asghar et al. (2011) indicate that countries which have succeeded in achieving high growth of Micro, Small & Medium Enterprises are those that have further emphasized Entrepreneurship Development Programs and consistently attempt to accumulate optimal utilization of their resources for such purpose.

Entrepreneurial Education

Another important factor to enhance entrepreneurial activity in territories is the relationship between education and entrepreneurship (Acs and Szerb, 2007; Naudé et al., 2008). Education has become one of the strategies that worldwide governments use to increase entrepreneurial activity (Von Graevenitza et al., 2010; Sánchez, 2013). Entrepreneurship education refers to instructing individuals on the attitudes and aptitudes that they need to experience and know to be entrepreneurs, run-manage a business and make it successful (OECD 1998; Duval-Couetil, 2013).

In this manner, studies have discussed the outcomes and approaches of entrepreneurial education. Regarding the outcomes of entrepreneurship education, these are normally measured in terms of: a) economic development: number of new firms, number of employees, innovation; b) firm performance: financial performance, relation to other firms, growth, innovation; and c) impact on individual participants: personal and career satisfaction, knowledge and skills acquisition, changes in attitudes, and identification of individual potential among others (Duval-Couetil, 2013). Yet according to O'Connor (2013), the economic benefit of entrepreneurship education has proven difficult to substantiate, partly due to the multi-definitional perspectives of entrepreneurship; a major challenge policymakers face is adjusting approaches used in entrepreneurship education to take into account economic and social objectives proposed by governments in relation to entrepreneurial activity (O'Connor,

2013). Consequently, still there is progress to be made in terms of successfully implementing strategies and practices related to entrepreneurship education. It is important to note, however, that studies have confirmed that education increases the intention of individuals to start a business and that the level of education and training of entrepreneurs is correlated with business growth and innovation (Graevenitza et al., 2010; Sánchez, 2013; Jun Bae et al., 2014).

Financial Support for Entrepreneurs

Previous studies have demonstrated that financial resources are crucial for the generation and consolidation of entrepreneurial activity (OECD, 2003, 2014; World Bank, 2004). Entrepreneurship finance is defined as the study of the resource allocation applied to new ventures; it is related to the mechanisms that entrepreneurs use to access the capital that they need to invest in start-ups or business growth (e.g.: bootstrapping, business angels, investors, ventures capital fund, risk capital fund, crowd funding, loans, public stock offering, among others).

Scholars have found that limited and difficult access to credit is a strong barrier to the birth and development of emerging companies (Colombo and Grilli, 2007). At the same time, some studies suggest that available financial alternatives have a positive impact on the propensity to create business. Yet Ho and Wong (2007) analyzed in 29 countries the availability of three types of financing sources: traditional debt financing, venture capital financing, and informal investments; it was found that only informal investments have statistically significant influence on entrepreneurial propensity. Precisely, in Latin America countries financial support for entrepreneurs is a big challenge to overcome, due to prevalent mistrust between those who have capital and entrepreneurs, besides the lack of regulation regarding investments and entrepreneurial activity (World Bank, 2013; World Economic Forum, 2014).

Business Growth and R&D Management

Entrepreneurial financial support is not only a tool for business startup but is also useful for business growth. Though, attention to high growth businesses involves other factors related to characteristics of entrepreneurs and their businesses, business climate and entrepreneurial ecosystem (Capelleras and Greene, 2008; Capelleras and Kantis, 2009). These authors indicate that the following features may affect business growth: the profile and human capital level of the founder(s) is one of the major determinants; the company being created by a team of entrepreneurs; size and quality of the entrepreneur's networking; access and characteristics of financial and human resources and financial resources available to the new company which are necessary to facilitate the development of their strategies, including the use of external funding sources (e.g.: banks, government agencies and venture capital). Finally, Capelleras and Kantis (2009) stated that growth and performance of new firms is related to their entrepreneurial orientation level.

Entrepreneurial orientation refers to the level at which companies adopt innovative behaviors (Covin y Slevin, 1989). Regarding innovative orientation, research and development (R&D) transfer or management is a key factor to generate a suitable climate for competitive entrepreneurial activity. R&D management is defined as the synergy between activities related to the management of innovation and technology (Brockhoff, 1994). It includes activities such as basic and fundamental research, technology development, new product and process development, prototyping, external and internal creation and retention of technological know-how, commercializing inventions, knowledge and technology transfer, etc. (Paukert et al., 2004).

Cummings and Bing-Sheng (2003) found that R&D knowledge transfer success is associated with several key variables in the workplace such as: linkages, embeddedness, physical distance, knowledge distance, norm distance, learning culture, project priority, organizational distance and transfer activities. Specifically, some studies have found empirical evidence about the positive correlation between business growth and R&D and knowledge transfer activities (Hölzl, 2009). In the context of Latin American countries and specifically for entrepreneurial activity in Colombia, a recent study has indicated that there is low R&D activity in startups and established firms, due to poor innovative culture in the country, lack of programs that encourage and support these activities and the lack of venture capital funds (Gómez-Núñez and Negrete-Escobar, 2013).

Requirements to Formally Start a Business

Finally, procedures required to formally establish and run a business are key to create a suitable climate for motivating entrepreneurial activity (World Bank, 2004; Ribeiro-Soriano and Galindo-Martín, 2012; OECD & LEED, 2014). The Doing Business Project defined starting a business as the number of steps entrepreneurs can expect to go through to start up and formally operate an industrial or commercial business (World Bank, 2014). Studies have found that as the number of procedures for starting a business increases, entrepreneurial activity decreases; conversely when the number of procedures decreases entrepreneurial activity increases (Klapper et al. 2010).

The World Bank (2014) studied the procedures, time, cost and paid-in minimum capital to start a business in 189 countries. According to World Bank (2014), a procedure is defined as any interaction of the company founders with external parties (this includes government agencies, lawyers, auditors or notaries); time is measured as the median duration that incorporation lawyers indicate is necessary in practice to complete a procedure with minimum follow-up by government agencies and no additional payments; cost is calculated as a percentage of the economy's income per capita that include all official, legal or professional fees required by law and the paid-in minimum capital requirement reflects the amount that entrepreneurs deposit in a bank or through a notary before registration and up to 3 months following incorporation (World Bank, 2014).

METHODS

Data Collection

This section presents the variables and datasets that were used to address the aim of this chapter: i.e. identifying opportunities and challenges of the entrepreneurial activity in Colombia between 2010 and 2012. This requires measuring the entrepreneurial activity per se and identifying aspects that might be associated with it, as explained below. It is important to note that four Colombian capital cities were used as observation units for this study, namely Barranquilla, Bogota, Cali and Medellin.

The GEM project gathers data on entrepreneurial activity through an adult population survey that is administered annually in 70 countries (Amorós, Bosma and GERA, 2014). The *TEA* (Total Entrepreneurial Activity) index is obtained from such survey and is used as a measure of entrepreneurial activity to compare countries, regions and cities worldwide. It is calculated as the proportion of nascent and new entrepreneurs among the surveyed sample (11.029 and 6.471 people between 18-64 years old for 2010 and 2012 respectively). The former refers to businesses created within the previous 3 months whereas the latter includes businesses created in the interval (3, 36] months. Given the wide use of *TEA*, intuitively it made sense to use such measure to define the change in entrepreneurial activity for city x between 2010 and 2012 as:

$$CEA_{x,1210} = \frac{\left(TEA_{x,2012} - TEA_{x,2010}\right)}{TEA_{x,2010}} \times 100\% \tag{1}$$

An alternative perspective focuses on individuals for which being entrepreneurs is not an option; this would be insightful to identify opportunities and challenges of starting a business in a given country. We define the non-entrepreneurial engagement in city x during year i as:

$$NEE_{x,i} = 1 - \left(PO_{x,i} + NA_{x,i} + NE_{x,i} + ES_{x,i} \right) \qquad (2)$$

where:

$PO_{x,i}$ = proportion of potential entrepreneurs (individuals that have the intention of starting a business) in the surveyed sample;

$NA_{x,i}$ = proportion of nascent entrepreneurs in the surveyed sample;

$NE_{x,i}$ = proportion of new entrepreneurs in the surveyed sample and

$ES_{x,i}$ = proportion of businesses established more than 36 months ago.

The change in NEE for city x between 2010 and 2012 is therefore defined as:

$$NEE_{x,1210} = \frac{\left(NEE_{x,2012} - NEE_{x,2010} \right)}{NEE_{x,2010}} \times 100\% \qquad (3)$$

Selected aspects that might be related with *CEA1210* and *NEE1210* were presented in the previous section. Data gathered from the National Expert Survey (NES) (GEM-Colombia, 2011, 2013) included 36 and 50 experts in total from the four capital cities during 2010 and 2012 respectively. Each respondent was presented a series of 30 Likert items related with the creation of new businesses and growth of established ones. Items included options which ranged from 1 ("Totally false") to 5 ("Totally true"); other options such as: "Not applicable", "Does not know" and "No answer" were also included. Therefore, each item (aspect) is an ordinal variable.

In order to reflect the opinion of experts for each city regarding each aspect, the median value per item was calculated; this was done to be consistent with data handling methods used in the Doing Business Report (World Bank, 2013). Also, using the mean value would not make sense as figures in the scale do not have numerical value per se. Following the experts' opinion for city x, an increase (decrease) in values for aspect i between 2010 and 2012 represents an improvement (decline) between 2010 and 2012:

$$NES(i)_{x,1210} = NES(i)_{x,2012} - NES(i)_{x,2010} \qquad (4)$$

Data related with the *ranking, processes, cost* and *time* associated with starting a business in each city were obtained from the Doing Business Study (World Bank, 2010; 2013). It should be noted that the variable *cost* used in this study is an adjusted value provided by the data supplier. This value is calculated using single base year conditions to avoid the effect of changes in exchange rates and other variables used for its calculation. An increase (decrease) in values for aspect j represents worse (better) conditions to start a business in city x between 2010 and 2012:

$$DOING(i)_{x,1210} = DOING(i)_{x,2012} - DOING(i)_{x,2010} \tag{5}$$

Data Analysis

Sommer's d correlation between each dependent variable (CEA_{1210}, NEE_{1210}) and each aspect ($NES(i)_{1210}$ for i=1 to 30, $DOING(j)_{1210}$ for j=1 to 4) was calculated. Such measure is asymmetric and hence allows assessing the association between variables defined as independent and dependent *a priori*; it does not require many points on the scale and both variables need to be at least ordinal (Argyrous, 2005, p 83; 101-102). This measure was chosen given the nature of the dataset used and the research aim of this study: all variables are ordinal or interval (hence ordinal), with specific values in the Likert scale used and ultimately the aim is to test if any change in the selected aspects is associated with changes in entrepreneurial activity and non-entrepreneurial engagement.

Sommer's d correlation ranks between -1 and +1. A positive (negative) value would suggest that a better (worse) opinion of experts or facility of starting a business is associated with an increase (decrease) in entrepreneurial activity or non-entrepreneurial engagement. It is important to note that this is not a measure of causation instead it quantifies the strength of association between variables. A final step included testing the significance of Sommer's d correlation. That is, did results arise per chance or not? This was done at $\alpha=0.10$ significance level. Only significant results were taken into consideration for analysis purposes.

FINDINGS AND DISCUSSION

This section presents the findings and discussion of results obtained from conducting the calculations presented in the Methods section. Table 1 presents only aspects that were significantly correlated with CEA_{1210} and NEE_{1210}.

Aspects Associated with Change in Entrepreneurial Activity

When analysing change in *entrepreneurial activity*, changes in 6 NES aspects were found to be significantly associated with it: *financial institutions' funding offer* (A02), *public policies to assist new and established companies* (B02), *access to*

Table 1. Description of aspects significantly correlated with CEA$_{1210}$ and NEE$_{1210}$

Variable	Category	Description
A02	NES (Financial Support)	Funds from private financial institutions are sufficient to support new and in-growth businesses.
A05	NES (Financial Support)	Risk capital offer for new and in-growth businesses is sufficient.
B02	NES (Government policies)	Supporting new and in-growth businesses is a central government policy priority.
B04	NES (Government policies)	Administrative and legal processes to start up a new business can be completed in about a week.
D06	NES (Education and training)	Higher and continuing education programmes are adequate to create new businesses and to make existing companies grow.
E02	NES (R&D transfer)	New and in-growth companies can access research and technologies available to established companies.
Q01	NES (Support to growth)	Many existing alternatives were specifically designed to support new high growth potential businesses.
Q03	NES (Support to growth)	Specialist teams that work in assisting the creation of high growth potential businesses are skilled and competent.
Q05	NES (Support to growth)	Public policies prioritise the creation of high growth businesses.
TIME	Doing Business Study	Number of days required to formally establish an SME.
PROC	Doing Business Study	Number of processes required to formally establish an SME.
RANK	Doing Business Study	Ranking of starting up a business.
COST	Doing Business Study	Cost as a % of GDP per capita.

novel research and technologies (E02), *initiatives* (Q01) *and specialist team* (Q03) *that assists new businesses with high growth potential* and *public policies that prioritise the creation of high growth businesses* (Q05). Changes in 3 aspects from the Doing Business report were found to be significantly associated with change in entrepreneurial activity: *ranking, procedures* and *cost of starting up a business*. See Table 2.

- *Offer of funds from financial institutions (A02).*

An improvement in the offer of funding alternatives from financial institutions for new and established companies has a strong negative correlation with entrepreneurial activity. At first instance, this result seems to be counter-intuitive as one

Table 2. Significant correlations

Aspect	Sommer's d	Significance
CEA$_{1210}$		
A02	-1.00	0.00
B02	**+1.00**	**0.08**
E02	-1.00	0.08
Q01	+0.60	0.00
Q03	**+1.00**	**0.08**
Q05	-0.67	0.05
PROC	**-1.00**	**0.00**
RANK	-0.67	0.05
COST	+0.67	0.05
NEE$_{1210}$		
A05	+1.00	0.00
B02	-1.00	0.08
B04	-1.00	0.00
D06	+0.60	0.00
Q03	-1.00	0.08
TIME	+0.67	0.05
PROC	+1.00	0.00

would expect that a wider offer of formal funding should enhance entrepreneurial activity. However, entrepreneurs are not necessarily well informed of such alternatives and hence do not use them. Additionally, it is important to differentiate offer from access to financial institutions in Colombia. Yet most of the population remains unbanked (Solo and Manroth, 2006) which results in lack of a credit history, which in turn leads to further exclusion from formal financial services. Conditions required from new businesses include evidence of trading activity, financial statements and commercial references; entrepreneurs lack these during the early stages of their businesses.

A limited group of entrepreneurs use personal banking loans (e.g. credit cards and overdrafts) to support their starting businesses; this alternative obviously relies on their personal finances and properties used as guarantees. Entrepreneurs excluded from formal banking usually rely on family, friends; another common source is informal lending which charge up to 150% AER for loans (Solo and Manroth, 2006). These lenders are serving excluded segments by adopting practices from formal institutions (e.g. loan approval system, close follow-up of funds' usage and referencing system) and others that are based on coercion (Sanchez-Barrios et al., in press).

A trade-off between risk and growth potential might be required from financial institutions to generate funding alternatives accessible to entrepreneurs.

- *Public policies that prioritise new and in-growth businesses (B02).*

The correlation between entrepreneurial activity and national policies that prioritise supporting new and in-growth businesses is positive and strong. Hence government efforts to enhance entrepreneurial activity in Colombia have been effective.

Public policy in Colombia focused on supporting micro, small and medium enterprises (MSME's) prior to the 2000's. The enforcement of Law 1014 (2006, Colombian Congress) and of subsequent policies released by the Colombian National Council for Economic and Social Policy-National Planning Department, *CONPES-DNP* (2004; 2007 and 2008) were decisive to raise national awareness of entrepreneurial topics. Such transition was the result of distinguishing between new businesses and MSME's. The former refers to newly created companies which grow up to a subsequent stage during a specific period of time; the latter includes companies that were created in the past and which might continue to be an MSME in the long term.

It is important to note, however, that until 2011 national policies were not differentiated; no direction was given in terms of the type of new businesses that should be supported. Instead, emphasis was given to creating businesses that could transform individuals into self-generators and hence reduce unemployment rates. Such businesses did not create multiple jobs and hence had a limited scope; furthermore, their growth potential was minimal and hence innovation and wealth generation were not necessarily enhanced.

Since 2011, the situation has changed as the Government is aware that the effects of starting a business go beyond solely generating self-employment for entrepreneurs. Specific programmes launched by the Colombian Congress (2011) and INNPULSA (http://www.innpulsacolombia.com/) have been implemented to support the creation of businesses with growth potential in the long term and therefore generate wealth. These programs provide more funding than previous alternatives (e.g. USD 50,000 in average versus USD 5,000 formerly) and focus on new businesses that offer differentiated products and/or services and belong to non-traditional sectors. This governmental strategy has therefore contributed positively to enhance entrepreneurial activity in cities that have properly embraced it.

- *Access to novel research and technologies available to established companies (E02).*

More access of new and in-growth businesses to new research and technologies available to established companies is strongly negatively correlated with entrepreneurial activity. At first instance, this result would not be anticipated; entrepreneurs should be motivated to start new businesses as barriers to knowledge are reduced.

Several reasons justify this result. First, newly created businesses in Colombia mostly belong to traditional industries which do not require or benefit from cutting-edge research and technologies (Gómez-Núñez and Negrete-Escobar, 2013).

Second, new businesses do not require such intangibles at early stages of their development unless their value proposition is based on science and technology (S&T) activities. At early stages, new businesses focus is on supplying market needs and to start trading; new technologies can be implemented at a subsequent stage (Hölzl, 2009; Gómez-Núñez and Negrete-Escobar, 2013).

Third, even if the activity of new businesses involved such resources, entry barriers in terms of intangibles (e.g. know-how and goodwill developed over the years by established businesses) could hinder new players from competing against established companies. (Cummings and Bing-Sheng, 2003). Such barriers might have a negative effect on competition and on the dynamics of the market, and might result in high prices and/or low quality and innovation. The Structuralism School argues that the effectiveness of potential competition depends on determinants of conditions of entry such as economies of scale, technological advantages and absolute cost advantages, among others. Entry barriers have basically a structural foundation, although the entry can often also be influenced by behaviour of the incumbents (Bain, 1956; Klapper et al., 2004; Santarelly and Vivarelli, 2007).

Finally, new businesses face financial entry barriers (e.g. patent royalties and implementation of new technologies) in contrast with established companies, which can deploy financial resources available. Hence the competitive arena at the industry level must be taken into account to assess the feasibility of new entrants (Porter, 1980).

Given the barriers explained above, it makes sense then for new businesses to engage in co-operation activities with larger (anchor) companies by supplying them with specific components and services within their value chain (OECD, 2005). An example of this strategy is that supported by the Inter-American Development Bank (IDB, 2013) and implemented by the National Association of Large Companies (ANDI) in Colombia; the objective is to create new businesses and support existing microenterprises that involve low-income segments which add value to anchor firms. Hence results explained before can be interpreted from a different perspective: cities in which new and in-growth businesses have less access to research and technologies available to established companies experience an increase in new business creation in Colombia.

183

- *Initiatives specifically designed to assist new high growth potential business-es (Q01).*

High growth potential businesses are dynamic, grow at least by 20% annually during 3 to 5 years and employ at least 10 people (Gilbert et al., 2006). Such growth is based on their competitive advantage within the market they operate in (Porter, 1980). High growth potential is not necessarily related with a specific industry; however it is usually related with S&T activities (Hölzl, 2009); hence it makes sense to interpret results under that lens. A moderate positive correlation shows that government efforts through specific initiatives to assist high growth businesses *(Q01)* have some degree of association and hence moderate impact on entrepreneurial activity in the Colombian cities considered in this study. Some reasons gathered from an expert's interview (Velasco, 2014) that might explain such results are presented below.

By 2013 investment in R&D and S&T activities is 0.724% of the GDP; it is mostly provided by the public sector (Colombian National Observatory of Science and Technology-*OCYT*, 2013). Investment in S&T is still incipient in the private sector as the domestic market is not sophisticated and hence highly developed products are not demanded; resources are limited and distributed through various sectors which results in lack of focus. This might be a reason for creating businesses more related with traditional activities than those related with S&T activities and hence the moderate impact of government initiatives in that direction.

Law 1286 (2009, Colombian Congress) was launched by the Government to strengthen the National System of Science, Technology and Innovation. It promotes the creation of incubators, technology parks and high growth firms based on S&T activities. However, its implementation is still ongoing; additionally, lack of bridge institutions that assist businesses in knowledge transfer activities might hinder the creation of high growth businesses. This might also explain moderate correlation results. It must be said however, that specific initiatives such as the creation of INNPULSA through Law 1450 (Colombian Congress, 2011) and regional committees that involve universities, businesses and the government are in place and support, among others, S&T activities (Colombian National Council for Economic and Social Policy-National Planning Department, 2008).

- *Specialist team that assists new businesses with high growth potential (Q03).*

Compared with public initiatives, correlation between the specialist team and entrepreneurial activity *(Q03)* is strong. This makes sense, as entrepreneurs actually interact with the specialist team at the operational level. Knowledge and skills of the team hence are relevant to enhance the creation of new businesses with high growth potential. An expert's interview (Velasco, 2014) was useful to shed light on these results, as explained below.

In general experts from public offices such as: The Ministry of Industry and Commerce, National Learning Service Agency *(SENA)*, *Bogota Connect*, *Ruta N*, *INNPULSA* and *TECNOVA* are well-educated and experienced professionals. This has been a common feature of President Santos's administration since 2010. A growing number of professionals are attaining master and doctoral degrees abroad, which equips them with technical skills required to adequately assist high growth firms. It is common to find experts who have previously worked in the private sector and have then migrated to the public sector to work as mentors for entrepreneurs; this is useful to understand the business operation context and hence to make sensible suggestions to entrepreneurs.

Regarding soft skills, experts are visionary and charismatic. Knowledge is transferred through focussed services and dissemination activities across the regions; this increases access of entrepreneurs to instruments and tools. Senior officers are directly involved in such activities and can be contacted through email; the aim is to reduce bureaucracy and also to increase access.

Finally, the stimulation of entrepreneurial competences among the general public as a result of the implementation of Law 1014 (Colombian Congress, 2006) has enhanced the interaction between entrepreneurs and expert teams. This might further justify the strong positive association between more qualified teams of experts and entrepreneurial activity at a city level.

- *Public policies that prioritise the creation of high growth businesses (Q05).*

Public policies that prioritise the creation of high growth businesses have a negatively moderate association with entrepreneurial activity. This result contrasts with that presented for aspect *(Q01)*; initiatives that assist new high growth potential businesses still may have a moderate effect on entrepreneurial activity whereas prioritising that type of businesses is a different strategy.

Interpretation of this result requires understanding S&T investment in Colombia, as presented previously within aspect *(Q01)*. Additionally, even though Colombia has intensified support to ST&I, the country still lags behind in the knowledge economy. In overall terms, investment in ST&I and R&D is low, with large gaps among regions and cities. Colombia ranks below other Latin American countries in investment in ST&I activities, and particularly in R&D (Caballero, 2011). Lack of research that provides knowledge inputs to generate impact on the productivity and weak innovation patterns and outputs compared to countries of similar size and level of income might also explain the prevalence of a traditional economy in which policies that prioritize the creation of high growth businesses do not have a positive effect on entrepreneurial activity (Gregson and Velasco, 2011).

Additional reasons include the fact that policies *per se* are not sufficient to create high growth businesses; they demand substantial financial resources due to the required investment. As explained before, more accessible funding alternatives are needed to create new businesses; the high risk nature of new high growth businesses further reduces their chances of obtaining funds and hence may reduce the effect of public policies (Audretsch and Lehman, 2004; Gómez-Núñez and Negrete-Escobar, 2013).

- *Ranking, processes and cost of starting a new business.*

Among significant negative correlations with entrepreneurial activity, processes have the strongest association, followed by the overall ranking of starting a new business. Entrepreneurial activity increases as fewer processes are required to start a business. Likewise, entrepreneurial activity increases as a specific city improves its position in the ranking (i.e. decreases in value). In contrast, the correlation between cost of starting a new business and entrepreneurial activity is positive and moderate. Interpretation of results is based on the Doing Business Report for Colombia (World Bank, 2013).

Prior to analysing results, it is important to explain that according to the Doing Business study, a new business is started when a small or medium enterprise (SME) is legally established. Such businesses have already been created and passed through various stages of the entrepreneurship process. Individuals surveyed through the APS from the GEM study may or may not have formally established their businesses; once a business is trading it is considered to be created under the GEM perspective (Reynolds et al., 2005). Additionally, microbusinesses constitute the majority of businesses trading in Colombia (Birch, 1979; GEM-Colombia, 2006). Therefore for interpretation purposes, aspects related with the Doing Business Study will be related with the formal establishment of SME's whereas those from the GEM Study will be related with creation of businesses in general.

Regarding the processes required to formalise an SME, cities with best practices were those in which 8 out of 9 processes are completed within 1 day. Such cities have in place business service centres (*CAE's*) in local offices of chambers of commerce to facilitate processes required to formally establish SME's. Other reasons for reduction in processes are information systems that integrate city halls, chambers of commerce and other public agencies related with formally establishing SME's; virtual completion and automatic processes resulting from the implementation of Process Simplification Decree 19 (Colombian Congress, 2012) and Law 1429 for formalising and generating jobs (Colombian Congress, 2010).

The moderate positive correlation between ranking and entrepreneurial activity resulted from the effect of other aspects such as cost and time, which did not exhibit a significant correlation with entrepreneurial activity.

An interesting result is that of correlation between cost and entrepreneurial activity. As costs related with formally establishing SME's increase (decrease), entrepreneurial activity also increases (decreases). This occurs because APS mostly captures the creation of either formal or informal businesses which are mostly microbusinesses; hence as it is more expensive to formalise SME's, entrepreneurs might be motivated to start up microbusinesses that provide services and products to SME's. This is related to the point made earlier for aspect *E02*. This reflects internal co-operation dynamics of the private sector.

Aspects Associated with Change in Non-Entrepreneurial Engagement

Changes in 5 NES aspects were significantly associated with changes in non-entrepreneurial engagement: *risk capital offer* (A05), *policies to assist new and established companies* (B02), *time required by new businesses to obtain licenses and permits* (B04), *training programmes to create new businesses and enhance the growth of established ones* (D06) and *specialist team*(Q03) *that assists new and existing businesses with high development potential*. Regarding the Doing Business report, 2 aspects were found to be significantly associated with change in entrepreneurial activity: *processes* and *time required to start up a business*. See Table 2.

Common aspects were found to be significantly correlated with entrepreneurial activity and non-entrepreneurial engagement, namely *B02*, *Q03* and *PROC*. As expected, correlation signs are opposite due to the definitions of CEA_{1210} and NEE_{1210} (see bold aspects in Table 2). Therefore correlations between these aspects and non-entrepreneurial engagement should be interpreted in the opposite direction. The remainder of this section focuses on interpretation of results related with other aspects presented in Table 2.

- *Risk capital offer (A05).*

An improvement in the offer of funding alternatives from risk capital alternatives (e.g. investor angels and venture capital funds) does not reduce non-entrepreneurial engagement. Similar to the situation explained for *(A02)*, an improved offer does not necessarily result in increased access. Some reasons might explain these results, as presented below.

First, it is important to note that such alternatives are still limited in Colombia: Bavaria Investment Angel Network and between 11 and 14 venture capital funds which include 3 national funds. This makes it difficult to fulfil the requirements to access them. Investor angels expect new businesses to sell innovative products/ services and to grow at a fast pace (Audretsch and Lehman, 2004; Gitonga-Imaita, 2013). This requires that funding for initial stages such as knowledge transfer, business valuation and in some cases designing and testing prototypes. Funds for these activities are limited in Colombia.

Second, investor angels are not willing to invest in microenterprises which constitute the majority of entrepreneurial engagement (Fracica-Naranjo et al., 2011; Gómez-Núñez and Negrete-Escobar, 2013). This might discourage potential entrepreneurs from starting a business and hence increase non-entrepreneurial engagement.

Therefore an issue to be tackled is the lack of access that entrepreneurs face when looking for funding via risk capital alternatives.

- *Time required by new businesses to obtain licenses and permits (B04, TIME).*

Non-entrepreneurial engagement decreases when the time required to create a business is closer to 1 week according to NES results. Likewise, non-entrepreneurial engagement increases when more time is required to formally establish an SME according to the Doing Business Study. Hence results are similar for both microbusinesses and SME's. Hence regardless if businesses are formally established or not, less time required motivates individuals to create new businesses. These results are somewhat related with the reduction in processes to formally establish companies explained before (*processes*).

- *Training programmes to create new businesses and enhance the growth of established ones* (D06).

More adequate and high quality professional and lifelong learning programmes do not necessarily decrease non-entrepreneurial engagement. In order to understand this result, it is important to distinguish among the competences associated with business creation, as follows.

Competences related with "being" an entrepreneur (e.g. having the will to start up a company, risk-taking attitude and perseverance) have the strongest impact in starting a business and are developed during early childhood and adolescence (Krueger and Brazeal, 1994; Douglas and Shepard, 2002; Markowska, 2011).

Technical competences related with the actual design of a product/service can be learned through training programmes or occupation. Managerial competences required to identify business ideas and deliver a product or service are usually acquired through education programmes. These two types of competences have the lowest impact on business creation compared with those related with "being" an entrepreneur (Lyngdoh, 2005; Xheneti, 2006).

Hence, training individuals in technical and managerial competences does not guarantee a decrease in non-entrepreneurial engagement. It is important to note, however, that training programmes are useful to identify and potentiate competences related with "being" an entrepreneur.

CONCLUSION AND IMPLICATIONS

In general, context conditions in Colombia are adequate to start a business. This was confirmed through high rates of entrepreneurial activity, low rates of non-entrepreneurial engagement, public policies that enhance business creation and reduced processes required to formally establish an SME. It should be noted, however, that even though conditions are being created, still substantial advance needs to be made for them to be ideal. Specifically, further advance needs to be made in terms of access to financial resources, access to technology that is relevant for microbusinesses, innovation policies and education in entrepreneurship. In particular, entrepreneurial ecosystems are mostly conceived to enhance traditional entrepreneurial activities and not those related with the creation of high growth businesses; this needs to be further enhanced.

Taking advantage of the opportunities and tackling the challenges presented in this section should contribute to enhance entrepreneurial activity and reduce non-entrepreneurial engagement. It is expected that useful insight is provided in terms of further research opportunities and the design of initiatives related with entrepreneurial activity in Colombia and other Latin American countries with similar conditions.

From an academic perspective, results show that results from the GEM database (i.e. entrepreneurial activity and non-entrepreneurial engagement) can be partly interpreted through the use of a different but complementary source: the Doing Business dataset. From a practitioner's point of view, results show that foreign and local entrepreneurs could benefit from reduced processes, time and cost required to formally establish an SME in Colombia as a result of modernization and anti-bureaucracy legislation. In cities where the cost of formally establishing an SME is more expensive, there should be opportunities to start-up innovative micro-businesses that are involved in the value chain of larger companies. This should be a two-way initiative in which entrepreneurs start new micro-businesses and large companies are motivated through governmental policies to buy products/services from newly created microbusinesses.

Regarding access to financial resources, formal financial institutions need to design a portfolio of funding alternatives that are more accessible to new businesses in terms of requirements. It is crucial that such institutions understand the different stages and hence the financial needs of new businesses to offer customised products to them. A similar standpoint needs to be adopted by investor angels and venture capital funds in terms of their expectations from new businesses at early stages; new businesses in Colombia might face similar challenges to those in other Latin American countries hence supporting them provides an opportunity to learn from their reality and performance and apply such knowledge to similar contexts. Further promotion of accessible funding sources at early stages of entrepreneurial activity in Colombia is also required. The Government should design policies and mechanisms to motivate risk capital investment in early stages through tax benefits or joint investment in which investors benefit from tax savings and/or profits. These initiatives should increase the chances of new businesses receiving funds.

It is important to highlight the effort made by the Colombian government in terms of investing in S&T activities through specific policies. This provides adequate context conditions for innovative start-ups. However, further advance is still required for the implementation of differentiated public policies that enhance the creation of innovative businesses through the articulation of R&D processes with the creation of new businesses. A major issue that new high growth potential businesses face for differentiated policies to be effective is lack of financial resources. Financial institutions and government agencies should jointly define strategies that are feasible in terms of being implemented from a policy and funding perspective. Additionally, a long term perspective needs to be adopted by both public and private sectors for this strategy to be permanent and for start-ups to be sustainable, especially as they face strong competition from foreign businesses as a result of Foreign Trade Agreements. Design and dissemination of new funding alternatives for high growth businesses are required accordingly. It is expected, however, that investment opportunities in specific industries are more evident at present; this should attract capital from foreign and local investors, provided the shift in expectations occurs, as explained above.

In terms of access to technology that is available to established companies, a challenge is to develop new technologies according to the possibilities of small businesses possibilities. As a result, they should be able to compete in specific niches and play an active role within the value chain of larger companies, which should also enhance access to funding. This requires enhancing the interaction between researchers in academic institutions and entrepreneurs to facilitate knowledge transfer; both parties benefit from such interaction as the former can invest in business opportunities at early stages and the latter save time and financial resources because of learning curve effects and savings from research expenses that are not affordable otherwise. This contrasts with existing public policies that mostly strengthen existing/large companies.

Finally, progress has been made since 2006 in terms of the human capital involved in entrepreneurial activity in Colombia. The entrepreneurial ecosystem involves highly qualified individuals that should be able to interact with entrepreneurs and investors. Yet developing an entrepreneurship culture is an ongoing topic in Colombia. Still more effort is required to develop an adequate platform that enhances not only technical and managerial entrepreneurial skills but most importantly those related with "being" an entrepreneur; a transversal strategy such as implementing initiatives to identify potential entrepreneurs since early childhood and continuing to develop their skills during adolescent and early adulthood would positively contribute towards cultivating an entrepreneurship culture in Colombia; this requires articulating initiatives from schools and higher education institutions.

REFERENCES

Acs, Z. (1996). Small Firms and Economic Growth. In Z. J. Acs, B. Carlsson, & R. Thurik (Eds.), *Small Business in the Modern Economy* (pp. 1–62). Oxford, UK: Blackwell Publishers.

Acs, Z., & Amorós, J. (2008). Entrepreneurship and competitiveness dynamics in Latin America. *Small Business Economics*, *31*(3), 305–322. doi:10.1007/s11187-008-9133-y

Acs, Z., & Szerb, L. (2007). Entrepreneurship, Economic Growth and Public Policy. *Small Business Economics*, *28*(2-3), 109–122. doi:10.1007/s11187-006-9012-3

Amorós, E., Bosma, N., & GERA. (2014). *Global Entrepreneurship Monitor 2013 Global Report*. Chile: GERA.

Asghar, A. J., Khaled, N., Seyed-Mohammad, S. K., & Amin-Reza, K. (2011). The Relationship between Government Policy and the Growth of Entrepreneurship in the Micro, Small & Medium Enterprises of India. J. *Technology of Managament & Innovation*, *6*(1), 66–76. doi:10.4067/S0718-27242011000100007

Audretsch, D., Falck, O., Feldman, M., & Heblich, S. (2012). Local Entrepreneurship in Context. *Regional Studies*, *46*(3), 379–389. doi:10.1080/00343404.2010.490209

Audretsch, D., & Keilbach, M. (2007). The Theory of Knowledge Spillover. *Entrepreneurship Journal of Management Studies*, *44*(7), 1242–1253. doi:10.1111/j.1467-6486.2007.00722.x

Audretsch, D., & Lehman, E. (2004). Financing High-Tech Growth: The Role of Banks and Venture Capitalists. *Schmalenbach Business Review, 56*, 340–357.

Audretsch, D., & Thurik, R. (2001). *Linking Entrepreneurship to Growth*. Paris: OECD, Directorate for Science, Technology and Industry Working Papers.

Bain, J. S. (1956). *Barriers to new competition*. Boston: Harvard University Press. doi:10.4159/harvard.9780674188037

Baumol, W. J. (2004). Four Sources of Innovation and Stimulation of Growth in the Dutch Economy. *The Economist, 152*(3), 321-351.

Birch, D. (1979). The Job Generation Process. M.I.T. Program on Neighborhood and Regional Change. Cambridge.

Bosma, N., Coduras, A., Litovsky, Y., & Seaman, J. (2012). *GEM Manual. Version 2012-9: May*. GEM.

Bosma, N., & Levie, J. Global Entrepreneurship Research Association-GERA. (2010). *Global Entrepreneurship Monitor 2009 Global report*. London: GEM.

Brockhoff, K. (1994). R&D Project Termination Decisions by Discriminant Analysis-An International Comparison. *IEEE Transactions on Engineering Management, 41*(3), 245–254. doi:10.1109/17.310139

Caballero, A. (2011). *Colombia -Science, Technology and Innovation: P117590-Implementation Status Results Report: Sequence 02*. Washington, DC: World Bank. Retrieved from http://documents.worldbank.org/curated/en/2011/05/14132146/colombia-science-technology-innovation-p117590-implementation-status-results-report-sequence-02

Capelleras, J. L., & Greene, F. J. (2008). The determinants and growth implications of venture creation speed. *Entrepreneurship and Regional Development, 20*(4), 311–337. doi:10.1080/08985620701855683

Capelleras Segura, J. L., & Kantis, H. D. (2009). *Nuevas empresas en América Latina: factores que favorecen su rápido crecimiento*. Barcelona: Universitat Autònoma de Barcelona, Servei de Publicacions.

Carree, M., & Thurik, R. (2002). The Impact of Entrepreneurship on Economic Growth. In *International Handbook of Entrepreneurship Research*. Boston: Kluwer Academic Publishers.

Colombian Congress. (2006). *Ley 1014* [Law 1014]. Retrieved from http://www.mineducacion.gov.co/1621/articles-94653_archivo_pdf.pdf

Colombian Congress. (2009). *Ley 1286* [Law 1286]. Retrieved from https://pwh. dnp.gov.co/LinkClick.aspx?fileticket=aN21z7FHE1o%3D&tabid=426

Colombian Congress. (2010). *Ley 1429* [Law 1429]. Retrieved from http://www. alcaldiabogota.gov.co/sisjur/normas/Norma1.jsp?i=41060

Colombian Congress. (2011). *Informe al Congreso* [Report to the Congress]. Retrieved from http://wsp.presidencia.gov.co/Publicaciones/Documents/Informe-Presidente2011.pdf

Colombian Congress. (2011). *Ley 1450* [Law 1450]. Retrieved from http://www. alcaldiabogota.gov.co/sisjur/normas/Norma1.jsp?i=43101

Colombian Congress. (2012). *Decreto 19* [Decree 19]. Retrieved from http://www. alcaldiabogota.gov.co/sisjur/normas/Norma1.jsp?i=45322

Colombian National Council for Economic and Social Policy- National Planning Department. (2004). *Documento CONPES 3280* [Document CONPES 3280]. Retrieved from http://www.sinic.gov.co/SINIC/CuentaSatelite/documentos/200981814348574. pdf

Colombian National Council for Economic and Social Policy- National Planning Department. (2007). *Documento CONPES 3484* [Document CONPES 3484]. http:// www.huila.gov.co/documentos/C/CONPES3484de2007.pdf

Colombian National Council for Economic and Social Policy- National Planning Department. (2008). *Documento CONPES 3527* [Document CONPES 3527]. Retrieved from http://wsp.presidencia.gov.co/sncei/politica/Documents/Conpes-3527-23jun2008.pdf

Colombian National Observatory of Science and Technology. (2013). *Indicadores Ciencia y Tecnologia* [Science and Technology Indicators]. Retrieved from http:// ocyt.org.co/Portals/0/Documentos/COLOMBIA_2013.pdf

Colombo, M., & Grilli, L. (2007). Funding Gaps? Access to Bank Loans by High-Tech Start-Ups. *Small Business Economics*, 29(1-2), 25–46. doi:10.1007/s11187-005-4067-0

Covin, J. G., & Slevin, D. P. (1989). Strategic management of small firms in hostile and benign environments. *Strategic Management Journal*, 10(1), 75–87. doi:10.1002/ smj.4250100107

Cummings, J., & Teng, B. S. (2003). Transferring R&D knowledge: The key factors affecting knowledge transfer success. *Journal of Engineering and Technology Management*, 20(1-2), 39–68. doi:10.1016/S0923-4748(03)00004-3

Davidsson, P. (1995). Culture, structure and regional levels of entrepreneurship. *Entrepreneurship and Regional Development, 7*(1), 41–62. doi:10.1080/08985629500000003

Douglas, E., & Shepard, D. (2002). Self-employment as a career choice: Attitudes, entrepreneurial intentions, and utility maximization. *Entrepreneurship Theory and Practice, 26*, 81–90.

Duval-Couetil, N. (2013). Assessing the Impact of Entrepreneurship Education Programs: Challenges and Approaches. *Journal of Small Business Management, 51*(3), 394–409. doi:10.1111/jsbm.12024

European Commision (2004). *Action Plan: The European Agenda for Entrepreneurship, Communication from the Commission to the Council, the European Parliament, the European Economic and Social Committee and the Committee of the Regions, COM (04) 70.* Brussels: EC.

Fracica-Naranjo, G., Matíz, F., & Hernández, G. (2011). Capital semilla para la financiación de start ups con alto potencial de crecimiento en Colombia [Seed capital to finance high growth potential start-ups in Colombia]. *Rev. esc.adm.neg., 71*, 126-147.

Freytag, A., & Thurik, R. (2007). Entrepreneurship and its determinants in a cross-country setting. *Journal of Evolutionary Economics, 17*(2), 117–131. doi:10.1007/s00191-006-0044-2

Fritsch, M. (2008). How does new business formation affect regional development? Introduction to the special issue. *Small Business Economics, 30*(1), 1–14. doi:10.1007/s11187-007-9057-y

Fritsch, M., & Mueller, P. (2008). The effect of new business formation on regional development over time: The case of Germany. *Small Business Economics, 30*(1), 15–29. doi:10.1007/s11187-007-9067-9

GEM-Colombia. (2006). GEM Colombia 2006. Reporte de Resultados [GEM Colombia 2006. Results Report]. Universidad Icesi, Universidad del Norte, Universidad de los Andes, Pontificia Universidad Javeriana Cali. Colombia: GEM.

GEM-Colombia. (2011). Reporte GEM Colombia 2011 [GEM Colombia 2011 Report]. Universidad del Norte, Universidad Icesi, Universidad de los Andes, Pontificia Universidad Javeriana Cali. Colombia: Editorial Universidad del Norte.

GEM-Colombia. (2013). Global Entrepreneurship Monitor Colombia 2012. Universidad de los Andes, Universidad Icesi, Universidad del Norte, Pontificia Universidad Javeriana Cali. Colombia: Ediciones Uniandes.

GEM-Colombia. (2014). Dinámica Empresarial Colombiana [Colombian Business Dynamics]. Universidad Icesi, Universidad del Norte, Universidad de los Andes, Pontificia Universidad Javeriana Cali. Colombia: GEM-Colombia.

Gilbert, B., McDougall, P., & Audretsch, D. (2006). New Venture Growth: A Review and Extension. *Journal of Management, 32*(6), 926–950. doi:10.1177/0149206306293860

Gitonga-Imaita, I. (2013). Financial resources as a factor influencing adoption of innovations along mango value chains in Meru County, Kenya. *European Scientific Journal,* (1), 49-56.

Gómez-Núñez, L., & Negrete-Escobar, I. (2013). GEM Colombia 2012: Empresas con Alto Potencial de Crecimiento [GEM Colombia 2012: High growth potential businesses]. Universidad del Norte y Fundación Bavaria, Colombia: Ediciones Uninorte.

Gregson, G., & Velasco, D. (2011) *Colombia's National System of Innovation: A Multi-theoretical Assessment of Structure, Policy and Performance.* Edinburgh Business School. Available at www.unid-sea.net

Grilo, I., & Thurik, R. (2008). Determinants of entrepreneurial engagement levels in Europe and the US. *Industrial and Corporate Change, 17*(6), 1113–1145. doi:10.1093/icc/dtn044

Ho, Y., & Wong, P. (2007). Financing, Regulatory Costs and Entrepreneurial Propensity. *Small Business Economics, 28*(2-3), 187–204. doi:10.1007/s11187-006-9015-0

Hölzl, W. (2009). Is the R&D behavior of fast-growing SMEs different? Evidence from CIS III data for 16 countries. *Small Business Economics, 33*(1), 59–75. doi:10.1007/s11187-009-9182-x

Isenberg, D. (2010). The Big Idea: How to start an Entrepreneurial Revolution. *Harvard Business Review, 88*(6), 41–50.

Isenberg, D. (2011). The entrepreneurship ecosystem strategy as a new paradigm for economy policy: principles for cultivating entrepreneurship. Babson Entrepreneurship Ecosystem Project, Babson College.

Jun Bae, T., Qian, S., Miao, C., & Fiet, J.O. (2014). The Relationship between Entrepreneurship Education and Entrepreneurial Intentions: A Meta-Analytic Review. *Entrepreneurship Theory and Practice,* (March), 217-254.

Karlsson, C., Friis, C., & Paulsson, T. (2004). *Relating entrepreneurship to economic growth.* Retrieved from http://www.infra.kth.se/cesis/documents/WP13.pdf

Klapper, L., Amit, R., & Guillén, M. (2010). Entrepreneurship and Firm Formation across Countries. In International Differences in Entrepreneurship. Chicago: University of Chicago Press. doi:10.7208/chicago/9780226473109.003.0005

Klapper, L., Laeven, L., & Rajan, R. (2004*). Barriers to Entrepreneurship.* Working Paper. World Bank.

Krueger, N., & Brazeal, D. (1994). Entrepreneurial potential and potential entrepreneurs. *Entrepreneurship: Theory and Practice, 18*(3), 91–104.

Lyngdoh, B. (2005). Skills for Work in the Future: A Youth Perspective. *Quarterly Review of Comparative Education, 35*(3), 311–316.

Malecki, E. (1994). Entrepreneurship in regional and local development International. *Regional Science Rewies, 16*(1-2), 119–153.

Markowska, M. (2011). *Entrepreneurial Competence Development: Triggers, Processes & Consequences.* (Doctoral dissertation). Jönköping: Jönköping International Business School.

Naudé, W., Gries, T., Wood, E., & Meintjies, A. (2008). Regional determinants of entrepreneurial start-ups in a developing country. *Entrepreneurship & Regional Development: An International Journal, 20*(2), 111–124. doi:10.1080/08985620701631498

O'Connor, A. (2013). A conceptual framework for entrepreneurship education policy: Meeting government and economic purposes. *Journal of Business Venturing, 28*(4), 546–563. doi:10.1016/j.jbusvent.2012.07.003

OECD. (2003). *Entrepreneurship and local economic development: Programme and policy recommendations.* Paris: OECD.

OECD. (2005). *Building Competitive Regions. Strategies and Governance.* Paris: Organisation for Economic Cooperation and Development.

OECD. (2009). *OECD Rural Policy Reviews: Spain.* Paris: OECD.

OECD & LEED. (2014). *Entrepreneurial Ecosystems and Growth Oriented Entrepreneurship.* The Hague, Netherlands.

Organisation for Economic Co-operation and Development (OECD). (1998). *Fostering Entrepreneurship*. OECD.

Paukert, M., Niederée, C., & Hemmje, M. (2004). *Adapting Organizational Knowledge Management Cultures to the Knowledge Life Cycle in Innovation Processes. Working-paper, Fraunhofer Institut für Integrierte Publikations- und Informationssysteme*. Darmstadt, Germany: IPSI.

Porter, M. (1980). *Competitive Strategy*. Free Press.

Reynolds, P., Bosma, N., Auio, E., Hunt, S., de Bono, N., Servais, I., & Chin, N. et al. (2005). Global Entrepreneurship Monitor: Data Collection Design and Implementation 1998–2003. *Small Business Economics*, *24*(3), 205–231. doi:10.1007/s11187-005-1980-1

Reynolds, P. D., Storey, D. J., & Westhead, P. (1994). Cross-national comparisons of the variation in new firm formation rates. *Regional Studies*, *28*(4), 443–456. doi:10.1080/00343409412331348386

Ribeiro-Soriano, D., & Galindo-Martín, M. A. (2012). Government policies to support entrepreneurship. *Entrepreneurship & Regional Development*, *24*(9–10), 861–864. doi:10.1080/08985626.2012.742322

Sánchez, J. (2013). The Impact of an Entrepreneurship Education Program on Entrepreneurial Competencies and Intention. *Journal of Small Business Management*, *51*(3), 447–465. doi:10.1111/jsbm.12025

Sanchez-Barrios, L. J., Giraldo-Oliveros, M., Khalik, M. A., & Manjarres, R. (in press). Services for the underserved: Unintended well-being. *Service Industries Journal*.

Santarelli, E., & Vivarelli, M. (2007). Entrepreneurship and the process of firms' entry, survival and growth. *Industrial and Corporate Change*, *16*(3), 455–488. doi:10.1093/icc/dtm010

Solo, T. M., & Manroth, A. (2006). *Access to financial services in Colombia: the "unbanked" in Bogota*. Policy Research working paper. The World Bank.

Terjesen, S., & Amorós, J. E. (2010). Female Entrepreneurship in Latin America and the Caribbean: Characteristics, Drivers and Relationship to Economic Development. *European Journal of Development Research*, *22*(3), 313–330. doi:10.1057/ejdr.2010.13

Thurik, R., & Wennekers, S. (2001). *A Note on Entrepreneurship, Small Business and Economic Growth*. Rotterdam: Erasmus Research Institute of Management Report Series.

Von Graevenitza, G., Harhoffa, D., & Weberb, R. (2010). The effects of entrepreneurship education. *Journal of Economic Behavior & Organization, 76*(1), 90–112. doi:10.1016/j.jebo.2010.02.015

Wennekers, S., & Thurik, R. (1999). Linking entrepreneurship and economic Growth. *Small Business Economics, 13*(1), 27–55. doi:10.1023/A:1008063200484

Wennkers, S., Van Stel, A., & Carree, M. (2010). *The relationship between entrepreneurship and economic development: is it U-shaped?* EIM Research Reports. The Netherlands: SCALES-initiative.

World Bank. (2004). *Doing Business in 2004: Understanding Regulation*. Washington, DC: World Bank and Oxford University Press.

World Bank. (2010). *Doing Business en Colombia 2010*. Washington, DC: World Bank Group.

World Bank. (2013a). *Doing Business en Colombia 2013: Regulaciones inteligentes para las pequeñas y medianas empresas*. Washington, DC: World Bank Group.

World Bank. (2013b). *Doing Business 2014: Understanding Regulation for Small and Medium Sizes Enterprises*. Washington, DC: International Bank for Reconstruction and Development/The World Bank.

World Bank. (2014). Retrieved from http://www.doingbusiness.org/about-us

World Economic Forum. (2014). *The Global Competitiveness Report 2013–2014*. Geneva: WEF.

Xheneti, M. (2006). Youth entrepreneurship in south east Europe: some policy recommendations. In J. Potter & A. Proto (Eds.), *Promoting Entrepreneurship in South East Europe, policies and tools*. Paris: OECD.

Chapter 10

Public–Private–Academic Cooperation as a Trust Building Mechanism:
The Case of Guatemala

Nicholas Virzi
Escuela de Gobierno, Guatemala

Juan Portillo
Universidad Rafael Landivar, Guatemala

Mariela Aguirre
Universidad Rafael Landivar, Guatemala

ABSTRACT

The chapter will be a case study from an Ordoliberal perspective of the conception, implementation and policy output of the newly created Private Council of Competitiveness (PCC) in Guatemala, a country wracked by mistrust of the public sector by the private sector. The PCC was founded as a private sector initiative, in conjunction with academia, to work with the government to spawn new efforts aimed at augmenting Guatemala's national competitiveness, by fomenting innovation, entrepreneurship and closer ties between academia and the public and private sectors. The chapter utilizes first hand interviews with the members of the PCC and key public sector players, academics, and other top representatives from the private sector to show how working together built the trust necessary to make the PCC a successful working body with the potential to produce important initiatives in matters of competitiveness, innovation and entrepreneurship.

DOI: 10.4018/978-1-4666-8820-9.ch010

THEORETICAL FRAMEWORK

Ordoliberalism

The present chapter takes an Ordoliberal approach to Public-Private Partnerships. Ordoliberalism looks to set up an ordered capitalist system that preserves the competition mechanism to safeguard political and economic liberty and ensure properly functioning markets work to the public good. In the Ordoliberal perspective, economic liberty leads to greater efficiency and productivity, but care should be taken so as market forces are not left to operate outside the reasonable norms and legal and regulatory framework of the state (Reyes, 2010).

Given its integral approach to political and economic stability and growth, Ordoliberalism should be considered as an important developmental alternative in the Third World, especially for countries such as Guatemala, where the full benefits of market institutions and forces do not reach in real time the majority of the population which is poor and marginalized. In Guatemala, state action is rationally suspect on account of poor performance due to public sector corruption, cronyism and clientelism (Virzi & Belteton, 2009 A). This situation leaves the country without the sufficient means to overcome collective action problems and suboptimal levels of public goods and infrastructure, which many argue is the proper purview of state action (Hardin, 1989). A more realistic approach to development would take into account the collective action problems that development actors face in the Third World (Booth, 2012).

An Ordoliberal approach takes attempts to balance the desire for liberty and market forces with the need for reasonable state action deemed necessary for the proper functioning of market forces. The founding principles of an Ordoliberal Social Market Economy (SME) are the primacy of the human person, general liberty, and the general welfare, for which it is deemed that a strong state is needed (Hoegen, 1999). The term SME was invented to refer to this new order that aspired to integrate and lead the main actors in society towards cooperation in benefit of the common good. In this regard, economic freedoms are to be fomented when they serve to promote competition (Somma, 2013). An Ordoliberal model posits as much market economics as possible, but as much state as necessary, to achieve a harmonious model of economic and social progress, marked by political stability (Christian Democratic Union [CDU], 2010).

Ordoliberalism was made famous by Ludwig Erhard, the Minister of Economics during the phase of Germany's economic miracle following World War II, when Germany was under American military occupation. To rebuild the destroyed German economy, Erhard oversaw the transition from a totalitarian demand economy to a more liberal, market economy oriented toward national development. Social inclusion safeguards and safety nets were included to blunt the appeal of communist, populist political and economic appeal. The main thrust was for the state to take an active role in benefit of market forces. In the Ordoliberal framework of a social market economy the state and the market work together toward a common goal (Hoegen, 1999). An important principle for the Ordoliberal SME is subsidiarity, whereby the government should not do what the private sector can well do, such as the production of goods and services (Hoegen).

Today, Germany stands as a bulwark and a standard bearer of a successful market economy, built upon the principles of free markets, republican democracy, and vigorous state action oriented towards national economic development, ever congruent with market oriented principles. Given its success for Germany in Europe, the German model of SME is put forth here as a viable developmental alternative for Third World developing economies such as Guatemala. The Social Market Economy is considered a potentially attractive option for developing countries because it has the end goal of satisfying human development needs within a framework of liberty and social compensation, accomplished via the mechanisms of constant cooperation between the public and private sectors.

The Role of Private-Public Partnerships in National Development

Inasmuch as Ordoliberalism posits public-private sector cooperation for national development, it is logical to consider Private-Public Partnerships (PPP) as congruent with an Ordoliberal framework. A PPP is a project that may be public or private and is funded by a partnership between the public and private sectors. Though it typically involves a formal contract, for present purposes a looser conception of PPP is adopted, meaning only that the public and private sectors actively work together towards some open, commonly-shared goals (Tan, 2012).

There are good reasons to combine private and public sector efforts. The private sector in any country is driven by the profit motive. Where poverty reigns, this will more likely be attending to the needs of the middle class or the rich, leaving significant portions of the population out of the developmental game. This is where the government can come in to complement the private sector. A government is, primarily, an organization dedicated to the provision of public goods (Olson, 1965).[1]

Markets strive to efficiently achieve the best possible outcomes, whereas governments strive, under premises of rational risk-aversion, avoid the worst possible outcomes, satisficing rather than optimizing. The private sector is concerned with efficiency, whereas the public sector overcomes collective action problems whereby public interest goods and projects might not be begun let alone completed under rational choice market perspectives.

The preceding argument marks the possible need for public and private cooperation in matters related to integral national development, where markets provide efficient management and oversight of public projects designed for the collective benefit. That said, in a Third World context marked by poor quality political leadership and institutional quality, the trust necessary for cooperation between the public and private sectors may be lacking.

From cyber-security to producing goods and providing services that were once considered 'public' there is increasing need for developing partnerships between the private sector and governments. PPP are used in many developing countries, as effective means to finance infrastructure investments, meet environmental business standards and even develop ecotourism. However, in a country like Guatemala, where lack of trust between the private sector and the government has been historically damaged by cases of corruption and poor quality service provision, it then becomes paramount to identify new consensus that can lead to effective partnership-building between the two main parties (Organization for Economic Co-operation and Development [OECD], 2013).

There is substantial theoretical and empirical backing in support of the notion of public-private cooperation working to fulfill comprehensive national development goals. The World Economic Forum's Global Competitiveness Report proposes that countries in the region of Latin America are developing an integrated vision which requires structural changes within each nation (World Economic Forum [WEF], 2014). These changes are understood as new strategies to spur economic growth through focalizing efforts in the most productive sectors and formalizing alliances between key players of the private and public sectors (WEF, 2014).

According to WEF framework, governments have a central role to play in articulating policies and constructing a climate of macroeconomic stability to build trust and consensus with the private sector. The necessary reforms should be not just in social spheres but also in smoothing the necessary structural adjustments as well as attending to the persistent imbalances across different productive sectors and industries. Government action will require improving state reach, via the fight against rampant public sector corruption, cronyism and clientelism. Unavoidably, in cases like Guatemala, with the lowest tax revenue as a percentage of GDP in the world,[2] tax hikes might be needed politically, a sure roadblock in a country like Guatemala where public sector transparency, efficiency and results are highly called into question.[3] In December, 2014 and January, 2015, the Guatemalan political scene was marked by rifts between the private sector and the government on the matter of proposed tax increases.[4]

There is hope for greater public and private cooperation, however. In recent years, Guatemala has followed similar trends in the region in which it has favored PPP and established a regulatory framework through the Partnership Law for Economic Infrastructure in 2010 (Cortez, 2014). This move was seen as an effort to institutionalize alliances in favor of economic growth, even though the private sector remained alert to the frequent changes in political factions (Cortez, 2014). The hope is that this initiative will lay down the foundations to build establish strategies for the government and private sector to work together.

This initiative is no mean feat. Although Guatemala features as a country with the characteristics of an emerging market economy with significant drawbacks in public sector transparency and accountability and corruption, she has nonetheless achieved the category of the most reformed country in terms of improving business climate according to the World Bank's Ease of Doing Business Index. This effort was undertaken by the Ministry of Economics, which, alongside the central bank, the Bank of Guatemala, is seen as a solidly pro-market public institution. As a general rule, the Ministry of Economics of Guatemala strongly promotes PPP initiatives, and this is particularly so in the case of the present Minister Sergio de la Torre.

PPP constitute key alliances to further advance public services, telecommunications, transport systems, infrastructure and even improve health and education systems (Pack & Saggi, 2006; Rondinelli & Iacono, 1996). Moreover, the positive linkages from PPP extend to developing the consensus of political economic dialogues. These are seen as key to demand accountability from government within their service provision as well as the means for the private sector to leverage government power (Bertucci & Alberti, 2003; Rondinelli, 2003).

In practical terms, PPP in Guatemala arise as the ideal means to form associations from which to develop social benefits if all partners establish their priorities for planning and negotiation. In turn, PPP become a development strategy that generate further trust eventually leading to a joint commitment in which broadly shared social and financial benefits are produced (Cortez, 2014).

EMPIRICAL BACKGROUND: BREACH OF CONFIDENCE BETWEEN PUBLIC AND PRIVATE SECTORS

Guatemala is a country that ranks on a medium scale on almost all international indicators. Guatemala is a lower middle income country, according to the World Bank,[5] is in the middle stage of development according to the paradigm established by the World Economic Forum, wherein competitiveness is based on efficiency in production (WEF, 2014), and has achieved a level of Human Development characterized as Medium by the United Nations (Malik, 2014). According to the Global Competitiveness Index elaborated by the World Economic Forum (WEF, 2014), Guatemala ranks 78th out of 144 countries in the world sample used to elaborate said index for the 2014-15 period. This ranking locates Guatemala as ranking better than 46% of the countries in the world sample, and worse than 54%.[6] Although this competitiveness ranking is better than El Salvador, Honduras and Nicaragua, it strongly lags the performance of Costa Rica (51) and Panama (48). In fact, if each country's ranking is weighted by its respective structural participation in the regional Gross Domestic Product, the region with Guatemala (CA) comes out with a hypothetical ranking of 72, and 70 if the region excludes Guatemala (CA no GT).[7] These figures indicate that, if one were to take the Central American region as a whole a hypothetical country, a single entity, that "country", amounting to one half percent of world GDP, would rank in the top half of countries in the world. However, including Guatemala would subtract from its integral competitiveness, instead of adding to it.[8]

According to the International Monetary Fund (IMF), Guatemala has a per capita Gross Domestic Product of roughly $3,800 in nominal terms, which is only one third the level of regional rivals like Panama and Costa Rica. These mediocre economic figures are not likely to change on their own. Guatemala has been grow-

Figure 1. Global Competitiveness Index Rank for Central America, Global Competitiveness Index (Rank)
Source: Global Competitiveness Report, 2014-2015 Graph by authors using World Economic Forum data

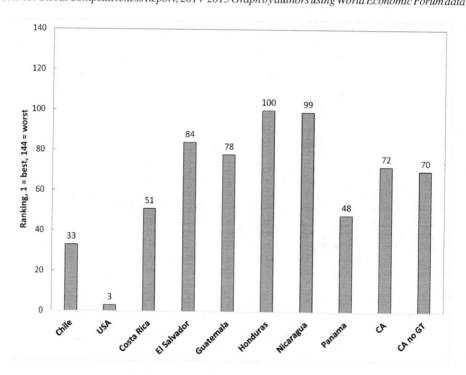

ing at a 3.4% annual rate for the last five years, whereas her population grows at an annual rate of 2.4%, a sad trend expected to continue for the next five years as well.[9]

Conventional economic arguments do not readily fit the Guatemalan case, unfortunately. Guatemala is considered to have solid macroeconomic fundamentals, but also many social deficiencies, like an extremely high rate of poverty 54% of the total population, malnutrition (almost half of children under five), poor quality educational and health systems, and high crime rates.[10] These are all problems which require political attention and a social consensus to design governmental solutions to these problems.[11]

Economic growth is not synonymous with human development, but it is a prerequisite, and, if economic history teaches us anything, national development will not be achieved without a leading role from the private sector. Planned economies where economic growth is spurred primarily from the state in the absence of private sector involvement or market incentives always end in disaster. Nonetheless, the private sector only attends three of the basic economic questions any society has to answer. These are: What to produce? How much to produce? How to produce? And For Whom to Produce? Consumer preferences, demand conditions and the profit motive and the efficiency imperative derived from it determine the answers to the first three questions, but the market economy alone does not provide a sufficiently acceptable answer to the last question, especially if political factors associated with unmet demands are taken into consideration, in the context of a liberal political and economic governing regime.

The following graph shows Guatemala's relative strengths and weaknesses when it comes to Global Competitiveness. As we have seen, Guatemala is slightly less competitive than the Central American region taken as a whole, as measured by the global ranking on the GCI as a whole (a ranking of 78 versus 70 for the region excluding Guatemala). Additionally, the country performance of Guatemala is highly uneven. On the second pillar of competitiveness, Infrastructure, Guatemala ranks even with the region. On the third pillar, Macroeconomic Stability, Guatemala outperforms the region. On the Fourth and Fifth pillars, Basic and Higher Education, Guatemala lags the region. On efficiency of markets, Goods, Labor and Financial (the 6th, 7th, and 8th pillars of Competitiveness), Guatemala outperforms the region. On Technological Readiness Guatemala performs worse than the weighted regional average, yet outperforms on Market Size and Business Sophistication, only to plummet again on the 12th pillar of the GCI, Innovation. Whereas Guatemala obtains a ranking of 95 on the 12th pillar of the GCI, Innovation, Costa Rica and Panama obtain rankings of 34 and 40, respectively, and the weighted average ranking for the region excluding Guatemala is calculated as 56.

Figure 2. Global Competitiveness Index Rank Across Pillars
Source: *Global Competitiveness Index, Scores across pillars 2014-2015, Authors' calculations and graph using data from World Economic Forum, 2014-2015*

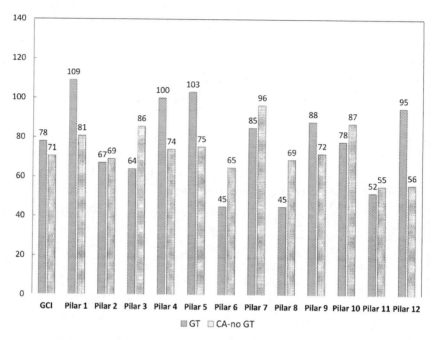

Figure 3. Cobweb Graph: Global Competitiveness Index Rank Across Pillars
Source: *Global Competitiveness Index, Scores, 2014-2015, Authors' calculations and graph using data from World Economic Forum, 2014-2015*

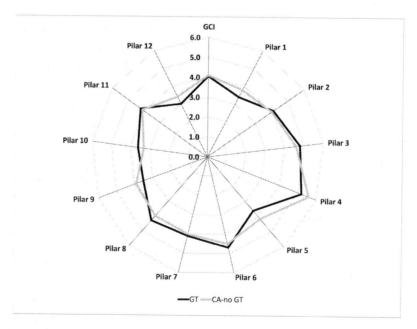

Figure 4. 12th Pillar, Innovation (Rank)
Source: *Global Competitiveness Report, 2014-2015, Graph by authors using World Economic Forum data*

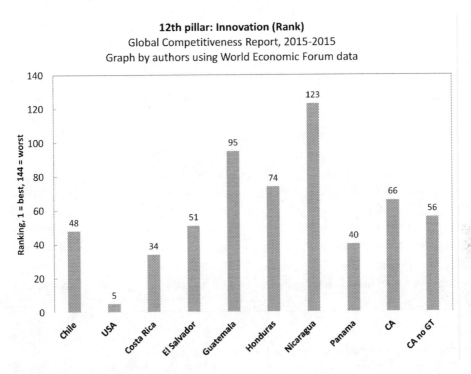

Guatemala lags the Central American region on the pillars of Basic Education, Higher Education, Technological Readiness and Innovation. Particularly worrisome is the lag of Guatemala on the matter of Innovation. Market can do many things to spur innovation, but, particularly in the Third World, to optimize they may require a supporting hand from the state. The question is how capable is the Guatemalan state to support development projects initiated by the private sector. A cursory glance at the available data suggests that state institutions in Guatemala for the most part are not up to the developmental task of fomenting innovation, economic growth and human development. In the worldwide sample of 144 countries used by the World Economic Forum, Guatemala ranked 109 in institutions, compared to an approximate calculated rank of 80 for the region without Guatemala. The First Pillar of Competitiveness, Institutions, is actually divided into two sub-pillars, Public and Private Institutions. Public Institutions cover a wide range of questions, but most telling for present purposes is the fact that Guatemala ranks 137 out of 144 countries in the world sample on the item labeled Public Trust in Politicians. This compares very unfavorably to 71 for Costa Rica and 102 for Panama. From these data, it can be deduced that in Guatemala there exists a breach of confidence between the private and public sectors. It is a logical matter that trust in public leaders' ability to contribute to the developmental progress of the nation would also be low among the enterprising sector in Guatemala.

Figure 5 shows a worldwide classification where the population answer the question 'how would you classify politician's ethical standards?' within a range from 1-7; where 1 denominates low versus 7 high ethical standards. From the countries in the region, Chile represent the best positioning in the table that places them in range 35 (WEF, 2014). As indicated by Figure.5 Guatemala shows the lowest classifications in the region. These results position Guatemala in place 137 out of 144 whilst El Salvador is the country that fares best in the region in place 68 (WEF, 2014).

We part from the premise that the private sector is always and in every place more efficient than the public sector … when it decides to do something. However, collective action problems exist, particularly in Third World countries with low quality institutions (Booth, 2012) The road of consensus, between the public and private sectors, requires that governments become more transparent and accountable, and that they build capacities and promote competitiveness in productive sectors with the aim of developing specialization and incorporating innovation to diversify productive structures (Lindergaard, 2011).

Figure 5. Public Trust in Politicians: Public Trust in Politicans
Source: Global Competitiveness Report, 2014-2015, Graph by authors using World Economic Forum data

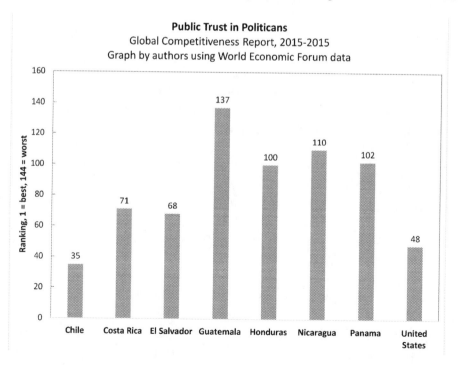

It is imperative that corruption be tamed, if trust is to emerge and development is to be achieved. Corruption distorts incentives, foments tax evasion, contributes to institutional weakness and feeds the rational perception that politics and policies are a zero sum game, where there would be no place for public and private cooperation in development projects (Virzi & Belteton, 2009).

Not only must corruption be mitigated, state action must produce concrete, widely recognized results towards amply shared aims. In this sense, innovation can be seen as a key factor to create and consolidate new sectors with more economic efficiency through diversifying capacities of the Small and Medium sized Enterprises (SMEs).

Staab (2003), argues that the persistent challenge is to implement policies that overcome the historical lack of trust on government initiatives.12 Historically in the region of Latin America, the lack of trust on the government is reflected in low tax collection as there is very little expectations that this would translate into more efficient public services (Overseas Development Institute [ODI], 2013). Similarly the embedded lack of trust is reflected in high absenteeism during elections and low participation in civil society organizations. The general perception amongst individuals is that they would not be able to demand accountability or influence

Figure 6. Public Trust in Politicians over time
Source: Global Competitiveness Report, 2014-2015, Graph by authors using World Economic Forum data

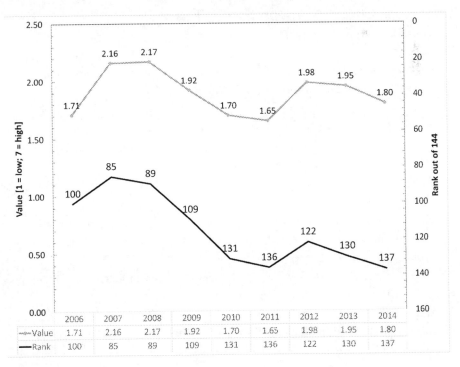

	2006	2007	2008	2009	2010	2011	2012	2013	2014
Value	1.71	2.16	2.17	1.92	1.70	1.65	1.98	1.95	1.80
Rank	100	85	89	109	131	136	122	130	137

government structures (ODI, 2013). This perception comes to a forefront in Latin America when we examine recent data in relation to trust indicators in Governments from the World Economic Forum (WEF) for the period of 2013-2014.

Pande and Udry (2005), argue that beyond public opinion the most damaging reflection of lack of trust in governments is the impact on economic growth. As a common denominator those countries that fare well in the trust invested in their governments, show high rates of economic growth (Leigh, 2006; Thompsom, 2004; Staab, 2003). In Guatemala the impact is seen through the flows of Foreign Direct Investment (FDI). Guatemala represents the 34% of the Central American population, yet only 27% of its GDP (already a significant productivity lag), and a paltry 12% of FDI in the region (WEF, 2014).[13]

Clearly, the Guatemalan public sector has a branding problem. It is widely perceived by the populace as corrupt. As such, trust is absent. This helps explain the widespread tax evasion and informal economy that leads Guatemala to have among the lowest government revenues as a percentage of national GDP in Latin America.[14] The country, it seems, is caught in a vicious negative spiral. Corruption breeds lack of confidence, which induces tax evasion, which dissipates funds for investment projects sorely needed to improve the national infrastructure, which, in turn, negatively impacts growth and perpetuates poverty. It was to solve precisely this problem that the PCC was originated.

The Private Council for Competitiveness: An Ordoliberal Approach

In this section the authors draw upon the opinions expressed by the group of experts interviewed for this study of the PCC. These experts are:

1. Fernando Paiz, is a Director of the Council of Directors for the Universidad del Valle (UVG) in Guatemala, and a member of the Technical Committee of the UVG-Texas A&M Project.
2. Jaime Diaz is the Director for the Program of National Competitiveness (Pronacom), a government initiative.
3. Roberto Canek, Coordinator for Educational Quality and Institutional Development for Universidad del Istmo (UNIS) in Guatemala. Canek represents UNIS on the Academic Sector of the PCC.
4. Hugo Alvarado, Professor of the Universidad de San Carlos of Guatemala, and participating member of the PCC's Academic Sector.
5. Humberto Olavarria is a Director on the Council of Trustees for the Foundation for National Development (FUNDESA) in Guatemala, a leading pro-business group in Guatemala.

6.   Juan Carlos Zapata is the Executive Director for FUNDESA in Guatemala.
7.   Salvador Biguria, Director of New Business from the Guatemalan Pantaleón sugar consortium.
8.   Otto Castillo is the Dean of the Engineering Faculty at UNIS.
9.   Fernando Lopez F. is President of the Chamber of Industry in Guatemala, and participating member of the PCC, representing the private sector.
10.   Maria Luisa Flores is the Vice Minister of Economics in Guatemala.

All interviewees were asked the same questions, to wit:

1.   What were the motivations behind the creation of the PCC?
2.   Why is the PCC constituted by the three sectors, academic, public and private.
3.   What are the concrete aims of the PCC? In what time frame?
4.   What deficiencies in national competitiveness in the actual system is the PCC expected to improve?
5.   What sectors is the PCC expected to benefit?
6.   How were the sectors selected?
7.   What are the motivations of the public, private and academic sectors to collaborate in the PCC?
8.   What is and will be the source of funding for the PCC? For how long?
9.   How will the progress of the PCC's actions be measured?
10.   What are the expected benefits of the National Program of Innovation[15]?
11.   In how much time and in what form will the work product of the PCC be reflected in the Guatemalan economy?
12.   How will the National Competitiveness Law[16] benefit the country? What national economic deficiencies is it expected to close?
13.   What economic sectors support the National Competitiveness Law? Where is the greatest resistance found?
14.   What public agencies support the PCC? Why these in particular?

The PCC is a joint effort involving the private, public and academic sectors, to promote a consensus behind the notion of achieving integral national development. The PCC was created under the organization Mejoremos Guate (Improve Guatemala), as part of its pillar known as Guatemala Mas Próspera (A More Prosperous Guatemala). The stated goals of the PCC are to achieve greater security, prosperity and solidarity for Guatemala.[17] The Private Council of Competitiveness (CPC in spanish) in Guatemala, was founded in 2012, and the lead author Nicholas Virzi was soon thereafter invited to integrate its academic sector. As its name implies, the PCC is a private initiative; it aims to promote employment generation in the country and create a multi-sectoral interaction that provides a favorable business climate, in order to improve the standard of living of citizens ("Guatemala: empresarios crean Consejo Privado de Competitividad", 2012). It is expected that the work of the PCC will increase performance of and confidence in the government, an improvement in tax revenue collections, so as to provide financing for development initiatives.[18]

According to Fanny D. Estrada, Director for Competitiveness of AGEXPORT, the Association of Guatemalan Exporters, and Acting Secretary for the PCC, the strategic objectives of the PCC are as follows:

- To establish a public-private competitiveness and innovation institution, for the continued promotion of competitiveness and job creation in the country.
- Strengthen the strategic vision and capacity deployment plans of productive sectors.
- Create a favorable business climate for the growth of local businesses and attracting foreign investment.
- Fostering a creative and competitive academic sector to promote innovation and a workforce with skills aligned with the needs of the productive sector.[19]

The emphasis on greater growth is essential to achieving the aims of greater prosperity and human development. Juan Carlos Zapata, Executive Director for Fundesa, believes that the results will be expected to build an innovation system that enable the country to achieve sustained growth above 6%.[20] Maria Luisa Flores, the Vice Minister of Economics, stated in her interview that she expected medium and long term results from the PCC, in conjunction with other public policies in the realm of competitiveness and innovation.[21]

The PCC is, in and of itself, a trust building mechanism inasmuch as it takes trust to constitute it, participate in it and implement the policies that it may inform. The involvement of government leaders to play a key role in support of market principles such as competitiveness and innovation are hallmarks of the Ordoliberal legacy. Coordination among sectors is a key component of Ordoliberal market economics. According to Humberto Olavarría, Director on the Fiduciary Council of Fundesa in Guatemala, the PCC involves the three key sectors of government, business and academia because the coordination of public and private efforts is essential to understanding labor needs and spurring innovation.[22] The fact that the cooperation of the public sector with the PCC is done through the Ministry of Economics is important, because this is the public agency which typically represents the private sector in most Guatemalan governments. Therefore, it is natural that greater trust would be found there.[23]

The main reason for why the PCC was constituted among the public, private and academic sectors was best summed up by Jaime Daíz, Director of the National Program for Competitiveness in Guatemala, PRONACOM, by its Spanish initials.

The PCC is conformed by these sectors so as to align the competiveness aims of each sector and include them in an agenda of sectorial development. The private sector chambers do not have mechanisms to align intersectorial agendas. In that sense, the PCC solves an intersectorial coordination problem.

... The PCC serves as a space to change the actual economic structure to one that most favors competitiveness, against specific sectorial interests. In this effort, academia serves a crucial role in investigating and analyzing PCC proposals and their possible impacts.[24]

The PCC was founded upon mainly the two pillars represented by the private sector and the academic sector, initially with six representatives of the former, and four representatives from the academic sector.[25] It was from the outset expected that the PCC would work closely with the government to guide and inform it on competitiveness matters. The idea that government and business work closely together under the guiding and supporting hand of government goes to the heart of Ordoliberal economics. The theory worked out in practice. From the work of the PCC the National Program of Innovation was spawned, a public sector endeavor that aims to diffuse business acumen and skills among the Guatemalan private sector, in compliance with Ordoliberal strictures that government action need be market conforming. (Siems & Schyner. 2013.) In only a few short years the PCC has, working closely, produced important results. One of the results is the National Competitiveness Law (Iniciativa de Ley 4647), as well as the National Program for Business Innovation, run by PRONACOM. Both initiatives were spawned under the sponsorship of the Ministry of Economics.[26] According to private sector leader Humberto Olavarría, the National Program of Innovation is expected to foment a climate that facilitates economic development, via innovation, so as to create a virtuous circle. As far as the Law of Competitiveness, Olavarría believes that it would create a stable structure to underpin public efforts that, today, still largely depend on the whim of the Executive and external financing.

The Vice Minister of Economics, Maria Luisa Flores, affirms that the Guatemalan government aims to support the private sector to confront the challenges that a globalized economy presents with research and development. Flores emphasizes that this would involve medium and long term processes, but that initial positive results were already being seen in international indicators like the Index of Global Competitiveness (World Economic Forum) and the Ease of Doing Business Index (World Bank).[27] On behalf of the private sector, Juan Carlos Zapata basically concurs that the participation of the three parts, the public, private and academic sectors, is necessary to maintain a balance in decision-making.[28] Salvador Biguria, also on behalf of the private sector, adds that the importance of these three sectors, public, private and academic, rests in the fact that these constitute the main sectors that impact and are impacted by the country's competitiveness; academics who form human talent and can be an important source of innovation; the business sector where companies and entrepreneurs considering the competitiveness of the country may be more or less successful in their industries are located; the public sector who helps define rules and should help remove barriers to competitiveness.[29] The integral approach to development, and the involvement of a guiding hand of government, in support of the proper functioning of markets is another hallmark of Ordoliberal thought.

The issue at hand is far from merely theoretical. The PCC`s stated vision is to achieve a competitive and innovative country that generates one million additional jobs by 2021, providing opportunities and wealth to all Guatemalans. Ben Sywulka, Executive Director of the PCC affirms that the PCC's mission is to contribute to improving the competitiveness and innovation capacity of the country and strengthening public-private institutions in charge of the subject.[30] On this matter, Zapata underscored Sywulka's point, affirming that the overarching aim of the PCC is to strengthen the national system of competitiveness.[31] According to the Vice Minister of Economics, Maria Luisa Flores, the Guatemalan government has and will continue to have a firm commitment to work closely with the PCC, through the Ministry itself, the National Program of Competitiveness (Pronacom), the foreign investment promotion program Invest in Guatemala, and the National Commission for the Promotion of Exports, CONAPEX.[32] It serves to emphasize that the emphasis on changing economic structures for the better and the market orientation towards the common good over particular interests is also a hallmark of Ordoliberal thought. The pragmatic emphasis on concrete, real world results, as opposed to theoretical concerns, let alone doctrinal purity among contending schools of economic thought, is another Ordoliberal hallmark.

The strong support the PCC enjoys among the private sector is not surprising given the heavy involvement of leading private personalities and institutions. This itself was key to the trust building across sectors which the PCC has uniquely accomplished in Guatemala. The stated aims of the PCC are completely congruent with the principles of market economics, and the involvement of the state in support of market development is a principal component of Ordoliberal economic thought. The congruence of stated motives and perceived intentions, in other words the alignment of interests has proven key to the success that the PCC has had in getting off the ground and meeting with the approval of a private sector otherwise extremely disdainful of public action in the economic sphere in Guatemala.

Quality matters. The business leaders intimately involved with the PCC are among the most renown in Guatemala. In the view of the president of the Chamber of Industry, Fernando López, the CPC seeks to generate proposals for development and innovation in the medium and long term, driven by the sector private.[33] Salvador Biguria concurs, affirming to the authors that one of the main reasons for the creation of the PCC in Guatemala was the integration of an entity to ensure that competitiveness issues took a salient public position in the country, and that this issue so important to the business sector not rely on solely on public funds and political appointments.[34] According to Humberto Olavarría, if the PCC is successful in the long run, it will change Guatemala. There will be greater job creation and economic growth, which is key to reducing the levels of poverty in the country and to generate state revenues.[35]

The Ordoliberal approach favors markets, and wants to see proper state action in furtherance of free market principles, so that the market economy can bring about the social benefits that it, in theory, promises. (Commun, 2014) In addition to its strongly pragmatic, pro-business focus, the PCC is open to input from the academic sector. Apparently to this end, the Executive Director of the PCC, Ben Sywulka, has been named the Executive Coordinator of MEGA Projects of Universidad del Valle, in addition to his functions as Director of Innovation for the PCC itself, and as instructor for the National Program of Innovation for Guatemala. This, under any light, is proof positive of a more intimate relationship and stronger ties between Universidad del Valle and the private sector (De Leon, 2014), if not, formally, the PCC itself, a clear private benefit of having participated in the PCC. This formal alliance between Ben Sywulka and Universidad del Valle, it is presumed, will work to advance the original stated aims of the PCC. The rational expectation would naturally be that such benefits become available to the other parties and institutions who cooperate with the PCC, in a timely manner. As always, the building of trust requires that information be freely shared in a timely manner, for which reason the PCC was officially created, to transmit information in real time between, and among, the key participating sectors, business, academia, and government.

The issue of academic involvement with the PCC, and clear communications among sectors of the PCC, is no small matter to its credibility in the future. To date, the PCC has accepted inputs from the academic sector. Hugo Alvarado, representative of the state university, Universidad de San Carlos, in the academic sector of the PCC considers the role of the academic sector in the PCC to be key, because he believes it is in academia where the future professionals who will be leading institutions and business in both private and public sectors are trained. Involving academia is fundamental to understanding the labor needs and to assist in innovation. Fernando Paiz, representative on the PCC's academic sector from the leading scientific research university in Guatemala, Universidad del Valle, considers the involvement of the academic sector important for the goals of technology transfer.[36] According to Roberto Canek of Universidad del Istmo, one of the chief aims of the PCC is to strengthen ties between academia and the private so as to make the nation more competitive.[37] The business leader, Fernando López, president of the Chamber of Industry, agrees with the leading Guatemalan academicians, affirming that the idea is to link business needs with academic preparation activity in both people and research and development.

The expectation is that these three sectors, public, private and academic will benefit from their involvement with the PCC. The ultimate aim is to benefit Guatemala from greater job creation. The universities represented in the Academic Sector gain much needed relevance with the future employers of their graduates in the private sector, as well as prestige with the research produced for the private sector. The private sector aims to become more competitive, thereby winning domestic and international market with improved products and services. The government will naturally benefit from any additional employment generated by the private sector and the concomitant amelioration of social ills ("Consejo Privado de Competitividad, n.d.). The cooperative nature and focus on the collective goal of national development are attributes congruent with an Ordoliberal perspective.

As a recent initiative, the strongest results in favor of the PCC is its mere existence. The mere existence of the PCC bears witness to the overcoming of a significant collective action problem and breach of confidence between the public and private sectors. Within the framework of the PCC, the private sector has adopted the code words of the social left, adding solidarity to their erstwhile favorite catch phrases, security and prosperity. This itself is an advance, given the distrust of the Guatemala private sector of government action professed to be in the name of the poor (Virzi & Belteton, 2009) and a strong lead indicator of the potential for consensus building between not just the private and public sectors, but academia as well.

The PCC will concentrate its initial efforts at spurring competitiveness among the 25 sectors that make up 80% of GDP.[38] These sectors were identified by the study of Dalberg and Ricardo Hausmann Signature, research proposed by the PCC.[39] Jaime Diaz refers to the Dalberg study indicating that it identified key gaps in competitiveness and the potential for employment generation. Some prioritization mechanisms used are those sectors that generate employment and that can grow in the short term.[40]

The work agenda for the PCC is ambitious. It involves CONAPEX, the national commission for exports, PRONACOM, the National Program for Competitiveness, the Ministry of Economics, Invest in Guatemala, a public agency designed to promote investment in Guatemala, CACIF, the Coordinating Committee for Agricultural, Commercial, Industrial and Financial Associations, and Fundesa, the Foundation for National Development. Agreements in principle are in place with all of these entities, again showing success for the PCC in trust-building across sectors in Guatemala. In addition to these achievements, it should be noted that the National Program for Competitiveness was developed in 2014 with the cooperation of the newly founded

Guatemalan School of Government, a private, nonpartisan institution dedicated to the identification and training of competent, ethical public servants.[41] All innovation workshops took place in the physical space of the School of Government. As well, so did an intensive, comprehensive course on PPP's.

Expectations for the PCC are high. According to Fernando Paíz, PCC representative from the Academic Sector, the results of the PCC should be measured in startups and growth in existing companies, Jaime Diaz believes that the results of the program should be new product development, increased company revenue, an increase in the number of jobs existing and increased private investment. Humberto Olavarria believes that if the CPC is successful, it will generate jobs and economic growth, it will help reduce poverty and generate resources for the state (tax collection), for private increases the purchasing power of the population.[42] PCC representative from the Academic Sector, Hugo Alvarado believes that strong economic results may result in greater foreign investment. The results oriented approach shows the clear, positive influence of the private sector. Jaime Diaz, National Competitiveness Director, says that the review and assessment progress of the PCC impact should be evaluated regarding the investment and employment generated in the growth sectors and worked at the national level, mainly explained by productivity.

The PCC focus is on the long term. Jaime Diaz believes it will take at least a decade to see concrete results.[43] Roberto Canek, representative from the Academic Sector on behalf of Universidad del Istmo, believes that the results of the work performed by the PCC will become clear after about 15 years, but it signals the direction is correct, in not more than 5 years.[44] The long run vision of the PCC notwithstanding, there have already been concrete results.

The PCC was instrumental in putting on the public agenda the National Competitiveness Law (Ley de la Competitividad y Productividad, Iniciativa de Ley No.4647), (*"Iniciativas 4644 a la 4648 - Presentadas por el Ejecutivo (enero 2013)"*, 2013). This bill proposes to tax formal businesses a 0.25% payroll tax to finance a National Competitiveness System, with a National Director of Competitiveness, to make sure that the competitiveness issue always remains politically salient, in a business-friendly way. Although this bill has not become law, it has succeeded in putting the issue of competitiveness on the political agenda and inserting it into the political discourse of the country.

Another result of the PCC initiative has been the well-received National Program of Business Innovation. The Executive Director of the PCC Benjamim Sywulka trains cadres of different business sectors on how to foment innovation in the workplace. This initiative has the explicit backing of the Ministry of Economics, through its National Program of Competitiveness, Pronacom. Juan Carlos Paiz, Presidential Commissioner for Competitiveness and Investment in Guatemala, stated publicly:

The Guatemalan government will accompany private enterprises, especially small-medium enterprises, in their processes of innovation. In a competitive world, invention is necessity and the process of continuous improvement should be implemented all along the value chain ("Lanzan programa de innovación empresarial", 2014).

It is too early to tell if the PCC will produce according to the high standards expected of it. However, its very existence is a hallmark that puts into evidence that trust between the private sector and a highly dysfunctional public sector can be achieved through the correct design mechanisms. The commitment undertaken by the private, academic and public sector is evidence of efforts to strengthen confidence, making the PCC a power example of just such a trust building mechanism.

CONCLUSION

The testimonies rendered by direct interviews from key economic, political and business players and leading academicians in Guatemala lend support to the notion that the PCC has already achieved a substantial measure of concrete success in a short time. The existence of the PCC in and of itself, and the intimate involvement of key leaders from the public, private and academic sectors is a key achievement in its own right, given the high levels of corruption and distrust of the public sector by the private sector in Guatemala. Trust is manifest in simply working together institutionally, under a long run vision.

Top business and political leaders on matters of competitiveness, and academicians concur that the work to which the PCC is dedicated is necessary to national development. The cooperative nature and focus on the collective goal of national development are attributes congruent with an Ordoliberal perspective. Whatever the future entails, the bringing together in Guatemala of the public, private and academic sectors on a common project is an example of positive consensus-building in a country where it is sorely lacking.

REFERENCES

Bertucci, G., & Alberti, A. (2003). Globalization and the Role of the State: Challenges and Perspectives. In Reinventing Government for the Twenty-First Century, State Capacity in a Globalizing Society. Kumarian Press Inc.

Blind, P. K. (2007). Building trust in government in the twenty-first century: Review of literature and emerging issues. In *Proceedings of 7th Global Forum on Reinventing Government Building Trust in Government* (pp. 26-29). Academic Press.

Booth, D. (2012). *Development as a Collective Action Problem. Synthesis report of the Africa Power and Politics Programme.* Overseas Development Institute. Retrieved from http://www.institutions-africa.org/filestream/20121024-appp-policy-brief-09-development-as-a-collective-action-problem

Christian Democratic Union. (2010). *German Democratic History in Documents and Images.* Retrieved from http://germanhistorydocs.ghi-dc.org/pdf/eng/Ch12Doc02(2)Eng.pdf

Commun, P. (2014). *German Ordoliberalism: Order versus Disorder in Röpke's Early Works.* Retrieved from www.i-lex.it

Consejo Privado de Competitividad. (n.d.). Retrieved from http://www.mejoremos-guate.org/cms/en/what-are-we-doing/consejo-privado-de-competitividad

De León, I. (2014). *Personaje del mes: Junio 2014 - Benjamin Sywulka.* Retrieved from http://uvg.edu.gt/publicaciones/personaje/2014/junio/index.html

Guatemala: empresarios crean Consejo Privado de Competitividad. (2012, June 13). Retrieved from http://www.estrategiaynegocios.net/csp/mediapool/sites/EN/CentroAmericayMundo/CentroAmerica/Guatemala/GTSociedad/story.csp?cid=472134&sid=1422&fid=330

Hardin, R. (1989). Rationally Justifying Political Coercion. *Journal of Philosophical Research, 15,* 1989–1990.

Hoegen, M. (1999). *La Economía Social de Mercado: Una opción para Guatemala?* Guatemala: IDIES.

Iniciativas 4644 a la 4648 - Presentadas por el Ejecutivo (enero 2013). (2013, January 21). Retrieved from http://www.congresovisible.com/index.php?option=com_k2&view=item&id=53:iniciativas-4644-a-la-4648-presentadas-por-el-ejecutivo-enero-2013

Kapsoli, J., Galindo, A., Márquez, G., Daude, C., Melo, A., Miller, M., ... Pérez, N. (2001). *Competitiveness: The Business of Growth.* Academic Press.

Lanzan programa de innovación empresarial. (2014, May 13). Retrieved from http://m.s21.com.gt/innovacion/2014/05/13/lanzan-programa-innovacion-empresarial

Leigh, A. (2006). Trust, inequality and ethnic heterogeneity. *The Economic Record*, *82*(258), 268–280. doi:10.1111/j.1475-4932.2006.00339.x

Lindergaard, S. (2011). *Making Open Innovation Work*. North Charleston, SC: CreateSpace.

Malik, K., & Jespersen, E. (2014). *Sustaining Human Progress: Reducing vulnerabilities and building resilience*. Human Development Report 2014. Retrieved from http://hdr.undp.org/en/2014-report/download

Olson, M. (1965). *The logic of collective action*. Harvard University Press Cambridge.

Organization for Economic Co-operation and Development. (2013). *Government at a Glance 2013*. Organization for Economic Co-operation and Development Publishing. doi: <ALIGNMENT.qj></ALIGNMENT>10.1787/gov_glance-2013-en

Overseas Development Institute. (2013). *Taxation in Developing Countries*. Overseas Development Institute.

Pack, H., & Saggi, K. (2006). *The case for industrial policy: a critical survey*. Washington, DC: World Bank Research Observer. doi:10.1596/1813-9450-3839

Pande, R., & Udry, C. (2005). *Institutions and development: A view from below*. (No. 928). Center discussion paper//Economic Growth Center.

Reyes, C. L. (2010, December). El deber del estado en el Ordoliberalismo de Walter Eucken. *Revista Chilena de Economía y Sociedad*, *4*(1), 15–27.

Rondinelli, D. A. (2003). Partnering for development: Government-private sector cooperation in service provision. In *Reinventing government for the twenty-first century: State capacity in a globalizing society*, (pp. 219-39). Academic Press.

Rondinelli, D. A., & Iacono, M. (1996). *Policies and institutions for managing privatization: International experience*. International Training Centre of the ILO.

Siems, M., & Schyner, G. (2013). Ordoliberal Lessons for Economic Stability: Different Kinds of Regulation, Not More Regulation. *Governance: An International Journal of Policy, Administration and Institutions*, *27*(3), 377–396. doi:10.1111/gove.12046

Somma, A. (2013). Private Law as Biopolitics: Ordoliberalism, Social Market Economy, and the Public Dimension of Contract. *Law and Contemporary Problems*, *76*, 105.

Staab, M. (2003). Public-Private Sector Relationships in Developing Countries. *Journal of Economic Development, 28*(2).

Tan, V. (2012*). Public-Private Partnership (PPP)*. Retrieved from http://a4id.org/sites/default/files/files/%5BA4ID%5D%20Public-Private%20Partnership.pdf

Virzi, N., & Belteton, A. (2009a). El impacto de la corrupción en la viabilidad del estado rector en Guatemala. En Cuadernos de Sociología, No. 7. Políticas publicas para una agenda de gobierno en Guatemala. Universidad Pontificia de Salamanca, Capitulo Guatemala. Centro de Estudios Sociales, UPSA Guate, Guatemala.

Virzi, N. & Belteton A. (2009b). *Un modelo keynesiano de los efectos macroeconomicos*. Facultad de Ciencias Económicas y Empresariales, Universidad Rafael Landívar. Septiembre, 2009, No. 4. Guatemala City, Guatemala.

World Economic Forum. (2014). *World Economic Forum, Global Competitiveness Report 2014-2015*. Author.

ENDNOTES

[1]   Where positive externalities exist in the production of a good or service, standard microeconomics dictates that the market will produce suboptimal levels of said good or service. In the case of negative externalities, the market with poorly defined property rights will produce too much, and in the case of positive externalities, too little.

[2]   Authors' calculations based on World Bank data. World Bank. 2014. World Development Indicators. Online database. http://databank.worldbank.org/data/views/variableSelection/selectvariables.aspx?source=world-development-indicators

[3]   Guatemala scores 29 out of 100 on the Transparency International Index score, for a percentile rank of 35%, worse than more than two thirds of the world sample on matters of public sector transparency. See http://www.transparency.org/country#GTM

[4]   The author Nicholas Virzi, Vice President of the American Chamber of Commerce in Guatemala was intimately involved in drafting the response of ASCABI, The Association of Bi-National Chambers of Commerce by its Spanish initials, to the government proposal of higher taxes on certain business sectors. See http://noticias.emisorasunidas.com/noticias/nacionales/camaras-comercio-binacionales-rechazan-presupuesto-2015. Also, see http://www.ascabi.org/?cat=3

[5]   World Bank. 2014. World Development Indicators. Online database. http://databank.worldbank.org/data/views/variableSelection/selectvariables.aspx?source=world-development-indicators

6   Authors' calculations based on the formula Percentile = 1-(R/N), where R is the Rank reported, and N is the simple size, which for 2014 is 144 countries.

7   Authors' calculations based on GCI data from the WEF and GDP data from the International Monetary Fund (IMF).

8   Authors' calculations based on GCI data from the WEF and GDP data from the International Monetary Fund (IMF).

9   Authors calculations based on data from the International Monetary Fund. 2014. World Economic Outlook database. Available online at: http://www. imf.org/external/pubs/ft/weo/2014/01/weodata/weoselgr.aspx

10   World Bank. 2014. World Development Indicators. Online database. http:// databank.worldbank.org/data/views/variableSelection/selectvariables. aspx?source=world-development-indicators

11   Interview with Oscar Avalle, Representative for the World Bank in Guatemala. Guatemala City, September, 2014.

12   Giddens (1990) defines trust in government as the confidence that the population has upon the system and the politicians to carry out their duties in a honourable and efficient way when they are in a position of power and have incentives to abuse it.

13   Authors' calculations based on data from the World Bank. 2014. World Development Indicators. Online database. http://databank.worldbank.org/data/views/variableSelection/selectvariables.aspx?source=world-development-indicators

14   See World Development Indicators. www.worldbank.org

15   The National Program of Innovation is a workproduct of the PCC. See http://m. s21.com.gt/innovacion/2014/05/13/lanzan-programa-innovacion-empresarial

16   The National Competitiveness Law, known in Guatemala as Iniciativa 4647 - Ley Marco del sistema nacional para la competitividad y productividad, is a workproduct of the PCC. See http://www.congresovisible.com/index. php?option=com_k2&view=item&id=53:iniciativas-4644-a-la-4648-presentadas-por-el-ejecutivo-enero-2013

17   http://www.mejoremosguate.org/cms/en/what-are-we-doing/consejo-privado-de-competitividad

18   Interview with Humbeto Olavarría, July 9, 2014.

19   Conversations of the author Nicholas Virzi in May of 2014.

20   Interview with Juan Carlos Zapata, in Guatemala City, Guatemala on July 10, 2014.

21   Interview with Maria Luisa Flores, in Guatemala City, Guatemala on July 29, 2014.

22   Interview with Humberto Olavarría, in Guatemala City, Guatemala on July 9, 2014.

23   Interview with Phillip Chicola, Director of Political Analysis for CACIF, the Coordination Committee of Agricultural, Commercial, Industrial and Financial Associations of Guatemala, the leading voice of private sector concerns in Guatemala. Guatemala City, Guatemala, November 1, 2014.

24   Interview with Jaime Díaz, in Guatemala City, Guatemala on July 8, 2014.

25   The author Nicholas Virzi was one of the original representatives from the Academic Sector.

26   Ultimately, the proposal for a National Competitiveness Law did not take effect as it was not approved by Congress. However, leading representatives of the national private sector were strongly in support of the measure and made serious lobbying efforts to enlist the support of all private sector chambers to present a united front in support of the initiative.

27   Interview with Maria Luisa Flores, in Guatemala City, Guatemala on July 29, 2014.

28   Interview with Juan Carlos Zapata, in Guatemala City, Guatemala on July 10, 2014.

29   Interview with Salvador Bigurria, in Guatemala City, Guatemala on July 10, 2014.

30   Conversations of the author Nicholas Virzi with Ben Sywulka, Executive Director of the Private Council of Competitiveness, August, 2013.

31   Interview with Juan Carlos Zapata, in Guatemala City, Guatemala on July 10, 2014.

32   Interview with Maria Luisa Flores, in Guatemala City, Guatemala on July 29, 2014.

33   Interview with Fernando Lopez, in Guatemala City, Guatemala on July 14, 2014.

34   Interview with Salvador Bigurria, in Guatemala City, Guatemala on July 10, 2014.

35   Interview with Humberto Olavarría, in Guatemala City, Guatemala on July 9, 2014.

36   Interview with Fernando Paíz in Guatemala City, Guatemala on July 8, 2014.

37   Interview with Roberto Canek in Guatemala City, Guatemala on July 9, 2014.

38   Interview with Salvador Bigurria.

39   Interview with Jaime Díaz, in Guatemala City, Guatemala on July 8, 2014.

40   Interview with Hugo Alvarado, in Guatemala City, Guatemala on July 9, 2014.

41   www.edg.org.gt

42   Interview with Humberto Olavarría, in Guatemala City, Guatemala on July 9, 2014.

43   Interview with Jaime Díaz, in Guatemala City, Guatemala on July 8, 2014.

44   Interview with Roberto Canek in Guatemala City, Guatemala on July 9, 2014.

Chapter 11

Commitment–Trust Dynamics in the Internationalization Process:
A Case Study of Market Entry in the Brazilian Market

António Carrizo Moreira
University of Aveiro, Portugal

Carolina Batista Alves
University of Aveiro, Portugal

ABSTRACT

This chapter describes the market entry process of Portuguese small and medium-sized enterprise (SME) into the Brazilian. This chapter explores an under-researched strand in the studies of internationalization of SMEs, namely how trust and commitment leveraged the relationship orientation of the Portuguese SME in entering into the Brazilian market. Through a Case Study the chapter explores the concept of relationship orientation, trust and commitment to analyze how a Portuguese SME managed to turn around a difficult situation transforming its associates in business partners and prevented a process of desinternationalization.

DOI: 10.4018/978-1-4666-8820-9.ch011

INTRODUCTION

Globalization has ignited the process of internationalization of firms. The main reason behind this internationalization process is both the increased instability of the contextual environment where firms operate and the increasing firm specialization around core competencies and/or core products.

One consequence of the growing importance of the internationalization of firms is the need to adapt to new environments namely reducing the psychic distance between the country of origin and the new market abroad.

Internationalization has been mainly analyzed as an outward perspective from the firm's point of view. It normally refers to the process of increasing involvement in foreign markets (Welch & Luostarinen, 1988) and related to the firm's export intensity.

Plenty of studies have been carried out analyzing the internationalization process of small and medium-sized enterprises (SMEs), including the Uppsala model and the resource allocating perspective.

The Uppsala model advocates an evolutionary, sequential and linear model with growing international involvement (Johanson & Wiedersheim-Paul, 1975; Bilkey & Tesar, 1977; Welch & Luostarinen, 1988). The resource allocation perspective understands the internationalization process as a strategic decision of allocating the firm resources *vis-à-vis* the firm's interaction with the environment.

Several international entry modes have been defined in the literature on internationalization (Calle-Fernández & Tamato-Bustamante, 2005; Moreira, 2009a); however the relational perspectives between partners of the country of origin and those of destination of exports have not been deeply analyzed.

Relationship marketing approaches inter-firm relationships based on trust, commitment and service, i. e., characterized by concern for the partner, contrary to the approach based on the unilateral exercise of power based on conflict, control and adversarial perspective. Clearly, the internationalization process can be understood as a relational process of entry into a foreign country but based on the relational commitment perspective that seeks to instill trust into the partner. The Commitment-Trust theory states that the commitment and trust are vital to the success of relationship marketing (Morgan & Hunt, 1994); trust and commitment are crucial for a successful relationship between the various partners.

There are several approaches for analyzing the quality of the relationship. For Van Bruggen et al. (2005) the quality of the relationship is composed of satisfaction, commitment, trust and conflict, where it is expected that for a successful relationship the levels of conflict be truly low and the levels of satisfaction, trust and commitment be high (Jap & Ganesan, 2000).

The contribution of this study stems from the analysis of the internationalization of a Portuguese SME entering the Brazilian market. Since the beginning of the relationship the quality of the relationship is assessed from a dynamic perspective, where the level of satisfaction, commitment, trust and conflict are analyzed.

Methodologically, the chapter follows a qualitative perspective. A case study is presented in which the level of satisfaction, commitment, trust and conflict are analyzed from a time-based perspective in which the partners' perspective is presented.

The document is structured in eight sections. After the introduction, the second section covers the two main strands of the internationalization process and the various dimensions related to internationalization strategies. The second section covers the network-based view of internationalization. The third section addresses market orientation. While the fourth section covers the topic of client orientation, the fifth section addresses relationship orientation.

Section six presents the research methodology. Section seven describes the case study pertaining to the evolving nature of the commitment, trust and conflict between the partners. Finally, the section eight finalizes this chapter with a summary of the main conclusions and challenges.

INTERNATIONALIZATION

The concept of internationalization has been evolving over time, incorporating the influences of different analytical and theoretical perspectives. According to Chetty and Hunt (2003), its definition varies according to the phenomenon under study as it may include sport exporting, continuous exporting, cross-border collaboration, alliances, green field investments, subsidiaries, branches and joint ventures following an outward perspective.

On the one hand, Calof and Beamish (1995) define internationalization as the process of adapting business operations to the international business environment. Luostarinen (1980), Welch and Luostarinen (1988) and Ruzzier et al. (2006) have defined internationalization as a process of increasing involvement in international operations outside the country of origin.

The classical theories studying the internationalization of firms focused their attention on trade among countries and the relationship among multinational players, which was quite limiting on what pertains to small firms behavior in international markets (Moreira, 2009a). They classically approached the life cycle theory (Vernon, 1966) and theories based on imperfect markets (Hymer, 1976; Kindleberger, 1969; Caves, 1971; Knickerbroker, 1973; Buckley & Casson, 1976) disregarding the operations of small and medium-sized firms.

Johanson and Vahlne (1977) realized that firms follow an evolutionary, sequential internationalization process in which firms move from occasional exporting activities to international production activities, based on a knowledge-based perspective. They defend that the four steps in this evolutionary process are based on experiential learning. As firms were able to internalize knowledge generated gained in unfamiliar foreign markets they were willing to move on to more resource encompassing stages of the outward international path (Johanson & Vahlne 1977; 1990).

The evolutionary, sequential, linear internationalization process model, known as Uppsala model (Johanson & Wierdersheim-Paul, 1975; Bilkey & Tesar, 1977), has been an important bedrock in explaining the growing international involvement of small and medium-sized firms. The network-based view of the firm (Håkansson, 1982; Håkansson & Johanson, 1984), based on a relational-based perspective among market players, has also been important in explaining how SMEs succeed in international markets.

The Uppsala model argues that firms follow a sequential path in their international operations. Basically, it is possible to identify four stages that differ regarding the company degree of involvement in the market (Johanson & Wiedersheim-Paul, 1975; Johanson & Vahlne, 1977): no regular export activities, exports through agents, sales through wholly owned subsidiary and international production subsidiaries. The degree of risk and commitment of resources increase as the internationalization process progresses.

Although this evolutionary, sequential perspective has been extensively used/supported (e.g. Welch & Luostarinen 1988; 1993; Gankema et al. 2010) it has been extensively criticized. Firstly, Andersen (1993) defends that while it describes the process of international expansion it does not explain why firms embark on each stage of the model. Secondly, the traditional pattern of the internationalization process, strongly affected by the globalization process, has been affected by born-global firms, infant multinationals and metanationals (e.g., Madsen & Servais 1997; Lindqvist, 1991; Doz, Santos & Williamson, 2001). Cuervo-Cazurra (2011) finds contradictory evidence and poses a model of non-sequential internationalization in which a firm selects a country that is dissimilar to its country of origin to start its first foreign expansion.

Based on an interactive approach, the importance of a relational perspective among market players throughout the value chain was popularized by Håkansson (1987). The network approach to internationalization, put forward by Johanson and Matsson (1988), claims that the internationalization of a firm is the result of the development of (internal and external) network relations with individuals and/or firms who have resources and experience/knowledge. They conclude that the networks established by the firm, the position of the firm in that network and the complementarity of resources of the firms involved in the network strongly influence the firm's degree of internationalization. As such, the international position the firm is strongly affected by the network in which the firm operates and its position in that network.

The network approach is important as it conditions the information and knowledge base the firm can have access to, especially in industrial, business-to-business (B2B) networks (Håkansson, 1982; Håkansson & Johanson, 1984) where interaction among firms are very important. According to Johanson and Mattsson (1988), there are two types of networks: internal and external. The external network involves all the relationships of the firm's subsidiaries with business partners such as, among others, suppliers and research institutions (Andersson, Forsgren, & Holm, 2002). The internal network involves all relationships within the firm's subsidiaries (Bjorkman & Forsgren, 2000). As the network approach is based on the importance of relationships, it is claimed that relationships underpin the firm's internationalization process and not the knowledge generated by the sequential entry mode proposed above. Consequently, this theory brings new ways of understanding internationalization highlighting a relational perspective.

Johanson and Mattsson (1988) argue that it is the diversity of production factors and competitive forces in internationalized markets where firms compete that create a wide pattern of entry opportunities for firms to expand abroad, which is a quite different explanation for firms to internationalize given by the traditional Uppsala model. As a consequence, the implementation of networks of relationships in new markets is important for firms to open new windows of opportunities abroad. Once the firms operates in one network, there are new possibilities in operating in new networks, as long as firms are able to fully exploit their international networking potential. Clearly, relationships can be used as entry modes in other networks.

According to the network approach, internationalization is no longer an outward movement of deploying resources and capabilities abroad, but the exploitation of potential cross-border relationships (Andersson, Johanson, & Vahlne, 1997). In this respect, internationalization is seen as a consequence of a relational-based approach in a network of firms. Trust-based activities in relational networked contacts are a mean to an end.

Factors like technology mastery (Burgel & Murray, 2000), knowledge and networks (Coviello & Munro, 1997), entrepreneurial orientation (Ibeh & Young, 2001) and sociocultural background (Leonidou & Katsikeas, 1996) have been growing in importance in recent studies on B2B internationalization.

There are several factors that might influence the internationalization process of SMEs (Young, Hamill, Wheeler, & Davies, 1989; Moreira, 2004): the type of products and activities; the international modes of entry and operation; the types of markets; internal competencies; the ability to manage cooperative relationships; financial constraints; and organizational structure.

Normally, the lack of resources is at the heart of the establishment of relationships among firms as business relationships can be considered a form of resource acquisition and international penetration (Neergaard, 1998). Analyzing the interaction of SMEs with multinational firms, Moreira (2007) found that SMEs managed to evolve in those external networks although there were clear differences in how SMEs performed in international business networks. Despite those differences, Moreira (2007) concluded that mutual trust and relationship orientation was mandatory for an evolutionary perspective in the supply chain in dyadic relationships. As a consequence, Moreira (2007) claims that trust-based dyadic relationships are important in the internationalization process of SMEs.

Johanson and Mattsson (1988) put forward a typology that analyzes the number and depth of relationships with clients, suppliers, distributors and competitors as firms internationalize: international expansion, in which firms try to build relationships abroad, international penetration, in which firms try to increase commitment abroad, and international integration, in which firms try to integrate their position in foreign networks.

Following the network perspective, Holmlund and Kock (1996) emphasize the existing unequal relationship in the supply chain, where suppliers (usually small firms) are dominated by clients (usually large companies). In a subsequent study, Holmlund and Kock (1998) also point that, despite some relational progression between suppliers and buyers, the supplier relationship and internationalization evolutionary patterns depend on the client.

As the chapter discusses the relationship between an industrial Portuguese SME and its international penetration in the Brazilian market, the internationalization process is going to be assessed based on the relationship the Portuguese firm with its Brazilian partner, namely, the conditions and opportunities that the Brazilian firm represents, and the performance achieved by the firm in this relationship in an evolutionary perspective. The relationship is going to be assessed in order to capture the intricacies of the entry mode in the Brazilian market where the partners' different perspectives are going to be assessed.

NETWORK-BASED VIEW OF INTERNATIONALIZATION

As mentioned before, when industrial firms take part in inter-organizational networks the firm's strategy is influenced by the position the firm has in the network, as it is the range of opportunities and constraints the firm faces (Johanson & Mattsson, 1988). This hinders or underpins the international position of the firm in the network. As such, the more profound the relationships are, the greater the firm's

Table 1. The network model of internationalization

		Market Level Internationalization	
		Low	High
Firm Level Internationalization	Low	Early Starter	Late Starter
	High	Lonely International	International Among Others

Source: Johanson and Mattsson (1988).

involvement in international markets, which is associated with the way the firm manages and internalizes the knowledge generated in international markets (Axelsson & Johanson, 1992).

Highly internationalized firms enjoy strong direct relationships with internationalized network actors (Johanson & Mattsson, 1988). Firms involved in foreign internationalized networks are more capable of developing relationships that can lead to further linkages with other actors (Axelsson & Johanson, 1992; Johanson & Vahlne, 1992) as firms are influenced by the level of internationalization of both the market and the network. Accordingly, Johanson and Mattsson (1988) put forward the following network model of internationalization, as shown in Table 1: the Early Starter, the Late Starter, the Lonely International and the International among Others.

The Early Starter firm, as well as the network the firm belongs to, possesses a low degree of internationalization (Johanson & Mattsson, 1988) and has weak links with foreign networks due to its low level of internationalization. The relationships that the Early Starter has within the international network are considered important for the accumulation of knowledge. The Early Starter's low level of involvement with foreign actors, either directly or indirectly, deters the acquisition and internalization of knowledge. Moreover, its weak position in the network further limits the internalization of foreign knowledge. As a consequence, knowledge feedback direct from foreign markets to the Early Starter is limited as the firm has hardly any experience operating in foreign markets and has weak relationships with international firms.

One of the main advantages of Lonely International firms is their high degree of internationalization, which provides them with greater levels of experiential knowledge in international markets, *vis-à-vis* Early Starters. As the Lonely International firms might be present in various relationships, they tap into knowledge resources from several partners. The main disadvantage of the Lonely International firm stems from its internationally inexperienced network.

Although Late Starter firms have some direct relationships overseas, they are characterized by a low level of commitment and activity in international markets and low levels of international experience (Johanson & Mattsson, 1995). As Late

Starters enjoy a knowledge advantage when compared to Early Starters as they are more committed to international operations and acquire knowledge from an international wider network (Holm, Eriksson, & Johansson, 1996) their participation in international networks give the Late Starter a valuable experience to develop and coordinate their position overseas.

Comparing Late Starters and Lonely Internationals is not simple. The Lonely International firm might exhibit higher levels of internationalization knowledge and foreign institutional knowledge relative to the Late Starter, based on the advantage of being a more highly internationalized firm. Nevertheless, it might exhibit a lower level of overseas business knowledge than a Late Starter firm due to the disadvantage of not residing in a highly internationalized network.

Finally, the International among Others enjoys a high degree of internationalization (Johanson & Mattsson, 1988). It has established and developed positions and resources in overseas markets and has a highly internationalized macro-position, which provides it with higher levels of experiential knowledge when compared with the Lonely International firm. The regular participation in cross-border activities enabled the International among Others the capabilities to coordinate and integrate international networks. Accordingly, the International among Others exhibits high levels of overseas institutional knowledge and business knowledge *vis-à-vis* the other three types of firms.

MARKET ORIENTATION

Market orientation is a fundamental concept in any marketing activity (Jaworski & Kohli, 1993). Like Firth (1998) and Deshpandé and Farley (2004) refer, market orientation is a central element of the management philosophy based on the marketing concept.

Deshpandé and Farley (2004) relate the marketing concept to the establishment of profitable relationships with the market agents. In truth it is a relational philosophy which aims at complementing the internal resources and capabilities of the firm in the generation of added value for the customer. Market orientation has been dealt with in literature in various ways, which include: a business philosophy; the acquisition of knowledge and intelligence; and a source of organizational learning (Deshpandé & Farley, 2004). If in an initial phase Deshpandé, Farley and Webster Jr. (1993) considered the customer as the focal point of market orientation, Kohli and Jaworski (1990) and Slater and Narver (1994a) adopted a more comprehensive perspective which includes competing firms and regulation.

Kohli and Jaworski (1990) conceived market orientation in terms of specific behavior including the set of activities, processes and behaviors resulting from the implementation of the marketing concept. Clearly, for them, information plays an important role. In turn, for Narver and Slater (1990) market orientation includes orientation for customers, for competitors and the inter-functional coordination, having profitability and long term as its main focus. This is clearly a behavioral perspective. And yet, these two concepts are completely different: whilst business profitability as an objective is fundamental for Narver and Slater (1990), for Kohli and Jaworski (1990) profitability is a consequence of market orientation.

Kohli and Jaworski (1990) and Narver and Slater (1990) developed two of the scales most frequently used for measuring the level of market orientation: MK-TOR (Narver & Slater, 1990) and MARKOR (Jaworski & Kohli, 1993). Kohli and Jaworski (1990) identified three major market intelligence factors: generation, dissemination and response. Narver and Slater (1990), in turn, suggest that market orientation consists of the following components: consumer orientation, competition orientation and inter-functional coordination.

The differences between the two concepts are clear for González-Benito and González-Benito (2005): while Narver and Slater (1990) focus their market orientation on the attitudes, values and beliefs of the managers, Kohli and Jaworski (1990) focus on the processes, activities and behavior of the firms. Clearly the first is more cultural based and the second is more operational based.

Webb, Webster and Krepapa (2000) argue that the total offer of the value of the firm's products reflects the market orientation. Thus, orientation for the customer and for the competitors and the firm's inter-functional coordination are the true drives of market orientation.

Heins (2000) claims that the effects of market orientation on performance depends on the importance given to the customer, the competitors or both. Hence, in growing markets, the more market orientation, the higher the market share reached. In turn, in stable and predictable markets, the more market orientation on the competitors, the higher the market share. Lastly, an orientation that is focused on competitors and customers, despite its higher results in market share, has a decrease in the investment return.

Langerak's (2001) perception of market orientation is broader. He states that continued creation of added value for the customers, in a cultural organization perspective, results in superior performance for both downstream and upstream markets oriented behaviors.

Market orientation can be reactive or proactive (Atuahene-Gima & Slater, 2001; Slater & Narver, 1994b). The first is related to the satisfaction of the customers' needs, while the latter is related to the satisfaction of the customers' latent needs. Another issue worthy of some study is the fact of a firm having a market driven orientation or a market driving orientation (Sheth & Sisodia, 1999; Day, 1999). Market driven firms reinforce the existing structures that define how the market is segmented, the market limits, who the main competitors are and what the customers want. In their essence firms are reactive. On the other hand market-driving firms have a proactive perspective trying to discover the latent needs of their current and potential customers.

The concept of market orientation has been widely analyzed (e.g. Matsuno, Mentzer, & Rentz, 2005; Liao et al., 2011; Sorjonen, 2011; Lings & Greenley, 2005; Panigyrakis & Theodoridis, 2007; Zhang et al., 2008; Dawes, 2000; González-Benito & González-Benito, 2005; Moreira & Silva, 2013), having debated the constructs that are part of the customer orientation, the assessment of performance, as well as the inclusion of the constructs that moderate the relationship between market orientation and performance.

In a broader perspective, international market orientation was analyzed by various authors (e.g. Deshpandé, Farley, & Webster Jr., 1993; Mavondo, 1999; Cadogan, Diamantopoulos, & Mortanges, 1999). Whilst Deshpandé, Farley, & Webster Jr. (1993) analyzed market orientation among different cultures, Mavondo (1999) analyzed it in different countries and Cadogan, Diamantopoulos and Mortanges (1999) analyzed it for the export market. The conclusion is clear: international market orientation is much more complex than it was thought to be. It is more than just adapting the constructs: one needs to include items in the constructs related to export markets, the type of international operations, the market destination, the firm's resources and capacities, its size and the strategies to enter those international markets (Cadogan & Diamantopoulos, 1995; Cadogan, Diamantopoulos, & Mortanges, 1999).

CUSTOMER ORIENTATION

The discussion about the range of the market orientation construct has been questioned by authors that defend that customer orientation is more objective.

Deshpandé, Farley and Webster Jr. (1993) claim that there is a clear conceptual distinction between market orientation and customer orientation and the scales proposed by Narver and Slater (1990) and Kohli and Jaworski (1990) are clearly different. Thus, Deshpandé, Farley and Webster Jr. (1993) state that, despite all the stakeholders being important, the customer's interest is in first place. Moreover, Deshpandé, Farley and Webster Jr. (2003) verified that the most successful North American and Japanese firms considered the focus on the customers as the main element of the market orientation.

Market orientation is considered diffused above all by the defenders of a relational perspective, in which the dyadic supplier-customer relationship is very important and objective (Payne, 1988), thus conforming to what is defended by Evans and Laskin (1994) in what concerns the importance of the customer in relational marketing.

According to Deng and Dart (1994), customer orientation seeks to increase the customer's long term satisfaction, so it is more focused than market orientation. Therefore, the scale defined by Narver and Slater (1990) will be more suitable for this construct than the one defined by Kohli and Jaworski (1990). This way, considering the quality of the relationship with the customer, in accordance with a dyadic performance, customer orientation is much more fruitful, especially for small and medium-sized firms (Zhao & Cavusgil, 2006; Gray et al., 1998). As an example, Zhao and Cavusgil (2006) demonstrated that competitor orientation does not have a significant impact on the customer's confidence, and claim that customer orientation is crucial for market orientation. In turn, Gray et al. (1998) claim that a small firm puts less emphasis on competitor orientation, thus customer orientation would be more objective than market orientation.

RELATIONSHIP ORIENTATION

As mentioned above, a network-based approach is based on the relationship between the different actors in the value chain and in international markets. In these circumstances the relationship between the actors is based on a relational perspective with a basis on dyadic businesses. Taking the market diversity into account, the potential of market orientation can be broader, since it can focus on macro-segments and pay less attention to important micro-segments. In the same way, being customer oriented, the option can be focusing on the customer so that, after having adjusted the company's resources and the needs of the customers, one may explore the resources and the needs of other customers, making the relationship with the customers more homogenous. However, one should consider that customer orientation can be relatively "unstable" since the dyadic relationship among businesses can be transactional or relational. So it is always important to take into account the need to direct towards a relationship and not a transaction.

It is not by chance that Zolkiewski and Turnbull (2006) claim that the basis of a business is the business-to-business relationship and not mere customer or market orientation. If a relationship is not successful all customer orientation is condemned.

In fact the problem is in the individual perspective of the firm and the researcher. As an example, Day and Van den Bulte (2002) considered relationship orientation as part of a global customer orientation. Deshpandé, Farley and Webster Jr. (1993) implemented the assessment of market orientation by resorting to the customers.

Helfert, Ritter and Walter (2002) argued that there are no markets and that it is necessary to adopt an orientation for individual customers. They also refer that market orientation does not take into account the inter-organizational relationships. Moreover, taking into account that the relationship is one of the most valuable resources of a business, a "general" market orientation can be questioned by the relational approach of markets. It is no longer possible to offer in the markets products that are thought to be desired without having a clear understanding of what the each individual customer wants (Helfert, Ritter, &Walter, 2002).

The issue of market orientation versus customer orientation has been widely addressed. According to a network perspective, Håkansson and Ford (2002) and Håkansson and Snehota (2006) claim that the orientation is not for the market since there are only individual customers. Thus the relationship should assume a primary role. Likewise, Gadde and Snehota (2000) claim that, according to a network perspective, as the firms deal with each supplier differently, based on the individual relationship with each supplier, the relationships with the customer should also be based on relational specificities.

Lamming's (1993) work gave dyadic relationships a new life. He demonstrated that this relationship is evolutionary and cumulative in nature and depends on: the mutual involvement of both the supplier and the client, the atmosphere of both firms' interaction and the environment in which the relationship takes place. Lamming (1993) made public that the relational challenge throughout the supply chain depends on multiple factors, not just in the two partners' convergent interests as originally thought. Based on NPD dyadic relationships, Moreira (2005) analyzed the evolutionary perspective of NPD and large multinational clients. He concluded that suppliers and clients have different perspectives and play different roles due to the bargaining power exercised by the latter and by the lack reciprocity of the former. Clearly, some relationships are "unbalanced".

The management of NPD process at inter-firm level is a key element of competitiveness. It involves the management of different a) strategic interests; b) knowledge and technological capabilities; c) perceptions of the external environment; and d) collaborative involvements. Therefore, the integration of the NPD process implies shared challenges at R&D level as well as common efforts at new product development level, which according to Nishiguchi (1994) involves an inter-firm co-specialization among participants. In such situations relationships are clearly specific and bound to influence the relationships among actors (Moreira, 2009b).

Day (2003) claims that a market driven approach makes the management of relationships with customers a key element of the marketing strategy. However, Yau et al. (2000) propose a relationship marketing orientation based on four different components: bonding, empathy, trust and reciprocity, making relationship orientation much more specific than market orientation. Yau et al. (2000) conclude that the impact of orientation for relational marketing on performance is greater than the one of market orientation in firms based on business-to-business marketing. Tuominen et al. (2004) refer that this concept of relationship orientation is linked to what they call customer intimacy, which assumes that the company is sufficiently flexible when responding to the customers' needs at an operational level, which in turn assumes a relationship orientation.

Clearly, relationship oriented firms consider the maintenance of their customers a priority strategy, trying to change from a market related capability to a customer-relating capability.

It is important to consider that small firms may need a more specific approach, mainly due to their own characteristics: they have little resources when compared to big multinational firms and their relationship with their customers is more important than market orientation (Moreira, 2007). Clearly, if the market orientation involves the scarce resources and knowledge that the small firm has, it is necessary to take into account that the firm will try to have a relationship orientation, mainly a business in which relationships prove to be advantageous to it, in detriment of a market orientation, *lato sensu*.

Mohr and Spekman (1994) proposed a model based on two basic assumptions:

1. Partnerships incorporate a set of behavioral characteristics that distinguish them from traditional transaction-based relationships, and
2. Successful partnerships have these characteristics with greater intensity.

Clearly, to achieve a relational perspective, the requirements imposed by Lamming (1993) need to be met: to achieve a relationship-based perspective, the parties involved must believe that all parties should act in order to fulfill their obligations. For the trust-based relationship to be achieved, both buyers and suppliers need to invest in the relationship so that it can be a stable one. Accordingly, all firms need to cooperate closely in order to achieve mutual and consistent objectives in such a way that interdependent relationships are generated in which all firms benefit from a synergistic cooperation. This only works if both firms are committed to achieving an interdependent relationship in which the dyad excels the performance of each firm. For Mohr and Spekman (1994) partnerships underpin long-term relationships and hinder opportunistic behaviors.

Trust is a belief, feeling or expectation about the other partner's loyalty resulting from its intention, integrity or competence, whenever there is any possibility of vulnerability or uncertainty (Moorman et al., 1992).

Morgan and Hunt (1994) argue that trust exists when one party believes in the integrity and reliability of the partner, which tends to reduce opportunistic behavior and can be seen as an important source of competitive advantage.

Considering the importance of trust for the quality of a relationship, Wang and Huff (2007) argue that uncertainty and vulnerability are important concepts in the emergence and sustenance of trust which derives a condition of uncertainty, risk, vulnerability and dependence in the relationship. Colquitt et al. (2012) concluded that trust reduces the behavioral and attitudinal uncertainty of the parties.

To achieve a relational behavior it is essential that commitment is present between the parties, i.e., both companies of the dyad must have a desire to develop a stable relationship and to realize short-term sacrifices to maintain long-term relationships (Anderson & Weitz, 1992). Mohr and Spekman (1994) refer to commitment as a desire of the parties to invest in the relationship, which will allow a greater allocation of resources to it.

Dwyer, Shurr and Oh (1998) state that the supplier-client commitment is often assessed by targeting resources in the form of time, money and facilities, specifically to meet the other party's requests. The commitment of resources depends on the allocation of the resources to the relationship. The long-term orientation indicates that partners are committed to the relationship. The commitment involves dissipation of doubts that the other party will not have difficulties in committing to achieving results and to prevent opportunistic behavior.

Brown, Lusch and Nicholson (1995) presents four dimensions of commitment: (i) the normative dimension involves the party's belief that it need to remain in the partnership; (ii) the instrumental dimension involves the analysis of the cost related to exiting the partnership or the cost of maintaining the relationship; (iii) the affective dimension involves favorable feelings about the continuity of the parties in the relationship; and (iv) the behavioral dimension is the perception that the parties will mutually support if necessary.

For the partnership to succeed it is necessary the parties to continually adapt to emerging situations, both intrinsic and extrinsic to the partnership, as the adaptation to changing market conditions is mandatory.

Clearly, for firms to have a relational perspective they have to be committed, adapt over time and cooperate in order to generate trust, commitment and reciprocity to achieve their common goals. In its evolutionary perspective firms will have to overcome all its conflicts, in order to maintain the relationship.

METHODOLOGICAL ASPECTS

A descriptive approach based on a descriptive single case study, as proposed by Yin (1984), was chosen in order to address the complexity of the relationship marketing orientation of the firm. The case study methodology is an empirical approach that investigates a contemporary phenomenon within its real-life context, when the boundaries between the phenomenon and context are not clearly evident and in which multiple sources of evidence are used (Yin, 1984). Case studies are also used as a way to obtain knowledge about a complex topic and check it regarding several research strands. They are appropriate in investigating industrial networks and international market entry strategies due to the complexity and dynamism that limit the application of positivist studies (Easton, Wilkinson, & Georgieva, 1997). Case studies have extensively been used over the years in business research as social scientists use this form of qualitative research to analyze real-world situations in order to obtain a basis for the application of ideas or theories, as well as for theory building.

Case study methodology helps in exploring concepts and situations in which positivistic studies cannot address adequately. Taking into account the advantages of using case study methodology, namely a single case study, it was decided to explore the behavior of a Portuguese firm in which it was possible to explore concepts such as market orientation, relationship orientation, commitment and trust in an international environment where a SME is trying to implement an internationalization strategy. This case study draws on a company from the electronics and telecommunications industry which operates in the B2B market.

Due to confidentiality reasons, it is not possible to disclose the name of the company. As such, BETA is going to be used throughout the chapter when referring to the firm. BETA was founded in 1995 in the Center of Portugal and has strong technical competences in the production of electronics and telecommunications products. The analysis of the case will generate knowledge about the evolution of the marketing strategy of the firm, how it has managed to internationalize its activities, the importance of its relationship orientation, mainly in its entry in the Brazilian market. The main objective of the chapter is then to address how BETA managed to muddle through the main difficulties when entering the Brazilian market using a relationship-oriented perspective, based in instilling a trust-based relationship.

Following the methodology suggested by Yin (2004), collecting data on case studies must allow the "triangulation", i.e., to obtain data from multiple sources in order to establish evidence or prove facts. The investigation was based on semi-structured interviews carried out with a senior executive. This allows a deep understanding of the company's evolution, skills and strategies adopted throughout time. Furthermore, secondary data was collected from the company's webpage, newspaper articles and internal reports as complementary information. Two semi-structured interviews and a tour on the company's facilities were conducted. These interviews allowed the characterization of the relationships between the company and its clients, as well as an overview of BETA's of internationalization process. After the interviews, data and results were validated by the company. This case study aims to contribute to the knowledge on how relationship-oriented, trust-based relationships facilitate the process of internationalization of an SME.

CASE STUDY

BETA is a small and medium sized firm that produces and sells electronic and communication equipment in a B2B context. The technology used is available all over the world.

BETA is a public limited company that has been in the market for 19 years, operating preferably in the field of telecommunications and transports (trains, buses and light duty vehicles). The firm resorts to products from other firms to create solutions that constitute an added value for their customers. BETA has always internalized values related to the confidence in partners, ethics, quality of their service and the professional development of their employees. They consider these values fundamental among the firms and the customers themselves.

The activities of provision of services with a strong emphasis on manpower and human capital have grown in the firm. This process reflects the power of the innovation of services and has allowed an increase in productivity in the firm.

When it was created in 1995, BETA did not have an international strategy. However, after some time that possibility arose. The firm had a small number of customers, in which the main one was responsible for 80% of the total sales of the firm. At the time, due to strong competencies in the making of electronic components, BETA aimed at fulfilling its main customers' orders. Due to its small dimension, BETA tried to make the most of its customers' orders to generate small economies of scale. However due to the decrease in the sales volume of its main customer (from 80% to 20% of BETA's total sales) the survival of the firm was at stake.

So, BETA had to react by analyzing ways by which it could solve this problem. After a market and industry analysis, various strategies were analyzed at a national level and, despite being a firm of reference in its operating area, the board of directors concluded that the market was saturated in Portugal, making the attraction of new customers unfeasible since their needs were already satisfied by the main competing firms. It was evident that an offensive strategy to gain market share would put BETA in a price war with its main competitors. Therefore the board of directors had no choice but to diversify or seek international customers.

Thus the opportunity of expanding the business internationally emerged, i.e. penetrate and/or invest in an external market experimenting on new territories and leaving their comfort zone.

It was then decided to initialize the process of internationalization so as to increase the client portfolio. This would only be possible with a wider diversification. Clearly, BETA would be able to avoid its dependence on important customers in the Portuguese market; it would diversify its range of products and avoid a direct conflict in the internal market and possible retaliation actions from important competitors. This way, BETA would avoid competing prices in the internal market and take on a leading role in the international market.

As soon as it was understood that going international was the most feasible measure it became necessary to define a strategy to enter the external market. As the firm had established a relationship with a contact in Germany, who was a connoisseur of this market that BETA wanted to explore, they decided to resort to this contact to make a detailed analysis of the market and then develop a network of contacts.

This initial contact was BETA's business promoter who did the market research in Germany and established the first contacts with potential customers while closely accompanying the relationship and communication between the German customers and their suppliers. With more detail, this promoter began by analyzing the market in accordance with the pre-established requirements and collected information about potential customers. Besides this analysis, the promoter researched the level of satisfaction that these potential customers had with BETA's competitors. This market research lasted for 6 months and it presented some opportunities since it identified potential clients for BETA in Germany.

With the internationalization, BETA's business volume increased substantially (30% of the business volume corresponds to direct exportation. Export of services given to international customers of BETA's Portuguese clients, should be added, therefore constituting more than 40% in an indirect way).

As BETA's production volume increased due to the internationalization of the firm they not only profited from economies of scale but also began to gain credibility in the German market and other markets such as the French, Swiss and Angolan. Since BETA was a business certified by the ISO 9001 and ISO TS 16949 Norms it was able to supply certified products, thus increasing its visibility and network of contacts. Due to its internationalization BETA was able to internalize its relational knowledge of international customers and transpose this experience into the firm. Equally, it was able to leverage its sales in Portugal, increasing its market to produce equipment made in Portugal.

Taking into account its experience of expansion to Germany, and because a direct investment in Germany was out of the question due to BETA's small dimension, it decided to try a different strategy and create a new firm in Brazil, due to the high import taxes on equipment. It would pose less of a risk to begin a process of internationalization in Brazil and thus diversify its market. To do so, it decides to use its contacts in Brazil. These contacts were first established when BETA began supplying the Brazilian market via its Portuguese clients that operated in Brazil. So in 2011, BETA's top management team decides to create a small structure in Brazil so as to provide services to its Portuguese customers with business in Brazil on the one hand, and initiate its own process of internationalization in South America on the other hand.

For various months, BETA's top management team met with Portuguese firms that operated in the market, and understanding the working modes in Brazil. Due to the country's size Brazil constitutes a promising market but at the same time a difficult one to work, since it is very fragmented and not very structured.

After making the decision of internationalizing to Brazil and acquiring knowledge through the customers that already worked in the market, BETA decided to create a firm in association with Brazilian citizens. This choice took into account the fact that three individuals had the best intrinsic knowledge of the market and so they could enter it rapidly. The entry into the Brazilian market was done with careful planning and a lot of research. BETA had almost one year to study the behavior of one of the possible partners. Thus, it signed a work contract with this partner in a Portuguese firm which was already a BETA customer in Brazil. In parallel, the administrators of BETA met weekly with Portuguese firms in Brazil, with other firms that had abandoned that market and still others who had the same aim of entering the Brazilian market. The intention was to acquire a wider knowledge of work experiences in Brazil.

At the end of 2011 the firm decided to extend the society to two other people, one of them brought by the first partner. The capital distribution among the various associates was 55% for BETA and 15% for each of the 3 Brazilian partners. The choice of the three partners was based on the fact that each of them was from a different field of work, namely the field of passive equipment for telecommunications (for example plugs, boxes and components), another from the field of active equipment for telecommunications (for example, modems, routers and set top box) and finally one from the field of education (hardware and software for schools). The aim was to expand, as far as possible, the intervention of the three partners in different markets, so as to, on the one hand, diversify the entry mode and, on the other hand, diminish the risk of intervention.

Clearly, the three markets have different operational perspectives and different customers. Whereas the passive equipment for telecommunications market is relatively aggressive in terms of price, the market for active equipment for telecommunications can be an intense relational perspective, since the equipment has to be developed taking into account the local B2B customers' needs. Lastly, the market of the educational field is an interesting market as it is in great expansion, but needs some lobbying activity among public decision makers.

The biggest problems in terms of entering this market was related to the knowledge of the laws, customs duties and the issue of labor laws since they are quite different from those in Portugal. To evaluate this issue BETA nominated an employee (using the promoter strategy) to study the laws and the market. Even so it was difficult since when this person, for example, spoke with three different accountants in Brazil about the same theme, he concluded that each of them did their work in a different way! The problem is that importing a product can be done in a certain way and after some time (sometimes years), the tax system can approach the firm claiming that the operation should have been done in a different manner. That is, these considerations caused some preoccupation in BETA's strategic approach.

BETA intended to maintain the strategy of seeking out new customers and follow a relational perspective. To do so, they sought to learn about the market and the implications that may derive from legislative and logistic issues in the context of developing business in this new market. So as to minimize any mistakes in entering the Brazilian market, BETA closely accompanied all the operations in Brazil. As an example, due to the great size of Brazil and the interstate infrastructural differences, BETA tried to understand how the firms' transport of merchandise was executed so as to avoid cost errors. It is of extreme importance to lower the costs of transport and avoid relational problems in an initial stage of a B2B relationship.

BETA had to invest in equipment, tools and the involvement of their partners in Portugal and in the support that they gave to the operations (budgeting, planning, and technical support among others). Besides their partners, BETA contracted four more people to develop projects in Brazil. It should be highlighted that as the production was done in BETA's facilities in Portugal, some BETA workers also participated in this effort. The difference in time zones played an important role in this initial stage as all employees involved in BETA had to be in sync with the difference in the time zone and with the collaboration with the Brazilian firms.

The work done by the firm was successful. However the Brazilian partners began to differ in what respected the strategies, operation management and the working modes in Brazil so the relationship among the three partners began to deteriorate. This bad relationship lead to a breech in confidence among all the partners and led to the emergence of differences in the BETA administrators in Portugal in what concerns the performance and the way to continue operations in Brazil. Some defended the decision of closing the firm and taking responsibility for the bad results, whereas others defended the idea of the importance of continuing their stay in Brazil, so as to find new solutions for this continuance.

As the problem was among the three Brazilian partners, in a first stage BETA decided to break the link with them and, given the expectations, this caused a discomfort among the directors.

In a second stage, and after a year, the business relationship was re-established with one of the Brazilian partners, having maintained sporadic contacts with the other two. Despite the problems of the breech of confidence among the partners involved, the directors of BETA chose "not to close the door" and maintain pre-established contacts. They thought about looking at the business and seeing what had not gone well and how to continue to act, on an individual relational basis with each of the partners.

In this way, BETA did not totally abandon the market or the three Brazilian partners: in the end BETA tried to maintain and find new contacts in consolidated areas. So as not to abandon the Brazilian market, BETA developed new solutions that were introduced in the Brazilian market. Despite everything that had happened, BETA tried to minimize the loss and so continued to work, not in a logic of partners in a traditional firm, but in a logic of a dyadic supplier/customer relationship, in which BETA plays a role of supplier and each of the three ex-partners that of the customers exploring their field of business in Brazil. The intention was, therefore, to work with each former partner individually, without discarding the knowledge acquired in the Brazilian market.

After understanding that working individually there would not be as many problems in customer orientation and for the market that they wanted to attain, BETA decided to continue in Brazil. At this moment the business relationship is more intense with the initial partners, despite continuing to establish business relationships and looking for new projects with the other two.

The decision to stay in Brazil to fulfill their commitments and begin an individual business relationship with each of the partners was made due to the fact that there were very interesting business opportunities for BETA and that it was worth trying to implement.

Brazil is a country undergoing a great expansion where investment continues to be made and there is a dire need of firms with competencies in advanced fields of technology, as is the case of BETA. At the moment there are changes in legislation that allow new services to be incorporated in businesses and in fields in which BETA has solutions. Leaving the Brazilian market would have been very negative in terms of investment and experience since not only would business opportunities be lost but the future process of entry would have to be repeated with similar costs and risks.

The main advantages in the process of internationalization are related to a successful entry with a substantial business volume, (despite the setbacks), and to the knowledge of the market and of other firms in Brazil. This would be impossible to attain if one was not present in the market.

BETA considers that one cannot say that it was not worth it, because it has a better knowledge of the laws and how one should work. It had access to firms that allowed it to believe that it will continue to do business in Brazil in a safer way.

Despite the breech of confidence with the three partners and the existing problems, the choice of this country was considered quite important and interesting for BETA. At this moment, BETA is present in the Brazilian market, but with new partners in new fields of business, namely in the area of energy efficiency and management of public lighting. So BETA wants to develop a new approach in Brazil, taking into account what was learnt during the long entry process in the Brazilian market.

In conclusion, BETA continued to try its luck in Brazil, because it intended to take advantage of the Brazilian market and did not want to feel regret if it had abandoned this market.

After all the years of work in Brazil, BETA concludes that for the process of internationalization to Brazil to be successful it was identical to the one used in Europe: to engage in business and be successful there has to be a relationship of confidence among all parts, you must have good references in the market and technological competencies that allow any firm to assert itself as a trustworthy partner, and only after comes price.

It should also be highlighted that internationalization to Brazil can be considered as successful, since it has brought to Portugal the senior management of large scale Brazilian companies, namely telecommunication operators, as well as Mayors from several large Brazilian cities with whom BETA has signed contracts, which has given value to BETA's name in the global market.

CONCLUSION

The firms' internationalization process is a very important issue for firms, especially for SMEs as they have very limited resources. Although several theories have been put forward to explain how firms thrive in international markets – e.g., the Porter's diamond (Porter, 1989), the Uppsala model, and the network model – very few times the relational aspects have been used to address the difficulties that most SMEs face in their path to foreign markets. As Crick and Spence (2005) defend, there is not a single theory explaining the process of internationalization strategies adopted by a company. Based on this perspective the case of BETA was used to address how the relational perspective can be used by SMEs to muddle the difficulties posed when entering foreign markets. A synthesis of the characteristics of BETA is put forward in Table 2.

The first conclusion is that BETA, *strictu sensu*, does not follow the concept of market orientation, it is rather customer oriented as it focused on the relationship with their customers. The lack of market orientation in the broadest sense means that BETA does not have resources that enable it to compete in a broader market and does not have a service or product that can cover the entire market. Moreover, given BETA's small size, the huge electronics and telecommunications marketplace and the global presence on many of their players, BETA's size deters it from developing a true market orientation, although it has competitive intelligence to analyze the market where it competes and pinpoints their main competitors.

The second conclusion is that the customer orientation concept can be more easily operationalized among SMEs as they seek more objectively their customers

Table 2. Synthesis of the case study

	BETA
Number of employees	225 employees.
Type of products for the automotive sector	Production and commercialization of electronics and telecommunications equipment
Quality Certifications granted	ISO9001; ISO TS 16949
Exports (%)	66% (2013)
International profile	Small and medium-sized firm. According to Johanson and Mattsson (1988) in can be considered a Lonely International as it has production operations in Portugal and it is present in the Brazilian market. It has market operations in Germany, France, Switzerland, Angola.
International mode of entry	Through agents in Germany, France, Switzerland, Angola. Direct presence in Brazil.
Market orientation	Although BETA is clearly an outward-oriented firm, its modus operandi involves working in close cooperation with its clients developing and producing electronics and telecommunications products. The concept of market orientation is not readily applicable to BETA as it does not develop market intelligence analytics or competition orientation metrics as proposed by Narver and Slater (1990) and Jaworski and Kohli (1993).
Client orientation	BETA is clearly a client oriented firm as it follows the typical dyadic perspective proposed by Deng and Dart (1994). As an SME of the electronics industry, BETA seeks a fruitful relationship with its clients so that a long-term relationship can be developed.
Relationship orientation	As Zolkiewski and Turnbull (2006) claim, if business relationships do not succeed, any customer relationship is doomed. In this respect BETA seeks not to serve the electronics market but rather to get involved in business relationships with its clients in order to create a long-term relationship. As such, BETA's orientation to its individual clients underpins the development of a trust-based relationship involving the commitment of both partners.
Trust	The firm needs to develop a high level of trust with their clients in the electronics and telecommunication market. This trust leads to a supplier-client relationship in the market that underpins sequential relationships with their clients. This way the firm avoids the typical cost leadership strategy that characterizes Asian firms.
Commitment	Beta seeks high level of commitment with clients based on reciprocal, relational, long-term relationships built basically on strong solution-oriented technological innovation capabilities. As seen before, this commitment is also present in stressful situations involving disagreements among business partners in which a long-term perspective is mandatory. Although the withdrawal of the Brazilian market could have been simpler, straight-forward solution in the short-term, the firm managed to turnaround the situation and not only did not withdraw from the Brazilian market, but also managed to work with their former partners and kept doing business with them.
Main resources	Human capital, relational capital, technological acumen, advanced technical equipment, technical skills, and quality.

continued on following page

Table 2. Continued

	BETA
Influence of the client in the market selection	Low. The client is very important for a relational perspective. However, BETA is opportunity driven and follows some personal contacts to deploy their international market entry strategies. In this way, BETA is not market driven but client oriented.
Factors that strengthen the relationship	Trust and commitment are built up since the development of new products/projects/businesses. They are based not on the supply of a product, but they involve supplier-client relationships that encompass the development of the product and post-production service activities. BETA seeks to develop long-term relationships that lead to a sequential business involvement. Strong technological capabilities increased the level of strength, trust and commitment between BETA and its clients.
Internationalization future perspective	Although other business opportunities in foreign markets are important BETA seeks to deepen its internationalization intensity in the Brazilian market in order to take on the opportunities of this fast growing electronics and telecommunications market. Internationalization also seeks to diversify BETA's main business base.

rather scanning the whole market, given its limited resources. Given the difficulty of conquering brand new markets, SMEs seek as a priority to deploy strategies to maintain their customers. As such, the relationship orientation guidance enables them to focus their attention on the relationship so that they retain their customers, increasing their level of satisfaction. It is focusing on the relationship that allows, as in BETA's case, to provide customer satisfaction and then take advantage of the network perspective proposed by Johanson and Mattsson (1998).

In its internationalization process BETA sought to enter the Brazilian market, as in the German market, reducing the risks of failure. The initial contacts were meant to generate commitment among the parties to try to generate trust. However, BETA was not expecting to face the difficulties it went through.

In an attempt to cover the market, three partners from different areas were completely sought for. However, given the importance of the Brazilian market for the BETA, it decided to stay in Brazil, even in adverse situations. BETA took advantage of its relational perspective to maintain the contacts with its three partners. In fact, the goal was to follow a relationship orientation involving its three former partners into business associates, thus preventing the failure of its entry into the Brazilian market.

One can say that the relationship orientation allowed BETA to circumvent the internal conflict generated. Despite the problems faced by BETA it managed to go over the instrumental dimension of commitment to safeguard its position in the Brazilian market and sowed it affective and behavioral dimension when it created the conditions for the former partners to keep working with BETA creating mutually supportive conditions for them as well as for BETA.

Finally, it is possible to conclude that if business relationships are important in leveraging the internationalization processes, it is more important to be aware of the importance of simple concepts such as trust, cooperation, and commitment as part of those business relationships. In their quest for international markets plenty of firms try to internalize concepts such as market orientation, and customer orientation disregarding the importance of how relationships are build up. Clearly, it is human beings that implement trust-based relationships that are underpinned on the commitment of businessmen to get involved on evolutionary cooperative agreements. Only when those cooperative agreements reach a relational partnership-like status, firms are aware of how important the relationship is for succeeding in a competitive world. As presented above, BETA is a good vivid example of how to operate in the market, with a relationship orientation following a long-term perspective.

REFERENCES

Andersson, U., Forsgren, M., & Holm, U. (2002). The strategic impact of external networks: Subsidiary performance and competence development in multinational corporation. *Strategic Management Journal*, *23*(11), 979–996. doi:10.1002/smj.267

Andersson, U., Johanson, J., & Vahlne, J.-E. (1997). Organic acquisitions in the internationalization process of the business firm. *Management International Review*, *37*(2), 67–84.

Atuahene-Gima, K., & Slater, A. (2001). *Dual core market orientation and radical innovation: A conceptual model and empirical test. European Marketing Academy Conference.*

Axelsson, B., & Johanson, J. (1992). Foreign market entry: The textbook vs. the network view. In B. Axelsson & G. Easton (Eds.), *Industrial Networks: A New View of Reality* (pp. 218–234). London: Routledge.

Bilkey, W. J., & Tesar, G. (1977). The export behavior of smaller-sized Wisconsin manufacturing firms. *Journal of International Business Studies*, *8*(1), 93–98. doi:10.1057/palgrave.jibs.8490783

Bjorkman, I., & Forsgren, M. (2000). Nordic international business research: A review of its development. *International Studies of Management & Organization*, *30*(1), 6–25.

Brown, J. R., Lusch, R. F., & Nicholson, C. Y. (1995). Power and relationship commitment: Their impact on marketing channel member performance. *Journal of Retailing*, *71*(4), 363–392. doi:10.1016/0022-4359(95)90019-5

Bruggen, G. H. (2005). The impact of channel function performance on buyer-seller relationships in marketing channels. *International Journal of Research in Marketing*, *22*(2), 141–158. doi:10.1016/j.ijresmar.2004.06.004

Buckley, P. J., & Casson, M. (1976). *The future of the multinational enterprise*. London: Macmillan.

Burgel, O., & Murray, G. C. (2000). The international market entry choices of start-up companies in high-technology industries. *Journal of International Marketing*, *8*(2), 33–62. doi:10.1509/jimk.8.2.33.19624

Cadogan, J., & Diamantopoulos, A. (1995). Narver & Slater, Kohli & Jaworski and the market orientation construct: Integration and internationalization. *Journal of Strategic Marketing*, *3*(1), 41–60. doi:10.1080/09652549500000003

Cadogan, J., Diamantopoulos, A., & Mortanges, C. (1999). A measure of export market orientation: Scale development and cross-cultural validation. *Journal of International Business Studies*, *30*(4), 689–707. doi:10.1057/palgrave.jibs.8490834

Calle-Fernández, A., & Tamayo-Bustamante, V. (2005). Estrategia e internacionalización en las PYMES: Caso Antioquia. *Cuadernos de Administración*, *18*(30), 137–164.

Calof, J., & Beamish, P. (1995). Adapting to foreign markets: Explaining internalisation. *International Business Review*, *4*(2), 115–131. doi:10.1016/0969-5931(95)00001-G

Caves, R. E. (1971). International corporations: The Industrial economics of foreign investment. *Economica*, *38*(149), 1–27. doi:10.2307/2551748

Chetty, S., & Campbell-Hunt, C. (2003). Paths to internationalisation among small-to medium-sized firms: A global versus regional approach. *European Journal of Marketing*, *37*(5/6), 796–820. doi:10.1108/03090560310465152

Coviello, N. E., & Munro, H. J. (1997). Network relationships and the internationalization process of small software firms. *International Business Review*, *6*(4), 361–386. doi:10.1016/S0969-5931(97)00010-3

Crick, D., & Spence, M. (2005). The Internationalisation of 'high performing' U.K. high-tech SMEs: A study of planned and unplanned strategies. *International Business Review*, *14*(2), 167–185. doi:10.1016/j.ibusrev.2004.04.007

Cuervo-Cazurra, A. (2011). Selecting the country in which to start internationalization: The non-sequential internationalization argument. *Journal of World Business*, *46*(4), 426–437. doi:10.1016/j.jwb.2010.10.003

Dawes, J. (2000). Market orientation and company profitability: Further evidence incorporating longitudinal data. *Australian Journal of Management, 25*(2), 173–200. doi:10.1177/031289620002500204

Day, G. (1999). Misconceptions about market orientation. *Journal of Market-Focused Management, 4*(1), 5–16. doi:10.1023/A:1009882027377

Day, G. S. (2003). Creating a superior customer-relating capability. *Sloan Management Review, 44*(3), 77–82.

Day, G. S., & Van den Bulte, C. (2002). *Superiority in customer relationship management: Consequences for competitive advantage and performance.* Marketing Science Institute Working Paper Series, Report No. 02-123.

Deng, S., & Dart, J. (1994). Measuring market orientation. A multi-factor, multi-items approach. *Journal of Marketing Management, 10*(8), 725–742. doi:10.1080/0267257X.1994.9964318

Deshpandé, R., & Farley, D. (2004). Organizational culture, market orientation, innovativeness, and firm performance: An international research odyssey. *International Journal of Research in Marketing, 21*(1), 3–22. doi:10.1016/j.ijresmar.2003.04.002

Deshpandé, R., Farley, D., & Webster, F. Jr. (1993). Corporate culture, customer orientation, and innovativeness in Japanese firms: A quadrad *analysis. Journal of Marketing, 57*(1), 23–37. doi:10.2307/1252055

Doz, Y., Santos, J., & Williamson, P. (2001). *From global to metanational: How companies win in the knowledge economy.* Boston, MA: Harvard Business Press.

Dwyer, F. R., Schurr, P. H., & Oh, S. (1987). Developing buyer-seller relationships. *Journal of Marketing, 51*(2), 11–27. doi:10.2307/1251126

Easton, G., Wilkinson, I., & Georgieva, C. (1997). Towards evolutionary models of industrial networks – a research programme. In H. Gemünden, T. Ritter, & A. Walter (Eds.), *Relationships and networks in international markets* (pp. 273–295). Oxford, UK: Pergamon.

Evans, J. R., & Laskin, R. (1994). The relationship marketing process: A conceptualization and application. *Industrial Marketing Management, 23*(2), 439–452. doi:10.1016/0019-8501(94)90007-8

Frith, J. R. (1998). The market orientation performance relationship in minority and woman-owned small firms. *Academy of Marketing Studies Journal, 2*(1), 35–56.

Gadde, L.-E., & Snehota, I. (2000). Making the Most of Supplier Relationships. *Industrial Marketing Management, 29*(4), 305–316. doi:10.1016/S0019-8501(00)00109-7

Gankema, H., Snuif, H., & Zwart, P. (2000). The internationalization process of small and medium sized enterprises: An evaluation of stage theory. *Journal of Small Business Management, 38*(4), 15–27.

González-Benito, O., & González-Benito, J. (2005). Cultural vs. operational market orientation and objective vs. subjective performance: Perspective of production and operations. *Industrial Marketing Management, 34*(8), 797–829. doi:10.1016/j.indmarman.2005.01.002

Gray, B. J., Matear, S., Boshoff, C., & Matheson, P. (1998). Developing a better measure of market orientation. *European Journal of Marketing, 32*(9), 884–903. doi:10.1108/03090569810232327

Håkansson, H. (1982). *International Marketing and Purchasing of Industrial Goods: An Interaction Approach*. Chichester, UK: Wiley.

Håkansson, H. (1987). *Industrial technological development. A network approach*. London: Croom Helm.

Håkansson, H., & Ford, D. (2002). How should companies interact in business networks? *Journal of Business Research, 55*(2), 133–139. doi:10.1016/S0148-2963(00)00148-X

Håkansson, H., & Johanson, J. (1984). Heterogeneity in industrial markets and its implications for marketing. In I. Hägg & F. Wiedersheim-Paul (Eds.), *Between market and hierarchy*. Uppsala: Department of Business Studies.

Håkansson, H., & Snehota, I. (2006). "No business is an island" 17 years later. *Scandinavian Journal of Management, 22*(3), 271–274. doi:10.1016/j.scaman.2006.08.001

Håkansson, H., & Snehota, J. (1995). *Developing Relationships in Business Networks*. London: Routledge.

Heins, R. A. (2000). Market orientation: Toward an integrated framework. *Academy of Marketing Science Review, 1*. Available http://www.amsreview.org/articles/heiens01-2000.pdf

Helfert, G., Ritter, T., & Walter, A. (2002). Redefining market orientation from a relationship perspective. Theoretical considerations and empirical results. *European Journal of Marketing, 36*(9/10), 1119–1139. doi:10.1108/03090560210437361

Holmlund, M., & Kock, S. (1996). Buyer dominated relationships in a supply chain: A case study of four small-sized suppliers. *International Small Business Journal, 15*(1), 26–40. doi:10.1177/0266242696151002

Holmlund, M., & Kock, S. (1998). Relationships and the internationalisation of Finnish small and medium-sized companies. *International Small Business Journal, 16*(4), 46–63. doi:10.1177/0266242698164003

Hymer, S. H. (1976). *The international operations of national firms: A study of direct investment.* MIT Press.

Ibeh, K. I., & Young, S. (2001). Exporting as an entrepreneurial act: An empirical study of Nigerian firms. *European Journal of Marketing, 35*(5/6), 566–586. doi:10.1108/03090560110388114

Jap, S., & Ganesan, S. (2000). Control Mechanisms and Relationship Life Cycle: Implications for Safeguarding Specific Investments and Developing Commitment. *JMR, Journal of Marketing Research, 37*(May), 227–245. doi:10.1509/jmkr.37.2.227.18735

Jaworski, B., & Kohli, A. (1993). Market orientation: Antecedents and consequences. *Journal of Marketing, 57*(3), 53–70. doi:10.2307/1251854

Johanson, J., & Mattsson, L.-G. (1987). Interorganizational relations in industrial systems: A network approach compared with the transaction-cost approach. *International Studies of Management & Organization, 17*(1), 64–74.

Johanson, J., & Mattsson, L.-G. (1988). Internationalisation in industrial system: a network approach. In N. Hood & J.-E. Vahlne (Eds.), *Strategies in global competition.* London: Croom Helm.

Johanson, J., & Vahlne, J.-E. (1977). The internationalization process of the firm – a model of knowledge development and increasing foreign market commitments. *Journal of International Business Studies, 8*(1), 23–32. doi:10.1057/palgrave.jibs.8490676

Johanson, J., & Vahlne, J.-E. (1990). The mechanism of internationalization. *International Marketing Review, 7*(4), 11–24. doi:10.1108/02651339010137414

Johanson, J., & Vahlne, J.-E. (1992). Management of foreign market entry. *Scandinavian International Business Review, 1*(3), 9–27. doi:10.1016/0962-9262(92)90008-T

Johanson, J., & Wiedersheim-Paul, F. (1975). The internationalization of the firm: Four Swedish cases. *Journal of Management Studies, 12*(3), 305–322. doi:10.1111/j.1467-6486.1975.tb00514.x

Kindleberger, C. P. (1969). *American business abroad: Six lectures on direct investment*. New Haven, CT: Yale University Press.

Knickerbocker, F. T. (1973). Oligopolistic reaction and multinational enterprise. *The International Executive, 15*(2), 7–9. doi:10.1002/tie.5060150205

Kohli, A., & Jaworski, B. (1990). Market orientation: The construct, research propositions, and managerial implications. *Journal of Marketing, 54*(2), 1–18. doi:10.2307/1251866

Lamming, R. (1993). *Beyond partnership: Strategies for innovation and lean supply*. London: Prentice Hall.

Langerak, F. (2001). Effects of market orientation on the behaviors of salespersons and purchasers, channel relationships, and performance of manufacturers. *International Journal of Research in Marketing, 18*(3), 221–234. doi:10.1016/S0167-8116(01)00040-4

Leonidou, L., & Katsikeas, C. (1996). The export development process: An integrative review of empirical models. *Journal of International Business Studies, 27*(3), 517–551. doi:10.1057/palgrave.jibs.8490846

Liao, S., Chang, W., Wu, C., & Katrichis, J. (2011). A survey of market orientation research (1995-2008). *Industrial Marketing Management, 40*(2), 301–310. doi:10.1016/j.indmarman.2010.09.003

Lindqvist, M. (1991). *Infant multinationals: The internationalization of young, technology-based Swedish firms*. Stockholm School of Economics, Institute of International Business.

Lings, I., & Greenley, G. (2005). Measuring internal market orientation. *Journal of Service Research, 7*(3), 290–305. doi:10.1177/1094670504271154

Luostarinen, R. (1980). *The Internationalization of the firm*. Helsinki: Helsinki School of Economics.

Madsen, T., & Servais, P. (1997). The internationalization of born globals: An evolutionary process? *International Business Review, 6*(6), 561–583. doi:10.1016/S0969-5931(97)00032-2

Matsuno, K., Mentzer, J., & Rentz, J. (2005). A conceptual and empirical comparison of three market orientation scales. *Journal of Business Research, 58*(1), 1–8. doi:10.1016/S0148-2963(03)00075-4

Mavondo, F. (1999). Market orientation: Scale invariance and relationship to generic strategies across two countries. *Journal of Market Focused Management, 4*(2), 125–142. doi:10.1023/A:1009835515831

Mohr, J., & Spekman, R. (1994). Characteristics of partnership success: Partnership attributes, communication behavior and conflict resolution techniques. *Strategic Management Journal, 15*(2), 135–152. doi:10.1002/smj.4250150205

Moorman, C., Deshpande, R., & Zaltman, G. (1992). Relationships between providers and users of marketing research: The dynamics of trust within and between organizations. *JMR, Journal of Marketing Research, 29*(3), 314–329. doi:10.2307/3172742

Moreira, A. (2004). Breve ensaio sobre a internacionalização. *Politécnica, 15*, 23–33.

Moreira, A. (2009b). Knowledge capability flows in buyer-supplier relationships: Challenges for small domestic suppliers in international contexts. *Journal of Small Business and Enterprise Development, 16*(1), 93–114. doi:10.1108/14626000910932908

Moreira, A. C. (2005a). A integração do desenvolvimento de novos produtos na cadeia de valor. Na senda de uma abordagem colaborativa. *Revista Portuguesa e Brasileira de Gestão, 4*(1), 56–66.

Moreira, A. C. (2005b). Supplier-buyer collaboration in new product development: Four case studies involving SMEs. *Brazilian Journal of Operations & Production Management, 2*(1), 5–24.

Moreira, A. C. (2007). La internacionalización de Pymes industriales a través de multinacionales. presentación de algunos casos de los sectores automotor y electrónico. *Cuadernos de Administración, 20*(34), 89–114.

Moreira, A. C. (2009a). The evolution of internationalisation: Towards a new theory? *Global Economics and Management Review, 14*(1), 41–59.

Moreira, A. C., & Carvalho, A. C. (2012). Internationalization approaches of the automotive innovation system. A historical perspective. In Technological change. Rijeka, Croacia: InTech.

Moreira, A. C., & Silva, P. M. (2013). Market orientation, innovation and organizational commitment in industrial firms. *Market, 25*(2), 123–142.

Morgan, R., & Hunt, S. (1994). The commitment-trust theory of relationship marketing. *Journal of Marketing, 58*(3), 20–38. doi:10.2307/1252308

Narver, J., & Slater, S. (1990). The Effect of a Market Orientation on Business Profitability. *Journal of Marketing, 54*(4), 20–35. doi:10.2307/1251757

Neergaard, H. (1998). *Networks as vehicles of internationalization: Network relationships and the internationalization process of small furniture manufacturers.* (Unpublished Doctoral Thesis). Aarhus School Business.

Nishiguchi, T. (1994). *Strategic industrial sourcing. The Japanese advantage.* Oxford, UK: Oxford University Press.

Panigyrakis, G., & Theodoridis, P. (2007). Market orientation and performance: An empirical investigation in the retail industry in Greece. *Journal of Retailing and Consumer Services, 14*(2), 137–149. doi:10.1016/j.jretconser.2006.05.003

Payne, A. F. (1988). Developing a marketing-oriented organization. *Business Horizons, 31*(May-June), 46–53. doi:10.1016/0007-6813(88)90008-0

Porter, M. (1989). *The competitive advantage of nations.* New York: The Free Press.

Ruzzier, M., Hisrich, R., & Antoncic, B. (2006). SME internationalization research: Past, present, and future. *Journal of Small Business and Enterprise Development, 13*(4), 476–497. doi:10.1108/14626000610705705

Sheth, J. N., & Sisodia, R. (1999). Revisiting marketing's lawlike generalizations. *Journal of the Academy of Marketing Science, 27*(1), 71–87. doi:10.1177/0092070399271006

Slater, S., & Narver, J. (1994a). Does competitive environment moderate the market orientation-performance relationship? *Journal of Marketing, 58*(1), 46–55. doi:10.2307/1252250

Slater, S., & Narver, J. (1994b). Market orientation, customer value, and superior performance. *Business Horizons, 37*(2), 22–28. doi:10.1016/0007-6813(94)90029-9

Sorjonen, H. (2011). The manifestation of market orientation and its antecedents in the program planning of arts organizations. *International Journal of Arts Management, 14*(1), 4–18.

Vernon, R. (1966). International investment and international trade in the product cycle. *The Quarterly Journal of Economics, 80*(2), 190–207. doi:10.2307/1880689

Webb, D., Webster, C., & Krepapa, A. (2000). An exploration of the meaning and outcomes of a customer-defined market orientation. *Journal of Business Research, 48*(2), 101–112. doi:10.1016/S0148-2963(98)00114-3

Welch, L., & Luostarinen, R. (1993). Internationalization: Evolution of a concept. In P. J. Buckley & P. N. Ghauri (Eds.), *The Internationalization of the firm: A reader* (pp. 155–171). Academic Press.

Welch, L. S., & Luostarinen, R. K. (1988). Internationalization: Evolution of a concept. *Journal of General Management*, *14*(2), 34–55.

Yau, O., McFetridge, P., Chow, R., Lee, J., Sin, L., & Tse, A. (2000). Is relationship marketing for everyone? *European Journal of Marketing*, *34*(9/10), 1111–1127. doi:10.1108/03090560010342494

Yin, R. K. (1984). *Case study research: Design and methods*. Newbury Park, CA: Sage.

Yin, R. K. (2004). *Case study methods. Complementary methods for research in education*. Washington, DC: American Educational Research Association.

Young, S., Hamill, J., Wheeler, C., & Davies, J. (1989). *International market entry and development*. Englewood Cliffs, NJ: Prentice Hall.

Zhang, D., Sivaramakrishnan, S., Delbaere, M., & Bruning, E. (2008). The relationship between organizational commitment and market orientation. *Journal of Strategic Marketing*, *16*(1), 55–73. doi:10.1080/09652540701794494

Zhao, Y., & Cavusgil, T. (2006). The effect of supplier's market orientation on manufacturer's trust. *Industrial Marketing Management*, *35*(4), 405–414. doi:10.1016/j.indmarman.2005.04.001

Zolkiewski, J., & Turnbull, P. (2006). Guest editorial. *European Journal of Marketing*, *40*(3/4), 241–247. doi:10.1108/ejm.2006.00740caa.001

KEY TERMS AND DEFINITIONS

Commitment: Commitment exists when both parties believe that the other party will invest in the relationship. This chapter is based on the theory that successful marketing relationships require both commitment and trust from both parties.

Relationship Orientation: Is a concept much more specific than market orientation. It involves the commitment of one party that believes that a relationship is worth working on to ensure that is endures throughout time. The relationship orientation is built on the foundation of mutual trust and commitment.

Trust: Trust exists when one party has confidence in the other party' reliability and integrity in business exchange processes.

Chapter 12

Business Development Opportunities and Market Entry Challenges in Latin America

Luis Rodrigo Asturias
Universidad Rafael Landivar, Guatemala

ABSTRACT

Considering Latin American economies have introduced various forms of attaining combat the economic crisis mostly through short-term policies based on credit incentive and increased public expenditure in order to revive the same; however, a long-term strategy where inclusive and sustainable growth which can be clearly discerned through innovation can play a key role prioritizing necessary. Thus in the course of this chapter create an analysis of the benefits of innovation and technological development taking into account the current state in Latin America and the possible scenarios in which technology serves as an important tool for economic and social development which translates into basic cornerstone for business and growth enhancer.

MACROECONOMIC CONSIDERATIONS IN LATIN AMERICA

As a starting point for analyzing potential business opportunities in the Latin American region is necessary to take into account macroeconomic basic variables to create a clear picture of the situation in the region is where macroeconomic variables thus

DOI: 10.4018/978-1-4666-8820-9.ch012

demonstrating the strengths, weaknesses, opportunities and economic threats in the region. Therefore the GDP of the Latin American and Caribbean region grew by 1.1% in 2014, its slowest rate of expansion since 2009. Considerable differences were observed between countries, with the sluggish regional rate largely determined by slow or negative growth in some of the largest economies: Argentina (-0.2%), the Bolivarian Republic of Venezuela (-3.0%), Brazil (0.2%) and Mexico (2.1%). The median GDP growth rate for the region was 2.8%, broadly in line with the 2013 figure. (2014, World Bank)

The region's fastest-growing economies were the Dominican Republic and Panama (6.0% in both cases), followed by the Plurinational State of Bolivia (5.2%), Colombia (4.8%) and Nicaragua (4.5%). Argentina, the Bolivarian Republic of Venezuela and Saint Lucia contracted by 0.2%, 3.0% and 1.4%, respectively, while the other economies grew at rates ranging from 0.5% to 4%.

In South America posted economic expansion of 0.7% (as against 2.8% in 2013), while Central America (including the Spanish-speaking Caribbean and Haiti) expanded by 3.7% (4.0% in 2013). The Mexican economy grew by 2.1% in 2014, compared with 1.1% in 2013. The English- and Dutch-speaking Caribbean likewise saw growth accelerate on previous years, reaching 1.9% in 2014.

One significant consequence of low economic growth was weak job creation, leading to a sharper-than-expected 0.4 percentage point fall in the urban employment rate. However, despite weak job creation, the urban open unemployment rate edged down from 6.2% to 6.0%. Until 2012, declining unemployment reflected a faster rise in employment than in participation, but since 2013 participation has fallen more heavily than employment. The labour performance of the region's countries was rather mixed. The regional outcome was determined by similar trends posted in Argentina, Brazil and Mexico, while a variety of results were observed in the other countries.

Although job creation has been weak —especially in wage employment— the labour market situation remains relatively benign. The open unemployment rate is at historically low levels, while other positive aspects include a widespread fall in the hourly underemployment rate, as well as real wage increases (measured at 1.3% according the weighted average of 10 countries, or 1.7% by the simple average of those countries.

Meanwhile the hydrocarbon exporters —Bolivarian Republic of Venezuela, Colombia, Ecuador and Plurinational State of Bolivia— also saw a significant decline (-4.6%) in their terms of trade. However, the countries that export agroindustrial products, Argentina, Paraguay and Uruguay, posted a smaller term-of-trade loss, at -0.4%, than the subregion overall. The Central American countries recorded a 1.1% terms-oftrade gain, thanks to higher prices for some of their export products and lower prices for energy imports. Terms of trade for the Caribbean food- and fuel- importing countries (that is, the Caribbean not including Trinidad and Tobago) are set to post a stable gain of 0.1%. Despite the large share of manufactures in its export structure, Mexico's terms of trade were down by 2.4%, similarly to the figure for the region overall, owing to the steep price drops for its export commodities (gold, silver, steel and oil).

Mexico regained its position as the second largest recipient of FDI in the region, with total inflows of US$ 38.286 billion, over double the amount received the year before. Mexico thus ranked behind Brazil, which received US$ 64.046 billion in FDI, 2% down on 2012 but ahead of Chile, which received US$ 20.258 billion, 29% less than in 2012.

By sector, services received the highest proportion of FDI inflows in 2013, with 38%, followed by manufacturing (36%) and natural resources (26%). However, these averages mask large differences between countries and subregions. Natural resources capture over 50% of FDI inflows in several countries, and as much as 70% in the Plurinational State of Bolivia. In fact, in South America (not including Brazil), natural resources receive more FDI than services, and manufacturing only small amounts. Inward FDI flows (left scale) Inward FDI flows as a percentage of GDP (right scale) Source: Economic Commission for Latin America and the Caribbean (ECLAC), on the basis of official figures and estimates at 8 May 2014.

The region's economies also vary greatly in terms of the origin of investments. The United States remains the largest investor in Latin America and the Caribbean generally, with a particularly prominent role in Central America (30% of inflows) and Mexico (32%). Europe overall is the largest investor in Brazil (46%), Mexico (54%) and Colombia (36%). In all the countries except Mexico, trans-Latin firms make significant contributions to FDI flows.

This is especially true in Ecuador (where FDI by trans-Latins accounts for 46% of inflows), Colombia (30%) and Central America (39%). Inflows from Asia have held steady (ECLAC, 2014).

Production Integration

Although the regional market has strong potential to boost production and export diversification, the region is not taking advantage of this. In 2013, just 19% of regional exports stayed within the region. This figure rises to 25% if Mexico is left out but, even so, the intraregional portion of total exports is far smaller in Latin America and the Caribbean than in other major regions of the world economy.

Despite the high manufacturing density of intraregional trade, most of it consists of finished products, as the small share of intermediate goods reveals. Intermediate goods account for over 30% of the value of goods traded between the countries of "factory Asia" and for almost 20% between the member countries of the North

American Free Trade Agreement (NAFTA), but for only 10% between the countries of Latin America and the Caribbean. This is evidence of a low degree of production integration between the Latin American and Caribbean economies. In fact, imports of parts and components by the region's largest economies originate mostly from extraregional suppliers.

Considering Latin American economies have introduced various forms of attaining combat the economic crisis mostly through short-term policies based on credit incentive and increased public expenditure in order to revive the same; however, a long-term strategy where inclusive and sustainable growth which can be clearly discerned through innovation can play a key role prioritizing necessary.

Indeed, you cannot think of long-term policies without considering the role pertaining to science, technology and innovation (TIC) in the economic recovery and growth in the coming years. Similarly joint TIC is accompanied by fiscal and monetary policies aimed at preventing the activity level continues to drop. Meanwhile industrial and technology policies must prevent technological and competitive asymmetries in the international economy deepen. So the short-term policy can focus on reducing unemployment and generations of capital, in case of the long-term can focus on reducing the gap between countries that are at the technological frontier (developed countries) and those in which the technology has only partially penetrated (developing countries).

ELAC mentions the short-term policy aimed at stabilizing output growth; the long term, in the case of developing economies, seeks to achieve growth rates that reduce, over time, international differences in income per capita (catching up). The international economic crisis causes several negative effects on innovation.

On one hand, the decline in growth rates strongly affects the rate of learning and the incorporation of innovations. It may be mentioned that there are created some negative effects occur by way of increased risk aversion and pessimistic expectations and unstable, which may reduce investment. Importantly, economic dynamism especially the export sector is key to innovation, and that international trade is an important source of learning.

Finally, the fall in tax revenue leads to a decrease of public resources devoted to basic and applied research. It is possible that, in this light, policies supporting innovation lost space.

It is worth noting that the economic crisis involves direct pressure to achieve greater efficiency and productivity. In other words, the crisis does not imply a break in innovation activities, as some opportunities become more visible.

Thus in the course of this chapter create an analysis of the benefits of innovation and technological development taking into account the current state in Latin America and the possible scenarios in which technology serves as an important tool for economic and social development which translates into basic cornerstone for business and growth enhancer.

1. Structural Change and Diversification in Latin America

When considering the development involves economic, social and political changes. As part of this process, productivity and change the production structure are closely interrelated with other areas of the economy and society. The close relationship between technology and income per capita requires moving towards more diversified, becoming more complex and higher-technology and knowledge production structures that advance in improving productivity and reducing structural heterogeneity. Building local capacities and reducing the economic and social gaps are complementary processes that require action by public policy.

As the industrial, technological and capacity building policies are needed to achieve those objectives. Thus, in Latin America, diversification policies with industrial and innovation policies are called to occupy a central position in the new development strategy. It is important that the agenda and policies to prioritize the development of long-term policies that are geared towards more intensive production structures in knowledge and innovation, and where social and environmental sustainability are priorities thereof.

Development involves quantitative and qualitative changes in the economic, social and political. It is a multidimensional process that democracy and citizenship are consolidated in a context of dynamic and insert virtuously economies in the international system.

It should be noted that the dimension of productivity and the change in the production structure is closely interrelated with other areas of the economy and society in the development process. The high technological convergence and income per capita in developed countries move requires more complex and diversified production structures with more technology and knowledge to advance in improving productivity and reducing structural heterogeneity.

Historical experience has relevance to all successful convergence (including the recent rise of China as a new world power and commercial) have been associated with the implementation and promotion of new sectors or activities.

Technology diffusion and productivity gains do not become to accumulate the same capital or produce more of the same goods, but rather relate to the emergence of new products and processes, and the consequent redefinition of production matrix.

Structural change is not only necessary to close the productivity gap and income with the developed world (external gap), is also necessary to reduce the income gap within economies (internal gap), especially in a region that stands out as one of the most unequal in the world. Distribution improvements can be achieved through social and redistributive policies, but these do not hold up in the long run without creating quality jobs. (ECLAC, 2013).

While it is true in Latin America have undertaken several initiatives conditional transfers have significantly lower levels of poverty, their sustainability, which depends heavily on revenues derived from activities related to the exploitation of natural resources, would be seriously compromised. The transfer of labor from low-productivity sectors and livelihood, and having a high level of informality towards higher productivity, more chain and with higher levels of spillover of knowledge is a central component of development. To achieve this it is necessary to create quality jobs so requires the transformation of the production base to be extended to include new activities and technological trajectories more technology-intensive and knowledge.

The two conditions that must assume the structural change for development-dynamism of the technological trajectory and dynamics of demand defined a productive structure with an dynamic science, which is what ensures that technological spillovers and expansion of effective demand promote not only a group of large companies, but also the whole of the economy through backward and forward. In this process of structural change are new agents and labor is increasingly shifting from low productivity sectors to new sectors that populate the space between the tip and the activities of subsistence (ECLAC, 2007, 2012; McMillan and Rodrik, 2011).

That said can automatically glimpsed a more homogeneous distribution of the activities of medium and high productivity, favorable outcome on equity. It is vital that in some cases there is tension between efficiency a country with excellent performance in sectors with few increasing returns can direct resources to the same (high fi static science) to the detriment of others who have lower productivity in the short term but trajectories highest productivity in the long run. The policies should focus transform fi science static dynamic, avoiding "effects lock" (lock-in) in less intense activities of knowledge.

In Latin America and the Caribbean, the challenge of competitiveness is extremely interesting as ever. Economic analysis of approximately 10 years back presented high levels of growth for certain countries in the Latin region. Although this continues to show significant limitations and shortcomings in terms of new technologies. The technological movement is presented as an exogenous reflection, without being given the necessary local efforts to fully exploit its potential.

Central to the new technological paradigms such as TIC, biotechnology and nanotechnology, is its cross impact in the production structure. They are general purpose technologies, which makes its impact is multiplied when there is a wide variety of sectors in which they may apply.

Thus new paradigms affect competitiveness, innovation and productivity of the entire production. However, it is necessary to incorporate the engines of economic growth in each country the development of new technologies, which will be able to create more diversified production structures that offer more opportunities for equitable and sustainable development.

2. Innovation and Social Inclusion

ECLAC sees social inclusion as an extended form of social integration, which defines, in turn, as a process that enables people a stake in the minimum level consistent with the development being achieved in a country. The concept of inclusion would be broader than that of social integration to the extent that instead of emphasizing on a structure to which individuals must adapt to join the systemic logic, is also an effort to adapt the system so you can incorporate a wide range of actors and individuals. In this sense, social inclusion involves interaction between the construction of a system to ensure at least a minimum of welfare to the entire population, on the one hand and, on the other hand, the reactions of the people who help to shape and redefine the system. Thus, social inclusion means not only improving the conditions of access to channels of integration but also promote and increase the possibilities of self-determination of the actors involved (ECLAC, 2007d).

Therefore the relationship between two concepts can be considered as dynamic and multifactorial innovation and social inclusion is not linear. Can be seen, at least two dimensions in such a relationship. As an instrument innovation as a tool for social inclusion and on the other, the goal of inclusion to guide innovation processes.

We can say that a first approximation between innovation and social inclusion is created from the consideration that, in the long run, one of the main engines of economic development is the invocation. Therefore it is not possible to conceive of a continuous improvement process being without innovation. In this sense, there can be no sustainable progress towards inclusion without continuous innovation processes.

It is necessary to consider the fundamental role played by information in both the construction of a system to enable greater inclusion and in the response of the population to that system, the way they organize and manage information, together with the possibilities and related costs, are determinants of efficiency is achieved.

Elsewhere innovation in TIC and management, can be analyzed by reducing the cost of creating, processing and distribution of information, which therefore has a positive impact on inclusion, as it allows the participation of a greater number of actors social assets and a higher density of communication. However, although in most cases an innovation in TIC or a management system cannot increase the exclusion of a group of populations in absolute terms, the relative position of that group it can deteriorate if others are benefiting at higher rates. That is why the need to ensure public policy through not only the massive access to the results of innovation, but also its use; this means that you have to transform it into a public service.

In general, ensure access and even more, the universal service involves two types of gap closing. The first, called market gap is the one between the situation of welfare that would result from the efficient functioning of the market system, and the actual situation in which they feel the effects of the faults of the system, such as concentration leading to have market power and externalities uncorrected. Another, called development gap is the distance between the optimal situation from the point of view of the role of social preference and the efficient market solution. Close the first breach involves correcting market failures; closing the second requires actions redistribution of income tangible or intangible.

The first gap can be controlled by regulatory policies and competition; while the second involves the implementation of redistributive policies or even productive development, to the extent that supposed to increase access obtains cost reductions through actions aimed at encouraging producers.

Finally it can be considered that social inclusion to guide innovation processes is a different way of approaching the relationship between innovation and inclusion is to conceive the latter as a social goal with ability to direct the allocation of human and financial resources to certain areas of innovation.

3. Innovation and Development

It is difficult to refer to the importance of innovation in economic analysis without mentioning the contribution of Schumpeter about it. For him, innovation is the driving force behind the development process of the countries in the long run. Schumpeter (1911) defines innovation as the emergence of new production functions, new markets and new means of transportation, feeding the process of "creative destruction" (some sectors decline while others are new and expand faster).

Some years ago the company was dependent on the individual genius of a certain type of employer (the innovator), with the passage of time becomes endogenous to large enterprises. These departments are established in research and development (R + D) systematically generate innovations as part of the ongoing quest to create competitive advantages. But these advantages are transient and diluted as a plethora of imitators who disseminates new knowledge and increases productivity and welfare levels of the economy as a whole emerges. Schumpeter is also due to the long cycles have associated growth to the emergence of a set of incremental innovations, with strong spillovers and interconnections with other sectors[1].

The original definition of innovation Schumpeter has been reworked by several authors. In particular, we have proposed different types of innovation, taking into account both the magnitude of its impact on the economic system and the intensity of their relationship with science and technology. Of the various typologies that have emerged, the most widespread is given by Freeman and Perez (1988), who divide innovations into four categories: i) progressive or incremental; ii) radicals; iii) changes in the technological system, and iv) changes in the techno-economic paradigm.

By nature itself, in many cases do not occur in formal R & D departments and patents are recorded; they are more related to processes of "learning" (learning by doing) and correction of problems (trouble shooting) in production.

Significantly, are not spontaneous, but require significant research efforts by the workers, engineers and technicians of the firm, without which it is not possible to transform experience into knowledge production and incremental innovations.

4. Productivity and Employment

The generation of quality employment is associated with two main objectives: to create sustained growth with increased productivity, and promote social inclusion (ECLAC, 2010). Primarily the first mentioned is linked to the type of economic structure, if the structure is more or less dynamic, whether or not power learning and knowledge, technological development and innovation.

Is worth to clarify that work for most countries in Latin America is the main source of household income necessary for their wellbeing, so it is in the labor market where people acquire and develop much of their skills and capabilities.

There are countries that have promoted structural change in direction of the dynamic efficiency, towards sectors with greater technological sophistication which has been reflected in increased growth of effective demand, have made, while employment gains and productivity. But when the economic structure is shifted towards sectors with low productivity, can increase employment but falling productivity.

For example, if workers leave higher productivity sectors to work in other lower productivity, there may be a fall in aggregate productivity, even though the product increases, because more employed workers. Conversely, if productivity increases, but so does the effective demand in equal or greater proportion, then there will be an increase in product with lower employment, which poses serious problems for opportunities to advance in the path of inclusive development.

So considering that product expansion has not always increased productivity, since the displacement of employment sectors with lower productivity. In the case of Latin American economies can be analyzed certain periods which increases the product but productivity falls showing a more volatile and erratic behavior. Meanwhile, those economies in Asia and Europe that have dynamic curves show that the two variables, output and productivity, jointly and steadily increase.

Latin America reflects a movement of employment towards sectors with lower productivity, which often represents a mere shelter to open unemployment. Latin America shows great heterogeneity within, and enlightened countries cannot really determine the variety of cases that exist in the region.

Figure 1. Dynamics of labor productivity and value added for selected countries (1980-2010): Denmark and Republic of Korea
Source: CEPALSTAT, World Bank (WB), World Development Indicators (WDI), Organization for Economic Cooperation and Development (OECD), The Labour Force Survey (MEI) 2012.

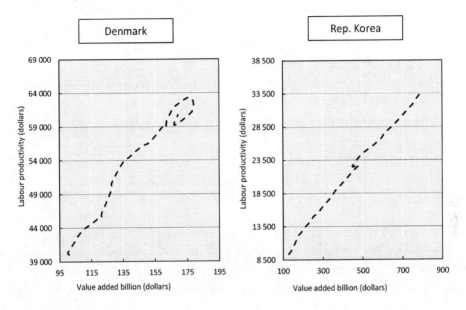

Figure 2. Dynamics of labor productivity and value added for selected countries (1980-2010): Costa Rica and Mexico
Source: CEPALSTAT, World Bank (WB), World Development Indicators (WDI), Organization for Economic Cooperation and Development (OECD), The Labour Force Survey (MEI) 2012.

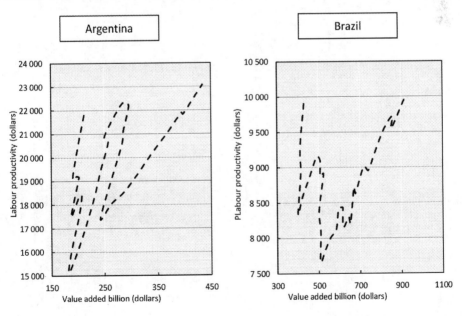

Even within the group of countries represented in the graph, there are very different stories: some achieve steady growth after 2004, while still others show very erratic movement.

In the Latin American case, the fall in productivity is well marked during the "lost decade" of the eighties. While such episodes occurred at other times in the economic history of the region (final of the nineties and early twenty-first century), they were not as long as the eighties.

Finally it can be seen that curve segments are almost horizontal, which responds to an almost exclusively based on the absorption of growth labor, and no absorption of technical progress or diversification.

5. The Technological Capabilities in the Region

There is a lot of literature showing consistently that the learning processes, generation and dissemination of endogenous technological capabilities are key elements for a sustained social inclusion and a more equitable income distribution. (Fajnzylber, 1990, ECLAC, 2007a) Growth in a global economy where knowledge is a major asset. The main elements that characterize the global knowledge economy are: i) increased codification of knowledge; ii) a closer relationship between technology

Figure 3. Dynamics of labor productivity and value added for selected countries (1980-2010): Argentina and Brazil
Source: *CEPALSTAT, World Bank (WB), World Development Indicators (WDI), Organization for Economic Cooperation and Development (OECD), The Labour Force Survey (MEI) 2012.*

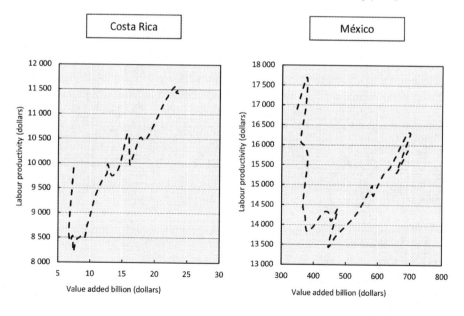

and science, with higher rates of innovation cycles and shorter product life; iii) increasing importance of innovation in GDP growth, as well as education and lifelong learning; iv) increased investment in intangibles (R & D, education, software, etc.) in fixed capital, and v) substantial changes in the demand for skills in the labor market.

While it is true Spain-Latin America-and particularly great technological advances in some of the above factors, meanwhile there are other economies around the world such as China and India that have focused efforts to build innovation capabilities.

In the case of Latin America, the limited technological capabilities are explained in most cases by factors related to the established economic pyramid that weighs more to other productive activities. As the dynamics of innovation, including the specialization pattern, the heavy weight of imports in sectors with high technological content, low positioning in global value chains and the consequent dependence on imported knowledge stands science, technology and innovation.

According to ECLAC, on average, Latin America is a very concentrated specialization in natural resources, although Mexico and Brazil are exceptions. In these countries the technology intensive industrial activities produce between 30% and 40% of manufacturing value added.

However, in the case of Mexico this is explained largely by the development of export manufacturing, which performs particularly assembly activities with low local added value per unit of product.

Meanwhile The Plurinational State of Bolivia, Honduras, Panama and Ecuador are the countries with the greatest weakness in terms of the importance of technology-intensive sectors, whose share does not exceed 10% of total value added in manufacturing country.

There example in Latin America and Peru, the Plurinational State of Bolivia, Paraguay, Panama, Ecuador, Chile and Uruguay that less than 20% of the total value of exports of goods corresponding to medium and high technological content, mainly due to the previous economic dependence on primary commodities and economic relationship with natural resources.

But in countries like Mexico, Costa Rica and Brazil assets medium and high technology represent between 35% and 65%, although it is worth noting that there are substantial differences between them: in Brazil reflect a production structure greater coordination and dissemination of technology between sectors, whereas in Mexico and Costa Rica have mainly focused on assembling activities and free trade zones.

Moreover, the regional companies that have managed to integrate into international production chains are positioned at lower hierarchical levels of them. Usually dealing with low-tech activities, such as processing of raw materials or basic assembly operations. Transnational companies maintain leadership in production networks based on outsourcing, outsourcing or relocating production activities based on static comparative advantages. This also appropriate the benefits derived from technological accumulation and innovation, but without transfer of knowledge and experiences within the countries where they are installed allow (ECLAC, 2008a).

In summary, the common denominator prevails in the region of specialization in production mode which is mainly based on the allocation of productive resources as static competitive advantages. The dynamic benefits claim the invention and diffusion of technical and organizational innovations that depend on access to all flows formed by advanced knowledge and links between businesses, which are rare in Latin American networks.

Comparing the investment on research and development (R & D) between the region and leading countries shows generally a very negative. While in recent expenditure on R & D reached values between 2% and 3.6% of GDP (ECLAC, 2008b), Latin America and the Caribbean do not exceed 0.5% of GDP (as in Costa Rica, the Plurinational State of Bolivia, Uruguay, Panama and Colombia) or are very close to that value (Argentina, Mexico and Cuba).

Given the need to improve products and processes, companies are no longer limited to the space of the domestic economy to get services they require and therefore the internationalization of services is increasingly important.

The companies they subcontract or purchase in other countries, motivated by the competitive advantages, a trend known as offshoring (offshoring) of business services. The origins of this trend are in the progress of TIC-through which businesses can overcome barriers between supply and demand geographically imposed by distance, requiring powerful competitive pressures to reduce costs and improve productivity, and progress in the liberalization of trade in such services (ECLAC, 2007b).

As a result of innovative TIC applications, the range and scope of business services are considerable and are constantly expanding (ECLAC, 2009). As services become increasingly tradable and diversity of market where you can get is quite broad.

6. Logistics Is a Key Element for Development and Competitiveness

A key to economic and competitive development of the Latin American region element is the issue of logistics which includes a variety of key elements in the marketing of goods. The logistics includes all services and processes needed to transport the goods and services from their point of production to the final consumer. Thus, the end point of transport within a country can be port or airport or final domestic destination.

Which includes various "soft" components such as administrative and customs procedures, organization and management of transport, packaging costs, warehouse and inventory tracking services and location as well as the use of TIC throughout the process.

Meanwhile logistics includes other "hard" items such as transport infrastructure, telecommunications and storage infrastructure that facilitates connectivity along the supply chain distribution. Thus, the current logistics concept encompasses both activities of the private sector and state action through public policy design, provision, facilitation and regulation of activity.

The different strategies for measuring logistics costs provide additional information depending on the levels of aggregation approaches and objectives. In particular, three measurement approaches: micro, macro and perceptions (Rantasila and Ojala, 2012). The macro approach is based on national accounts and measures the contribution to GDP of the logistics industry, providing an overview of the importance of the sector in relative terms. However, macro measures the size of the informal sector provide a clear indicator of logistics performance, since the relationship between the size of the logistics industry and its performance is not monotonous. Similarly, there is no systematic relationship between the sector's contribution to GDP and economic performance (Shepherd, 2011).

The micro-level perspective of industry, product or provides supply chain logistics costs compared with the value of the final product.

A higher contribution of logistics costs indicates a greater dependence on logistics industry input and influence on their competitiveness. However, an existing challenge in the region is how to monitor and evaluate micro consolidated databases in order to make comparisons between countries.

Finally the third analysis strategy is based on perceptions that may be generated directly with fillers, with the portability compared by country, considering various aspects such as the efficiency of the customs process, the quality of transport infrastructure, competence and quality of logistics services, and the ability to track and trace shipments.

The cost and quality of logistics have fundamental implications for sustainable economic growth. Better logistics performance benefits facilitating domestic and international trade. First, facilitates national connectivity and reduces transaction costs. This is critical, since the domestic competitiveness of signatures is affected by transportation costs, thus impacting on the potential of integration with suppliers.

Second, promotes trade integration, contributing to the increase in exports, to reduce import costs, the diversification of products and partners. These benefits translate, among others, the increase in employment-intensive sectors of logistics, support the competitiveness of SMEs, the reduction in the cost of food and the provision of essential services to remote regions (Rodriguez, 2012 services; OECD / WTO, 2013).

So if all countries improved even halfway to international best practices and in just two key aspects of the supply chain (administration on the barriers of borders and transport infrastructure and communications-related services), world GDP could increase by about 5% (equivalent to USD 2.6 billion) and exports by 14.5% (WEF, World Bank and Bain, 2013).

In the case of Latin America, then take into account the level of development of countries, thanks to improvements in logistics services could increase labor productivity similarly reducing trade costs that may be associated with greater sophistication exported goods.

That is once we control for other variables that affect economic development, improving logistics performance is significantly associated with productivity gains and sophistication of exports. In particular, the increase of the index ranks logistics (which is between 1 and 5) implies a gain in labor productivity of about 35% for the average country in the sample.

REFERENCES

ECLAC. (2007a). *Economic Commission for Latin America and the Caribbean 2006. Trends 2007 (LC / G.2341-P / E)*. Santiago, Chile: ECLAC.

ECLAC. (2007b). Social Cohesion: Inclusion and a Sense of Belonging in Latin America and the Caribbean (LC / G.2335 / Rev.1). Santiago, Chile: ECLAC.

ECLAC. (2008a). Productive 20 Years Later: Old problems, new opportunities (LC / G.2367 (SES.32 / 3)). Santiago, Chile: ECLAC.

ECLAC. (2008b). *Iberoamerican spaces: the knowledge economy (LC / G.2392)*. Santiago, Chile: ECLAC / General Secretariat (SEGIB).

ECLAC. (2009). Foreign direct investment in Latin America and the Caribbean, 2008 (LC / G.2406-P). Santiago, Chile: ECLAC.

ECLAC. (2010). *The Time for equality: closing gaps, opening trails*. Santiago, Chile: Economic Commission for Latin America and the Caribbean, United Nations.

ECLAC. (2013). *Broadband in Latin America: Beyond Connectivity*. Santiago, Chile: Economic Commission for Latin America and the Caribbean, United Nations.

ECLAC. (2014). Global value chains and world trade. In *Prospects and challenges for Latin America*. ECLAC.

Fajnzylber, F. (1990). *Industrialización en América Latina: de la 'caja negra' al 'casillero vacío': comparación de patrones contemporáneos de industrialización, books of ECLAC, N° 60 (LC/G.1534/Rev.1-P).* Santiago de Chile. Publication of the United Nations.

Freeman, C., & Pérez, C. (1988). Structural crises of adjustment, business cycles and investment behavior. In Technical Change and Economic Theory. Pinter Publisher.

McMillan, M. & Rodrik, D. (2011). *Globalization, structural change and productivity growth.* Joint ILO-WTO paper, February.

Rantasila, K., & Ojala, L. (2012). *Measurement of national-level logistics costs and performance.* International Transport Forum Discussion Papers, No. 2012/04. OECD Publishing. doi:10.1787/5k8zvv79pzkk-en

Rodrigue, J.-P. (2012). *The benefits of logistics investments: Opportunities for Latin America and the Caribbean.* Technical Notes IDB-TN-395, Department of Infrastructure and Environment.

Schumpeter, J. (1911). *The Theory of Economic Development.* Cambridge, MA: Harvard University Press.

Shepherd, B. (2011). Logistics costs and Competitiveness: Measurement and trade policy applications. In *MPRA Paper 38254.* University Library of Munich.

WEF, Bain, & Banco Mundial. (2013). *Enabling Trade Valuing Growth Opportunities.* World Economic Forum.

ENDNOTE

[1]   These cycles of approximately 50 years, are referred to as cycles Kondratieff.18 ECLAC / SEGIB.

Chapter 13
Online Tools for the Modern Entrepreneurs Fueled by Trust:
Crowdfunding and Investor Angels

Nery Fernando Guzmán
Universidad Rafael Landivar, Guatemala

Sergio Martínez
Universidad Rafael Landivar, Guatemala

Helen Michelle Monzón
Universidad Rafael Landivar, Guatemala

ABSTRACT

Latin America and the Caribbean (LAC) as an emergent region has showed a high economic growth at the recent history. Its economic growth has been higher than the world general performance during a half of a century. Since 1960 to 1980, LAC was the region with the highest economic growth per decade. Unfortunately, the great economic growth stopped with the Debt Crisis which macroeconomic non desirable effects were sensible during the next decade. As a solution at international level. One of the barriers to start a business is the financial factor. The crowdfunding is a group of people dedicated to create a network in order to get financial help from people that are willing to support a business idea.

DOI: 10.4018/978-1-4666-8820-9.ch013

INTRODUCTION

The following chapter it's an effort to show the different and modern tools that can be used and replicated in Latin America to create business opportunities based on trust and transparency models. One of the main difficulties for the immature business it's the procedure of getting financial capital to expand or to put their ideas to work in real life, that's because for the banks there is too many risk and there are no guaranties for the solicited credit.

This prevents new ideas to get money to grow and this may slow down the economy in countries where credit access for small business it's difficult such as Latin America.

Therefore they are alternatives that can be used to obtain such financial capital; they are tools like crowdfunding and angel investors networks that are willing to take a moderate risk that the entrepreneur has to prove with a solid business plan and transparency to obtain trust from the investors.

The bonus with dealing with these online technologies is that business people can get their ideas posted and many investors around the world can see them and evaluate them.

It's a great lesson as well for the investors that are willing to explore other areas because they need to be organized in networks that can have a constant flow of ideas to select the best ones and to periodically be showing them in a systematic way to the members of the investor network, this can drastically reduce the risk and it's a cost that can be very beneficial to the network.

BACKGROUND

Latin America and the Caribbean Investment Overview: Overall Performance at the Beginning of the XXI Century

General Macroeconomic Context

Latin America and the Caribbean (LAC) as an emergent region has showed a high economic growth at the recent history. Its economic growth has been higher than the world general performance during a half of a century. Since 1960 to 1980, LAC was the region with the highest economic growth per decade. Unfortunately, the great economic growth stopped with the Debt Crisis which macroeconomic non desirable effects were sensible during the next decade. As a solution at international level, The Washington Consensus was established in order to stimulate economies with more liberalization mechanisms to financial and commercial transactions around the world. By this way, at the beginning of the XXI Century, LAC started to grow quickly, although not to the same levels of the previous century and not better than the other world emergent regions, like Asia. In this context, LAC face actually very challenges about its welfare sustainability to the next decade of the XXI century. For this issue, it's important to note that investment has a key role, identifying its well dynamism after the international financial crisis of 2008.

World Investment Overview

The world investment has risen exponentially since the half of the XX Century. In spite of several economic and financial international crises occurred, the investment always recovered gradually until to achieve higher levels than before its fall. In this sense, the history teaches to consider to several crises as an opportunity to raise the investment level in order to stimulate economy and improve the population welfare.

The world requires now to stimulate the investment as occurred in 1990 when the global leaders established the Washington Consensus. The issue come from that the world investment has lost dynamism over the years. After the financial international crisis of 2008, the most several since the Great Depression of 1929, the investment growth has showed a gradual slowdown. However, the international organisms actually show optimistic expectations about investment to the second decade of XXI Century. In this sense, the United Nations Conference on Trade and Development lays out the importance to promote investment policy and action plans in order to face the global economic, social and environmental challenges (UNCTAD, 2014).

In order to follow the previous world investment overview, the next figure presents the investment performance of world's regions at the period since 2004 to 2012.[1]

As presented in Figure 1, every world region has showed the same trend of investment slowdown, which results more clear after the financial international crisis of 2008. But, the investment performance varies between world's regions. Before the crisis, South Asia showed the highest investment growth rate. However it's the region with the most clear investment slowdown. During the crisis, Sub-Saharan Africa and East Asia & Pacific have showed the lowest shrinkage. Both regions have reported the intermediate investment growth rates during the period of reference. After the crisis, Latin America & the Caribbean had the best recovering. It showed the highest investment growth rates in 2010 and 2011.

Although Latin America & the Caribbean (LAC) region have the forth investment position with 6% of total, its volatility and growth improved in comparison with the other emergent regions with higher investment positions. By this sense, the next figure presents the average results of volatility and growth investment for the world's regions, during the post-crisis period since 2010 to 2012.

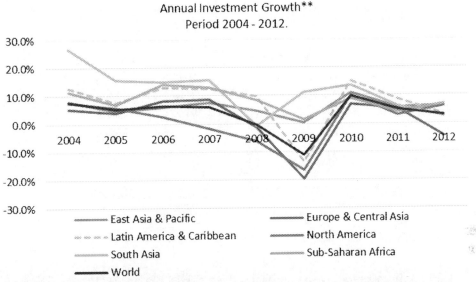

Figure 1. World investment overview by regions: annual investment growth

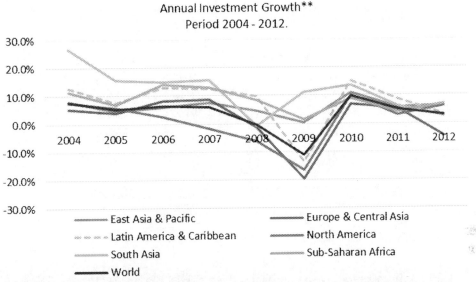

*The regions used correspond to World Bank's criteria. Middle East & North Africa is not included due to its information unavailability.
**The indicator is the annual growth of gross capital formation expressed in constant 2005 dollars.
Source: Authors based on World Development Indicators by World Bank.

Evaluating the left side of Figure 2, LAC showed the highest investment growth rate with an average of 9%, followed by East Asia & Pacific with 7.7%, South Asia with 7.4%, Sub-Saharan Africa with 6.6%, North America with 6.3%, the World with 5.9% and the Europe & Central Asia with 2.5%. Furthermore, the right side of Figure 2 presents that LAC showed the lowest investment volatility with 31.7% in comparison with South Asia with 33.5%, East Asia & Pacific with 35.0% and Sub-Saharan Africa with 39.2% as an emergent regions.

LAC Investment Overview: Important Features

Latin America & the Caribbean as an emergent region could have greater opportunities to enforce the investment dynamism. For that issue, the regional leaders should establish policy measures and action plans about the investment environment. In this sense, the Economic Commission for Latin America & the Caribbean recommends a better coordination policy in order to reduce uncertainty in markets due to natural resource's prices falling and the not clear signals transmitted by the monetary policy of United States as the most important trading partner of the majority of region's countries (ECLAC, 2014).

Figure 2. World investment overview by regions: general annual investment growth after financial crisis and investment volatility

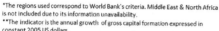

The LAC investment environment show the general following features: a) A higher growth than the other GDP components by the expenditure side, b) A progressive global interaction with the foreign investment direct inflows) A strong relationship with the entrepreneurship as an engine to create new business.

LAC Investment Overview: General Indicators by Country

Table 1 presents the general investment indicators absolutes and relatives by country of the Latin America & the Caribbean.

Figure 3. LAC investment Dinamism

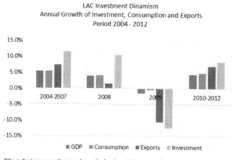

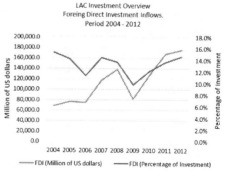

Table 1. Latin American and the Caribbean. General investment indicators by country (2012).

Country	Gross Domestic Product (Current, Millions US Dollars)	Gross Capital Formation (Current, Millions of US Dollars)	Gross Capital Formation as a Percentage of Gross Domestic Product	Foreign Direct Investment Inflow (Millions of US Dollars)	Foreign Direct Investment Inflow as a Percentage of Gross Domestic Product	Foreign Direct Investment Inflow as a Percentage of Gross Capital Formation
Antigua Y Barbuda	1,194.00	265.4	22.20%	129.4	10.80%	48.80%
Argentina	477,028.30	114,442.00	24.00%	12,115.80	2.50%	10.60%
Bahamas	8,149.00	2,699.80	33.10%	360.2	4.40%	13.30%
Barbados	4,224.90	602.1	14.30%	0	0.00%	0.00%
Belize	1,572.60	251.9	16.00%	194.2	12.30%	77.10%
Bolivia	27,067.40	4,774.70	17.60%	1,060.00	3.90%	22.20%
Brazil	2,249,090.90	394,097.40	17.50%	65,271.90	2.90%	16.60%
Chile	266,410.00	66,854.30	25.10%	28,541.70	10.70%	42.70%
Colombia	370,328.40	88,584.00	23.90%	15,529.00	4.20%	17.50%
Costa Rica	45,374.80	9,848.30	21.70%	2,332.30	5.10%	23.70%
Cuba[1/]	68,990.10	5,726.80	8.30%	n.d	n.d	n.d
Dominica	495.7	73.9	14.90%	19.6	4.00%	26.50%
Dominican Republic	58,897.80	9,657.20	16.40%	3,609.60	6.10%	37.40%
Ecuador	87,494.70	24,843.50	28.40%	582.4	0.70%	2.30%
El Salvador	23,813.60	3,367.80	14.10%	447.6	1.90%	13.30%
Grenada	801.5	130.7	16.30%	31.5	3.90%	24.10%
Guatemala	50,388.40	7,535.40	15.00%	1,244.60	2.50%	16.50%
Guyana	2,851.20	710.5	24.90%	293.7	10.30%	41.30%
Haiti	7,820.30	2,310.50	29.50%	178.8	2.30%	7.70%
Honduras	18,564.20	4,800.40	25.90%	1,058.60	5.70%	22.10%
Jamaica	14,794.80	2,942.60	19.90%	272.5	1.80%	9.30%
Mexico	1,181,633.40	275,066.60	23.30%	17,223.70	1.50%	6.30%
Nicaragua	10,507.70	2,673.00	25.40%	804.6	7.70%	30.10%
Panama	35,938.20	10,288.60	28.60%	2,887.40	8.00%	28.10%
Paraguay	24,595.30	3,813.60	15.50%	479.5	1.90%	12.60%
Peru	203,976.70	57,524.70	28.20%	12,239.70	6.00%	21.30%
St. Kitts and Nevis	731.9	194.3	26.50%	92.4	12.60%	47.60%

continued on following page

Table 1. Continued

Country	Gross Domestic Product (Current, Millions US Dollars)	Gross Capital Formation (Current, Millions of US Dollars)	Gross Capital Formation as a Percentage of Gross Domestic Product	Foreign Direct Investment Inflow (Millions of US Dollars)	Foreign Direct Investment Inflow as a Percentage of Gross Domestic Product	Foreign Direct Investment Inflow as a Percentage of Gross Capital Formation
St. Lucia	1,318.30	347.2	26.30%	75.8	5.70%	21.80%
St. Vincent and the Grenadines	694.4	164.1	23.60%	115.4	16.60%	70.30%
Suriname[2]	4,366.80	1,581.50	36.20%	62.8	1.40%	4.00%
Trinidad Y Tabago[3]	18,369.10	2,874.70	15.60%	2,553.20	13.90%	88.80%
Uruguay	50,003.30	11,787.20	23.60%	2,687.30	5.40%	22.80%
Venezuela	381,286.20	101,409.70	26.60%	3,216.00	0.80%	3.20%
Latin America	5,643,708.40	1,193,678.80	21.20%	171,510.20	3.00%	14.40%
Caribbean	64,961.30	8,382.60	12.90%	4,200.70	6.50%	50.10%
Latin America & The Caribbean	5,708,669.70	1,202,061.40	21.10%	175,710.90	3.10%	14.60%

[1]Information availability until 2011
[2]Information availability until 2010
[3]Information availability until 2006
Source: Authors based on Cepal stat

Figure 4. LAC investment toward entrepreneurship

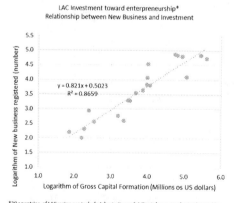
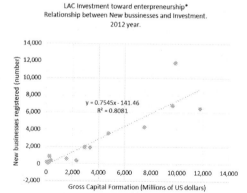

*20 countries of LAC region are included due to its availability information for both variables.
Note: The variables expressed as a logarithm allow to reduce the graphic distortion of outliers.
Source: Authors based on World Bank Indicators and Cepalstat.

*14 countries of the left graph are included due to its variable's absolute values are not outliers.
Source: Authors based on World Bank Indicators and Cepalstat.

Entrepreneurship in Latin America and the Caribbean: What Being an Entrepreneur Means

According to Richard Cantillon, an entrepreneur is a person who pays certain price and sells a product at an uncertain price, therefore he makes decisions about how to get and how to use the resources also admits the risks in the process.

Jean-Baptise Say, described an entrepreneur as an economic agent that unites all means of production such as land, work and capital in order to produce a product. An entrepreneur for Joseph Schumpeter is an innovative person who seeks to destroy the status-quo of the existent products to create new ones.

As a conclusion, an entrepreneur is that person who knows his objective and set goals in order to get to it, he has the power of decision and the initiative to take actions despite the risk they might represent. He also knows how to identify a business opportunity and will find the necessary resources to start it.

LAC faces actually the challenge of reaching better conditions of development and sustainability. As the previous section mentioned, the region has not showed yet the economic growth rates and investment performance reached during the past century. However, the region through its emergent condition has a high potential to improve its economic dynamism. For this issue, the present section has the purpose to highlight the entrepreneurship in Latin America & the Caribbean as a progressive opportunity of welfare taken by people who live in the region.

Entrepreneurship has been taking a more important role around the world by the society. Its general context is highlighted by the Global Entrepreneurship Monitor of 2013 as it follows: "According to a broad spectrum of key players in society, including policymakers, academics, entrepreneurs themselves as well as for the population at large, entrepreneurship tends to be associated with economic development and well-being of society". The benefits of entrepreneurship are perceived at the way of how entrepreneurs are ambitious and spur innovation, speed up structural changes in the economy, introduce new competition and contribute to productivity, job creation and national competitiveness (Amorós & Bosma, 2014).

For the challenges LAC faces, entrepreneurship has a key role in strategies toward reaching a better economic dynamism and sustainable development. The leaders of the regions are conscious about the challenge of improving investment and economic through domestic productivity. They have shared that the pathway to boost domestic productivity consist in creating a strong environment which allow entrepreneurs to establish, innovate and compete through business (Lederman, Messina, Pienknagura, & Rigolini, 2014).

Entrepreneurship in LAC show the characteristic of vitality. This is because the region has the highest number of entrepreneurs as a percentage of population in comparison with others countries and regions under emergent economic conditions

(Lederman, Messina, Pienknagura, & Rigolini, 2014). However, the region has a lack of performance expected of firms created by entrepreneurs. When firms born, they are commonly smaller than the ones in other regions similar to LAC. At the same way, bigger firms use to create lower employment with the same comparison focus. By this way, entrepreneurship in LAC faces a lack of innovation as a situation of stagnation seen at general business performance.

Barriers to Entrepreneurship

1. **Financial Barriers:** The lack of financial support is one of the main barriers for the entrepreneurs. To start their business, the entrepreneurs need to have financial resources. There are several ways to find funding sources, such as online tools like crowdfunding, crowdsourcing and business angels.

The online tools are based on trust and to gain confidence the investor needs to know who is behind the project that is requesting financial aid, what they are looking forward to accomplish, how they are going to invest the money they are getting.

2. **Cultural Barriers:** One of the characteristics of Latin America is that it is a region where different cultures predominate. An entrepreneurship must know the target and the market he is getting into, which means, he must know the cultural aspects before getting started with his business.
3. **Administrative Barriers:** The administrative barriers are those that have to do with the country conditions to start a business, unlike the cultural barriers, the administrative barriers refer to the difficulties or support that the country can provide to the entrepreneurship. In this case, the entrepreneurship must get professional support (legal, economic...) in order to start the business perfectly.

FUTURE RESEARCH DIRECTIONS

Corruption Perception and the Impact on Trust in the Private Sector in Guatemala

The civil society organization called Acción Ciudadana, founded on the year 1996 with the objective to awareness the society about transparency, made a study called "Indicator for perception and experiences of corruption in Guatemala" in the year 2006.

The study was about a survey in which the civil society was the study sample. It was made in order to analyze their perception about which sectors are the most corrupt. As a result, the 4 sectors (out of 11) more corrupt and the ones that help the less to fight against it are: 1) political parties, 2) the police, 3) the unions and 4) private sector (Acción Ciudadana, 2006)

How to Measure the Corruption According to Transparency International

Transparency International is an organization specialized on the corruption measurement. Their vision is about a world where governments, politicians, entrepreneurs and civil society are free of the corruption scourge. This movement began in 1993 by a group of individuals that decided to fight against those dishonest actions, not only in the public sector but also in the private sector.

Transparency International analyzes 18 subjects that are more vulnerable to fall in corruption. Those subjects are:

1. Sports,
2. Whistleblowing,
3. Oil and gas,
4. Climate change,
5. Intergovernmental bodies,
6. Health,
7. International conventions,
8. Humanitarian assistance,
9. Education,
10. Judiciary,
11. Access to information,
12. Forestry,
13. Politics and government,
14. Water,
15. Poverty and development,
16. Private sector,
17. Public procurement,
18. Defense and security.

The organization builds the Bribe Payers Index, this one has the distinction of being built from the opinion of entrepreneurs that are operating their business in the 28 biggest economies of the world. It shows the entrepreneurs perception about the possibility to bribe in another country. The index scores the country in a scale from 0 to 10, the more close to 10 means that the companies in that country doesn´t bribe in another one.

According to Transparency International, the corruption not only distorts the market but also creates an unfair competition and affects the business climate, which can negatively impact on the society and leave as a consequence economic instability. Also, affects the company's reputation leaving it vulnerable to suits because of frauds, felony and other crimes. It is also necessary to mention that the corruption in the private sector is not only to pay bribes, it is also fraud, money laundering, collusion, the use of political influence, tax shields and other factors (Transparency International, 2011).

Online Tools for the Modern Entrepreneurs Fueled by Trust

Crowdfunding

One of the barriers to start a business is the financial factor. The crowdfunding is a group of people dedicated to create a network in order to get financial help from people that are willing to support a business idea. One of the differences between crowdfunding and investment is that the crowdfunding is a type of donation because the people that are giving the financial help don´t expect any kind of profit in return; they give the money because they actually believe in the project to develop.

The crowdfunding model awards the donators in order to motivate them to keep helping new entrepreneurs. The best known sites to get crowdfunding are IndieGoGo, Kickstarter, RocketHub, Broota, and others.

The interesting point about crowdfunding is that it is dedicated to any type of project. It not only supports profit business projects but also non-profit projects, such as ideas with solidarity purposes (for example the Argentinean crowdfunding site "Nobleza Obliga"). There are crowdfunding sites that also support projects that promote art, education, cultural events and many others.

There Are 3 Types of Crowdfunding

1. **Donations, Philanthropy, and Sponsorship:** This is de kind of crowdfunding that is used by non-profit organizations. The donators give their money to a cause they believe in and don't expect anything in return.
2. **Lending:** This type of crowdfunding (also known as crowdlending) is when a person requests an amount of money and sends his information to a platform specialized in lending by a group of people. It´s characteristic is that if a person has saved money, he can lend it at a higher interest rate; he can decide the interest rate or the crowdlending platform can indicate it for him and the person who borrowed the money has to return it.

3.   **Investment in Exchange for Equity, Profit, or Revenue Sharing:** The entrepreneurs that request money offers shares in exchange for money. People who finance the project not only support the entrepreneur but also gain money in the future if the project succeeds.

Everyone Is Going to Crowdfunding

The famous Google's platform YouTube has its own platform for crowdfunding named Fan Funding. It consists about donations that the followers of a channel can donate only through Google Wallet. This is a proof that crowdfunding is started to be used by every sector and organization.

In order to get donations, the channel owner has to able the support function so their fans can donate.

Angel Investor in Latin America

Also called business angels are key agents in financing projects to entrepreneurs. Business capitalization it's more dependent from the angel investors now a day because they provide capital to business segments that are still immature for the traditional capital and are out of the selection from traditional banking systems. One of the big problems is the risks and the lack of guaranties to provide credit (EBAN, 2014)

This type of angel investors are often anonymous and don't have open offices like banks and traditional capital schemes. They are hard to detect for the entrepreneurs unless they belong to a certain business circle or club.

The door of entry for this investors are the networks of Business Angels, through this networks the angel investors get a limited number of projects, that have been carefully evaluated. These networks are of great interest for government because they are a good instrument to boost economic growth and business development in the early stages (FOMIN, 2013)

According to FOMIN in the publication called Las redes de inversionistas ángeles en América Latina y el Caribe, they consulted with 665 investors that have realized 99 investments between 2005 and 2011, 70% of those investments where post 2008 and the total amount of investment in Latin America its around 17 million dollars with 64 from the 99 investments in place. If the global number of investments its 99 then the operations would be close to 26 million dollars.

One of the weakness for Latin America is that not every country has one angel investor network, Argentina, Chile, Colombia and Mexico are the countries that possesses the most evolved business networks. Chile it's a remarkable example where the growth it's very aggressive and fast for this business networks we can see that in the Foreign Investment Statute, Decree Law 600 from Chile that shows the rules and regulations for doing business facilitating this type of interchange.

Therefore the market for angel investors in Latin America it's very poor. A great number of networks don't have many transactions in a year. In Chile the public support for the creation of these networks offers a very important lesson to all the country's in the region.

According to FOMIN the lack of quality and preparation from the entrepreneurs it's not attractive for the investors due to the short preparation and to not say the adequate words.

Therefore the most important things for this kind of networks live it's to make the company to have government support to attract potential investors, support the entrepreneurs and to facilitate the investment in business.

EBAN (Asociación Europea de Redes de Inversionistas) gathers 20,000 investors in associated networks, with 75,000 investors in Europe and 250,000 investors in United States. (EBAN)

The Process for Investors to Decide and Gain Trust

It is important for the entrepreneurs to develop a strategy according to the behavior of the investors.

- According to FOMIN the investors first encounter the business opportunity in the idea and they evaluate if the time lapse proposes is corrects.
- It must fit the priorities of the investor.
- The third step is trust they will have a series of questions and transparency standards that will generate trust.
- After they have trust they will evaluate if there will be a market for the ideas they are presented and then they will go with a business idea.

For every 100 business ideas usually 2 are financed through angel investors. And only 10 percent of the opportunities that get to an investor get financing opportunities. It's a very high risk process for the investor as well if only few of the enterprises are able to produce profit it may get losses and non-profitable investments.

For the investors it's useful to have a diverse investment portfolio to minimize the risk.

Business Angels Networking

In Europe they are more than 390 networks and 340 in United States. In Latin America and the Caribbean they are 21 networks (EBAN, White Paper, 2010). In Latin America the networks are ruled by a professional that assumes command of the activities of the networks and covers the firs process or the investor decision: identification of the opportunity, depuration of opportunities and the organization and coordination for the project presentation to the investors.

The tasks according to FOMIN that the investor will go it's the following

- Identification of the project.
- Selection of the project.
- Support to the presentation.
- Investment forum.
- Negotiation.
- Deal Closure and participation on the business.

Business Angels Network in Latin America

Business needs a high environment of trust and transparency in order to boost creativity and innovation of entrepreneurs. Sharing useful information is a way through that entrepreneur could enforce business plans with other partners potentially involved. This issue requires efficiency as every business step. By this way, online resources could enforce the activity of sharing useful information by entrepreneurs. Additionally, online resources provide trust and transparency to the extent that an increasing number of entrepreneurs interact and validate the information published.

The Latin American model is very similar to Europe; it's not as advanced as the United States model. Yet the Latin American networks offers organizations as a platform for an investor club. There will be a professional management from the club members. (BID, 2013)

If Latin America wishes to enter the game of the business investment networks there must be a constant effort between government and private institutions with one common goal: to seek economic development and business proliferation. The task for the businessman that needs financial capital relies on the capability to demonstrate transparency, clear objectives and a business plan that can be demonstrated to the investors. From the investor part the creation of organized networks are essential to guaranty the flow of ideas and the selection of the more robust ones.

The immature business can be accelerated with this kind of process but it requires effort and commitment.

All These Tools Are Fueled by Trust

The reason this tools need to have a high emphasis on trust and transparency is because they have to prove that the business operation are going as planned and in order to have more funds entrepreneurs need to have an strategic transparency to be able to provide another path to economic growth in Latin America (Alves, 2004) this kind of path allows the firms to signal and provide information that may reinforce the perception and trust to attract more funding.

Therefore to follow the traditional marketing and business strategy it will not be enough to have impact in entrepreneurship and business promotion. Strategic transparency helps to form the foundations for global investors and financial flows into Latin America (Alves, 2004) Electronic tools can help to facilitate the sharing of information and provide a cheap channel of information that can boost the goals for the entrepreneurs in developing countries.

CONCLUSION

The Bribe Payers Index is a helpful tool for Latin entrepreneurs that want to establish business relationships with foreign markets, such as suppliers, clients, competitors and others. By applying this tool the entrepreneurs will have a clear outlook because they will have the knowledge about with which country they are going to be more secure or more vulnerable to the opacity of a foreign company.

Once stablished the framework for transparency the entrepreneurs can begin to create a robust business plan that must be the ultimate tool to deliver trust with concise ideas that can be easily understood by the investors. The local entrepreneurs must be organized and be motivated to create crowdfunding sites to improve their probabilities of getting capital for the business startups or expansion.

The investors that are willing to explore new areas of business should build a network that needs to have a systematic approach to new ideas so it can have a constant flow of business proposals and must be in touch with several investors to minimize the risk and optimize the investors time. It may have a cost but if it is well organized and backed by government policies it can be great for economic development for Latin America.

All the players in the game of business must learn to think as their counterparts for the investors it is better to have a platform that can centralize the ideas from the entrepreneurs. And from the entrepreneur side they must be willing to build trust with transparency and solid business plans. Government must give the right rules for this interaction to happen to maximize its effect.

REFERENCES

Alves, & Choi. (2004). *Facilitating Entrepreneurship in Emerging Markets: Economic Policy*. International Business and Strategic Transparency.

BID. (2013). *Las redes de inversionistas ángeles en América Latina y el caribe*. BID.

Ciudadana, A. (2006). Indicadores de percepción y experiencias de corrupción de Guatemala -IPEC-. Guatemala.

EBAN. (n.d.). *EBAN. Recuperado el 2014, de EBAN*. Retrieved from http://www. eban.org

ECLAC. (2014). *Foreign Direct Investment in Latin America and The Caribbean*. Retrieved from http://www.cepal.org/publicaciones/xml/8/52978/ForeignDirectInvestment2013.pdf

Transparency International. (2011). *Bribe payers index 2011*. Author.

UNCTAD. (2014). *World Investment Report: Investing in the SDGs: An action plan*. Retrieved from http://unctad.org/en/PublicationsLibrary/wir2014_en.pdf

KEY TERMS AND DEFINITIONS

Angel Investor: They are also known as business angel, it consist in a person that provides capital for business startups. The investor and the entrepreneur define the conditions of the agreement and the amount of capital that's being granted.

Business Plan: A formal statement that compiles goals and the method to be achieved. The more detailed the plan the better to gain trust.

ECLAC: Economic Commission of Latin America and the Caribbean.

Economic Growth: The annual growth rate of the Gross Domestic Product.

Entrepreneur: The person that develops a business model and a business plan that guides to acquire the human and other required resources, and is responsible for the success of failure of the project.

Gross Domestic Product: The value of all goods and services produced by an economy.

Investment: The gross capital formation that measures the gross fixed capital formation and changes in inventories and acquisitions less disposals of valuables for a unit or sector. Also, the resources spent in the hope of future benefits within a date or time frame. For an investment to take place it is important to reach a previous agreement in negotiation.

LAC: Latin America and the Caribbean.

Negotiation: The dialogue between two or more people or parties that want to understand, resolve points or to close a business deal.

Transparency: A concept that implies openness, communication and accountability. This is generated through clean financial processes that can build trust to the investors of a business idea.

UNCTAD: United Nations Conference on Trade and Development.

ENDNOTE

[1]   The period 2004 – 2012 is selected due to its present a sub period before and other after of the crisis of 2008. The both sub periods reflects generally a great economic and financial growth under a cycle around the crisis time.

Chapter 14
Remittances:
A Key Factor for Economic Change and the Reduction of Poverty in Latin America – The Case of Guatemala

Reny Mariane Bake
Universidad Francisco Marroquin, Guatemala

ABSTRACT

International remittances to developing countries are growing and are more than foreign direct investment or the official development aid. More of the 3.2% of global population are living abroad and the trends will increase in the next decades, involving skilled and no skilled workers. Developing countries in Latin America receives 15% of all international remittances and six countries (México, Guatemala, Dominican Republic, Colombia, El Salvador and Honduras) in the region received more of the 70% of all the remittances in 2013. By coincidence, this six countries have a lack to develop and large pockets of poverty, much of which is concentrated in those areas from which migrants come. The remittances are palliatives to poverty in their countries and help their families to reduce their poverty. In many cases, the remittances are the seed for new small and medium enterprises in Latin America, with not enough access to financial services.

DOI: 10.4018/978-1-4666-8820-9.ch014

MIGRANTS AND THE REMITTANCES

Migration is not quite a new phenomenon. From Africa to Asia to Europe and to America, migration is part of the human history. The new phenomenon is the State as we understood today. This has its origins after the war of the thirty years (1648), with the signing of the agreements of Westphalia, which give rise to the modern state, the concept of national sovereignty and the concept of the nation state.

The independence of the United States was in 1776 and more than half of the member countries of the United Nations did not exist as such until after the end of World War II in 1945, which also founded the United Nations. The world's largest economy, USA, was founded by migrants and is one of the main recipients of them today. The United States Census Bureau estimated that the number of foreigners born in the USA calculated nearly 13% of total population (United States Census Bureau, 2012).

According to World Bank (2014) nearly 1 of 7 persons in the world is an international or an internal migrant, growing awareness of the importance of migration around the world. To 2013, 3.2% of the world population is living abroad. The same study destroyed a myth about migrations: "In contrast with common perceptions, South-South migration was larger than South-North migration: 82.3 million (or 36 percent) of migrants from developing countries lived in another developing country, compared to 81.9 million (or 35 percent of migrants from the South) lived in a developed country" (World Bank, 2014, pp. 2).

The movement of people across borders is and will remain part of humanity, which is considered "new" in the term migrant, as stated in the UNESCO Glossary on Migrants and Migration: "any person who lives temporarily or permanently in a country where he or she was not born, and has acquired some significant social ties to this country". (UNESCO. International Migration and Multicultural policies, 2015).

In the same web page, the UNESCO mentioned the United Nations Convention on the Rights of Migrants (unesco.org) and defines in the article 2.1 a *migrant worker* as: "a person who is to be engaged, is engaged or has been engaged in a remunerated activity in a State of which he or she is not a national". The UNESCO also clarifies the term to make a difference with migration by political situations: "The term 'migrant' in article 1.1 (a) should be understood as covering all cases where the decision to migrate is taken freely by the individual concerned, for reasons of 'personal convenience' and without intervention of an external compelling factor."

With the definitions explained above, for these analysis, a migrant means: "any person who lives temporarily or permanently in a country where he or she was not born, who voluntarily chose to live and work in a remunerated activity in the State of which he or she is not a national".

Remittances

Table 1.

3.2% of the world's population or 232 million people are living abroad worldwide, compared with 175 million in 2000 and 154 million in 1990.
The United States remains the most popular destination, but Europe and Asia host nearly two-thirds of all international migrants worldwide.
• Europe remained the most popular destination region with 72 million international migrants in 2013, compared to 71 million in Asia. • Asia saw the largest increase of international migrants since 2000, adding some 20 million migrants in 13 years. This growth was mainly fuelled by the increasing demand of foreign labor in the oil-producing countries of Western Asia and in South-Eastern Asian countries with rapidly growing economies, such as Malaysia, Singapore and Thailand.
However, the world's largest corridor of international migration is between United States and Mexico. US gained the largest absolute number of international migrants between 1990 and 2013—nearly 23 million, equal to one million additional migrants per year.
Seventy four per cent of international migrants are of working age, between 20 and 64 years of age.
Women represent the 48% of all international migrants.

Source: Author's compilation based on (UN, 2014)

As the United Nations (2015) states, migration and its importance to the world has increased in recent decades and more people than ever are living abroad (www. un.org). In a conference of the UN Department of Economic and Social Affairs (UN-DESA), the highlights of the press release in the next summary presented in Table 1.

The purpose of the international migration of workers going to places where they are more productive, is looking to increase their income; with this increase of income, the family remittances reduce poverty in their countries of origin. According to the website of the World Bank "Generally, remittances reduce the number and severity of poverty, and lead to: increased human capital accumulation; increased spending on health and education; better access to information technology and communications and formal financial services; best investments in small businesses; greater entrepreneurial training; better preparation for adverse contingencies, earthquakes and cyclones, and less child labor. Diasporas can be an important source of trade, capital, technology and knowledge to the countries of origin and destination." (World Bank).

The migrants are skilled or not skilled workers, because of the economic globalization and demographic changes in different regions of the planet, the international migration will increase in the next decades. According to the German Federal Employment Agency, the country will have a shortage of two hundred thousand qualified workers, especially doctors, nurses and engineers. As the mobility of people increases worldwide, the remittances are a growing trend worldwide and it is expected that this trend continues for decades.

Table 2.

For 2014, the international migrants from developing countries are expected to send $436 billion in remittances to their home countries.
To 2014 the remittance flows to developing countries will have an increase of 7.8% over the 2013 volume of $404 billion, rising to $516 billion in 2016.
Global remittances, including those to high-income countries, are estimated at $581 billion this year, from $542 billion in 2013, rising to $681 billion in 2016.
Remittances remain a key source of external resource flows for developing countries, far exceeding official development assistance and more stable than private debt and portfolio equity flows.
For many developing countries, remittances are an important source of foreign exchange, surpassing earnings from major exports, and covering a substantial portion of imports.
In Nepal, remittances are nearly double the country's revenues from exports of goods and services, while in Sri Lanka and the Philippines they are over 50% and 38%, respectively. In India, remittances during 2013 were $70 billion, more than the $65 billion earned from the country's flagship software services exports. In Uganda, remittances are double the country's income from coffee, its main export.
Remittances have become a major component of the balance of payments of nations.
There is no doubt that these flows act as an antidote to poverty and promote prosperity. Remittances and migration data are also barometers of global peace and turmoil.
Additional to the remittances, migrants living in high income countries are estimated to hold savings in excess of $500 billion annually.
Nigeria is readying a diaspora bond issue to mobilize diaspora savings and boost financing for development.

Source: Author's compilation based on (Remittances-developing-countries-deportations-migrant-workers-wb, 2014).

In 2014 the international migrants from developing countries are expected to send $436 billion in remittances to their home countries, 7.8% over the 2013 volume of $404 billion. (World Bank, 2014)

This confirmed the projections of Dillip Rapha (World Bank), at the Tenth Meeting on Migration and Remittances (Rapha, 2012): to 2014, the global flow of remittances to developing countries would be U.S. $ 441 billion and a growth rate from 7-8% annually in the period 2012-2014. A summary of the World Bank projections is presented in Table 2.

The same study of the World Bank defines the top ten remittances receiving countries globally in 2013, as presented in Table 3.

For some countries, the remittances mean a high share of the gross domestic product GDP, as shown Table 4.

Latin America and the Caribbean regions, in 2014, grew just 1.9% and $61 billion from 2013. According to the World Bank (2014), the remittance flows to the region began recovering in the second half of 2013, after a 13-month decline. Mexico is the largest remittance recipient country in the region and the fourth world largest recipient of remittances after India, China and The Philippines. This means a change, because in 2012, Mexico was the third largest recipient of remittances

Remittances

Table 3. Top ten remittances receiving countries 2013 in US $

Country	Remittances Received
India	$70 billion
China	$60 billion
The Philippines	$25 billion
Mexico	$22 billion
Nigeria	$21 billion
Egypt	$17 billion
Pakistan	$15 billion
Bangladesh	$14 billion
Vietnam	$11 billion
Ukraine	10 billion

Source: Author's compilation based (World Bank, 2014).

after India and China. According to the World Bank "The positive impetus from the US economic recovery was partly offset by removals of migrants from the US. The economic slowdown and unemployment in Spain and Italy, which are also large destinations of Latin American migrants, contributed to the slowdown in remittances to the region. For 2016, remittances are expected to reach $81 billion by 2016" (World Bank, 2014).

In some countries of Latin America, the importance of remittances represents a significant contribution to GDP, much higher than traditional exports, as in the case of El Salvador, where remittances represent 16% of GDP (Rapha, 2012). Analyzing

Table 4. Remittances as share of GDP: top ten recipients.

Country	Share OF GDP
Tajikistan	52 percent
Kyrgyz Republic	31 percent
Nepal	25 percent
Moldova	25 percent
Samoa	23 percent
Lesotho	23 percent
Armenia	21 percent
Haiti	21 percent
Liberia	20 percent
Kosovo	17 percent

Source: Author's compilation based on (World Bank, 2014).

Table 5. International migrant remittances in Latin America and the Caribbean –LAC

Year	International Migrant Remittances to Developing Countries	To Latin America and the Caribbean	% LAC /Global International Migrant Remittances
2013	$ 404 billions	$ 61 billions	15.1%
2016	$516 billions	$ 81 billions	15.7%

Source: Author's compilation based on (World Bank, 2014)

the data of the Central Banks in 2014, for Honduras remittances represent 15% GDP (Honduras, 2014) or Guatemala remittances represent almost 10% GDP (Banco Central de Guatemala, 2014). The poorest countries in the Western Hemisphere have a greater dependence of remittances than the less poor countries.

The remittances to Latin America generate questions that remain unresolved as: How can be and make the most of these remittances for poverty reduction and generate new business opportunities in every country?

Today, part of these remittances are used for consumption and investment, like spending for education, to buy houses, small farms and to open small businesses. In some countries they are the main sources of seed capital for new ventures for SMEs.

REMITTANCES, A KEY FACTOR FOR ECONOMIC CHANGE IN LATIN AMERICA AND REDUCING POVERTY: THE CASE OF GUATEMALA

Remittance flows to countries in the Latin America and the Caribbean (LAC) means 15% of the global international migrant remittances in 2013 and will remain the same in 2016, as shown in the next table:

Latin America and the Caribbean remittances have a different kind of importance and impact in their economies. For example, the four countries of LAC (Haiti, El Salvador, Honduras and Guatemala) are in the group of the 20 countries in which the remittances cover more than 20% of imports and 30% of the exports in 2013, as shown in the next tables, taken from the *Migration and Remittances: Recent Developments and Outlook* (World Bank, 2014).

According to the Banco Central de Guatemala (2014), if we focus just in Latin American sixth countries (México, Guatemala, Dominican Republic, Colombia, El Salvador and Honduras) they received 76% of all the remittances in 2013, as shown in the next table:

In Table 6, the sum of the remittances received by three countries (Guatemala, El Salvador and Honduras) is $12,151 million dollars in 2013, equal to 20% of all

Remittances

Figure 1. Remittances cover more than 20% of imports in 20 countries.
Source: Taken from the April 2014 issue of Migration and Remittances: Recent Developments and Outlook (Figure 2b: Page 3) (World Bank, 2014).

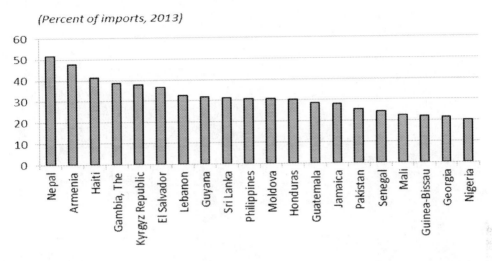

Figure 2. Remittances are equivalent to more than 30 percent of exports in 20 countries.
Source: Taken from the April 2014 issue of Migration and Remittances: Recent Developments and Outlook (Figure 2b: Page 3), (World Bank, 2014).

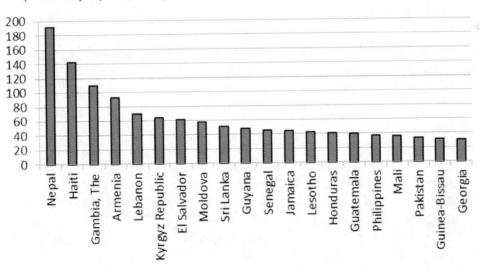

Table 6. Remittances by country in Latin America

No.	Countries	US Millions of Dollars					
		2009	2010	2011	2012	2013	Structure 2013
	Total	53,466	53,704	55,552	56,075	55,330	100.0%
1	Mexico	21,306	21,304	22,803	22,438	21,892	39.6%
2	Guatemala	3,912	4,127	4,378	4,783	5,105	9.2%
3	Dominican Republic	3,042	3,683	4,008	4,045	4,262	7.7%
4	Colombia	4,134	4,023	4,168	4,073	4,071	7.4%
5	El Salvador	3,387	3,431	3,649	3,911	3,953	7.1%
6	Honduras	2,403	2,540	2,749	2,842	3,093	5.6%
						Subtotal	76.6%
	Other LAC countries	15,283	14,597	13,797	13983	12,953	
	% Other LAC / remittances to region	28.58%	27.18%	24.84%	24.94%	23.4%	

Source: (Banco Central de Guatemala, 2014).

remittances received by Latin American and Caribbean countries (World Bank, 2014) and 3% of all international migrant remittances to developing countries in 2013. The three countries have an estimated population of 31.2 million of inhabitants, less than half of one percent of global population and 6% of Latin American. For those countries mentioned, remittances in 2013 were more than 10% of the GDP and at least, one of four households received international remittances.

The Northern Triangle (Guatemala, El Salvador and Honduras) have at least, half of the population below the poverty line; in 2013, these countries were placed among the last six countries in the Human Development Index –HDI- in Latin America and the Caribbean, just a little better than Haiti and Nicaragua (UNDP, 2013).

The 97% of international remittances to Guatemala come from the United States and mainly are focused in the rural area, especially in the departments of San Marcos, Quetzaltenango and Huehuetenango and the department of Guatemala (Banco Central de Guatemala, 2014). One of the departments (Huehuetenango) had 67.6% of rural poverty (Segeplan, 2014).

For Guatemalan, the main reason for migration is economic, since 52% sought to improve economic conditions and 37% were looking for a job, 2% wanted to build a house and 1% tried to save for a business (Banco Central de Guatemala, 2014).

Remittances

Table 7. Guatemalan migrants in USA (2012)

In 2012 the number of Guatemalan immigrants was 3.8 times more than in 1990.
More than half of Guatemalan in the United States arrived to the country after the 2000's.
Migrants from Guatemala in the United States are concentrated in the working age.
Over 60% are men.
The migrants from Guatemala have a smaller percentage of women than that observed in other groups of immigrants, from 80 countries in the analysis.
In 2012, the total income of Guatemalan immigrant population in the United States was
15,558,000 of dollars, equivalent to 31 percentage points of GDP in Guatemala.
Guatemalan in the United States sent more than 30% of their income to their origin country, nearly the triple of the average of all migrants living in USA.

Source: Author's compilation based on (Cemla, 2014).

In almost half of rural municipalities in Guatemala (44%), the majority of the population (over 75%) live in poverty (Segeplan, 2014). The migrants from Guatemala are going to USA and their characteristics are described in Table 7.

In Guatemala, the frequency of receiving remittances is monthly, in 65% of the cases, with the immediate family receiving the money; the remittances are received in 32% by parents, 22% by partners, 19% by brothers and 15% by children. Remittances are used in consumption by 49.4% of the cases, investment and savings 20.4%, 11.8% in social investment and intermediate consumption 18.4% (Banco Central de Guatemala, 2014).

The Guatemalan Migrants are among the largest investors in the country. It is estimated that no less than one billion dollars were invested in housing and small businesses in 2013 by the migrants. The same year, according to the Central Bank of Guatemala, the Foreign Direct Investment in the same period was US $ 1.3 billion.

In many villages of the Guatemalan countryside, remittances have meant a reduction in poverty and a change in the landscape of the country; in many cases, migrants invest their money to build or improve their houses in the homeland. This is seen in the picture below:

Santa Eulalia is a small town in Huehuetenango, Guatemala, near the border with Mexico. It is located in one of the most remote areas of the country's economic center which is the city of Guatemala. Its population is 100% indigenous. Almost 30% of the Santa Eulalia villagers are migrants in the United States and of those, just 5% are women.

During a field visit to the village, after a journey of over 10 hours by a regular road from the capital city, when asked about the presence or type of services offered by the state, the answer was no, they do not get many visits even less by the government officials, much less any support.

Figure 3. The changing landscape of Santa Eulalia, Huehuetenango, Guatemala
Picture by Reny M. Bake, May 2014.

In many public schools, migrants in the United States had donated their desks, because schools had none for the children. Santa Eulalia, as many villages and small towns with a group of migrants in USA, shows new houses built by the migrants. In many cases, the migrants are the main source to build new public constructions, as a new church or school.

Walking through the area, it was easy to see signs of the relation with USA; the USA flag or the American eagle is a common decoration in the front of their houses.

At the same time, it was observed that the population had access to smartphones and computers as well as younger people who handled quite well communication programs such as Skype, Facebook or WhatsApp. The migrants, to stay in touch with their families, often send computers and cell phones. Even by the concern and interest of migrants in the United States not to lose their roots and the Mayan language, there is an online radio, www.topfmsantaeulalia.com that can be heard there and is not the only case. In contrast, because of the distance to other areas of Guatemala, you cannot hear the national radios in Santa Eulalia, but you have an online radio to listen to in Santa Eulalia or USA.

Also, in an interview with a human smuggling organization "coyote", member of the town, a possible reason why there are fewer female migrants in the United States when compared with the percentage of men is because of culture, women do not want to stop using their native dress and don't want to go to the USA to adapt. On the other hand, there is the culture that men migrate seasonally, saving to build a house and to marry within their own ethnic group. Very few tend to marry in the

United States and usually return to their village of origin to find a wife who will wait as he works in the United States.

With the support of the migrants in USA, the Santa Eulalia people reduced the poverty and have access to the technology and knowledgeable society in a new economy. In addition they have their own networks to keep their own culture and language. The crucial question is how to generate economic opportunities for its inhabitants in their own Santa Eulalia, as well as in Guatemala with the support and in a network with the migrants in USA. In the case of Guatemala, at least of 20% of all remittances are used for investment, especially in housing or SMEs.

So far, on international migration, remittances sent to developing countries, have their impact on Latin America and especially in Guatemala. For this country, remittances are key in reducing poverty and reducing inequality in the country. In many cases, remittances are new opportunities of business creation in Guatemala and USA.

Each year, the migration of Guatemalans to the United States increases, seeking opportunities for a better life and remittances to their homeland are growing. More than 90%, Guatemalans migrate due to lack of economic opportunities at home.

As we see in Table 6, Guatemala, El Salvador and Honduras Received in 2013 20% of all Remittances received by Latin American and Caribbean countries according the World Bank (World Bank, 2014).

This migration is growing without an observed reduction but it is changing. In the past usually just adults were traveling, but now, even children are going illegally to USA, as we saw with the crisis of migrant children in mid-2014.

This phenomenon of unaccompanied children migration, is a cultural aspect that is not yet fully explained by scholars or by the governments. Indeed, the cultural aspect should not be forgotten in the case of migration and to do business in the region. Some of the reasons for these are next:

For those interested in the phenomenon of migration of native people from the Northern Triangle to the United States, sooner or later will doubt about the kind of business or investment that can be made in those countries related to remittances. Then briefly explored this question:

The phenomenon of increasing migration of Northern Triangle citizens to the United States has to do with poverty and lack of opportunities, and a state that does not fulfill its basic function, safety.

If people migrate looking for opportunities, what public policy proposals involving remittances are necessary to accelerate their impact on the region and help the economy?

Table 8. Cultural issues: Key to doing business in Latin America

It is important to remember the cultural differences between Latin American and other non-Hispanic cultures, especially for those looking for business opportunities in Latin America related to migrants and remittances. Also, there are cultural differences between Latin American countries themselves or even within different geographic areas in the same country.
In their book, "International Marketing", Czinkota and Ronkainen wrote about the importance of the cultural aspects to do-international business. It is a classic example of the failure of Euro Disney. At the beginning it was because they did not take into account the cultural characteristic aspects of each country or region. (Czinkota, 2008).
The United States Census itself in "The Hispanic Population 2010", mentions the diversity of origins of Latinos in this country (United States Census Bureau, 2012). In the case of Latin America, although most countries have in common the Hispanic culture, the cultural and social aspects of each country can vary greatly, as it affects the geography or the fact that in certain areas there are more indigenous than others and the Spanish cannot be the only language spoken in the area.
This is the case of Guatemala, with 22 Mayan languages, a language of African -American origin "Garifuna" and Spanish, which is the official language.
Another important cultural aspect to consider in doing business in Latin America is conceived as a family. Hispanic usually tends to prefer doing business with family members, individuals previously known or referred by a family member or friend. And family for a Latino, is understood in a broad way and not reduced as in the United States.
The classic example of "the Cousin of the Cousin is family too" made many jokes in the Latin America idiosyncrasy, but is true. This situation is very different from American culture, where the family is seen as a small circle. Remember this is important if you want to do business with or related to migrant remittances to Latin American businesses; rarely, they accept to invest their money with people who do not know or are not referred by a family member or a friend.
In the case of Guatemala and the migrants in USA, most of them are men, because women, especially from indigenous areas, do not want to lose their language and traditional clothes. Many men are going to work to USA, but with the hope to go back to their families in Guatemala.

Some Public Policies Proposals Related to Remittances as an Engine of Change in Latin America

Not all the Latin American countries have the same dependence on remittances as the Northern Triangle countries. The remittances, for Guatemala, El Salvador and Honduras, are almost or more than the 10% of the GDP. And have more of the 10% of the Northern Triangle inhabitants living in USA as migrants.

The crisis of unaccompanied migrant children in 2014 has resulted for governments of Guatemala, El Salvador, Honduras and the United States in an initiative to develop a proposed plan for prosperity, seeking to create opportunities in countries of origin and reduce migration.

The successful design and implementation of a plan of this nature is of interest, not only for politicians from the region, but also for those who want to do business with it. By accelerating regional development, the possibilities and business options increase.

Remittances

Table 9. Potential business opportunities and investment in Latin America related to remittances

- As previously analyzed in this paper, not all Latin American countries have the same flow of remittances or this means the same to their economies, as shown in the Table 6. The Latin American countries receiving more remittances in the region are Mexico, Guatemala, Dominican Republic, Colombia, El Salvador and Honduras; these six countries are almost the 77% of the total of remittances received in the region.
- If we focus on the countries called "Northern Triangle" (Guatemala, El Salvador and Honduras) they account over 20% of total remittances received in Latin America.
- The three countries are listed as small economies in the region, and do not have large natural resources like Venezuela or major exporters of commodities such as Argentina.
- Since the point of view of competitiveness, the most valuable asset of the Northern Triangle is the geographical location, it is the natural bridge connecting the two American subcontinents and between two oceans. In addition, they have good weather and a huge touristic potential.
- The three countries of the Northern Triangle have a Free Trade Agreement with the United States for nearly a decade, the DR CAFTA and they have common poverty and a lack of free markets and rule of law problems that affect the migration to USA.
- Many of the migrants in the United States from the Northern Triangle come from rural areas in their countries. Some business opportunities related to remittances can be services for migrants and their families. Also, there is a huge potential for investment or co-investment in production and export of food and beverages to the migrant market, as one of the strongest aspects of the cultural differences is the food. Other market opportunities related to remittances are products and services related to technology.
- A potential investment that has not been explored yet, is the possibility of joint investment in rural areas to create jobs in their communities, and export goods to the US, using the knowledge of the US market learned by migrants.

The region has received by many years enormous amounts of development cooperation and that has not resulted in a clear reduction of poverty. It is time to break the classical circle of international cooperation projects and take into account two principles:

First principle: The basis of any project or plan for prosperity must be based on the concept of Aid for Trade. In other words, the international cooperation and projects to be included in that plan for prosperity should be based on seeking support trade and entrepreneurship in Northern triangle, linking, somehow, also with US businesses, or "AID for Trade".

The *second principle* is to break with the traditional approximation of design development from above to establish guidelines to be done. In other words, the traditional approximation is from top to bottom. In this case, especially in Guatemala, with many cultures and languages, plans need to involve local communities and to partake of what is designed for development.

The Northern Triangle have largest groups of migrants in the United States helping now their communities individually; these groups should also be involved in the plan. Who are the best to link their communities in Guatemala with the United States than those born in said communities and now residing in USA? They are those who know the grief and anguish of migration, as well as the needs of their communities. An issue with the second principle is that the plan is developed below (local) up (the dome), breaking the traditional mold of "top down". It must be "bottom up".

With these two principles, "Aid for Trade" and "bottom-up", are a must to design and implement any plans to reduce economic migration to the United States. Until now, none of the three Northern Triangle countries understand clearly the importance of economic migrants and the factor of change that has involved them in the fight against poverty. Even, the migrants can be a factor of change in social issues, as the possibility of building a society or closer to the US model culture, such as the division of powers and accountability, which can help to develop a culture of republic and democracy.

The three Northern Triangle countries have a Central American integration process by decades; then, they could analyze together the migration issues to negotiate with the United States the benefits for their migrants and share information and support with their communities.

The question is, Why the Northern Triangle countries, with their dependency on remittances, do not develop a group of countries with similar interests and provide joint services for their migrants in the United States, a country where the majority of Northern Triangle migrants are?

The three countries, with differences, have many things in common and can develop projects to support the use of the remittances to develop the rural areas. We must remember that migrants work for them and their families, now, they are investing millions of dollars in their countries of origin, as real estate and SMEs. How can you develop public policies to support these new projects, moving the migrants, from "just the remittances" to "seed capital for new businesses" which usually will be with family and friends? If you do not take into account migrants and local communities, the chances of success for any plan of prosperity will be minimal.

CONCLUSION

The migration from Northern Triangle citizens to USA will not stop until the development of the countries of the region becomes a reality. Migrants send remittances, which, in the short run, benefit the local economies of the Northern Triangle. The Northern Triangle countries have shown a strong short run dependence on the ingress of remittances in their economies. The receipt of remittances has contributed to the mitigation of poverty and social instability that would normally arise from conditions of poverty and marginalization. Remittances help ameliorate social, cultural and economic issues for the countries of Guatemala, El Salvador and Honduras. Migration to USA has, in certain areas, become almost an informal custom, which has accentuated in recent years, aided by the phenomenon of globalization and the economic crises in the countries of origin.

Remittances

Remittances constitute a short run panacea, but hide a long run problem. The remittances for Guatemala, El Salvador and Honduras have translated into elevated consumption patterns in said countries, with mixed results for the war on poverty in the region during the last decade. Even local politicians have not yet been able to gauge the real importance to their national economies of the remittances sent by nationals living in the United States. Countries that depend heavily on remittances are those that expel emigrants, so are naturally unable to attract new migrants, and much less, foreign direct investment.

For short run purposes, the remittances to the Northern Triangle countries are akin to the Marshall Plan for the region, except that the monetary transfers occur on a microeconomic level, person to person, family to family. As the Marshall Plan positively changed Europe in the postwar period, the remittances have become the safety nets for the emigrant-emitting countries of the region. The main difference is that, in the case of remittances, it is individuals who are directly making the important, defining choices, it is individuals who are making the difference, not states.

The governments of Guatemala, El Salvador and Honduras, and USA, must understand that remittances represent over 20% of the value of their imports and more than 30% of exports. Remittances are almost or more than 10% of the GDP of these countries. Any plan for "prosperity" must involve the local communities and their own migrants.

Mexico provides a strong example of how migrant communities can get involved to benefit their communities, not only for business but for social projects, it is the project called "three to one". The 3x1 program for migrants supports the initiatives of Mexicans living abroad and gives them the opportunity to channel resources into works of social impact that directly benefit their communities of origin.

The only countries in Latin America with this dependence of remittances in their economies are the Northern Triangle countries and Dominican Republic. The four countries have a Free Trade Agreement with USA. If we want to see long term solutions for these countries, the governments should be a strong focus in AID for Trade and try to exploit the commercial relationship to develop greater business between the countries involved.

Remittances have been shown to be a key factor for the social stability in the countries and a key factor in the war against poverty. As such, migrants should be a central issue of government foreign affairs, for economic and social reasons. For the USA, the Northern Triangle countries are the closest countries of the North Command and are key to national security issues for the USA. Also with more of 10% of the adult population of the Northern Triangle countries living in the USA, this can be a key factor to support and promote democracies, a key pillar of United States foreign policy.

As the Northern Triangle countries have common dependence of remittances to their economies, similar geographic position in the world, shared problems of poverty, crime, drugs and violence, the development of public policies in coordination with USA will be in benefit of the four main countries. This theme needs to be emphasized by the USA in the planned "Prosperity plan" for Northern Triangle countries.

REFERENCES

Banco Central de Honduras. (2014). Retrieved 10 08, 2014, from http://www.bch.hn/remesas_familiares.php

Banco de Guatemala. (2014). *Banguat. Remesas familiares.* Guatemala: Banco de Guatemala.

Cemla, E. P. (2014). *Cemla.* Retrieved from http://www.cemla-remesas.org/principios/pdf/PrincipiosRemesas-Guatemala-2014.pdf

Czinkota, M., & Ronkainen, I. (2008). Marketing Internacional. México: C. Learning.

Rapha, D. (2012). *Tenth meeting on migration and remittances.* Retrieved from World Bank: http://www.worldbank.org/en/news/press-release/2014/04/11/remittances-developing-countries-deportations-migrant-workers-wb

Segeplan. (2014). Retrieved from Segeplan.gob.gt: http://www.segeplan.gob.gt/2.0/index.php?option=com_content&view=article&id=1321:mapas-de-pobreza-rural-herramienta-relevante-para-el-combate-a-la-pobreza-y-a-la-desigualdad-dice-secretaria-de-planificacion&catid=25:ultima&Itemid=115

UN. (2014). Retrieved from un.org: http://www.un.org/en/development/desa/news/population/number-of-international-migrants-rises.html

UNDP. (2013). Retrieved from undp.org: http://hdr.undp.org/es/content/human-development-index-hdi-table

UNESCO. (1990). *Full Text of the International Convention on the Protection of the Rights of All Migrant Workers and Members of Their Families (no yet in force).* Retrieved from unesco.org: http://www.unesco.org/most/migration/mwc_toc.htm

UNESCO. (2014). *International Migration and Multicultural policies.* Retrieved from unesco.org: http://www.unesco.org/most/migration/glossary_migrants.htm

UNESCO. (n.d.). Retrieved from unesco.org: http://www.unesco.org/new/en/social-and-human sciences/themes/international-migration

Remittances

United States Census Bureau. (2012). *The foreign born population in 2010*. Retrieved from census.gov: https://www.census.gov/prod/2012pubs/acs-19.pdf

United States Census Bureau. (2012). *La población hispana: 2010*. Retrieved from census.gov: http://www.census.gov/prod/cen2010/briefs/c2010br-04sp.pdf

World Bank. (2014). *Migration and Remittances: Recent developments and Outlook*. Retrieved from World Bank: http://siteresources.worldbank.org/INTPROSPECTS/Resources/334934-1288990760745/MigrationandDevelopmentBrief22.pdf

World Bank. (2014). Press release: *World Bank*. Retrieved from World Bank: http://www.worldbank.org/en/news/press-release/2014/04/11/remittances-developing-countries-deportations-migrant-workers-wb

Compilation of References

Acs, Z. (1996). Small Firms and Economic Growth. In Z. J. Acs, B. Carlsson, & R. Thurik (Eds.), *Small Business in the Modern Economy* (pp. 1–62). Oxford, UK: Blackwell Publishers.

Acs, Z., & Amorós, J. (2008). Entrepreneurship and competitiveness dynamics in Latin America. *Small Business Economics, 31*(3), 305–322. doi:10.1007/s11187-008-9133-y

Acs, Z., & Szerb, L. (2007). Entrepreneurship, Economic Growth and Public Policy. *Small Business Economics, 28*(2-3), 109–122. doi:10.1007/s11187-006-9012-3

Akula, V. (2008). Business basics at the Base of the Pyramid. *Harvard Business Review, 86*(6), 53–57.

Alesina, A., & La Ferrara, E. (2005). Preferences for redistribution in the land of opportunities. *Journal of Public Economics, Elsevier, 89*(5-6), 897–931. doi:10.1016/j.jpubeco.2004.05.009

Alexandre, C., Mas, I. & Radcliffe, D. (2010). *Regulating New Banking Models that can Bring Financial Services to All.* Bill & Melinda Gates Foundation.

Allen, F., McAndrews, J., & Strahan, P. (2002). E-Finance: An Introduction. *Journal of Financial Services Research, 22*(1/2), 5–27. doi:10.1023/A:1016007126394

Altman, D. G., Rego, L., & Ross, P. (2009). Expanding opportunity at the Base of the Pyramid. *People & Strategy, 32*(2), 46–51.

Alves, & Choi. (2004). *Facilitating Entrepreneurship in Emerging Markets: Economic Policy.* International Business and Strategic Transparency.

Amorós, E., Bosma, N., & GERA. (2014). *Global Entrepreneurship Monitor 2013 Global Report.* Chile: GERA.

Anderson, E., & Gatignon, H. (1986). Modes of foreign entry: A transaction cost analysis and propositions. *Journal of International Business Studies, 51*(1), 71–82.

Anderson, J., & Billou, N. (2007). Serving the world's poor: Innovation at the Base of the Economic Pyramid. *The Journal of Business Strategy, 28*(2), 14–21. doi:10.1108/02756660710732611

Compilation of References

Andersson, U., Forsgren, M., & Holm, U. (2002). The strategic impact of external networks: Subsidiary performance and competence development in multinational corporation. *Strategic Management Journal*, *23*(11), 979–996. doi:10.1002/smj.267

Andersson, U., Johanson, J., & Vahlne, J.-E. (1997). Organic acquisitions in the internationalization process of the business firm. *Management International Review*, *37*(2), 67–84.

Anechiarico, F., & Jacobs, J. (1996). *The Pursuit of Absolute Integrity*. Chicago: Chicago University Press.

Aorcena, R., & Sutz, J. (2000). *Interactive Learning spaces and development policies in Latin America*. DRUID Working Paper, 00-13, Department of Business Studies: Aalborg.

Arroyo, A. C., & Walker, D. H. T. (2010). The Role of Atlantic Corridor Project as a Form of Strategic Community of Practice in Business Transformations in Latin America. *International Journal of Managing Projects in Business*, *3*(2), 333–348. doi:10.1108/17538371011036626

Asghar, A. J., Khaled, N., Seyed-Mohammad, S. K., & Amin-Reza, K. (2011). The Relationship between Government Policy and the Growth of Entrepreneurship in the Micro, Small & Medium Enterprises of India. J. *Technology of Managament & Innovation*, *6*(1), 66–76. doi:10.4067/S0718-27242011000100007

Atkinson, R. D. (2013). *Competitiveness, Innovation and Productivity: Clearing up the Confusion*. Washington, DC: The Information Technology & Innovation Foundation.

Attis, D. (2014). *Higher education and the future of U.S. competitiveness*. Educause.

Atuahene-Gima, K., & Slater, A. (2001). *Dual core market orientation and radical innovation: A conceptual model and empirical test.European Marketing Academy Conference*.

Aubert, J.-E. (2005). *Promoting Innovation in Developing Countries: A Conceptual Framework*. World Bank Policy Research Working Paper, No. 3554.

Audretsch, D., & Thurik, R. (2001). *Linking Entrepreneurship to Growth*. Paris: OECD, Directorate for Science, Technology and Industry Working Papers.

Audretsch, D., Falck, O., Feldman, M., & Heblich, S. (2012). Local Entrepreneurship in Context. *Regional Studies*, *46*(3), 379–389. doi:10.1080/00343404.2010.490209

Audretsch, D., & Keilbach, M. (2007). The Theory of Knowledge Spillover. *Entrepreneurship Journal of Management Studies*, *44*(7), 1242–1253. doi:10.1111/j.1467-6486.2007.00722.x

Audretsch, D., & Lehman, E. (2004). Financing High-Tech Growth: The Role of Banks and Venture Capitalists. *Schmalenbach Business Review*, *56*, 340–357.

Axelsson, B., & Johanson, J. (1992). Foreign market entry: The textbook vs. the network view. In B. Axelsson & G. Easton (Eds.), *Industrial Networks: A New View of Reality* (pp. 218–234). London: Routledge.

Ayyagari, M., Demirguc-Kunt, A., & Maksimovic, V. (2007). *Formal versus informal finance: Evidence from China*. World Bank Mimeo.

Bain, J. S. (1956). *Barriers to new competition*. Boston: Harvard University Press. doi:10.4159/harvard.9780674188037

Balasubramanyam, V., Salisu, M., & Sapsford, D. (1999). Foreign Direct Investment as an Engine of Growth. *The Journal of International Trade & Economic Development*, *8*(1), 27–40. doi:10.1080/09638199900000003

Banco Central de Honduras. (2014). Retrieved 10 08, 2014, from http://www.bch.hn/remesas_familiares.php

Banco de Guatemala. (2014). *Banguat. Remesas familiares*. Guatemala: Banco de Guatemala.

Banerjee, A. V., & Duflo, E. (2007). The economic lives of the poor. *The Journal of Economic Perspectives*, *21*(1), 141–167. doi:10.1257/jep.21.1.141 PMID:19212450

Banerjee, A. V., & Duflo, E. (2011). *Poor economics: A radical rethinking of the way to fight global poverty*. New York: PublicAffairs.

Barron, J. (2014). All in the Family: Trading Legal Security for Trust and Export Growth in Latin America. *Business Credit*, *116*(5), 31–32.

Bas, T., Amoros, E., & Kunc, M. (2008). Innovation, Entrepreneurship and Clusters in Latin America Natural Resource-Implication and Future Challenges. *Journal of Technology Management and Innovation*, *3*(3), 52–65.

Bateman, M., & Chang, H. J. (2009). *The Microfinance Illusion*. Available online at: http://www.microfinancetransparency.com/evidence/PDF/App.3%20Chang%20Bateman%20article.pdf (accessed 15 October 2014)

Bateman, M. (2010). *Why doesn't microfinance work? The destructive rise of local neoliberalism*. New York: Zed Books.

Baumol, W. J. (2004). Four Sources of Innovation and Stimulation of Growth in the Dutch Economy. *The Economist*, *152*(3), 321-351.

Behrman, J. (1974). *Decision criteria for foreign direct investment in Latin America*. New York: Council of the Americas.

Berger, M., Goldmark, L., & Miller-Sanabria. (Eds.). (2006). *An inside view of Latin American microfinance*. Washington, DC: Inter-American Development Bank.

Bergstrand, J. (1990). The Heckscher-Ohlin-Samuelson Model, The Linder Hypothesis and the Determinants of Bilateral Intra-Industry Trade. *The Economic Journal*, *100*(403), 1216–1229. doi:10.2307/2233969

Compilation of References

Bertucci, G., & Alberti, A. (2003). Globalization and the Role of the State: Challenges and Perspectives. In Reinventing Government for the Twenty-First Century, State Capacity in a Globalizing Society. Kumarian Press Inc.

Bevan, A., Estrin, S., & Meyer, K. (2004). Foreign investment location and institutional development in transaction economies. *International Business Review, 13*(1), 43–64. doi:10.1016/j.ibusrev.2003.05.005

Bhattacharya, R., Devinney, T. M., & Pillutla, M. M. (1998). A Formal Model of Trust Based on Outcomes. *Academy of Management Review, 23*(3), 459–472.

Bialaszewski, D., & Giallourakis, M. (1985). Perceived Communication Skills and Resultant Trust Perceptions Whiting the Channel Distribution. *Journal of the Academy of Marketing Science, 13*(1/2), 206–217. doi:10.1007/BF02729715

Bibb, S., & Kourdi, J. (2004). *Trust Matters for Organizational and Personal Success*. New York: Palgrave.

BID. (2013). *Las redes de inversionistas ángeles en América Latina y el caribe*. BID.

Biglaiser, G., & De Rouen, K. (2006). Economic reforms and inflows of foreign direct investment in Latin America. *Latin American Research Review, 41*(1), 51–75. doi:10.1353/lar.2006.0001

Bilkey, W. J., & Tesar, G. (1977). The export behavior of smaller-sized Wisconsin manufacturing firms. *Journal of International Business Studies, 8*(1), 93–98. doi:10.1057/palgrave.jibs.8490783

Birch, D. (1979). The Job Generation Process. M.I.T. Program on Neighborhood and Regional Change. Cambridge.

Bjorkman, I., & Forsgren, M. (2000). Nordic international business research: A review of its development. *International Studies of Management & Organization, 30*(1), 6–25.

Blanco, L. (2012). The Spatial Interdependence of FDI in Latin America. *World Development, 40*(7), 1337–1351. doi:10.1016/j.worlddev.2012.02.003

Blind, P. K. (2007). Building trust in government in the twenty-first century: Review of literature and emerging issues. In *Proceedings of 7th Global Forum on Reinventing Government Building Trust in Government* (pp. 26-29). Academic Press.

Blonigen, B. (2005). A Review of the Empirical Literature on FDI Determinants. *Atlantic Economic Journal, 33*(4), 383–403. doi:10.1007/s11293-005-2868-9

Blonigen, B., & Wang, M. (2005). Inappropriate pooling of wealthy and poor countries in empirical studies. In T. Moran, E. Graham, & M. Blomstron (Eds.), *Does Foreign Direct Investment Promote Development?* (pp. 221–244). Washington, DC: Institute for International Economics.

309

Booth, D. (2012). *Development as a Collective Action Problem. Synthesis report of the Africa Power and Politics Programme.* Overseas Development Institute. Retrieved from http://www. institutions-africa.org/filestream/20121024-appp-policy-brief-09-development-as-a-collective-action-problem

Booth, J. A., & Seligson, M. A. (2009). *The Legitimacy Puzzle: Political Support and Democracy in Latin America.* New York: Cambridge University Press. doi:10.1017/CBO9780511818431

Borensztein, E., De Gregorio, J., & Lee, J. (1998). How does foreign direct investment affect economic growth? *Journal of International Economics, 45*(1), 115–135. doi:10.1016/S0022-1996(97)00033-0

Bosma, N., Coduras, A., Litovsky, Y., & Seaman, J. (2012). *GEM Manual. Version 2012-9: May.* GEM.

Bosma, N., & Levie, J.Global Entrepreneurship Research Association-GERA. (2010). *Global Entrepreneurship Monitor 2009 Global report.* London: GEM.

Breschi, S., & Malerba, F. (1997). Sectoral Innovation Systems: Technological Regimes, Schumpeterian Dynamics and Spatial Boundaries. In C. Edquist (Ed.), *Systems of Innovation Pinter.* London.

Brockhoff, K. (1994). R&D Project Termination Decisions by Discriminant Analysis-An International Comparison. *IEEE Transactions on Engineering Management, 41*(3), 245–254. doi:10.1109/17.310139

Brown, J. R., Lusch, R. F., & Nicholson, C. Y. (1995). Power and relationship commitment: Their impact on marketing channel member performance. *Journal of Retailing, 71*(4), 363–392. doi:10.1016/0022-4359(95)90019-5

Bruggen, G. H. (2005). The impact of channel function performance on buyer-seller relationships in marketing channels. *International Journal of Research in Marketing, 22*(2), 141–158. doi:10.1016/j.ijresmar.2004.06.004

Bruton, K., Khavul, S., & Chavez, H. (2011). Microlending in emerging economies: Building a new line of inquiry from the ground up. *Journal of International Business Studies, 42*(5), 718–739. doi:10.1057/jibs.2010.58

Buckley, P. J. (2002). Is the International Business research agenda running out of steam? *Journal of International Business Studies, 33*(2), 365–373. doi:10.1057/palgrave.jibs.8491021

Buckley, P. J., & Casson, M. (1976). *The future of the multinational enterprise.* London: Macmillan.

Buckley, P. J., & Ghauri, P. N. (2004). Globalisation, economic geography and the strategy of multinational enterprises. *Journal of International Business Studies, 35*(2), 81–98. doi:10.1057/palgrave.jibs.8400076

Buckley, P., & Casson, M. (1976). *The Future of Multinational Enterprises.* London: MacMillan.

Compilation of References

Buckley, P., Clegg, L. J., Cross, A. R., Liu, X., Voss, H., & Zheng, P. (2007). The Determinants of Chinese Outward Foreign Direct Investment. *Journal of International Business Studies, 38*(4), 499–518. doi:10.1057/palgrave.jibs.8400277

Burgel, O., & Murray, G. C. (2000). The international market entry choices of start-up companies in high-technology industries. *Journal of International Marketing, 8*(2), 33–62. doi:10.1509/jimk.8.2.33.19624

Caballero, A. (2011). *Colombia -Science, Technology and Innovation: P117590-Implementation Status Results Report: Sequence 02*. Washington, DC: World Bank. Retrieved from http://documents.worldbank.org/curated/en/2011/05/14132146/colombia-science-technology-innovation-p117590-implementation-status-results-report-sequence-02

Caballero, K., & Melgarejo, M. (2005). La estrategia de recuperación, 2000 - 2004. In INCAE Business School (Eds.), *CGAP Portal de Microfinanzas*. Available at: http://www.microfinancegateway.org/sites/default/files/mfg-es-documento-caso-bancosol-2-2005.pdf

Cadogan, J., & Diamantopoulos, A. (1995). Narver & Slater, Kohli & Jaworski and the market orientation construct: Integration and internationalization. *Journal of Strategic Marketing, 3*(1), 41–60. doi:10.1080/09652549500000003

Cadogan, J., Diamantopoulos, A., & Mortanges, C. (1999). A measure of export market orientation: Scale development and cross-cultural validation. *Journal of International Business Studies, 30*(4), 689–707. doi:10.1057/palgrave.jibs.8490834

Calle-Fernández, A., & Tamayo-Bustamante, V. (2005). Estrategia e internacionalización en las PYMES: Caso Antioquia. *Cuadernos de Administración, 18*(30), 137–164.

Calof, J., & Beamish, P. (1995). Adapting to foreign markets: Explaining internalisation. *International Business Review, 4*(2), 115–131. doi:10.1016/0969-5931(95)00001-G

Capelleras Segura, J. L., & Kantis, H. D. (2009). *Nuevas empresas en América Latina: factores que favorecen su rápido crecimiento*. Barcelona: Universitat Autònoma de Barcelona, Servei de Publicacions.

Capelleras, J. L., & Greene, F. J. (2008). The determinants and growth implications of venture creation speed. *Entrepreneurship and Regional Development, 20*(4), 311–337. doi:10.1080/08985620701855683

Cardenas, J. C., Chong, A., Nopo, H., Horowitz, A. W., & Lederman, D. (2009). To What Extent Do Latin Americans Trust, Reciprocate and Cooperate? Evidence from Experiments in Six Latin American Countries/ Comments. *Economia, 9*(2), 45–94.

Cardoso, F. & Faletto, E. (1979). *Dependency and Development in Latin America*. Berkeley, CA: Berkeley University Press.'

Carree, M., & Thurik, R. (2002). The Impact of Entrepreneurship on Economic Growth. In *International Handbook of Entrepreneurship Research*. Boston: Kluwer Academic Publishers.

Carreras, M. (2013). The impact of criminal violence on regime legitimacy in Latin America. *Latin American Research Review, 48*(3), 85–107. doi:10.1353/lar.2013.0040

Carruthers, B. G., & Kim, J. C. (2011). The sociology of finance. *Annual Review of Sociology, 37*(1), 239–259. doi:10.1146/annurev-soc-081309-150129

Caves, R. (1971). International Corporations: The Industrial Economics of Foreign Investment. *Economica, 38*(179), 1–27. doi:10.2307/2551748

Cemla, E. P. (2014). *Cemla.* Retrieved from http://www.cemla-remesas.org/principios/pdf/PrincipiosRemesas-Guatemala-2014.pdf

Central American Institute for Fiscal Studies. (2014). *Participación de las remesas en salud.* Central American Instititute for Fiscal Studies. Central American Instititute for Fiscal Studies.

Central American Institute for Fiscal Studies. (n.d.). *Gasto Público, tendencias recientes y su impacto en equidad.* Central American Institute for Fiscal Studies.

Central American Institute of Fiscal Studies. (2014a). *Public Expenditure in Education.* Central American Institute of Fiscal Studies.

Central American Institute of Fiscal Studies. (2014b). *To a new vision of competitiveness.* Central American Institute of Fiscal Studies.

CGAP. (2011). What do we know about the impact of microfinance? In *Consultative group to assist the poor - About microfinance.* Available online at: www.cgap.org/p/site/c/template.rc/1.26.1306

CGAP. (2012). *The Consultative Group to Assist the Poor.* [online] Available at: http://www.cgap.org/blog/biggest-social-experiment-planet

CGAP. (2014). *Financial Inclusion and Development: Recent Impact Evidence.* Available online at: http://www.cgap.org/sites/default/files/FocusNote-Financial-Inclusion-and-Development-April-2014.pdf

Chacholiades, M. (1992). *Economía Internacional.* Bogotá, Colombia: McGraw-Hill.

Chaminade, C., & Vang, J. (2008). Globalisation of knowledge production and regional innovation policy: Supporting specialized hubs in the Bangalore software industry. *Research Policy, 37*(10), 1684–1696. doi:10.1016/j.respol.2008.08.014

Chang, H.-J. (2007). *Institutional Change and Economic Development* (H.-J. Chang, Ed.). New York: United Nations University Press.

Chang, H.-J. (2010). *23 Things They Don't Tell You about Capitalism.* New York: Bloomsbury Press.

Chao, C. M., Yu, C. T., Cheng, B. W., & Chuang, P.-C. (2013). Trust and Commitment in Relationships among Medical Equipment Suppliers: Transaction Cost and Social Exchange Theories. *Social Behavior and Personality, 4*(7), 1057–1070. doi:10.2224/sbp.2013.41.7.1057

Compilation of References

Cheng, L., & Kwan, Y. (2000). What are the determinants of the location of foreign direct investment? The Chinese experience. *Journal of International Economics*, *51*(2), 379–400. doi:10.1016/S0022-1996(99)00032-X

Chetty, S., & Campbell-Hunt, C. (2003). Paths to internationalisation among small-to medium-sized firms: A global versus regional approach. *European Journal of Marketing*, *37*(5/6), 796–820. doi:10.1108/03090560310465152

Christian Democratic Union. (2010). *German Democratic History in Documents and Images.* Retrieved from http://germanhistorydocs.ghi-dc.org/pdf/eng/Ch12Doc02(2)Eng.pdf

Citrin, J. (1974). The Political Relevance of Trust in Government. *The American Political Science Review*, *68*(3), 973–988. doi:10.2307/1959141

Ciudadana, A. (2006). Indicadores de percepción y experiencias de corrupción de Guatemala -IPEC-. Guatemala.

Collins, J., & Uhlenbruck, K. (2004). *How firms respond to government corruption: Insights from India.* Academy of Management Best Paper Procedings.

Colombian Congress. (2006). *Ley 1014* [Law 1014]. Retrieved from http://www.mineducacion. gov.co/1621/articles-94653_archivo_pdf.pdf

Colombian Congress. (2009). *Ley 1286* [Law 1286]. Retrieved from https://pwh.dnp.gov.co/LinkClick.aspx?fileticket=aN21z7FHE1o%3D&tabid=426

Colombian Congress. (2010). *Ley 1429* [Law 1429]. Retrieved from http://www.alcaldiabogota. gov.co/sisjur/normas/Norma1.jsp?i=41060

Colombian Congress. (2011). *Informe al Congreso* [Report to the Congress]. Retrieved from http://wsp.presidencia.gov.co/Publicaciones/Documents/InformePresidente2011.pdf

Colombian Congress. (2011). *Ley 1450* [Law 1450]. Retrieved from http://www.alcaldiabogota. gov.co/sisjur/normas/Norma1.jsp?i=43101

Colombian Congress. (2012). *Decreto 19* [Decree 19]. Retrieved from http://www.alcaldiabogota. gov.co/sisjur/normas/Norma1.jsp?i=45322

Colombian National Council for Economic and Social Policy- National Planning Department. (2004). *Documento CONPES 3280* [Document CONPES 3280]. Retrieved from http://www. sinic.gov.co/SINIC/CuentaSatelite/documentos/200981814348574.pdf

Colombian National Council for Economic and Social Policy- National Planning Department. (2007). *Documento CONPES 3484* [Document CONPES 3484]. http://www.huila.gov.co/documentos/C/CONPES3484de2007.pdf

Colombian National Council for Economic and Social Policy- National Planning Department. (2008). *Documento CONPES 3527* [Document CONPES 3527]. Retrieved from http://wsp. presidencia.gov.co/sncei/politica/Documents/Conpes-3527-23jun2008.pdf

Colombian National Observatory of Science and Technology. (2013). *Indicadores Ciencia y Tecnologia* [Science and Technology Indicators]. Retrieved from http://ocyt.org.co/Portals/0/Documentos/COLOMBIA_2013.pdf

Colombo, M., & Grilli, L. (2007). Funding Gaps? Access to Bank Loans by High-Tech Start-Ups. *Small Business Economics, 29*(1-2), 25–46. doi:10.1007/s11187-005-4067-0

Commun, P. (2014). *German Ordoliberalism: Order versus Disorder in Röpke's Early Works.* Retrieved from www.i-lex.it

Consejo Privado de Competitividad. (n.d.). Retrieved from http://www.mejoremosguate.org/cms/en/what-are-we-doing/consejo-privado-de-competitividad

Cotler, P., & Aguilar, G. (2013). The microfinance sectors in Peru and Mexico: Why have they followed different paths? In R. Manos, J.-P. Gueyie, & J. Yaron (Eds.), *Promoting microfinance: Challenges and innovations in developing countries and countries in transition.* Palgrave Macmillan. doi:10.1057/9781137034915.0008

Council on Competitiveness. (2007). *Competitiveness Index: Where America Stands.* Boston: Council on Competitiveness.

Coviello, N. E., & Munro, H. J. (1997). Network relationships and the internationalization process of small software firms. *International Business Review, 6*(4), 361–386. doi:10.1016/S0969-5931(97)00010-3

Covin, J. G., & Slevin, D. P. (1989). Strategic management of small firms in hostile and benign environments. *Strategic Management Journal, 10*(1), 75–87. doi:10.1002/smj.4250100107

Crick, D., & Spence, M. (2005). The Internationalisation of 'high performing' U.K. high-tech SMEs: A study of planned and unplanned strategies. *International Business Review, 14*(2), 167–185. doi:10.1016/j.ibusrev.2004.04.007

Crowards, T. (2002). Defining the Category of 'Small' States. *Journal of International Development, 14*(2), 143–179. doi:10.1002/jid.860

Cruz, J. M. (2003). Violencia y democratización en Centroamérica: El impacto del crimen en la legitimidad de los regímenes de posguerra. *América Latina Hoy, 35,* 19–59.

Cuervo-Cazurra, A. (2011). Selecting the country in which to start internationalization: The non-sequential internationalization argument. *Journal of World Business, 46*(4), 426–437. doi:10.1016/j.jwb.2010.10.003

Cummings, J., & Teng, B. S. (2003). Transferring R&D knowledge: The key factors affecting knowledge transfer success. *Journal of Engineering and Technology Management, 20*(1-2), 39–68. doi:10.1016/S0923-4748(03)00004-3

Curat, P., Lupano, J., & Adúriz, I. (2006). *Demanda potencial por microcréditos en el Conurbano Bonaerense.* Fundación Andares.

Compilation of References

Curevo-Cazurra, A. (2008). Better the Devil You Don't Know: Type of Corruption and FDI in Transition Economies. *Journal of International Management, 14*(1), 12–27. doi:10.1016/j. intman.2007.02.003

Czinkota, M., & Ronkainen, I. (2008). Marketing Internacional. México: C. Learning.

Dahlstrom, R., & Nygaard, A. (1995). An Exploratory Investigation of Interpersonal Trust in New and Mature Markets. *Journal of Retailing, 71*(4), 339–361. doi:10.1016/0022-4359(95)90018-7

Davidsson, P. (1995). Culture, structure and regional levels of entrepreneurship. *Entrepreneurship and Regional Development, 7*(1), 41–62. doi:10.1080/08985629500000003

Dawes, J. (2000). Market orientation and company profitability: Further evidence incorporating longitudinal data. *Australian Journal of Management, 25*(2), 173–200. doi:10.1177/031289620002500204

Day, G. S., & Van den Bulte, C. (2002). *Superiority in customer relationship management: Consequences for competitive advantage and performance.* Marketing Science Institute Working Paper Series, Report No. 02-123.

Day, G. (1999). Misconceptions about market orientation. *Journal of Market-Focused Management, 4*(1), 5–16. doi:10.1023/A:1009882027377

Day, G. S. (2003). Creating a superior customer-relating capability. *Sloan Management Review, 44*(3), 77–82.

De León, I. (2014). *Personaje del mes: Junio 2014 - Benjamin Sywulka.* Retrieved from http://uvg.edu.gt/publicaciones/personaje/2014/junio/index.html

De Sierra, G. (1999). Limitaciones y potencialidades de un pequeño país en el marco de la integración regional. *Futuro de la sociedad uruguaya, CEE 1815.* EBO, Mdeo.

De Soto, H. (2000). *The mystery of capital: Why Capitalism triumphs in the West and fails everywhere else.* London: Bantam Press – Black Swan edition.

De Wever, S., Martens, R., & Vandenbempt, K. (2005). The impact of trust on strategic resource acquisition through interorganizational networks: Towards a conceptual model. *Human Relations, 58*(12), 1523–1543. doi:10.1177/0018726705061316

Deng, S., & Dart, J. (1994). Measuring market orientation. A multi-factor, multi-items approach. *Journal of Marketing Management, 10*(8), 725–742. doi:10.1080/0267257X.1994.9964318

Deshpandé, R., & Farley, D. (2004). Organizational culture, market orientation, innovativeness, and firm performance: An international research odyssey. *International Journal of Research in Marketing, 21*(1), 3–22. doi:10.1016/j.ijresmar.2003.04.002

Deshpandé, R., Farley, D., & Webster, F. Jr. (1993). Corporate culture, customer orientation, and innovativeness in Japanese firms: A quadrad *analysis. Journal of Marketing, 57*(1), 23–37. doi:10.2307/1252055

315

Diamanti, I. (2014). *Democrazia Ibrida*. Rome: Editori Laterza.

DiMaggio, P., & Powell, W. (1983). The iron cage revisited: Institutional isomorphism and collective rationality in organizational fields. *American Sociological Review, 48*(2), 147–160. doi:10.2307/2095101

Diniz, E., Birochi, R., & Pozzebon, M. (2012). Triggers and barriers to financial inclusion: The use of ICT-based branchless banking in an Amazon County. *Electronic Commerce Resource Application, 11*(5), 484–494. doi:10.1016/j.elerap.2011.07.006

Diplomat Magazine. (2013). *Guatemala Land of the Eternal Spring...Land for Investments*. Available at http://www.diplomatmagazine.nl/2013/12/01/guatemala-land-eternal-springland-investments/

Doh, J., Rodriguez, P., Uhlenbruck, K., Collins, J., & Eden, L. (2003). Coping with corruption in foreign markets. *The Academy of Management Executive, 17*(3), 114–127. doi:10.5465/AME.2003.10954775

Dolan, C., & Scott, L. (2009). Lipstick evangelism: Avon trading circles and gender empowerment in South Africa. *Gender and Development, 17*(2), 203–218. doi:10.1080/13552070903032504

Douglas, E., & Shepard, D. (2002). Self-employment as a career choice: Attitudes, entrepreneurial intentions, and utility maximization. *Entrepreneurship Theory and Practice, 26*, 81–90.

Douma, S., George, R., & Kabir, R. (2006). Foreign and domestic ownership, business groups, and firm performance: Evidence from a large emerging marke. *Strategic Management Journal, 27*(7), 637–657. doi:10.1002/smj.535

Doz, Y., Santos, J., & Williamson, P. (2001). *From global to metanational: How companies win in the knowledge economy*. Boston, MA: Harvard Business Press.

Dunning, J. (1988). *Explaining international production*. London: Unwin Hyman.

Dunning, J. (1998). Location and the multinational enterprise: a neglected factor. *Journal of* Dunning, J., 2000. The Eclectic (OLI) Paradigm of International Production: Past, Present and Future. *International Journal of the Economics of Business, 8*(2), 173–190. doi:10.1080/13571510110051441

Duval-Couetil, N. (2013). Assessing the Impact of Entrepreneurship Education Programs: Challenges and Approaches. *Journal of Small Business Management, 51*(3), 394–409. doi:10.1111/jsbm.12024

Dweyer, F. R., Schurr, P. H., & Oh, S. (1987). Developing Buyer-Seller Relationships. *Journal of Marketing, 51*(2), 11–27. doi:10.2307/1251126

Easterly, W., & Kraay, A. (2000). Small States, Small Problems? Income, Growth, and Volatility in Small States. *World Development, Elsevier, 28*(11), 2013–2027. doi:10.1016/S0305-750X(00)00068-1

Compilation of References

Easton, D. (1975). A Re-Assessment of the Concept of Political Support. *British Journal of Political Science*, 5(04), 435–457. doi:10.1017/S0007123400008309

Easton, G., Wilkinson, I., & Georgieva, C. (1997). Towards evolutionary models of industrial networks – a research programme. In H. Gemünden, T. Ritter, & A. Walter (Eds.), *Relationships and networks in international markets* (pp. 273–295). Oxford, UK: Pergamon.

EBAN. (n.d.). *EBAN. Recuperado el2014, de EBAN*. Retrieved from http://www.eban.org

ECLAC (Economic Commission for Latin America and Caribbean). (2014). Retrieved from http://www.eclac.org

ECLAC. (2007a). *Economic Commission for Latin America and the Caribbean 2006. Trends 2007 (LC / G.2341-P / E)*. Santiago, Chile: ECLAC.

ECLAC. (2007b). Social Cohesion: Inclusion and a Sense of Belonging in Latin America and the Caribbean (LC / G.2335 / Rev.1). Santiago, Chile: ECLAC.

ECLAC. (2008a). Productive 20 Years Later: Old problems, new opportunities (LC / G.2367 (SES.32 / 3)). Santiago, Chile: ECLAC.

ECLAC. (2008b). *Iberoamerican spaces: the knowledge economy (LC/G.2392)*. Santiago, Chile: ECLAC / General Secretariat (SEGIB).

ECLAC. (2009). Foreign direct investment in Latin America and the Caribbean, 2008 (LC / G.2406-P). Santiago, Chile: ECLAC.

ECLAC. (2010). *Foreign Direct Investment in Latin America and the Caribbean*. [Online] Available at: http://www.eclac.org/publicaciones/xml/0/43290/2011-138-LIEI_2010-WEB_INGLES.pdf

ECLAC. (2010). *The Time for equality: closing gaps, opening trails*. Santiago, Chile: Economic Commission for Latin America and the Caribbean, United Nations.

ECLAC. (2012). *Economic Comission for Latin America and the Caribbean*. [Online] Available at: http://www.eclac.cl/prensa/noticias/comunicados/4/46574/tabla_ied2011_en.pdf

ECLAC. (2013). *Broadband in Latin America: Beyond Connectivity*. Santiago, Chile: Economic Commission for Latin America and the Caribbean, United Nations.

ECLAC. (2013). *Chinese Foreign Direct Investment in Latin America and the Caribbean*. ECLAC.

ECLAC. (2014). *Foreign Direct Investment in Latin America and The Caribbean*. Retrieved from http://www.cepal.org/publicaciones/xml/8/52978/ForeignDirectInvestment2013.pdf

ECLAC. (2014). Global value chains and world trade. In *Prospects and challenges for Latin America*. ECLAC.

Emirbayer, M., & Mische, A. (1998). What is Agency? *American Journal of Sociology*, 103(4), 962–1023. doi:10.1086/231294

Ernst, D. (2002). Global production networks and the changing geography of innovation systems. Implications for developing countries. *Economics of Innovation and New Technology, 11*(6), 497–523. doi:10.1080/10438590214341

European Commision (2004). *Action Plan: The European Agenda for Entrepreneurship, Communication from the Commission to the Council, the European Parliament, the European Economic and Social Committee and the Committee of the Regions, COM (04) 70*. Brussels: EC.

European Social Fund in the Czech Republic. (2013). *Education for Competitiveness OP (ECOP)*. Recuperado el 23 de 10 de 2014, de The Education for Competitiveness Operational Programme (ECOP): http://www.esfcr.eu/07-13-en/ecop

Evans, J. R., & Laskin, R. (1994). The relationship marketing process: A conceptualization and application. *Industrial Marketing Management, 23*(2), 439–452. doi:10.1016/0019-8501(94)90007-8

Evans, P., & Rauch, J. E. (1999). Bureaucracy and Growth: A Cross-National Analysis of the Effects of "Weberian" State Structures on Economic Growth. *American Sociological Review, 64*(5), 748–765. doi:10.2307/2657374

Fajnzylber, F. (1990). *Industrialización en América Latina: de la 'caja negra' al 'casillero vacío': comparación de patrones contemporáneos de industrialización, books of ECLAC, Nº 60 (LC/G.1534/Rev.1-P)*. Santiago de Chile. Publication of the United Nations.

Felipe, J., & Kumar, U. (2011). *Unit Labor Costs in the Eurozone: The Competitiveness Debate Again*. New York: Levy Economics Institute.

Fracica-Naranjo, G., Matíz, F., & Hernández, G. (2011). Capital semilla para la financiación de start ups con alto potencial de crecimiento en Colombia [Seed capital to finance high growth potential start-ups in Colombia]. *Rev. esc.adm.neg., 71*, 126-147.

Freeman, C., & Pérez, C. (1988). Structural crises of adjustment, business cycles and investment behavior. In Technical Change and Economic Theory. Pinter Publisher.

Freytag, A., & Thurik, R. (2007). Entrepreneurship and its determinants in a cross-country setting. *Journal of Evolutionary Economics, 17*(2), 117–131. doi:10.1007/s00191-006-0044-2

Friman, M., Garling, T., Millet, B., Mattson, J., & Johnston, R. (2002). An Analysis of International Business- to Business Relationship Based on the Commitment-Trust Theory. *Industrial Marketing Management, 31*(5), 403–409. doi:10.1016/S0019-8501(01)00154-7

Frith, J. R. (1998). The market orientation performance relationship in minority and woman-owned small firms. *Academy of Marketing Studies Journal, 2*(1), 35–56.

Fritsch, M. (2008). How does new business formation affect regional development? Introduction to the special issue. *Small Business Economics, 30*(1), 1–14. doi:10.1007/s11187-007-9057-y

Fritsch, M., & Mueller, P. (2008). The effect of new business formation on regional development over time: The case of Germany. *Small Business Economics, 30*(1), 15–29. doi:10.1007/s11187-007-9067-9

Compilation of References

Gadde, L.-E., & Snehota, I. (2000). Making the Most of Supplier Relationships. *Industrial Marketing Management*, *29*(4), 305–316. doi:10.1016/S0019-8501(00)00109-7

Gajdzik, B., & Grzybowska, K. (2012). Example Models of Building Trust in Supply Chains of Metallurgical Enterprises. *Metalurgija*, *51*(4), 563–566.

Gambetta, D. (1988). Can we trust 'Trust'?. In D. Gambetta (Ed.), Trust, Making and Breaking Cooperative Relations, (pp. 213-237). Basil Blackwell.

Ganesan, S. (1994). Determinants of Long-Term Orientation in Buyer-Seller Relationships. *Journal of Marketing*, *58*(2), 1–19. doi:10.2307/1252265

Gankema, H., Snuif, H., & Zwart, P. (2000). The internationalization process of small and medium sized enterprises: An evaluation of stage theory. *Journal of Small Business Management*, *38*(4), 15–27.

Geels, F. W. (2004). Sectoral systems of innovation to socio-technical systems: Insights about dynamics and change from sociology and institutional theory. *Research Policy*, *33*(6-7), 897–920. doi:10.1016/j.respol.2004.01.015

GEM-Colombia. (2006). GEM Colombia 2006. Reporte de Resultados [GEM Colombia 2006. Results Report]. Universidad Icesi, Universidad del Norte, Universidad de los Andes, Pontificia Universidad Javeriana Cali. Colombia: GEM.

GEM-Colombia. (2011). Reporte GEM Colombia 2011 [GEM Colombia 2011 Report]. Universidad del Norte, Universidad Icesi, Universidad de los Andes, Pontificia Universidad Javeriana Cali. Colombia: Editorial Universidad del Norte.

GEM-Colombia. (2013). Global Entrepreneurship Monitor Colombia 2012. Universidad de los Andes, Universidad Icesi, Universidad del Norte, Pontificia Universidad Javeriana Cali. Colombia: Ediciones Uniandes.

GEM-Colombia. (2014). Dinámica Empresarial Colombiana [Colombian Business Dynamics]. Universidad Icesi, Universidad del Norte, Universidad de los Andes, Pontificia Universidad Javeriana Cali. Colombia: GEM-Colombia.

Ghauri, P. N., & Buckley, P. J. (2006). Globalization, multinational enterprises and world poverty. In S. C. Jain & S. Vachani (Eds.), *Multinational corporations and global poverty reduction* (pp. 204–232). Cheltenham, UK: Edward Elgar Publishing.

Gibson, S. (2007). Microfranchising: The Next Step on the Development Ladder. In J. Fairbourne, S. Gibson, & G. Dyer (Eds.), *Microfranching: Creating Wealth at the Bottom of the Pyramid* (pp. 235–239). Northampton, MA: Edward Elgar Publishing. doi:10.4337/9781847205360.00012

Gilbert, B., McDougall, P., & Audretsch, D. (2006). New Venture Growth: A Review and Extension. *Journal of Management*, *32*(6), 926–950. doi:10.1177/0149206306293860

Gitonga-Imaita, I. (2013). Financial resources as a factor influencing adoption of innovations along mango value chains in Meru County, Kenya. *European Scientific Journal*, (1), 49-56.

Godinez, J., & Liu, L. (2014). Corruption distance and FDI flows into Latin America. *International Business Review.*

Gómez-Núñez, L., & Negrete-Escobar, I. (2013). GEM Colombia 2012: Empresas con Alto Potencial de Crecimiento [GEM Colombia 2012: High growth potential businesses]. Universidad del Norte y Fundación Bavaria, Colombia: Ediciones Uninorte.

González-Benito, O., & González-Benito, J. (2005). Cultural vs. operational market orientation and objective vs. subjective performance: Perspective of production and operations. *Industrial Marketing Management, 34*(8), 797–829. doi:10.1016/j.indmarman.2005.01.002

Gray, B. J., Matear, S., Boshoff, C., & Matheson, P. (1998). Developing a better measure of market orientation. *European Journal of Marketing, 32*(9), 884–903. doi:10.1108/03090569810232327

Gray, C., & Kaufman, D. (1998). *Corruption and Development.* Washington, DC: World Bank.

Gregson, G., & Velasco, D. (2011) *Colombia's National System of Innovation: A Multi-theoretical Assessment of Structure, Policy and Performance.* Edinburgh Business School. Available at www.unid-sea.net

Griffith, D. A., Harvey, M. G., & Lisch, R. F. (2006). Social Exchange in Supply Chain Relationships: The Resulting Benefit of Procedural and Distributive Justice. *Journal of Operations Management, 24*(2), 85–98. doi:10.1016/j.jom.2005.03.003

Grilo, I., & Thurik, R. (2008). Determinants of entrepreneurial engagement levels in Europe and the US. *Industrial and Corporate Change, 17*(6), 1113–1145. doi:10.1093/icc/dtn044

Grosse, R. (1989). *Multinational in Latin America.* London: Routledge.

GSMA. (2010). *Mapping and Effectively Structuring Operator-Bank Relationships to Offer Mobile Money for the Unbanked.* [online] Available at: http://www.gsma.com/mobilefordevelopment/wp- content/uploads/2012/03/mappingandeffectivestructuringfinal2643.pdf

GSMA. (2013). *State of the Industry 2013: Mobile Financial Services for the Unbanked.* [online] Available at: http://www.gsma.com/mobilefordevelopment/wp- content/uploads/2014/02/SOTIR_2013.pdf

GSMA. (2014). *Financial Inclusion in Paraguay: New Mobile Money Regulation.* [online] Available at: http://www.gsma.com/latinamerica/financial-inclusion-in-paraguay-new-mobile-money-regulation

Guatemala: empresarios crean Consejo Privado de Competitividad. (2012, June 13). Retrieved from http://www.estrategiaynegocios.net/csp/mediapool/sites/EN/CentroAmericayMundo/CentroAmerica/Guatemala/GTSociedad/story.csp?cid=472134&sid=1422&fid=330

Gullett, J., Do, L., Canuto-Caranco, M., Brister, M., Turnet, S., & Caldwell, C. (2009). The Buyer-Supplier Relationship: An Integrative Model of Ethics and Trust. *Journal of Business Ethics, 90*(S3), 329–341. doi:10.1007/s10551-010-0430-4

Compilation of References

Habib, M., & Zurawicki, L. (2002). Corruption and Foreign Direct Investment. *Journal of International Business Review, 33*(2), 291–307. doi:10.1057/palgrave.jibs.8491017

Håkansson, H. (1982). *International Marketing and Purchasing of Industrial Goods: An Interaction Approach.* Chichester, UK: Wiley.

Håkansson, H. (1987). *Industrial technological development. A network approach.* London: Croom Helm.

Håkansson, H., & Ford, D. (2002). How should companies interact in business networks? *Journal of Business Research, 55*(2), 133–139. doi:10.1016/S0148-2963(00)00148-X

Håkansson, H., & Johanson, J. (1984). Heterogeneity in industrial markets and its implications for marketing. In I. Hägg & F. Wiedersheim-Paul (Eds.), *Between market and hierarchy.* Uppsala: Department of Business Studies.

Håkansson, H., & Snehota, I. (2006). "No business is an island" 17 years later. *Scandinavian Journal of Management, 22*(3), 271–274. doi:10.1016/j.scaman.2006.08.001

Håkansson, H., & Snehota, J. (1995). *Developing Relationships in Business Networks.* London: Routledge.

Hammond, A. L., Kramer, W. J., Katz, R. S., Tran, J. T., & Walker, C. (2007). The next 4 billion: Market size and business strategy and the Base of the Pyramid. World resources institute and international finance corporation/World bank. *Group.*

Handel, M. (1981). *Weak States in the International System.* London: Frank Cass Publishers.

Hardin, R. (1989). Rationally Justifying Political Coercion. *Journal of Philosophical Research, 15*, 1989–1990.

Hardin, R. (1993). The Street-Level Epistemology of Trust. *Politics & Society, 21*(4), 505–529. doi:10.1177/0032329293021004006

Hart, S. L. (2005). *Capitalism at the Crossroads. The Unlimited Business Opportunities in Solving the World's Most Difficult Problems.* Upper Saddle River, NJ: Wharton School Publishing.

Hausman, A., & Johnston, W. J. (2010). The Impact of Coercive and Non-Coercive Forms of Influence on Trust, Commitment, and Compliance in Supply Chains. *Industrial Marketing Management, 39*(3), 519–526. doi:10.1016/j.indmarman.2009.05.007

Heffernan, T., O'Neill, G., Travaglione, T., & Droulers, M. (2008). Relationship Marketing: The Impact of Emotional Intelligence and Trust on Bank Performance. *International Journal of Bank Marketing, 26*(3), 183–199. doi:10.1108/02652320810864652

Heins, R. A. (2000). Market orientation: Toward an integrated framework. *Academy of Marketing Science Review, 1.* Available http://www.amsreview.org/articles/heiens01-2000.pdf

Helfert, G., Ritter, T., & Walter, A. (2002). Redefining market orientation from a relationship perspective. Theoretical considerations and empirical results. *European Journal of Marketing*, *36*(9/10), 1119–1139. doi:10.1108/03090560210437361

Helms, B. (2006). *Access for all: Building inclusive financial systems*. Washington, DC: World Bank. doi:10.1596/978-0-8213-6360-7

Hennart, J. (1982). *A theory of multinational enterprise*. Ann Arbor, MI: University of Michigan Press.

Hermes, N., Lensink, R., & Meesters, A. (2011). Outreach and efficiency of microfinance institutions. *World Development*, *39*(6), 938–948. doi:10.1016/j.worlddev.2009.10.018

Heterington, M. J. (1998). The Political Relevance of Political Trust. *The American Political Science Review*, *92*(4), 791–808. doi:10.2307/2586304

Hobday, M. (1994). Technological learning in Singapore: A test case of leapfrogging. *The Journal of Development Studies*, *30*(4), 831–858. doi:10.1080/00220389408422340

Hobday, M., Rush, H., & Bessant, J. (2004). Approaching the innovation frontier in Korea: The transition phase to leadership. *Research Policy*, *33*(10), 1433–1457. doi:10.1016/j.respol.2004.05.005

Hoegen, M. (1999). *La Economía Social de Mercado: Una opción para Guatemala?* Guatemala: IDIES.

Hofstede. (2014). Retrieved from http://geert-hofstede.com/organisational-culture-dimensions.html

Hofstede, G. (1980). *Culture's Consequences: International Differences in Work-Related Values*. Newbury Park, CA: Sage Publications.

Holmlund, M., & Kock, S. (1996). Buyer dominated relationships in a supply chain: A case study of four small-sized suppliers. *International Small Business Journal*, *15*(1), 26–40. doi:10.1177/0266242696151002

Holmlund, M., & Kock, S. (1998). Relationships and the internationalisation of Finnish small and medium-sized companies. *International Small Business Journal*, *16*(4), 46–63. doi:10.1177/0266242698164003

Hölzl, W. (2009). Is the R&D behavior of fast-growing SMEs different? Evidence from CIS III data for 16 countries. *Small Business Economics*, *33*(1), 59–75. doi:10.1007/s11187-009-9182-x

Hoskisson, R., Eden, L., Lau, C., & Wright, M. (2000). Strategy in Emerging Economies. *Academy of Management Journal*, *43*(3), 249–267. doi:10.2307/1556394

Hosseini, H. (1994). Foreign Direct Investment, Decision, Transaction-cost Economics and Political Uncertainty. *Humanomics*, *10*(1), 61–82. doi:10.1108/eb018745

Ho, Y., & Wong, P. (2007). Financing, Regulatory Costs and Entrepreneurial Propensity. *Small Business Economics*, *28*(2-3), 187–204. doi:10.1007/s11187-006-9015-0

Compilation of References

Hung, S. W., Cheng, M. J., & Chen, P. C. (2012). Reexamining the Factors for Trust in Cultivating Online Customer Repurchase Intentions: The Moderating Effect of Perceived Waiting. *International Journal of Human-Computer Interaction*, 28(10), 666–677. doi:10.1080/104473 18.2011.654201

Hurtado, O. (2010). Latin America in the Mirror of Culture. *The American Interest*, (Jan/Feb), 92-102.

Hymer, S. H. (1976). *The international operations of national firms: A study of direct investment*. MIT Press.

Ibeh, K. I., & Young, S. (2001). Exporting as an entrepreneurial act: An empirical study of Nigerian firms. *European Journal of Marketing*, 35(5/6), 566–586. doi:10.1108/03090560110388114

IDB. (2013). *Global Microscope: Continued Growth and Innovation in Financial Markets for Low-income Populations*. Available online at: http://www.iadb.org

Iniciativas 4644 a la 4648 - Presentadas por el Ejecutivo (enero 2013). (2013, January 21). Retrieved from http://www.congresovisible.com/index.php?option=com_ k2&view=item&id=53:iniciativas-4644-a-la-4648-presentadas-por-el-ejecutivo-enero-2013

Inter-American Development Bank. (2010). *Labor Costs and Competitiveness*. Washington.

Isenberg, D. (2011). The entrepreneurship ecosystem strategy as a new paradigm for economy policy: principles for cultivating entrepreneurship. Babson Entrepreneurship Ecosystem Project, Babson College.

Isenberg, D. (2010). The Big Idea: How to start an Entrepreneurial Revolution. *Harvard Business Review*, 88(6), 41–50.

Ivatury, G., & Mas, I. (2008). *The Early Experience with Branchless Banking. Focus Note 46*. Washington, DC: CGAP.

Jagad, S. (2010). Balancing Trust and Control in Organizations: Towards a Process Perspective. *Society and Business Review*, 5(3), 259-269.

Jain, A. (2001). Journal of Economic Surveys. *Corruption. RE:view*, 15, 71–121.

Jain, S. C., & Vachani, S. (2006). The role of MNCs in alleviating global poverty. In S. C. Jain & S. Vachani (Eds.), *Multinational corporations and global poverty reduction* (pp. 3–28). Cheltenham, UK: Edward Elgar Publishing.

Jambulingam, T., Kathuria, R., & Nevin, J. R. (2011). Fairness-Trust-Loyalty Relationship Under Varying Conditions of Supplier-Buyer Interdependence. *Journal of Marketing Theory and Practice*, 19(1), 39–56. doi:10.2753/MTP1069-6679190103

Jamison, G. D. (2011). Interpersonal Trust in Latin America: Analyzing Variations in Trust Using Data from the Lationbarometro. *Journal of Multidisciplinary Research*, 3(3), 65–80.

Jap, S., & Ganesan, S. (2000). Control Mechanisms and Relationship Life Cycle: Implications for Safeguarding Specific Investments and Developing Commitment. *JMR, Journal of Marketing Research, 37*(May), 227–245. doi:10.1509/jmkr.37.2.227.18735

Jaworski, B., & Kohli, A. (1993). Market orientation: Antecedents and consequences. *Journal of Marketing, 57*(3), 53–70. doi:10.2307/1251854

Johanson, J., & Mattsson, L.-G. (1987). Interorganizational relations in industrial systems: A network approach compared with the transaction-cost approach. *International Studies of Management & Organization, 17*(1), 64–74.

Johanson, J., & Mattsson, L.-G. (1988). Internationalisation in industrial system: a network approach. In N. Hood & J.-E. Vahlne (Eds.), *Strategies in global competition*. London: Croom Helm.

Johanson, J., & Vahlne, J.-E. (1977). The internationalization process of the firm – a model of knowledge development and increasing foreign market commitments. *Journal of International Business Studies, 8*(1), 23–32. doi:10.1057/palgrave.jibs.8490676

Johanson, J., & Vahlne, J.-E. (1990). The mechanism of internationalization. *International Marketing Review, 7*(4), 11–24. doi:10.1108/02651339010137414

Johanson, J., & Vahlne, J.-E. (1992). Management of foreign market entry. *Scandinavian International Business Review, 1*(3), 9–27. doi:10.1016/0962-9262(92)90008-T

Johanson, J., & Wiedersheim-Paul, F. (1975). The internationalization of the firm: Four Swedish cases. *Journal of Management Studies, 12*(3), 305–322. doi:10.1111/j.1467-6486.1975.tb00514.x

Jones, K. (1996). Trust as an affective attitude. *Ethics, 107*(1), 4–25. doi:10.1086/233694

Jones, S., Wilikens, M., Morris, P., & Masera, M. (2000). Trust Requirements in e-Business. *Communications of the ACM, 43*(12), 80–87. doi:10.1145/355112.355128

Jun Bae, T., Qian, S., Miao, C., & Fiet, J.O. (2014). The Relationship between Entrepreneurship Education and Entrepreneurial Intentions: A Meta-Analytic Review. *Entrepreneurship Theory and Practice,* (March), 217-254.

Kalvet, T. (2012). Innovation: a factor explaining e-government success in Estonia. Electronic Government, 9(2), 142 - 157.

Kang, Y., & Jiang, F. (2010). FDI location choice of Chinese multinationals in East and Southeast Asia: Traditional economic factors and institutional perspective. *Journal of World Business, 47*(1), 45–53. doi:10.1016/j.jwb.2010.10.019

Kapsoli, J., Galindo, A., Márquez, G., Daude, C., Melo, A., Miller, M., ... Pérez, N. (2001). *Competitiveness: The Business of Growth*. Academic Press.

Karlsson, C., Friis, C., & Paulsson, T. (2004). *Relating entrepreneurship to economic growth*. Retrieved from http://www.infra.kth.se/cesis/documents/WP13.pdf

Compilation of References

Karnani, A. (2007). The mirage of marketing to the Bottom of the Pyramid: How the private sector can alleviate poverty. *California Management Review, 49*(4), 90–111. doi:10.2307/41166407

Karnani, A. (2009a). Romanticizing the poor. *Business Strategy Review, 19*(2), 48–53. doi:10.1111/j.1467-8616.2008.00535.x

Karnani, A. (2009b). Romanticizing the poor harms the poor. *Journal of International Development, 21*(1), 76–86. doi:10.1002/jid.1491

Kelli, A., Mets, T., Jonsson, L., Pisuke, H., & Adamsoo, R. (2013). The Changing Approach in Academia-Industry Collaboration: From Profit Orientation to Innovation Support. *TRAMES, 17*(3), 215–241.

Khodyakov, D. (2007). Trust as a Process: A Three Dimensional Approach. *Sociology, British Sociological Association, 41*(1), 115–132.

Kindleberger, C. P. (1969). *American business abroad: Six lectures on direct investment.* New Haven, CT: Yale University Press.

Kistruck, G. M., Webb, J. W., Sutter, C., & Duane Ireland, R. (2011). Microfranchising in Base-of-the- Pyramid markets: Institutional challenges and adaptations to the franchise model. *Entrepreneurship Theory and Practice, 35*(3), 503–531. doi:10.1111/j.1540-6520.2011.00446.x

Kiva. (2014). *About Us.* Available online at: www.kiva.org

Klapper, L., Amit, R., & Guillén, M. (2010). Entrepreneurship and Firm Formation across Countries. In International Differences in Entrepreneurship. Chicago: University of Chicago Press. doi:10.7208/chicago/9780226473109.003.0005

Klapper, L., Laeven, L., & Rajan, R. (2004). *Barriers to Entrepreneurship.* Working Paper. World Bank.

Knack, S. (2000). *Social Capital and The Quality of Government: Evidence from the United States.* World Bank Policy Research Working Paper (2504).

Knickerbocker, F. T. (1973). Oligopolistic reaction and multinational enterprise. *The International Executive, 15*(2), 7–9. doi:10.1002/tie.5060150205

Kohli, A., & Jaworski, B. (1990). Market orientation: The construct, research propositions, and managerial implications. *Journal of Marketing, 54*(2), 1–18. doi:10.2307/1251866

Koh, T. K., Fichman, M., & Kraut, R. E. (2012). Trust Across Borders: Buyer-Supplier Trust in Global Business-to-Business E-Commerce. *Journal of the Association for Information Systems, 13*(11), 886–922.

Kolk, A., Rivera-Santos, M., & Rufin, C. R. (2013). Reviewing a Decade of Research on the 'Base/Bottom of the Pyramid' (BOP) Concept. *Business & Society, 20*(10), 1–40.

Kolstad, I., & Wiig, A. (2012). What determines Chinese outward FDI? *Journal of World Business, 47*(1), 26–34. doi:10.1016/j.jwb.2010.10.017

Korzeniowski, P., (2013). The Complex Challenge of Repairing Customer Trust. *Customer Relationship Management*, 26-30.

Kostova, T., & Zaheer, S. (1999). Organisational legitimacy under conditions of complexity: The case of the multinational enterprise. *Academy of Management Review, 24*, 64–81.

Kotschwar, B., Moran, T., & Muir, J. (2012). *Chinese Investment in Latin American Resources: The Good, The Bad and The Ugly*. Peterson Institute for International Economics.

Krot, K., & Lewicka, D. (2012). The Importance of Trust in Manager-Employee Relationships. *International Journal of Electronic Business Management, 10*(3), 224–233.

Krueger, N., & Brazeal, D. (1994). Entrepreneurial potential and potential entrepreneurs. *Entrepreneurship: Theory and Practice, 18*(3), 91–104.

Krugman, P. (1999). The Role of Geography in Development.*Annual World Bank Conference on Development Economics 1998*. Washington, DC: Published by the World Bank.

Kumar, A., Nair, A., Parsons, A., & Urdapilleta, E. (2006). *Expanding Bank Outreach through Retail Partnerships: Correspondent Banking in Brazil*. World Bank Working Paper No. 85. Washington, DC: World Bank.

Kumar, N., Scheer, L. K., & Steenkamp, J. B. E. M. (1995). The Effects of Perceived Interdependence on Dealer Attitudes. *JMR, Journal of Marketing Research, 32*(3), 348–356. doi:10.2307/3151986

Kurer, O. (2005). Corruption: An Alternative Approach to its Definition and Measurement. *Political Studies, 53*(1), 222–239. doi:10.1111/j.1467-9248.2005.00525.x

Kusari, S., Hoeffler, S., & Iacobucci, D. (2014). Trusting and Monitoring Business Partners throughout the Relationship Life Cycle. *Journal of Business-to-Business Marketing*. Retrieved from http://www.tandfonline.com/loi/wbbm20

Kwon, I.-W. G., & Suh, T. (2004). Factors Affecting the Level of Trust and Commitment in Supply Chain Relationships. *Journal of Supply Chain Management, 40*(2), 4–14. doi:10.1111/j.1745-493X.2004.tb00165.x

Kwon, Y.-C. (2008). Antecedents and Consequences of International Joint Venture Partnerships: A Social Exchange Perspective. *International Business Review, 17*(5), 559–573. doi:10.1016/j.ibusrev.2008.07.002

LAB. (2012). *An Overview of Microfinance in Latin America*. Latin American Bureau. Available online at: http://lab.org.uk

Laeequddin, M., Sahay, B. S., Sahay, V., & Waheed, K. A. (2010). Measuring Trust in Supply Chain Partners' Relationships. *Measuring Business Excellence, 14*(3), 53–69. doi:10.1108/13683041011074218

Lagos, M. (2001). Between Stability and Crisis in Latin America. *Journal of Democracy, 12*(1), 137–145. doi:10.1353/jod.2001.0009

Compilation of References

Laguna, C. (2003). Undamentos de la teoría clásica del comercio internacional. Buenos Aires: EUMED.

Lamming, R. (1993). *Beyond partnership: Strategies for innovation and lean supply*. London: Prentice Hall.

Lancastre, A., & Lages, L. F. (2006). The Relationship between Buyer and B2B e-Marketplace: Cooperation Determinants in an Electronic Market Context. *Industrial Marketing Management, 35*(6), 774–789. doi:10.1016/j.indmarman.2005.03.011

Langerak, F. (2001). Effects of market orientation on the behaviors of salespersons and purchasers, channel relationships, and performance of manufacturers. *International Journal of Research in Marketing, 18*(3), 221–234. doi:10.1016/S0167-8116(01)00040-4

LANIC (Latin American Network Information Center). (n.d.). Retrieved from http://lanic.utxas.edu

Lanzan programa de innovación empresarial. (2014, May 13). Retrieved from http://m.s21.com.gt/innovacion/2014/05/13/lanzan-programa-innovacion-empresarial

Latinobarometro Corporation. (2013). *2013 Report*. Retrieved from http://www.latinobarometro.org/latino/LATDatos.jsp

Lee, E., Rhee, Y., & Lee, S. (2013). Beyond Ricardian Model: An Optimal Commodity Distribution Based on Absolute Advantage for Multi-Country Multi-Commodity. *International Journal of Business and Management, 8*(14), 110–114. doi:10.5539/ijbm.v8n14p110

Leigh, A. (2006). Trust, inequality and ethnic heterogeneity. *The Economic Record, 82*(258), 268–280. doi:10.1111/j.1475-4932.2006.00339.x

Leonidou, L., & Katsikeas, C. (1996). The export development process: An integrative review of empirical models. *Journal of International Business Studies, 27*(3), 517–551. doi:10.1057/palgrave.jibs.8490846

Levi, M. (1998). A state of trust. *Trust and Governance*, 77-101.

Liao, S., Chang, W., Wu, C., & Katrichis, J. (2011). A survey of market orientation research (1995-2008). *Industrial Marketing Management, 40*(2), 301–310. doi:10.1016/j.indmarman.2010.09.003

Lindergaard, S. (2011). *Making Open Innovation Work*. North Charleston, SC: CreateSpace.

Lindqvist, M. (1991). *Infant multinationals: The internationalization of young, technology-based Swedish firms*. Stockholm School of Economics, Institute of International Business.

Lings, I., & Greenley, G. (2005). Measuring internal market orientation. *Journal of Service Research, 7*(3), 290–305. doi:10.1177/1094670504271154

London. (2007). *A base of-the-pyramid perspective on poverty Alleviation*. The William Davidson Institute-University of Michigan.

London. (2010). Business Model Development for the base of the pyramid market entry. *Academy of Management Proceedings*, (1), 1-6.

London, T. (2009). Making better investments at the base of the pyramid. *Harvard Business Review*, *87*(5), 106–113.

London, T., & Hart, S. L. (2004). Reinventing strategies for emerging markets: Beyond the transnational model. *Journal of International Business Studies*, *35*(5), 350–370. doi:10.1057/palgrave.jibs.8400099

Lundvall, B.-A., Joseph, K. J., Chaminade, C., & Vang, J. (Eds.). (2009). *Handbook of Innovation Systems and Developing Countries. Learning*. Edward Elgar. doi:10.4337/9781849803427

Luostarinen, R. (1980). *The Internationalization of the firm*. Helsinki: Helsinki School of Economics.

Luo, Y. (2007). Are joint venture partners more opportunistic in a more volatile environment? *Strategic Management Journal*, *28*(1), 39–60. doi:10.1002/smj.564

Luo, Y., Xue, Q., & Han, B. (2010). How emerging market governments promote outward FDI: Experience from China. *Journal of World Business*, *45*(1), 68–79. doi:10.1016/j.jwb.2009.04.003

Lyngdoh, B. (2005). Skills for Work in the Future: A Youth Perspective. *Quarterly Review of Comparative Education*, *35*(3), 311–316.

MacIntosh, G. (2009). Examining the Antecedents of Trust and Rapport in Services: Discovering New Relationships. *Journal of Retailing and Consumer Services*, *16*(4), 298–305. doi:10.1016/j.jretconser.2009.02.001

Madsen, T., & Servais, P. (1997). The internationalization of born globals: An evolutionary process? *International Business Review*, *6*(6), 561–583. doi:10.1016/S0969-5931(97)00032-2

Malecki, E. (1994). Entrepreneurship in regional and local development International. *Regional Science Rewies*, *16*(1-2), 119–153.

Malerba, F. (2002). Sectoral systems of innovation and production. *Research Policy*, *31*(2), 247–264. doi:10.1016/S0048-7333(01)00139-1

Malerba, F., & Mani, S. (2009). Sectoral systems of innovation and production in developing countries: an introduction. In F. Malerba & S. Mani (Eds.), *Sectoral Systems of Innovation and Production in Developing Countries: Actors, Structure and Evolution* (pp. 3–24). Cheltenham, UK: Edward Elgar. doi:10.4337/9781849802185.00006

Malik, K., & Jespersen, E. (2014). *Sustaining Human Progress: Reducing vulnerabilities and building resilience*. Human Development Report 2014. Retrieved from http://hdr.undp.org/en/2014-report/download

Mani, S. (2007). *Innovation Capability in Developing Countries, A study of the Telecommunications Industry*. Cheltenham, UK: Edward Elgar.

Compilation of References

Mankiw, G. (2009). *Healthcare and Competitiveness*. Boston: Harvard.

Markowska, M. (2011). *Entrepreneurial Competence Development: Triggers, Processes & Consequences*. (Doctoral dissertation). Jönköping: Jönköping International Business School.

Martin, R. L. (2007). *A Study on the Factors of Regional Competitiveness*. Cambridge, UK: Academic Press.

Mathews, J. (2006). Dragon multinationals: New players in 21st century globalization. *Asia Pacific Journal of Management, 23*(1), 5–27. doi:10.1007/s10490-006-6113-0

Matsuno, K., Mentzer, J., & Rentz, J. (2005). A conceptual and empirical comparison of three market orientation scales. *Journal of Business Research, 58*(1), 1–8. doi:10.1016/S0148-2963(03)00075-4

Mavondo, F. (1999). Market orientation: Scale invariance and relationship to generic strategies across two countries. *Journal of Market Focused Management, 4*(2), 125–142. doi:10.1023/A:1009835515831

Mayer, R. C., Davis, J. H., & Schoorman, F. D. (1995). An integrative model of organizational trust. *Academy of Management Review, 20*(3), 709–734.

McCann, D. (1995). Small states, open markets, and the organization of business interests. Aldershot, UK: Dartmouth.

McMillan, M. & Rodrik, D. (2011). *Globalization, structural change and productivity growth*. Joint ILO-WTO paper, February.

Mexico, F. (2014). *Los 12 millonarios más importantes de Centroamérica*. Available at from http://www.forbes.com.mx/los-12-millonarios-mas-importantes-de-centroamerica/

Meyer, K. (2001). Institutions, transactions and entry mode choice in Eastern Europe. *Journal of International Business Studies, 32*(2), 357–367. doi:10.1057/palgrave.jibs.8490957

MIF-IDB. (2013). *Fondo Multilateral de Inversiones (FOMIN) - Banco Interamericano de Desarrollo (BID) - Microfinanzas Americas, Las 100 Mejores, 2013*. Available at: http://www10.iadb.org/intal/intalcdi/PE/2013/12790es.pdf

Migliorisi, S., & Prabhu, A. (2011). *Guatemala: World Bank Country-Level Engagement in Governance and Anticorruption*. Washington, DC: World Bank.

Miller, A. H. (1974). Political Issues and Trust in Government: 1964-1970. *The American Political Science Review, 68*(3), 951–972. doi:10.2307/1959140

Miller, L. (2014). A Value-based Approach to Sustainability: The Role of Values and Culture in the Pursuit of Wealth. *Development and Society, 43*(1), 143–161.

Mirriam-Webster. (2014). *Encyclopedia Britannica*. Mirriam-Webster.

329

Mohr, J., & Spekman, R. (1994). Characteristics of partnership success: Partnership attributes, communication behavior and conflict resolution techniques. *Strategic Management Journal, 15*(2), 135–152. doi:10.1002/smj.4250150205

Moorman, C., Deshpande, R., & Zaltman, G. (1992). Relationships between providers and users of marketing research: The dynamics of trust within and between organizations. *JMR, Journal of Marketing Research, 29*(3), 314–329. doi:10.2307/3172742

Moorman, C., Deshpande, R., & Zaltman, R. (1993). Factors Affecting Trust in Market Relationships. *Journal of Marketing, 57*(1), 81–101. doi:10.2307/1252059

Moran, E. K. & Gossieaux, F. (2013). How Employee Trust Affects the Bottom Line. *Communication World*, 18-21.

Moreira, A. C., & Carvalho, A. C. (2012). Internationalization approaches of the automotive innovation system. A historical perspective. In Technological change. Rijeka, Croacia: InTech.

Moreira, A. (2004). Breve ensaio sobre a internacionalização. *Politécnica, 15*, 23–33.

Moreira, A. (2009b). Knowledge capability flows in buyer-supplier relationships: Challenges for small domestic suppliers in international contexts. *Journal of Small Business and Enterprise Development, 16*(1), 93–114. doi:10.1108/14626000910932908

Moreira, A. C. (2005a). A integração do desenvolvimento de novos produtos na cadeia de valor. Na senda de uma abordagem colaborativa. *Revista Portuguesa e Brasileira de Gestão, 4*(1), 56–66.

Moreira, A. C. (2005b). Supplier-buyer collaboration in new product development: Four case studies involving SMEs. *Brazilian Journal of Operations & Production Management, 2*(1), 5–24.

Moreira, A. C. (2007). La internacionalización de Pymes industriales a través de multinacionales. presentación de algunos casos de los sectores automotor y electrónico. *Cuadernos de Administración, 20*(34), 89–114.

Moreira, A. C. (2009a). The evolution of internationalisation: Towards a new theory? *Global Economics and Management Review, 14*(1), 41–59.

Moreira, A. C., & Silva, P. M. (2013). Market orientation, innovation and organizational commitment in industrial firms. *Market, 25*(2), 123–142.

Morgan, R. M., & Hunt, S. D. (1994). The Commitment-Trust Theory of Relationship Marketing. *Journal of Marketing, 58*(3), 20–38. doi:10.2307/1252308

Mudambi, R., & Navarra, P. (2002). Institutions and internation business: A theoretical overview. *International Business Review, 11*(6), 635–646. doi:10.1016/S0969-5931(02)00042-2

Murphy, K., Shleifer, A., & Vishny, R. (1993). Why is Rent-Seeking so Costly to Growth? *The American Economic Review*, 409–414.

Myint, U. (2000). Corruption: Causes, consequences and cures. *Asia-Pacific Development Journal, 7*(2), 1020–1046.

Compilation of References

Narasimhan, R., Nair, A., Griffith, D. A., Arlbjorn, J. S., & Bendoly, E. (2009). Lock-in Situations in Supply Chains: A Social Exchange Theoretical Study Sourcing Arrangements in Buyer-Supplier Relationships. *Journal of Operations Management, 27*(5), 374–389. doi:10.1016/j.jom.2008.10.004

Narver, J., & Slater, S. (1990). The Effect of a Market Orientation on Business Profitability. *Journal of Marketing, 54*(4), 20–35. doi:10.2307/1251757

Naudé, W., Gries, T., Wood, E., & Meintjies, A. (2008). Regional determinants of entrepreneurial start-ups in a developing country. *Entrepreneurship & Regional Development: An International Journal, 20*(2), 111–124. doi:10.1080/08985620701631498

Navajas, S., & Tejerina, L. (2006). *Microfinance in Latin America and the Caribbean: How Large Is the Market?* Washington, DC: Inter-American Development Bank. Sustainable Development Department Best Practices Series.

Neace, M. B. (2004). The Impact of Low Trust on Economic Development: The Case of Latin America. *Review of Policy Research, 21*(5), 699-713.

Neergaard, H. (1998). *Networks as vehicles of internationalization: Network relationships and the internationalization process of small furniture manufacturers.* (Unpublished Doctoral Thesis). Aarhus School Business.

Nghia, N. C. (2010). Management research about solutions for the eradication of global poverty: A literature review. *Journal of Sustainable Development, 3*(1), 17–28. doi:10.5539/jsd.v3n1p17

Niazi, M., Ikram, N., Bano, M., Imtiaz, S., & Khan, S. U. (2013). Establishing Trust in Offshore Software Outsourcing Relationships: An Exploratory Study Using a Systematic Literature Review. *IET Software, 7*(5), 283–293. doi:10.1049/iet-sen.2012.0136

Nishiguchi, T. (1994). *Strategic industrial sourcing. The Japanese advantage.* Oxford, UK: Oxford University Press.

Nordqvist, M., Marzano, G., Brenes, E., Jimenez, G., & Fonseca-Paredes, M. (2011). *Understanding entrepreneurial family businesses in uncertain environment: Opportunities and resources in Latin America* (pp. 1–29). Cheltenham, UK: Elgar Publishing in Association with the Global STEP Project. doi:10.4337/9781849804738

Norris, P. (1999). *Critical citizens global support for democratic government.* Oxford, UK: Oxford University Press. doi:10.1093/0198295685.001.0001

North, D. (1990). *Institutions, institutional change and economic performance.* Cambridge, UK: Cambridge University Press. doi:10.1017/CBO9780511808678

Nye, J. S., Zelikow, P. D., & King, D. C. (1997). *Why People Don't Trust Government.* Cambridge, MA: Harvard University Press.

O'Brien, J., & Beamish, P. W. (2006). Linking poverty and Foreign Direct Investment in developing countries. In S. C. Jain & S. Vachani (Eds.), *Multinational corporations and global poverty reduction* (pp. 105–122). Cheltenham, UK: Edward Elgar Publishing.

O'Connor, A. (2013). A conceptual framework for entrepreneurship education policy: Meeting government and economic purposes. *Journal of Business Venturing, 28*(4), 546–563. doi:10.1016/j.jbusvent.2012.07.003

OECD & LEED. (2014). *Entrepreneurial Ecosystems and Growth Oriented Entrepreneurship.* The Hague, Netherlands.

OECD. (2003). *Entrepreneurship and local economic development: Programme and policy recommendations.* Paris: OECD.

OECD. (2005). *Building Competitive Regions. Strategies and Governance.* Paris: Organisation for Economic Cooperation and Development.

OECD. (2009). *OECD Rural Policy Reviews: Spain.* Paris: OECD.

OECD. (2014). *Secretary General's Report to Ministers.* Paris: Organization for Economic Cooperation and Development.

Olsen, J. (2009). Change and continuity: An institutional approach to institutions of democratic government. *European Political Science Review, 1*(1), 3–32. doi:10.1017/S1755773909000022

Olson, M. (1965). *The logic of collective action.* Harvard University Press Cambridge.

Ondrus, J., & Lyytinen, K. (2011). Mobile payments market: Towards another clash of the Titans? *10th International Conference on Mobile Business*, (pp. 166-172). Academic Press.

Organisation for Economic Co-operation and Development (OECD). (1998). *Fostering Entrepreneurship.* OECD.

Organization for Economic Co-operation and Development. (2013). *Government at a Glance 2013.* Organization for Economic Co-operation and Development Publishing. doi: <ALIGNMENT.qj></ALIGNMENT>10.1787/gov_glance-2013-en

OSEAS. (2014). *Educational system of Ukraine.* Tallin, Ukraine: OSEAS.

Overseas Development Institute. (2013). *Taxation in Developing Countries.* Overseas Development Institute.

Pack, H., & Saggi, K. (2006). *The case for industrial policy: a critical survey.* Washington, DC: World Bank Research Observer. doi:10.1596/1813-9450-3839

Pande, R., & Udry, C. (2005). *Institutions and development: A view from below.* (No. 928). Center discussion paper//Economic Growth Center.

Panigyrakis, G., & Theodoridis, P. (2007). Market orientation and performance: An empirical investigation in the retail industry in Greece. *Journal of Retailing and Consumer Services, 14*(2), 137–149. doi:10.1016/j.jretconser.2006.05.003

Pantelić, A. (2013). The implications of a growing microfinance market in Latin America and the Caribbean. In R. Manos, J.-P. Gueyie, & J. Yaron (Eds.), *Promoting microfinance: Challenges and innovations in developing countries and countries in transition*. Palgrave Macmillan. doi:10.1057/9781137034915.0006

Patel, S. (2006). Transfer of Technology to Developing Countries. *Mainstream Weekly., 45*(1), 1–6.

Paukert, M., Niederée, C., & Hemmje, M. (2004). *Adapting Organizational Knowledge Management Cultures to the Knowledge Life Cycle in Innovation Processes. Working-paper, Fraunhofer Institut für Integrierte Publikations- und Informationssysteme*. Darmstadt, Germany: IPSI.

Payne, A. F. (1988). Developing a marketing-oriented organization. *Business Horizons, 31*(May-June), 46–53. doi:10.1016/0007-6813(88)90008-0

Peacock, S., & Beltrán, A. (2003). *Hidden Powers in Post Conflict Guatemala – Illegal Armed Groups and the Forces Behind Them*. Washington, DC: Washington Office on Latin America.

Peng, M. (2010). The global strategy of emerging multinationals from China. *Global Strategy Journal, 2*(2), 97–107. doi:10.1002/gsj.1030

Peng, M., Wang, D., & Jiang, Y. (2008). An institution-based view of international business strategy: A focus on emerging economies. *Journal of International Business Studies, 39*(5), 920–936. doi:10.1057/palgrave.jibs.8400377

Perez, C. (2004). Technological revolutions, paradigm shifts and socio-institutional change. In E. Reinert (Ed.), *Globalization, Economic Development and Inequality: An alternative Perspective* (pp. 217–242). Cheltenham, UK: Edward Elgar. doi:10.4337/9781845421625.00016

Pérez, O. J. (2004). Democratic Legitimacy and Public Insecurity: Crime and Democracy in El Salvador and Guatemala. *Political Science Quarterly, 118*(4), 627–644. doi:10.1002/j.1538-165X.2003.tb00408.x

Phelps, S. F., & Campbell, N. (2012). Commitment and Trust in Librarian-Faculty Relationships: A Systematic Review of the Literature. *Journal of Academic Librarianship, 38*(1), 13–19. doi:10.1016/j.acalib.2011.11.003

Polanyi, K. (1992). The Economy as Instituted Process. In The Sociology of Economic Life. Boulder, CO: Westview Press.

Porter, M. (2012). *Regional competitiveness*. Obtenido de Harvard Business School: http://www.isc.hbs.edu/pdf/2012-0427---Michael_Porter_Puebla.pdf

Porter, M. (1980). *Competitive Strategy*. Free Press.

Porter, M. (1989). *The competitive advantage of nations*. New York: The Free Press.

Porter, M. (2005). *What is Competitiveness?* Spain: IESE Business School.

Pournarakis, M., & Varsakelis, N. (2004). Institutions, internationalization and FDI: The case of economies in transition. *Transnational Corporations, 13*, 77–94.

Powell, W. (2007). The new institutionalism. The International Encyclopedia of Organization Studies. Sage Publishers. Available at http://www.stanford.edu/group/song/papers/NewInstitutionalism.pdf

Power, T. J., & Jamison, J. D. (2005). Political Mistrust in Latin America. *Comparative Sociology*, *4*(1-2), 47–72.

Prahalad, C. K., & Hart, S. L. (2002). The fortune at the Bottom of the Pyramid. *Strategy and Business*, (26), 1-13.

Prahalad, C. K. (2005). *The fortune at the Bottom of the Pyramid: Eradicating Poverty Through Profits*. Upper Saddle River, NJ: Wharton School Publishing.

Prahalad, C. K. (2010). *The fortune at the Bottom of the Pyramid: Eradicating poverty through profits (5th Anniversary Edition)*. Upper Saddle River, NJ: Wharton School Publishing.

Prahalad, C. K., & Hammond, A. (2002). Serving the World's Poor, profitably. *Harvard Business Review*, (September), 4–11. PMID:12227146

Putnam, R. D. (1994). Social Capital and Public Affairs. *Bulletin - American Academy of Arts and Sciences. American Academy of Arts and Sciences*, *47*(8), 5–19. doi:10.2307/3824796

Ramasamy, B., Yeung, M., & Laforet, S. (2012). China's outward foreign direct investment: Location choice and firm ownership. *Journal of World Business*, *47*(1), 17–25. doi:10.1016/j.jwb.2010.10.016

Ransi, G. S., & Kobti, Z. (2014). A Hybrid Artificial Reputation Model Involving Interaction Trust, Witness Information and the Trust Model to Calculate the Trust Value of Service Providers. *Axioms*, *3*(1), 50–63. doi:10.3390/axioms3010050

Rantasila, K., & Ojala, L. (2012). *Measurement of national-level logistics costs and performance*. International Transport Forum Discussion Papers, No. 2012/04. OECD Publishing. doi:10.1787/5k8zvv79pzkk-en

Rapha, D. (2012). *Tenth meeting on migration and remittances*. Retrieved from World Bank: http://www.worldbank.org/en/news/press-release/2014/04/11/remittances-developing-countries-deportations-migrant-workers-wb

Reed, L. R. (2011). *State of the Microcredit Summit Campaign Report*. Washington, DC: Microcredit Summit Campaign. Available online at: http://www.microcreditsummit.org/uploads/resource/document/socr-2011-english_41396.pdf

Reinert, E. (2007). *How Rich Countries Got Rich... and Why Poor Countries Stay Poor*. London: Constable & Robinson Ltd.

Reyes, C. L. (2010, December). El deber del estado en el Ordoliberalismo de Walter Eucken. *Revista Chilena de Economía y Sociedad*, *4*(1), 15–27.

Compilation of References

Reynolds, P. D., Storey, D. J., & Westhead, P. (1994). Cross-national comparisons of the variation in new firm formation rates. *Regional Studies*, *28*(4), 443–456. doi:10.1080/0034340941 2331348386

Reynolds, P., Bosma, N., Auio, E., Hunt, S., de Bono, N., Servais, I., & Chin, N. et al. (2005). Global Entrepreneurship Monitor: Data Collection Design and Implementation 1998–2003. *Small Business Economics*, *24*(3), 205–231. doi:10.1007/s11187-005-1980-1

Ribeiro-Soriano, D., & Galindo-Martín, M. A. (2012). Government policies to support entrepreneurship. *Entrepreneurship & Regional Development*, *24*(9–10), 861–864. doi:10.1080/089 85626.2012.742322

Rice, T., & Sumberg, A. (1997). Civic Culture and Government Performance in the American States. *The Journal of Federalism*, *27*(1), 99–114. doi:10.1093/oxfordjournals.pubjof.a029899

Rivera-Batiz, F. (2000). *Foreign Direct Investment in Latin America: Current Trends and Future Prospects*. New York: Columbia University Press.

Roberts, P., & Greenwood, R. (1997). Integrating Transaction Cost and Institutional Theories: Toward a Constrained-Efficiency Framework for Understanding Organizational Design Adoption. *Academy of Management Review*, 346–373.

Rodrigue, J.-P. (2012). *The benefits of logistics investments: Opportunities for Latin America and the Caribbean*. Technical Notes IDB-TN-395, Department of Infrastructure and Environment.

Rodriguez, P., Uhlenbruck, K., & Eden, L. (2005). Government Corruption and the Entry Strategies of Multinationals. *Academy of Management Review*, *30*(2), 383–396. doi:10.5465/ AMR.2005.16387894

Rodrik, D. (1996). Understanding Economic Policy Reform. *Journal of Economic Literature*, *34*, 9–41.

Rondinelli, D. A. (2003). Partnering for development: Government-private sector cooperation in service provision. In *Reinventing government for the twenty-first century: State capacity in a globalizing society*, (pp. 219-39). Academic Press.

Rondinelli, D. A., & Iacono, M. (1996). *Policies and institutions for managing privatization: International experience*. International Training Centre of the ILO.

Roodman, D. M. (2012). *Due diligence: An impertinent inquiry into microfinance*. Washington, DC: Center for Global Development.

Rose-Ackerman, S., (2008). Corruption and Government. *Journal of International Peacekeeping*, 328-343.

Rose-Ackerman, S. (2008). *Corruption and Post-Conflict Peace-Building*. New Haven, CT: Yale Law School Legal Scholarship Repository.

Rugman, A. (2010). Reconciling internatinalization theory and the eclectic paradigm. *Multinational Business Review, 18*(2), 1–12. doi:10.1108/1525383X201000007

Rugman, A., & Verbeke, A. (1992). A Note on the Transnational Solution and the Transaction Cost Theory of Multinational Management. *Journal of International Business Studies, 23*(4), 761–771. doi:10.1057/palgrave.jibs.8490287

Ruzzier, M., Hisrich, R., & Antoncic, B. (2006). SME internationalization research: Past, present, and future. *Journal of Small Business and Enterprise Development, 13*(4), 476–497. doi:10.1108/14626000610705705

Sanchez-Barrios, L. J., Giraldo-Oliveros, M., Khalik, M. A., & Manjarres, R. (in press). Services for the underserved: Unintended well-being. *Service Industries Journal*.

Sánchez, J. (2013). The Impact of an Entrepreneurship Education Program on Entrepreneurial Competencies and Intention. *Journal of Small Business Management, 51*(3), 447–465. doi:10.1111/jsbm.12025

Santarelli, E., & Vivarelli, M. (2007). Entrepreneurship and the process of firms' entry, survival and growth. *Industrial and Corporate Change, 16*(3), 455–488. doi:10.1093/icc/dtm010

Schiff, M. (2002). *Regional integration and development in small states.* Policy Research Working Paper Series 2797. The World Bank.

Schumpeter, J. (1911). *The Theory of Economic Development.* Cambridge, MA: Harvard University Press.

Schumpeter, J. (1986). *History of Economic Analysis.* Abingdon, UK: Routledge Publishing.

Schumpeter, J. A. (1939). *Business Cycles: A Theoretical, Historical and Statistical Analysis of the Capitalist Process.* London: McGraw-Hill.

Scott, W. (2002). The Changing World of Chinese Enterprises: An Institutional Perspective. In A. Tsui & M. Lau (Eds.), *Management of Enterprises in the People's Republic of China* (pp. 59–78). Boston: Kluwer Academic Press. doi:10.1007/978-1-4615-1095-6_4

Searing, E. A. M. (2013). Love Thy Neighbor? Recessions and Interpersonal Trust in Latin America. *Journal of Economic Behavior & Organization, 94*, 68–79. doi:10.1016/j.jebo.2013.07.010

Segeplan. (2014). Retrieved from Segeplan.gob.gt: http://www.segeplan.gob.gt/2.0/index.php?option=com_content&view=article&id=1321:mapas-de-pobreza-rural-herramienta-relevante-para-el-combate-a-la-pobreza-y-a-la-desigualdad-dice-secretaria-de-planificacion&catid=25:ultima&Itemid=115

Selingson, M. (2006). The Measurement and Impact of Corruption Victimization: Survey Evidence from Latin America. *World Development, 34*(2), 381–404. doi:10.1016/j.worlddev.2005.03.012

Compilation of References

Sen, A. (1997). *Development thinking at the beginning of the 21st century* London, UK: Suntory and Toyota International Centres for Economics and Related Disciplines, London School of Economics and Political Science.

Sen, A. (1999). *Development as Freedom*. Oxford, UK: Oxford University Press.

Shepherd, B. (2011). Logistics costs and Competitiveness: Measurement and trade policy applications. In *MPRA Paper 38254*. University Library of Munich.

Sheth, J. N., & Sisodia, R. (1999). Revisiting marketing's lawlike generalizations. *Journal of the Academy of Marketing Science*, 27(1), 71–87. doi:10.1177/0092070399271006

Shiau, W. L., & Luo, M. M. (2012). Factors Affecting Online Group Buying Intention and Satisfaction: A Social Exchange Theory Perspective. *Computers in Human Behavior*, 28(6), 2431–2444. doi:10.1016/j.chb.2012.07.030

Shionoya, Y. (2008). Schumpeter and Evolution: an ontological exploration. In Marshall and Schumpeter on Evolution: Economic Sociology of Capitalistic Development. Cheltenham, UK: Edward Elgar Press.

Shleifer, A., & Vishny, R. (1993). Corruption. *The Quarterly Journal of Economics*, 108(3), 599–617. doi:10.2307/2118402

Siems, M., & Schyner, G. (2013). Ordoliberal Lessons for Economic Stability: Different Kinds of Regulation, Not More Regulation. *Governance: An International Journal of Policy, Administration and Institutions*, 27(3), 377–396. doi:10.1111/gove.12046

Simanis, E. & Milstein, M. (2012). Back to Business Fundamentals: Making BoP Relevant to Core Business. *Field Actions Science Report*, (4), 8.

Simanis, E., & Hart, S. L. (2009). Innovation from the inside out. *MIT Sloan Management Review*, 50(4), 77–86.

Slater, S., & Narver, J. (1994a). Does competitive environment moderate the market orientation-performance relationship? *Journal of Marketing*, 58(1), 46–55. doi:10.2307/1252250

Slater, S., & Narver, J. (1994b). Market orientation, customer value, and superior performance. *Business Horizons*, 37(2), 22–28. doi:10.1016/0007-6813(94)90029-9

Smith, A. (1976). An Inquiry into the Nature and Causes of the Wealth of Nations (2 vols.). Oxford.

Smith, A. (1979). The Theory of Moral Sentiments. Oxford.

Solo, T. M., & Manroth, A. (2006). *Access to financial services in Colombia: the "unbanked" in Bogota*. Policy Research working paper. The World Bank.

Somma, A. (2013). Private Law as Biopolitics: Ordoliberalism, Social Market Economy, and the Public Dimension of Contract. *Law and Contemporary Problems*, 76, 105.

Sorjonen, H. (2011). The manifestation of market orientation and its antecedents in the program planning of arts organizations. *International Journal of Arts Management, 14*(1), 4–18.

Srinivasan, T. N. (1986). *The Cost and Benefits of Being a Small, Remote, Island, Landlocked, or Ministate Economy.* World Bank, Development Policy Issues Series Discussion Paper. Number ERS 2.

Srinivas, S., & Sutz, J. (2008). Developing countries and innovation: Searching for a new analytical approach. *Technology in Society, 30*(2), 129–140. doi:10.1016/j.techsoc.2007.12.003

Sriram, M. S. (2005). Information Asymmetry and trust: A framework for understanding microfinance in India. *Vikapla, 30*(4), 77–85.

Staab, M. (2003). Public-Private Sector Relationships in Developing Countries. *Journal of Economic Development, 28*(2).

Stanfield, J. (2010). *Self Help and Sustainability in Education in Developing Countries, E.G. West Centre EFA Working Paper, 10.* Available online at: http://egwestcentre.com/publications-3/working-papers/

Stoian, F., & Filippaios, F. (2008). Dunning's eclectic paradigm: A holistic, yet context specific framework for analysing the determinants of outward FDI. Evidence from international Greek investments. *International Business Review, 17*(3), 349–367. doi:10.1016/j.ibusrev.2007.12.005

Streeten, P. (1979). Development Ideas in Historical Perspective. In K. Hill (Ed.), *Toward a New Strategy for Development.* New York: Pergamon Press.

Streeten, P. (1985). Development Economics: The Intellectual Divisions. *Eastern Economic Journal, 11*(3), 235–247.

Streeten, P. (1993). The Special Problems of Small Countries. *World Development, 21*(2), 197–202. doi:10.1016/0305-750X(93)90014-Z

Sukhtankar, S., & Graham, C. (2004). Does Economic Crisis Reduce Support for Markets and Democracy in Latin America? Some Evidence from Surveys of Public Opinion and Well Being. *Journal of Latin American Studies*, 349–377.

Sutton, P., & Payne, A. (1993). Lilliput under Threat: The Security Problems of Small Island and Enclave Developing States. *Political Studies, 41*(4), 579–593. doi:10.1111/j.1467-9248.1993.tb01657.x

Swift, J. S., & Lawrence, K. (2003). Business Culture in Latin America: Interactive Learning for UK SME's. *Journal of European Industrial Training, 27*(8/9), 389–397. doi:10.1108/03090590310498522

Tan, V. (2012). *Public-Private Partnership (PPP).* Retrieved from http://a4id.org/sites/default/files/files/%5BA4ID%5D%20Public-Private%20Partnership.pdf

Compilation of References

Tan, D., & Meyer, K. (2011). Country-of-origin and industry FDI agglomeration of foreign investors in an emerging economy. *Journal of International Business Studies*, *42*(4), 504–520. doi:10.1057/jibs.2011.4

Terjesen, S., & Amorós, J. E. (2010). Female Entrepreneurship in Latin America and the Caribbean: Characteristics, Drivers and Relationship to Economic Development. *European Journal of Development Research*, *22*(3), 313–330. doi:10.1057/ejdr.2010.13

The Ecomomist. (2012). *The Economist Intelligence Unit*. [Online] Available at: https://www.eiu.com/public/topical_report.aspx?campaignid=LatAmFDI2012

Theron, E., Terblanche, N., & Boshoff, C. (2011). The Antecedents of Trust in Business-to Business Financial Services. *Journal of Business-To-Business Marketing*, *18*(2), 188–213. doi:10.1080/1051712X.2010.499837

Thompsom, C. E. M., Barbosa Júnior, C. L., & Frota, I. L. N. (2003). *A parceria Bradesco e Correios no Bando Postal: uma abordagem estratégica, tecnológica e social*. Bauro, Brazil: X Simpósio de Engenharia de Produção.

Thompson, D. M. (2008). Is the Internet a Viable Threat to Representative Democracy? *Duke Law & Technology Review*, *23*(1).

Thurik, R., & Wennekers, S. (2001). *A Note on Entrepreneurship, Small Business and Economic Growth*. Rotterdam: Erasmus Research Institute of Management Report Series.

Tõnurist, P. (2010). What Is a "Small State" in a Globalizing Economy? *Halduskultuur – Administrative Culture*, *11*(1), 8-29.

Transparency International. (2011). *Bribe payers index 2011*. Author.

Transparency International. (2011). *Transparency International*. [Online] Available at: http://www.transparency.org/cpi2011/in_detail

Trevino, L., & Mixon, F. Jr. (2004). Strategic factors affecting foreign direct investment decisions by multi-national enterprises in Latin America. *Journal of World Business*, *39*(3), 233–243. doi:10.1016/j.jwb.2004.04.003

Trevino, L., Thomas, D., & Cullen, J. (2008). The three pillars of institutional theory and FDI in Latin America: An institutionalization process. *International Business Review*, *17*(1), 118–113. doi:10.1016/j.ibusrev.2007.10.002

Trilateral Commission. (1975). *The crisis of democracy*. New York: New York University Press.

Tsai, K. S. (2004). Imperfect Substitutes: The local political economy for informal finance and microfinance in rural China and India. *World Development*, *32*(9), 1487–1507. doi:10.1016/j.worlddev.2004.06.001

U.S. Bureau of Labor Statistics. (2007). *Competitiveness in Manufacturing*. Washington, DC: U.S. Bureau of Labor Statistics.

Uhlenbruck, K., Rodriguez, P., Doh, J., & Eden, L. (2006). The impact of corruption on entry strategy: Evidence from telecommunication projects in emerging economies. *Organization Science*, *17*(3), 402–414. doi:10.1287/orsc.1060.0186

UN. (2014). Retrieved from un.org: http://www.un.org/en/development/desa/news/population/number-of-international-migrants-rises.html

UNCTAD. (2009). *World investment report 2009: Transnational corporations, agricultural production and development*. New York: UN Publications.

UNCTAD. (2013). Global Investment Trends Monitor. Geneva: *United Nations Conference on Trade and Development*.

UNCTAD. (2014). *World Investment Report: Investing in the SDGs: An action plan*. Retrieved from http://unctad.org/en/PublicationsLibrary/wir2014_en.pdf

UNDP. (2004). *La democracia en América Latina: Hacia una democracia de ciudadanas y ciudadanos*. New York: UNPD.

UNDP. (2008). *Creating value for all: strategies for doing business with the poor - Growing Inclusive Markets*. New York: United Nations Development Programme. Available at http://growinginclusivemarkets.org/media/gimlaunch/Report_2008/GIM%20Report%20Final%20August%202008.pdf

UNDP. (2013). Retrieved from undp.org: http://hdr.undp.org/es/content/human-development-index-hdi-table

UNDP-OAS. (2011). *Our democracy in Latin America*. Mexico: Fondo de Cultura Económica.

UNESCO. (1990). *Full Text of the International Convention on the Protection of the Rights of All Migrant Workers and Members of Their Families (no yet in force)*. Retrieved from unesco.org: http://www.unesco.org/most/migration/mwc_toc.htm

UNESCO. (2014). *International Migration and Multicultural policies*. Retrieved from unesco.org: http://www.unesco.org/most/migration/glossary_migrants.htm

UNESCO. (n.d.). Retrieved from unesco.org: http://www.unesco.org/new/en/social-and-human sciences/themes/international-migration

United Nations. (2009). *Rethinking Poverty: Report on the World Social Situation*. Available online at: www.un.org/esa/socdev/rwss/docs/2010/fullreport.pdf

United States Census Bureau. (2012). *La población hispana: 2010*. Retrieved from census.gov: http://www.census.gov/prod/cen2010/briefs/c2010br-04sp.pdf

United States Census Bureau. (2012). *The foreign born population in 2010*. Retrieved from census.gov: https://www.census.gov/prod/2012pubs/acs-19.pdf

Compilation of References

Uslaner, E. M. (2003). Trust, Democracy and Governance: Can Government Policies Influence Generalized Trust? In M. Hooghe & D. Stolle (Eds.), *Generating Social Capital: Civil Society and Institutions in Comparative Perspective*. Palgrave Macmillan.

Vassolo, R. S., De Castro, J. O., & Gomez-Mejia, L. (2011). Managing in Latin America: Common issues and a research agenda. *The Academy of Management Perspectives, 25*(4), 22–36. doi:10.5465/amp.2011.0129

Vernon, R. (1966). International investment and international trade in the product cycle. *The Quarterly Journal of Economics, 80*(2), 190–207. doi:10.2307/1880689

Virzi, N. & Belteton A. (2009b). *Un modelo keynesiano de los efectos macroeconomicos*. Facultad de Ciencias Económicas y Empresariales, Universidad Rafael Landívar. Septiembre, 2009, No. 4. Guatemala City, Guatemala.

Virzi, N., & Belteton, A. (2009a). El impacto de la corrupción en la viabilidad del estado rector en Guatemala. En Cuadernos de Sociología, No. 7. Políticas publicas para una agenda de gobierno en Guatemala. Universidad Pontificia de Salamanca, Capitulo Guatemala. Centro de Estudios Sociales, UPSA Guate, Guatemala.

Von Graevenitza, G., Harhoffa, D., & Weberb, R. (2010). The effects of entrepreneurship education. *Journal of Economic Behavior & Organization, 76*(1), 90–112. doi:10.1016/j.jebo.2010.02.015

Von Hippel, E. (1988). *The Sources of Innovation*. New York: Oxford University Press.

Vonortas, N. (2002). Building competitive firms: Technology policy initiatives in Latin America. *Technology in Society, 24*(4), 433–459. doi:10.1016/S0160-791X(02)00034-9

Wagner, S. M., Coley, L. S., & Lindemann, E. (2011). Effects of Suppliers' Reputation on the Future of Buyer-Supplier Relationships: The Mediating Roles of Outcome Fairness and Trust. *Journal of Supply Chain Management, 47*(2), 29–48. doi:10.1111/j.1745-493X.2011.03225.x

Watkins, K. (2005). *Human Development Report- International Cooperation at Crossroads: Aid, Trade and Security in an Unequal World*. Retrieved from http://www.undp.org/en/reports/global/hdr2005

Webb, D., Webster, C., & Krepapa, A. (2000). An exploration of the meaning and outcomes of a customer-defined market orientation. *Journal of Business Research, 48*(2), 101–112. doi:10.1016/S0148-2963(98)00114-3

Weck, M., & Ivanova, M. (2013). The Importance of Cultural Adaptation for the Trust Development within Business relationships. *Journal of Business and Industrial Marketing, 28*(3), 210–220. doi:10.1108/08858621311302868

WEF, Bain, & Banco Mundial. (2013). *Enabling Trade Valuing Growth Opportunities*. World Economic Forum.

Wei, S. (1997). *Why is corruption so much more taxing than tax? Arbitrariness Kills*. Cambridge, MA: National Bureau of Economic Research. doi:10.3386/w6255

Welch, L. S., & Luostarinen, R. K. (1988). Internationalization: Evolution of a concept. *Journal of General Management*, *14*(2), 34–55.

Welch, L., & Luostarinen, R. (1993). Internationalization: Evolution of a concept. In P. J. Buckley & P. N. Ghauri (Eds.), *The Internationalization of the firm: A reader* (pp. 155–171). Academic Press.

Wennekers, S., & Thurik, R. (1999). Linking entrepreneurship and economic Growth. *Small Business Economics*, *13*(1), 27–55. doi:10.1023/A:1008063200484

Wennkers, S., Van Stel, A., & Carree, M. (2010). *The relationship between entrepreneurship and economic development: is it U-shaped?* EIM Research Reports. The Netherlands: SCALES-initiative.

Westney, D. (1993). Institutionalization theory and the multinational corporation. In *Organization theory and the multinational corporation* (pp. 53–75). New York: St. Martin's Press.

Weyland, K. (1998). The politics of corruption in Latin America. *Journal of Democracy*, *2*(2), 108–121. doi:10.1353/jod.1998.0034

Wharton. (2009). *A world transformed: What are the top 30 innovations of the last 30 years?* Knowledge@wharton - University of Pennsylvania. Available online at: http://knowledge.wharton.upenn.edu

Wildavsky, B. (2010). *The Great Brain Race: How Global Universities Are Reshaping the World.* Princeton University Press.

Williams, H., & Torma, M. (2007). Trust and Fidelity: From "under the mattress" to the mobile phone. In Vodafone policy paper series The Transformational Potential of M- Transactions, 6.

Williamson, O. E. (1989). Transaction Cost Economics. In R. Schmalensee & R. Willig (Eds.), Handbook of Industrial Organization, (pp. 136-182). Elsevier.

Wood, R. (2014). *Eurozone: Competitiveness Indicators and the Failure of Internal Devaluation.* EconoMonitor. EconoMonitor.

World Bank. (2004). *Doing Business in 2004: Understanding Regulation.* Washington, DC: World Bank and Oxford University Press.

World Bank. (2005). *Diagnostico Sobre Transparencia, Corrupcion y Gobernabilidad en Latinoamerica.* Washington, DC: World Bank.

World Bank. (2010). *Doing Business en Colombia 2010.* Washington, DC: World Bank Group.

World Bank. (2013a). *Doing Business en Colombia 2013: Regulaciones inteligentes para las pequeñas y medianas empresas.* Washington, DC: World Bank Group.

World Bank. (2013b). *Doing Business 2014: Understanding Regulation for Small and Medium Sizes Enterprises.* Washington, DC: International Bank for Reconstruction and Development/ The World Bank.

Compilation of References

World Bank. (2014). *Migration and Remittances: Recent developments and Outlook*. Retrieved from World Bank: http://siteresources.worldbank.org/INTPROSPECTS/Resources/334934-1288990760745/MigrationandDevelopmentBrief22.pdf

World Bank. (2014). *Poverty Data*. [online] Available at: http://data.worldbank.org/topic/poverty

World Bank. (2014). Press release: *World Bank*. Retrieved from World Bank: http://www.worldbank.org/en/news/press-release/2014/04/11/remittances-developing-countries-deportations-migrant-workers-wb

World Bank. (2014). Retrieved from http://www.doingbusiness.org/about-us

World Economic Forum. (2002). *The Global Competitiveness Report 2001-2002*. Oxford, UK: Oxford Press.

World Economic Forum. (2014). *The Global Competitiveness Report 2013–2014*. Geneva: WEF.

World Economic Forum. (2014). *The Global Competitiveness Report 2013–2014*. World Economic Forum.

World Economic Forum. (2014). *World Economic Forum, Global Competitiveness Report 2014-2015*. Author.

World Population Data Sheet Interactive World Map. (2014). Retrieved from www.prb.org

World Values Survey Association. (2014). *WVS - Wave 6* and *WVS - Wave 5*. Retrieved from http://www.worldvaluessurvey.org/WVSContents.jsp

World Values Survey. (2010-2014). Retrieved from http://www.worldvaluessurvey.org/

WVS 6. (2012). *WV6 Official Questionnaire v4*. Retrieved from http://www.worldvaluessurvey.org/WVSDocumentationWV6.jsp

Xheneti, M. (2006). Youth entrepreneurship in south east Europe: some policy recommendations. In J. Potter & A. Proto (Eds.), *Promoting Entrepreneurship in South East Europe, policies and tools*. Paris: OECD.

Yau, O., McFetridge, P., Chow, R., Lee, J., Sin, L., & Tse, A. (2000). Is relationship marketing for everyone? *European Journal of Marketing, 34*(9/10), 1111–1127. doi:10.1108/03090560010342494

Ybarra, C. E., & Turk, T. A. (2009). The Evolution of Trust in Information Technology Alliances. *The Journal of High Technology Management Research, 20*(1), 62–74. doi:10.1016/j.hitech.2009.02.003

Yin, R. K. (1984). *Case study research: Design and methods*. Newbury Park, CA: Sage.

Yin, R. K. (2004). *Case study methods. Complementary methods for research in education*. Washington, DC: American Educational Research Association.

Young, S., Hamill, J., Wheeler, C., & Davies, J. (1989). *International market entry and development*. Englewood Cliffs, NJ: Prentice Hall.

Zapata, C. P., Olsen, J. E., & Martin, L. L. (2013). Social Exchange From the supervisor's Perspective: Employee Trustworthiness as a Predictor of Interpersonal and Informational Justice. *Organizational Behavior and Human Decision Processes*, *121*(1), 1–12. doi:10.1016/j.obhdp.2012.11.001

Zhang, D., Sivaramakrishnan, S., Delbaere, M., & Bruning, E. (2008). The relationship between organizational commitment and market orientation. *Journal of Strategic Marketing*, *16*(1), 55–73. doi:10.1080/09652540701794494

Zhao, Y., & Cavusgil, T. (2006). The effect of supplier's market orientation on manufacturer's trust. *Industrial Marketing Management*, *35*(4), 405–414. doi:10.1016/j.indmarman.2005.04.001

Zillifro, T., & Morais, D. B. (2004). Building Customer Trust and Relationship Commitment to a Nature-Based Tourism Provider: The Role of Information Investments. *Journal of Hospitality & Leisure Marketing*, *11*(2/3), 159–172. doi:10.1300/J150v11n02_11

Zolkiewski, J., & Turnbull, P. (2006). Guest editorial. *European Journal of Marketing*, *40*(3/4), 241–247. doi:10.1108/ejm.2006.00740caa.001

Zurawicki, L., & Habib, M. (2010). Corruption and Foreign Direct Investment: What Have We Learned? *International Business and Economics Research Journal*, *9*(7), 1–10.

About the Contributors

Mauricio Garita is a researcher at the Universidad del Valle de Guatemala. He has a PhD from the Universidad Pontificia de Salamanca in sociology and politics and an MS from Manchester Business School in International Business and Management. His research centers on economic policy and its impact on the business environment. As a consequence he has developed research concerning economic growth and equality, business and politics and the impact of economic and political issues on the financial aspects of companies. He has worked with the private sector of Guatemala, the Secretariat for Economic Integration, the World Bank and the Central American Institute of Fiscal Studies.

Jose Godinez is an Assistant Professor of Management at Merrimack College. He has a PhD from the University of Edinburgh Business School, a BS in Business Administration from the Johns Hopkins University, and an MS from the University of Manchester. His research centers on the intersection of the international business, strategy, and entrepreneurship disciplines. Specifically, he focuses on strategies designed to minimize the detrimental effects of corruption on businesses; strategies to successfully operate in institutional voids; and value creation for all stakeholders of firms targeting the bottom of the pyramid. He has presented his research at the Academy of Management and the Academy of International Business annual meetings. Jose Godinez also advises policymakers in his native Guatemala and serves on the board of directors of a Massachusetts-based nonprofit focusing on financial literacy for traditionally non-banked populations.

* * *

Carolina Alves holds a degree in Management and a Master in Management - Marketing and International Business - at the University of Aveiro, Portugal. She has developed her final project at Portugal Telecom Inovação e Sistemas, where she specialized in the field of Smart Cities. She is currently managing partner at Talents & Treasures, where she brings expertise in project management, social innovation and open source software.

Luis Rodrigo Asturias graduated from the University Rafael Landivar, Master in Public Administration from the University of Barcelona, work experience in Public Policy job as economic adviser to the Secretary of Planning and Programming of the Presidency in Guatemala, is currently an economic adviser in the Ministry Social Development particularly in the Vice Ministry of Policy, Planning and Evaluation, writer since 2012 in the Diario de Centro America in addition in Perspective Magazine on economic issues.

Reny Mariane Bake is Guatemalan born of a Dutch father and a Guatemalan mother, raised in the rural area of Guatemala. Reny has been traveling to USA and Europe, learning about many cultures and lifestyles. She has worked in several analysis related to the Guatemalan and Central America economies. Reny is an International Visitor Leadership Program Alumni of the US Department of State, 2005. During the last years she has studied at William J. Perry Center for Hemispheric Defense studies, National Defense University the following courses: Strategy & Defense Policy (2009), Civil-Political-Military Relations and Democratic Leadership (2011), and Perspectives on Homeland Security and defense (2014). In addition to security matters, Reny is a national known expert on Free Trade Agreements, with extensive experience working on the DR-CAFTA negotiations and other FTAs for Guatemala. She is currently an analyst in economic issues on the Guatemalan television circuit. For more than eleven years, she was a weekly Economic columnist in the most prestigious Guatemalan newspaper, Prensa Libre. Her research focuses on international business, development and geopolitical issues.

Marco Bottone was born in Piedimonte Matese on September 27, 1988. He graduated in Economy at the Second University of Naples before completing a Masters' Degree in Economics organized by Tor Vergata University of Rome. He is currently a second-year graduate student of Sapienza PhD program of Economic Statistics. Bottone collaborated with the directorate for studies and economical-fiscal research of Ministry of Finance and has received numerous awards, such as the national award for the best dissertation in the area of fiscal equity. His current research focuses on Statistical and Bayesian Inference, Econometrics, Finance, Mixture Model, Quantile Regression, and Risk Measures.

Harish C. Chandan is Professor of Business at Argosy University, Atlanta. He was interim chair of the business program in 2011. He received President's award for excellence in teaching in 2007, 2008 and 2009. His teaching philosophy is grounded in the learner needs and life-long learning. His research interests include research methods, leadership, marketing, and organizational behavior. He has published 20 peer-reviewed articles in business journals and five chapters in business reference books. Dr. Chandan has presented conference papers at Academy of Management, International Academy of Business and Management, Southeast Association of Information Systems, and Academy of International Business. Prior to joining Argosy, Dr. Chandan managed optical fiber and cable product qualification laboratories for Lucent Technologies, Bell Laboratories. During his career with Lucent, he had 40 technical publications, a chapter in a book and five patents.

Liyis Gómez has a PhD in Entrepreneurship and Management from the Autonomous University of Barcelona. She has taught stragegy and entrepreneurship courses since 1995. She has been director of Doing Business in Colombia. Her research interests include entrepreneurial contexts, entrepreneurial competencies and business development of high impact.

Eduardo Gómez-Araujo has a PhD in Entrepreneurship and Management from Universidad Autónoma de Barcelona. He has taught Entrepreneurship and Business History courses since 2006 at Universidad del Norte (Barranquilla-Colombia). He has worked as senior researcher in the Global Entrepreneurship Monitor (GEM)-Catalunya and currently he is working in the GEM-Colombia Project. His research interests include Entrepreneurship and Territorial Development (Rural and Regional areas), Young Entrepreneurs and Regional Development and Business History.

Nery Fernando Guzmán is an Economist from Guatemala. With experience in private sector in the import/export business in Guatemala. As the CFO of General Express, S.A. in Guatemala coordinated the strategy and logistics for an international freight company dedicated to international commerce. As for the consulting experience for the last years in the area of business intelligence, data mining, data base and information managing in order to execute strategy for the decision making.

Mahmoud Khalik is a Teaching Fellow at the University of St Andrews School of Management where he teaches courses in International Business, Strategy, and Marketing. He has taught International Business and Strategy to undergraduate and postgraduate students at the University of Edinburgh Business School for four years. His research interests revolve around firm internationalization from developed economies and emerging markets, firm strategies targeting the base of the pyramid and undeserved communities, and qualitative research methods adopting case study designs.

Michele Lobina is an Italian economist specializing in International and Development Economics. His studies include a Master of Arts in Political Economy and he is currently a PhD candidate in Economy and Finance at Sapienza University of Rome. He has collaborated with the Chamber of Commerce and the Italian Embassy in Guatemala, and has held a role of an Associate Professor of Macroeconomics at Rafael Landivar University of Guatemala City. His current research regards the impact of free trade agreements on competitive capacities of small and medium-sized enterprises in developing countries.

Helen Michelle Monzón studied Economics in Rafael Landívar University, Guatemala. Actually working in the Central American Institute for Fiscal Studies (ICEFI, Guatemala).

António C. Moreira obtained a Bachelor's degree in Electrical Engineering and a Master's degree in Management, both from the University of Porto, Portugal. He received his PhD in Management from UMIST-University of Manchester Institute of Science and Technology, England. He has a solid international background in industry leveraged working for a multinational company in Germany as well as in Portugal. He has also been involved in consultancy projects and in research activities. He is an Assistant Professor at the Department of Economics Management and Industrial Engineering, University of Aveiro, Portugal, where he headed the Bachelor and Master Degrees in Management for five years.

Milo Paviera is a Doctoral Researcher and Teaching Assistant at the University of Edinburgh Business School within the Strategy and International Business Group. He is investigating Entrepreneurship in the Informal Economy, collective forms of action and informal firms acting as social movements. He looks at emerging forms of Capitalism and Employees Ownership and how they become a source of competitive advantage. His broad interests are in Strategy and Public Policy in Emerging Economies.

Juan Carlos Portillo is a Guatemalan industrial engineer. Graduated from the Universidad de San Carlos in Guatemala and possesses a master in quantitative finance by the Universidad Rafael Landivar.

Sandra Rodríguez is a Professor of economics at Universidad del Norte, Colombia. Sandra obtained her doctoral degree in applied economics at Autonomous University of Barcelona (UAB-Barcelona) in 2012. Her current research and teaching interests are related to health economics, public regulation, institutions and game theory, focusing in particular on the issue of health and health care systems.

Luis Sanchez-Barrios has a PhD in Management from the University of Edinburgh, UK. He has taught finance courses since 2003. His research interests include microfinance, entrepreneurial scorecards, financial education and regression methods for scoring purposes.

Theodore Terpstra is pursuing a degree in International Relations at the University of Connecticut.

Nicholas Virzi is a Professor of Economics at Universidad Rafael Landívar, in the Master´s Program of the Faculty of Engineering, and at the Escuela de Gobierno (School of Government) in Guatemala. He is Vice President of the American Chamber of Commerce in Guatemala, where he is President of the Investment Promotion Committee. Mr. Virzi is also a member of the Private Council of Competitiveness in Guatemala, representing the Academic Sector. He is a graduate of U.C., Berkeley in Political Science and has a Master´s Degree from San Francisco State University in Economics. He has published various works and is active on the regional conference circuit on matters of political economy, investment and innovation.

Heather C. Webb is a lecturer in business at Higher Colleges of Technology in Dubai, UAE where she teaches strategy and international business. She has a PhD from the University of Edinburgh Business School, a MSc in International Business and Emerging Markets from the University of Edinburgh, and a BA in History from the University of Washington. Her research focuses on aspects of strategy, international business and entrepreneurship. Her research interest concentrates on strategies, business models, developing countries and innovation. Specifically, she researches mobile payment systems in developing countries as well as bottom of the pyramid consumers. She has presented her work at the Academy of Management and at the Academy of International Business.

Index

S

sectoral system of innovation 107-109, 115
small states 48-54, 56-60, 63-65
SMEs 4-5, 9, 17, 23-24, 195, 209, 224-
    225, 227-229, 244, 246, 248, 253,
    269, 294, 299, 302
social agenda 116
Social Capital 63, 105, 129-130, 145-146,
    156
Social Cohesion 130, 157, 270
Stakeholder Trust 82-83

T

Third World, 200, 207
Transparency 31, 40-41, 43, 46, 127, 131,
    148, 151, 155, 202-203, 221, 273,
    280-282, 284-287

U

unbanked 109, 112, 114-117, 119-120,
    122-123, 125, 181, 197
UNCTAD 37, 39, 43, 46, 67, 69, 81, 274,
    287

V

Venezuela 3, 70, 85, 100, 257
vision 54, 158-162, 165-168, 202, 212,
    214, 217-218, 281

W

World Values Survey 82, 84-85, 105, 127,
    132-133, 136, 147, 153-154, 157

Information Resources Management Association

Become an IRMA Member

Members of the **Information Resources Management Association (IRMA)** understand the importance of community within their field of study. The Information Resources Management Association is an ideal venue through which professionals, students, and academicians can convene and share the latest industry innovations and scholarly research that is changing the field of information science and technology. Become a member today and enjoy the benefits of membership as well as the opportunity to collaborate and network with fellow experts in the field.

IRMA Membership Benefits:

- **One FREE Journal Subscription**
- **30% Off Additional Journal Subscriptions**
- **20% Off Book Purchases**
- Updates on the latest events and research on Information Resources Management through the IRMA-L listserv.
- Updates on new open access and downloadable content added to Research IRM.
- A copy of the Information Technology Management Newsletter twice a year.
- A certificate of membership.

IRMA Membership $195

Scan code to visit irma-international.org and begin by selecting your free journal subscription.

Membership is good for one full year.

www.irma-international.org

Printed in the United States
By Bookmasters